Clinical Legal Education in Asia

Clinical Legal Education in Asia
Accessing Justice for the Underprivileged

Edited by
Shuvro Prosun Sarker

palgrave
macmillan

CLINICAL LEGAL EDUCATION IN ASIA

First published in 2015 by PALGRAVE MACMILLAN® in the United States—a division of St. Martin's Press LLC, 175 Fifth Avenue, New York, NY 10010.

Where this book is distributed in the UK, Europe and the rest of the world, this is by Palgrave Macmillan, a division of Macmillan Publishers Limited, registered in England, company number 785998, of Houndmills, Basingstoke, Hampshire RG21 6XS.

Palgrave Macmillan is the global academic imprint of the above companies and has companies and representatives throughout the world.

ISBN: 978-1-137-51752-4

Library of Congress Cataloging-in-Publication Data

Clinical legal education in Asia : accessing justice for the underprivileged / by Shuvro Prosun Sarker, B.A. LL.B (Calcutta), LL.M (NUJS) Assistant Professor, School of Law, KIIT University, Bhubaneswar, Odisha, India.
pages cm
Includes bibliographical references and index.
ISBN 978-1-137-51752-4 (hardback)
1. Law—Study and teaching (Clinical education)—Asia. I. Sarker, Shuvro Prosun, editor.
KNC47.5.C55C58 2015
340.071'15—dc23

2014047883

A catalogue record of the book is available from the British Library.

Design by Amnet.

First edition: September 2015

10 9 8 7 6 5 4 3 2 1

To the two teachers who have inspired my life and education . . .
Professor N. R. Madhava Menon
and
Professor Mahendra Pal Singh

Contents

List of Tables and Figures ix

Preface xi

List of Contributors xiii

1 Introduction: Clinical Legal Education and Its Asian Characteristics 1
Bruce Avery Lasky and Shuvro Prosun Sarker

2 Better Lawyers, Better Justice: Introducing Clinical Legal Education in the Maldives 17
Marium Jabyn and Rogena Sterling

3 Chinese Clinical Legal Education: Globalizing and Localizing 37
Cecily E. Baskir, Ma Liqun, and Li Ao

4 Clinical Education in South Korean Law Schools: Challenges and Hopes 53
Helen Haekyong Kang and Kyung Sin Park

5 Clinical Education in Taiwanese Law Schools 75
Thomas Chih-hsiung Chen

6 Clinical Legal Education in Israel 91
Yael Efron

7 Clinical Legal Education in Palestine: A Clinical Case under Military Occupation 113
Mutaz M. Qafisheh

8 Clinical Legal Education in Singapore 137
Rathna N. Koman and Helena Whalen-Bridge

9 Clinical Legal Education in Thailand: A Pedagogy Whose Time Has Come 159
Panarairat Srichaiyarat, Lisa Radtke Bliss, and Withoon Taloodkum

10 Empowering the Underprivileged: The Social Justice Mission for Clinical Legal Education in India 177
Shuvro Prosun Sarker

11 Legal Clinical Education in Japan: A Work in Progress 195
Matthew J. Wilson

12 Legal Clinics in Turkey 215
Julian Lonbay and Musa Toprak

13 Pathways to Social Transformation through Clinic: Developing a "Social Justice" Culture in Hong Kong 229
Luke Marsh and Michael Ramsden

Index 249

List of Tables and Figures

Tables

12.1 Survey results from the Anadolu legal clinic 220

12.2 Survey results from the Children's Rights in Practice street law course 221

Figures

8.1 Why do you choose to volunteer at the legal clinics? 147

8.2 Volunteer take-aways from the clinics. 148

8.3 Effectiveness of SMU legal clinics in developing below-mentioned skills and interests. 149

8.4 What have you gained from the clinics as a volunteer? 150

8.5 How would you describe your experience consulting with lawyers on duty about the client work you handled? 151

8.6 Whether experience at the clinics inspired you to take or maintain an interest in volunteer legal work? 153

Tables

Figures

Preface

After I completed the work on my first edited book, *Legal Education in Asia* (Eleven International Publishing, The Hague, 2014), in early 2013, Professor N. R. Madhava Menon, in sending his foreword for the book, advised me to take a similar initiative to come up with a comparative study on clinical legal education, concentrating on Asia. His advice was like a command to me, and I started working on a next book and here is the reality.

While working on this book, I received the help of very sensible and scholarly colleagues from all over the world who have experience in clinical legal education in the Asian region. I am extremely thankful for their scholarly writings and for their association with me not only as contributors but also as good friends.

The contributors to this book would like to acknowledge some important persons who helped or assisted them in preparing the chapters. Matthew Wilson extends his sincere gratitude to the University of Wyoming College of Law and the Kyung Hee University Law School for the support provided to him. Yael Efron thanks Shauna Naghi for her assistance in preparing the chapter on Israel. She expresses gratitude for the data collected and shared by Adv. Debbi Sadeh and the dedicated clinicians at the Israeli Board of Clinicians. Helen Kang would like to thank her assistant, Angelina Torres, for her commendable work. Rathna Koman would like to thank Eugene Neo Zhi Wei, an SMU final-year student, for his excellent research assistance. Cecily Baskir would like to acknowledge my coauthors, Li Ao and Ma Liqun, Robin Runge, and Zhang Lining, for their assistance, and Jeffrey Lehman for giving her the opportunity to teach as a clinician in China.

I am very happy to acknowledge the research assistance of Ms. Arpita Sengupta, B.A. LL.B (Hons.) student of National University of Juridical Sciences, for her excellent and timely work. Thank you very much, Arpita!

I would like to acknowledge the help of my colleagues at the School of Law, KIIT University, Bhubaneswar, India, for their all-round inspiration and good words. I would also like to express my sincere gratitude to Professor Manoj Kumar Sinha, Professor N. K. Chakrabarti, Professor Jane Schukoske, Professor M. R. K. Prasad, Professor Anirban Chakraborty, and Shounak Chatterjee for their comments on various occasions regarding the preparation of the book.

Finally, I would like to thank Roustavi, my wife, for her incredible support for my work.

Shuvro Prosun Sarker
Assistant Professor
School of Law, KIIT University, India
November 15, 2014

List of Contributors

Bruce Avery Lasky, Director, BABSEA CLE, Thailand

Cecily E. Baskir, Attorney, New York Bar, United States and Affiliated Faculty, Peking University School of Transnational Law, China

Helen Haekyong Kang, Professor of Law, Golden Gate University School of Law and Director, Environmental Law and Justice Clinic, Golden Gate University School of Law, United States

Helena Whalen-Bridge, Associate Professor of Law, National University of Singapore

Julian Lonbay, Senior Lecturer, Birmingham Law School, The University of Birmingham, Edgbaston, England

Kyung Sin Park, Professor of Law and Founder, Center for Clinical Legal Education of Korea University Law School, South Korea

Li Ao, Professor of Law, Wuhan University Law School, China

Lisa Radtke Bliss, Director of Experiential Education and Associate Clinical Professor, Georgia State University College of Law, United States

Luke Marsh, Assistant Professor, Chinese University of Hong Kong, Hong Kong

Ma Liqun, Lecturer, Southwest University of Political Science and Law, China

Marium Jabyn, PhD Candidate, Te Piringa—Faculty of Law, University of Waikato, New Zealand

Matthew J. Wilson, Dean and Professor of Law, University of Akron Law School, United States

Michael Ramsden, Associate Professor, Chinese University of Hong Kong, Hong Kong

Musa Toprak, Baskent University, Faculty of Law, Baglica Kampusu, Ankara, Turkey

Mutaz M. Qafisheh, Dean of the College of Law and Professor of International Law, Hebron University, Palestine

Panarairat Srichaiyarat, Deputy Director of the Centre for ASEAN Studies at Khon Kaen University, Thailand

Rathna N. Koman, Associate Professor of Law (Practice), Singapore Management University

Rogena Sterling, PhD Candidate, Te Piringa—Faculty of Law, University of Waikato, New Zealand

Shuvro Prosun Sarker, Assistant Professor, School of Law, KIIT University, India and DAAD Doctoral (Dr. Jur.) Scholar at the Faculty of Law, Justus Liebig University Giessen, Germany

Thomas Chih-hsiung Chen, Associate Professor of Law, School of Law, National Chiao Tung University, Taiwan

Withoon Taloodkum, Lecturer, School of Law, University of Phayao, Thailand

Yael Efron, Faculty, Hebrew University and Zefat Academic College School of Law, Israel

CHAPTER 1

Introduction: Clinical Legal Education and Its Asian Characteristics

Bruce Avery Lasky and Shuvro Prosun Sarker

The Early Wave of Clinical Legal Education

The history of clinical legal education (CLE) in the United States is more than one hundred years old, and the United States is regarded as the first country to start such an experiential learning method of law teaching.[1] The Dean of Harvard Law School, Christopher Columbus Langdell, in 1870 started the case method of law teaching, which replaced the earlier apprenticeship training or study of law as an abstraction.[2] Langdell's method of teaching resulted in law students "study[ing] selected appellate opinions and distill[ing] from them the evolution of legal principles."[3] George S. Grossman described Langdell's method as one in which a mental process was involved in the analysis, synthesis, and distinction of appellate opinions, which created a dialogue between student and teacher designed to elicit the underlying reasoning and principles involved.[4] Margaret Martin Barry described the method in the following way:

> The casebook method's emphases on appellate judicial decisions and the Socratic method as the means to teach the skill of legal analysis . . . and an analytical and systematized approach to the law as interconnected rational principles, taught primarily through lectures at proprietary law schools.[5]

Consequently Langdell's newly invented method of law teaching supported the emergence of full-time law teachers in universities, and practitioner law teachers were seen to be as a poverty of the law school. Langdell is quoted as having said,

> What qualifies a person to teach law is not experience in the work of a lawyer's office, not experience in dealing with law, not experience in the trial or

> argument of cause-not experience, in short, in using law, but experience in learning law.[6]

The case method of law teaching was criticized as an "aggressive, demeaning and destructive of group cohesion"[7] and "wasteful of class time."[8] Jerome Frank described Langdell's model:

> Unfortunately, attempted reform of legal pedagogy is frequently in the hands of the "library-law" teacher. With the best will in the world, such a teacher often finds it almost impossible to warp over the old so-called case system so as to adapt it to the needs of the future practicing lawyer. For, as above noted, that system is centered in books. So long as teachers who know nothing except what they learned from books under the old case-system are in control of a law-school, the actualities of the lawyer's life are likely in that school to be considered peripheral and as of secondary importance.[9]

The case method of law teaching was not able to help a future lawyer develop the skills required in an actual situation as it emphasized a client-less analysis in a situation of competition and isolation.[10] Students were taught to prepare only for exams, which resulted in a system of "every man for himself." This isolation narrowed the opportunity for the students to learn the necessary skills of teamwork, which is a very important factor in actual legal practice.[11] These elements of the case method prompted legal scholars of that time to consider bringing something more to law teaching pedagogy that Langdell[12] had missed, as they believed his method had represented a "narrow view of legal education."[13]

Consequently, in the early 1900s several law schools started legal aid centers to provide an opportunity for students to acquire firsthand experience in learning lawyering skills and legal analysis. The other mission, apart from the curricular objective, behind this initiative was to play a social justice role by providing legal assistance to the underprivileged sections of society.[14] The New York State Bar Association in 1916 adopted a resolution requiring that "every law school shall make earnest clinical work, through legal aid societies or other agencies, a part of its curriculum for its full course."[15] This was obviously a crucial decision following the misery caused to human life in World War I.[16]

William V. Rowe in 1917 was one of those persons who first talked about the importance of clinical education in law schools and put forward the jurisprudence behind it. He emphasized analysis of the issues of the day by students and offered a moral argument, saying that

> it will be the purpose of the clinic, not merely to educate in practice and to develop, in general, the true professional spirit, but, in the interest of the commonwealth and of good citizenship, to lay the foundations in the individual student for sound personal character and business honor, to make clear, in the concrete, the lawyer's duty to society and to his fellow men, and, in so doing, to combat the idea, prevalent for two generations past, that the law is simply one means, like any trade, of making a living, and is freely open to the world without serious restrictions as to qualifications, and with no special resulting social obligations.[17]

Rowe put forward the idea that the honor of the legal profession and social responsibility should be implanted in the minds of students from the beginning of their law school instruction with the help of the bar, much like an internship system. But he anticipated the problem of connecting a law clinic with a lawyer's office and, finally, argued that clinical work should be done by law schools alone with the help of the State.[18]

Following World War I, the emergence of a realist school of jurisprudence played a crucial role in developing CLE in America. The realist movement influenced law schools to start teaching the social sciences, and the research method began moving toward being empirical in nature.[19] Advocates of realism do not believe that judicial opinions are the result of rules of logic based on precedent, but rather that "access to a body of fact and comment on the basis of which decisions can be made to implement effectively democratic values."[20] According to realists, law students should go beyond the letter of the law or the wording of a judicial opinion to understand the social and psychological forces on the basis of which a law or judicial opinion is made.[21] However, after World War II, neorealists started to propagate a new idea of teaching the law that would better equip students to be policymakers in society.[22]

While the earlier realist movement emphasized the training of law students in a functional social-legal setting, the neorealists shifted training "away from the purpose of technical competence."[23] The neorealists' idea of developing law students into policymakers did not gain sufficient momentum; however, the teaching of ethics and professional responsibility as a part of law school curriculum came about as a result of their influence.[24] Moreover, the realists' efforts at "turning the legal or human knowledge into action" received consistent support through various reports and professional bodies. The Carnegie Foundation for the Advancement of Teaching in 1921 funded a study on legal education in America by Alfred Z. Reed. Reed's report supported the ideas of the realists and emphasized the need to provide law students with a general education, theoretical knowledge of the law, and practical skills training.[25] In 1944, the Committee on Curriculum of the Association of American Law Schools produced a report titled "The Place of Skills in Legal Education" and supported the earlier report prepared by Reed and based on the ideas of the realists.[26]

The "Social Justice"[27] Orientation Abinitio

There was no particular vision of CLE during the first 50 years of its existence.[28] The early advocates of CLE campaigned for the skills training of law students and for providing access to justice for the underprivileged population, and supported the legal realism movement.[29] The neorealists' notion of developing future lawyers as policymakers led to the addition of new courses like professional ethics to the law school curriculum.[30] But the movement for social relevance in the law school curriculum in the United States in the 1960s became the primary objective of CLE, of "us[ing] law as an instrument for social justice and change."[31] Charles E. Ares found that there was a desire among law students "to help make the law serve the needs of the poor. Only the techniques for meeting that desire are missing."[32] Therefore, it was then necessary to start thinking about developing the curriculum by starting a dialogue among law teachers. Frank's idea of establishing clinics inside the law school was really welcomed at that time because of its potential for uniting theory and practice.[33] Most of the clinicians were not interested in teaching the skills of legal practice; rather, they wanted to put the students into the real world to experience the feeling of representing a client and thus learn the complexities and essentials of law practice.[34] Law schools in the 1960s and 1970s "expanded clinics to demystify law for students and to represent client communities with claims that thrust clinical programs into the civil rights, consumer rights, environmental rights, and poverty rights movements."[35] Their aim was to represent the indigent client, as there is different market for legal professionals who represent paying clients. So the commitment to a CLE was intended to be strictly attached to concerns for social justice, and this would be helpful not only for the indigent client but also for the student who experienced real-world circumstances.[36] This movement for social justice education is considered to be a return to the roots of CLE.[37] Thus "clinics play a critical role, both in terms of educating students to their professional obligations and sensitizing them to the needs of people."[38] Jane H. Aiken, describing the goal of social justice education, quotes Lee Anne Bell, who said that

> The goal of social justice education is full and equal participation of all groups in a society that is mutually shaped to meet their needs. Social justice includes a vision of society in which the distribution of resources is equitable and all members are physically and psychologically safe and secure. We envision a society in which individuals are both self-determining (able to develop their full capacities) and interdependent (capable of interacting democratically with others). Social justice involves social actors who have a sense of their own agency as well as a sense of social responsibility toward and with others and the society as a whole.[39]

According to Jon Dubin, clinical legal education promotes the essentials of social justice primarily by three ways:[40]

1. By promoting access to justice for the underprivileged through representing them in various forums
2. By exposing law students to the responsibility for public service or pro bono work
3. By creating an understanding of the relationship between law and social justice among the law students.

All three ways have some effect on the learning of a law student about social justice values because the unique experience that is gained cannot properly be explained by the student's prior understanding of law and legal procedure.[41] The student is required to properly follow up on a process that can help him to think critically beyond any beliefs, values, and norms.[42] In this phase, clinicians have to play a greater role by shaping the student's reflective thinking. Finally, through this reorientation, the student's perspective is changed, and he can explain the unusual experiences he has gained. When a student is representing a client and understands the client requires legal representation, without which his or her problems cannot be solved, this makes the student much more responsible. This responsibility to an individual client will be transformed into social responsibility when the student's understanding of society is increased by representing the underprivileged. Therefore, to generate this type of understanding among law students, it is necessary to educate them in order to secure social justice. The Report of the Committee on the Future of In-House Clinics of the American Association of Law Schools 1992, quoting Gary Palm, urges clinicians to include instruction on this aspect that

> they will never otherwise receive. This instruction includes learning about poverty. . . . They should confront the failure of our government to provide equal justice and fair legal procedures for the poor. We should help them structure their careers to include pro bono work through community group representation, litigation and legislative advocacy.[43]

Frank Bloch, discussing the benefits of instructing students on the social justice responsibility of the legal profession by involving students in legal aid activities, states that the

> merger of legal aid and legal education through the clinical movement has been important because a lawyer's professional life really begins when he or she enters law school . . . the law school years represent for most the first time in their lives that self-identification as a lawyer can have any real meaning. This self-identification as a lawyer is particularly important for law students when they are first exposed to legal aid activities and the notion of professional public service.[44]

The lack of access to justice for the underprivileged is a problem rooted deep in any legal system in the world. Thus, it is always important as a law student to find the reasons behind it, the solutions behind it. Clinical teachers should take the initiative in teaching students to fight for the underprivileged. They should expound on the ideas of justice, morality, and rights, and expose how these noble ideas are getting scattered by the inequitable distribution of wealth. These all can create sensitivity to human suffering among law students, and show the original roots of CLE and its further direction for the next century or so.

The Asian Characteristic of Clinical Legal Education —Empowerment, Justice, and Skills

This chapter began with a consideration of the history and an evaluation of CLE in the United States, and it now moves on to evaluate the characteristics of CLE in Asia. However, "Asian characteristic" is somewhat amorphous. It can be quite vexing to try to define what is meant by Asia, as it is a broad continent with many nationalities, religions, ethnicities, languages, and cultures. The same can be said for Asian legal systems, which possess a mixture of common law, civil law, Shari'ah law, and customary law structures, often with a number of these structures existing within a single nation state. These legal systems have a multitude of roots and origins, with some dating back centuries and others having a more recent strong colonialist influence.

The same may also be said for the multifaceted characteristics of Asian legal education. Yet, although there exists a multitude of unique legal education practices, many common attributes concurrently exist as well. Often, these similarities have been most apparent when looking at the challenges faced by Asian law schools, which have included the need to balance legal education and interdisciplinary perspectives, to provide sufficient comparative material, to reform teaching and assessment methodology, and to juggle competing needs with very limited resources.[45] One primary legal education challenge, for example, which cuts across most Asian national borders, is that students are often passive learners, and teachers are seen as "gurus imparting knowledge." This scenario not only exists at the law school level but is most often also true of the basic education level of most students prior to entering their law study.[46] Moreover, law being a bachelor-level program in most Asian countries, it is common that lawyering skills and the professional lawyering ethic and societal responsibility are not taught until after students graduate from their undergraduate programs.

Yet, within these common challenges there exists a growing change in many Asian countries and law programs, which has included a CLE movement. This trend has fervently developed and currently continues to expand at a rapid pace.

An examination of this regional CLE movement would show that it reflects its own Asian characteristics. For example, one contemporary core commonality of most of these Asian university CLE programs can be found in their focused social justice mission of delivering legal assistance and empowerment to the poor and marginalized, while simultaneously developing legal knowledge, skills, ethics, and pro bono values within the participating university students.

A number of CLE programs, including the Ateneo University Human Rights Center (AHRC)[47] in the Philippines, train students to use a participatory method of representation when working with clients. Rather than utilizing a top-down approach, clients are treated as equals throughout the representation process. The lawyer's role is not just to solve a client's problem and deliver the answers or solutions through a one-way exchange. Rather, the client is involved as a co-decision-maker.

This mode of alternative lawyering enables clients to do for themselves and understand and find solutions to their own problematic situations. It is a means of achieving a break in the often cycle of need. Conventionally, clients meet with lawyers and look to simply have their legal problems solved. In these scenarios, once the immediate need is worked out, it is not unusual for these persons to return to the same environment from which they came. This frequently leads again, often only a short time later, to the development of similar or identical problems. It is a type of Band-Aid approach to problem solving. Traditional lawyering is seen as a mechanism that "promotes a client dependency on the lawyer instead of encouraging legal self-reliance on the part of marginalized groups."[48]

Alternative lawyering, which is a client-focused representation method, is a tool for lowering the rate at which clients' needs are repeated. Students in clinic programs, employing alternative lawyering techniques, are taught to listen to clients and hear what they are saying. They are taught to learn from their clients, and to sit back and allow the client to guide the decision-making process, which is often a difficult technique for the control-minded personalities that many attorneys possess.

Moreover, in working to further empower communities, these alternative lawyering methods often focus on group representation rather than individuals. They center on the "social or structural problems" of "the poor and vulnerable groups." Along with the representation of the groups, a primary goal is empowerment in the social, economic, and political sphere.

Historically, many CLE programs throughout Asia, like those in the Philippines, have played a significant role in ensuring this empowerment principle. Yet, although a number of programs throughout Asia possess this regional commonality, the same cannot be said for CLE being structured educational programs. Rather, although the Philippines developed accredited CLE course structures early on, another common Asian CLE characteristic was that most other clinic-type programs existing in the region were more service-related clinics, in which little to no jurisprudential pedagogy was used. Many of them were developed outside the formal curriculum as volunteer, extracurricular, initiatives.

This problematic situation can be demonstrated through a review of the Thammasat University, Thailand, legal clinic. Started in 1949, it has for years in Thailand often been hailed as a model CLE program, which focuses on providing a broad variety of legal services to the public.[49] Yet, to this day, the clinic has yet to be integrated into a structured, credit-bearing course. For many years, similar to Thammasat, there has seemed to be a lack of connection between universities developing CLE programs that provide both a social justice mission and, simultaneously, and integrated program with an accredited legal education course.

Moreover, comparable to the lack of CLE-accredited programs, there was also no common movement to apply and use CLE methods in the traditional, doctrinal, or elective courses. Rather than use these methods, which apply an interactive, student-centered, reflective approach, and include a focus on social justice, ethics, and professionalism, lectures continued to be the primary mode of teaching. At best, CLE methods were often limited to being used for students in clinic programs.

Early in the twenty-first century, this situation started to shift as universities in a number of Asian countries began to align both the pedagogy and the social justice mission in their CLE programs with the methods. Building on these experiences, a regional breakthrough occurred in 2005 when the First Southeast Asia Clinical Legal Education Conference was held in Phnom Penh, Cambodia. The conference, which used the Pannasastra University of Cambodia Legal Clinic as a prototype of a social justice and accredited course model, was attended by a broad range of legal educators, legal professionals, members of civil society, and government representatives from throughout Asia and globally. The event provided the first regional venue for exchanging experiences by both those new to the CLE movement and persons already engaged in CLE who were interested in expanding their programs to include both a social justice theme and an accredited course program.

This event was soon followed by the First Southeast Asia Clinical Legal Education Training of Trainers Workshop in 2007, hosted by the University of Ateneo and co-organized by the Open Society Justice Initiative and Bridges Across Borders Southeast Asia Community Legal Education Initiative (BABSEA CLE).Like the forum in Cambodia in 2005, this event concentrated on ensuring that the participants in attendance appreciated the need to try to guarantee both academic and social justice CLE program components. As well, there was a strong concentration on the ways and means of utilizing CLE methods in traditional law teaching subjects.

Following these forums, similar CLE-related regional events have occurred, including in Indonesia, China, India, Indonesia, Laos, Malaysia, Singapore, Thailand, and Vietnam. As a result, and almost a decade since the 2005 Phnom Penh Conference, there is a clear indication that the objectives laid out in Cambodia have begun to be achieved. Social justice-oriented CLE-accredited programs are moving toward a more standardized practice throughout Asia, and CLE methods are much more widely appreciated, accepted, and used in law school instruction.

In addition to these collective regional CLE forums, there have been other factors involved in ensuring these CLE successes. One of these, while not necessarily unique to the Asian culture, but clearly known as a part of it, is the idea of community and working together. Throughout this past decade, one of the most successful driving forces supporting the development of CLE in Asia has been the collaboration of universities at both the national and the regional level. CLE-related study visits, exchanges, and other knowledge, experience, and product sharing has been common in the region. These collaborations have resulted in an ardent regional sense of familial unity. Examples are too numerous to list. Some of the more noted ones include the visit to both Ateneo University and the University of Philippines by the Pannasastra University of Cambodia in 2004, followed by the University Malaya and Universiti Teknologi Mara (Malaysia) in 2007. The growth of CLE in Vietnam is often attributed to a 2009 study visit to Thailand hosted and organized by the Chiang Mai University Legal Consultation Centre. The visit was attended by a number of deans and high-level professors from throughout Vietnam, who soon after began to provide core support for the development of CLE at their home institutions. More recent examples are the study visits made by delegations of Myanmar legal education representatives to universities in Thailand, Vietnam, and India in 2013, and to Laos and Singapore in 2014.

This community character has also brought about the creation of CLE associations and networks, which have further been a factor in fueling the CLE movement. This can be exemplified in part in the earlier years by the creation the Committee of Chinese Clinical Legal Educators (CCCLE) in 2003, and more recently the Indonesia Clinical Legal Education Association in February 2013, the Vietnam Clinical Legal Education Network in April 2013, and the Southeast Asia Clinical Legal Education Association (SEACLEA) in November 20013.

Moreover, the regional CLE advancements have also been due to the concerted efforts of organizations and institutions promoting the expansion of CLE. In addition to the Ford Foundation, which began to promote and back clinics in China starting in 2000,[50] others began to follow suit, and have included BABSEA CLE, the Global Alliance for Justice Education (GAJE), the *International Journal of Clinical Legal Education*, the Open Society Foundation/Justice Initiative, and the United Nations Development Programme (UNDP). Working with a common mission of developing pedagogically sound, justice-oriented CLE programs, and often strategizing collaboratively, they have continually worked with Asian university representatives to organize, host, and attend regional and globally related CLE events.

CLE-related research and academic writing has also begun to play a significant role in its regional development. This factor is often stressed to nascent CLE law lecturers as one of the many benefits of being involved in CLE programs, as well as the need to use CLE methods.[51] In the past few years, it has become more common for publications with a sole or substantial focus on CLE development in the Asian context, to be produced. The strategic advocacy value of such publications should not be minimized. They have been both useful in gaining support from policymakers, who are often reluctant to approve progressive, social justice–related educational CLE programs,[52] as well as in other ways, including providing access to justice-focused donor agencies that have historically not funded such initiatives. Moreover, the publications also serve the purpose of assisting legal educators in the professional advancement of their academic careers.

As a result of this combination of factors, CLE has begun to develop a solid foundation throughout Asia as an initiative aimed at building formal legal education, access to justice, and the rule of law. The demand for the introduction of new programs and the strengthening of existing ones continues to increase with the appreciation of CLE's value in assisting in the reform of legal education while simultaneously providing new tools for strengthening civic engagement in schools and communities. There is a much greater understanding that these programs directly foster inclusive participation by strengthening awareness of core development goal principles, especially access to justice, rights-based approaches, and legal empowerment of the poor. At the same time, CLE builds capacities for advocacy and civil engagement, at both the grass-roots level and nationally.

These successes have also been accompanied by a number of common challenges throughout Asia. Because CLE is still somewhat unfamiliar to more traditional educators and policymakers, there has been a hurdle at a number of institutions in receiving approval for accredited clinical courses. This has a direct impact on the amount time that both law teachers and students can be engaged in the programs due to their not receiving remuneration or credit for their involvement.

Other challenges have included a lack of training, both in the progressive teaching methods of many of law teachers as well as practical lawyering skills. This has been coupled with the fact that in Asia, unlike with clinic programs in the United States and a number of other countries, which often have eight to ten students per clinic course, class sizes may exceed 100 students.

There also exists a prohibition in most Asian countries on university law teachers' practicing law. As a result, many CLE direct client service programs only provide initial consultation and referral services rather than direct client representation. These challenges, however, have often been turned into a strength, as many CLE programs have developed teaching methods and community service focuses that do not follow some of the more traditional direct client service clinics often seen in the United States and other Western countries. As an example, many CLE programs throughout Asia are engaged in community legal education activities, as this provides a forum for many more students to be involved, with many student groups participating in community legal education activities with a number of different communities throughout a semester.

Finally, a constant challenge is ensuring the educational goals of the CLE programs are not trumped by those who mistakenly see them primarily as legal aid and community service projects. As most Asian countries have, at best, fledgling government-supported legal aid systems, this is often a situation that is frequently encountered. This circumstance is often used as a strength by CLE advocates. They are able to express the point that if the programs are properly developed with a primary focus on quality educational, rather than quantity delivery services, they will help ensure the exponential development of many more future ethically and professionally trained legal aid-oriented actors. This provides the basis for an at-scale paradigm shift that will positively strengthen the legal profession and legal system.

Present State of CLE in Asia and New Initiatives

Within the pages of this chapter, it is not possible to provide a complete view of the present state of CLE in Asia. At best, it is fair to say that against the backdrop of successes and challenges described herein, there has been much forward movement and growth. New CLE initiatives have begun, and many others are being considered. One such example includes Myanmar, which has embarked on a nationwide CLE development program involving all 18 law departments. This program has move forward with the broad support of the Myanmar government, United Nations Development Programme (UNDP), BABSEA CLE, and private sector legal partners, including Herbert Smith Freehills, DLA Piper, and their nonprofit initiative, New Perimeter. Other developments have included universities that thematically focus on specific access to justice issues, including migrant[53] and sex workers, transgender communities,[54] People Living with HIV (PLHIV),[55] and land-related issues.[56] Transnational CLE programs involving partnerships between two or more universities, working cross-borders, have begun as well.[57]

When looking at current the CLE systematic programs and methods being applied throughout much of Asia, it is important to note a particular model employed by BABSEA CLE. This approach strives to transcend tolerance and strengthen access to justice through CLE. This model

1. Ensures the growth of university-based CLE programs focusing on legal empowerment for socially vulnerable and marginalized individuals and communities;
2. Assists in developing a networked cadre of pro bono and community service-minded law graduates and civil society advocates for justice;
3. Encourages the embodiment of CLE approaches that transcend the notion of tolerance, enabling advocates for justice to stand in solidarity with poor, vulnerable, and marginalized communities; and
4. Facilitates local and global linkages between CLE programs as well as nonstate actors (NSAs), including civil society organizations, law firms, corporations, and local state actors (LSAs), including governmental policymakers, municipalities, and justice sector institutions;.

The BABSEA CLE model draws on critical pedagogy to assist prospective lawyers and advocates for justice to develop a critical stance challenging exclusion based on biases and the practice of "othering." BABSEA CLE-supported CLE programs in Asia are committed to the development of critical epistemologies, ethics of caring, compassion, and solidarity, and actively strive to heighten law students' and faculty members' understanding of social disparities and consideration of alternatives to existing structural arrangements that are conducive to legal inequality.[58]

BABSEA CLE views social justice as an individual, collective, and institutional journey. This involves developing multicultural/multiethnic/multinational knowledges to challenge racism, sexism, disablism, homophobia, transphobia, and other biases, and taking a critical stance on injustice and exclusion. The model is also working to make access to justice resources more widely available through open and distance learning (ODL) and open educational resources (OERs). The model's success is, in part, the result of working within a networked community of critical friends and advocates who promote a transparent rule of law and increased access to justice within NSAs and LSAs both locally and globally.[59]

Other new regional developments have included the intersection between the CLE movement and the emerging global pro bono movement. Both the public and private sector have come to understand how pro bono initiatives can work in conjunction with and support CLE programs. They furthermore comprehend that CLE programs develop the next generation of pro bono leaders and advocates, and thereby support the pro bono movement. Seen as mutually supportive, these regional and global energies were formally joined, beginning at the Inaugural Asia Pro Bono Conference held in Laos (September, 2012) and co-organized by the National University of Laos Faculty of Law and Political Science. Since that time, two similar Asia regional events have been co-organized by universities, including in Vietnam (October 2013) and, more recently, in Singapore (September 2014). In September 2015, the 4th Asia Pro Bono Conference and Legal Ethics Forum will be co-organized by three Myanmar university law departments located in Mandalay.

Another recent development, which is greatly attributed to the regional CLE movement, has been the effort to integrate legal ethics, professional responsibility, pro bono work, and access to justice teachings into the formal law curricula of many law schools throughout the region. Many Asian university legal education institutions do not have a mandated legal ethics, professional responsibility course. For those that do, they often fail to connect the teaching of legal and professional standards with the lawyer's pro bono obligation, and role, in guaranteeing access to justice to the poor and marginalized. The move to incorporate this curriculum is often being first introduced and initiated through university CLE programs.

Conclusion

While CLE could initially have been described as an Anglo-Western style of legal education teaching, its current status in Asia no longer places it within this framework. Rather, CLE throughout the Asia region, although still in an early development stage, has managed to incorporate many of the core values set out by early Western legal education theorists, and has concurrently developed its own Asian characteristics. These characteristics have developed through national, regional, and international collaborations. As a result, the programs possess a mixed synergistic set of objectives, including the reform of legal education, which has been beneficial for both students and legal educators alike. Moreover, these programs provide direct legal service and legal empowerment for individuals and communities that are faced with access to justice obstacles. Finally, the programs focus on assisting in strengthening a more ethical and socially conscious legal profession and legal system in an area of the world often seen in great need of this reinforcement.

The movement forward will likely face a number of surges and stalls. Yet, based upon what has already occurred, it will be a forward movement nonetheless. It will also be a movement that will likely continue to evolve in a particularly Asian characteristic way.

Notes

1. See generally Margaret M. Barry, Jon C. Dubin, and Peter A. Joy, "Clinical Education for this Millennium: The Third Wave" (2000) 7 *Clinical L. Rev.* 1, 5.
2. George S. Grossman, "Clinical Legal Education: History and Diagnosis" (1973–1974) 26 *J. Legal Educ.* 162, 163. See generally Jerome Frank, "Why Not

a Clinical Lawyer-School?" (1932–1933) 81 *U. Pa. L. Rev.* 907. But some scholars, such as John Norton Pomeroy, Professor at the University of New York City (now known as New York University), used a case method of instruction several years before Langdell introduced this method of instruction at Harvard. However, Langdell was credited as he had satisfactorily used this method as the Dean of Harvard Law School. See Joel Seligman, *The High Citadel: The Influence of Harvard Law School* (Houghton, Mifflin, 1978) 32–42; Anthony Chase, "The Birth of the Modern Law School" (1979) 23 *Am. J. Legal Hist.* 329, 333; Robert Stevens, *Law School: Legal Education in America from the 1850s to the 1980s* (The University of North Carolina Press, 1983) 3, 52.
3. Ibid.
4. Ibid.
5. Barry et al. (n 1) 5.
6. J.W. Hurst, *Growth of American Law: The Law Makers* (Little, Brown and Company, 1950) 263.
7. Alan A. Stone, "Legal Education on a Couch" (1971) 85 *Harv. L. Rev.* 392.
8. "Modern Trends in Legal Education" (1964) 64 *Colum. L. Rev.* 710, 713. See Louis L. Jaffe, "Commentaries on Mr. Shea's Lecture" (1962–1963) 12 *Buff. L. Rev.* 280, 287.
9. Jerome Frank, "Why Not a Clinical Lawyer-School?" (1932–1933) 81 *U. Pa. L. Rev.* 915.
10. Jennifer Howard, "Learning to 'Think Like a Lawyer' Through Experience" (1995) 2 *Clinical L. Rev.* 167, 172.
11. Ibid.
12. Grossman (n 2).
13. Barry et al. (n 1) 6. See Charles R. McManis, "The History of First Century American Legal Education: A Revisionist Perspective" (1981) 59 *Wash. U. L.Q.* 597.
14. Legal aid centers were established by law students at schools such as University of Denver, The George Washington University, Harvard University, University of Minnesota, Northwestern University, University of Pennsylvania, and University of Tennessee. See John S. Bradway, "The Nature of a Legal Aid Clinic" (1930) 3 *S. Cal. L. Rev.* 173, 174; William V. Rowe, "Legal Clinics and Better Trained Lawyers—A Necessity" (1917) 11 *Ill. L. Rev.* 591.
15. Rowe, ibid. 595.
16. Grossman (n 2).
17. Rowe (n 14) 607.
18. See William V. Rowe, "The People's Law Bureau" (1920–1921) 15 *Ill. L. Rev.* 424, 430–431.
19. Grossman (n 2) 167; Jerome Frank and Llewellyn were the proponents of Realist School in America.
20. Harold D. Lasswell and Myres S. Mcdougal, "Legal Education and Public Policy: Professional Training in the Public Interest" (1942–1943) 52 *Yale L.J.* 203, 229.
21. See Grossman (n 2) 167; ibid. 230.
22. Ibid. 203; Harold D. Lasswell and Myres S. Mcdougal of Yale were the prominent figures of neo realist movement. See also Grossman (n 2) 167.
23. R. F. Boden, "Is Legal Education Deserting the Bar?" (1970) 37 *Ins. Counsel J.* 97, 99.
24. Note (n 8) 723.
25. Barry et al. (n 1) 7.
26. "Place of Skills in Legal Education" (1945) *45 Colum. L. Rev.* 345.

27. Justice has no absolute meaning because it, too, like all knowledge, is grounded in context. At a minimum, however, those of us who dedicate ourselves to social justice must ask ourselves if our proposed action as a lawyer will support and increase human dignity. See Jane H. Aiken, "Provocateurs for Justice" (2000–2001) 7 *Clinical L. Rev.* 287, 296.

    I believe that teaching law students to be socially conscious practitioners is at the heart of clinical education and should be at the heart of a good legal education. Equal access to justice cannot be achieved if legal services are not made available to the poor and subordinated and if the barriers they face are not challenged. For many schools, community service and social justice are very much an aspect of the mission of CLE. See Antoinette S. Lopez, "Learning Through Service in a Clinical Setting: The Effect of Specialization on Social Justice and Skills Training" (2000–2001) 7 *Clinical L. Rev.* 307, 310.
28. Barry et al. (n 1) 9.
29. Barry et al. (n 1) 9.
30. Lasswell and Mcdougal (n 20) 206.
31. Barry et al. (n 1) 13.
32. Charles E. Ares, "Legal Education and the Problem of the Poor" (1964–1965) 17 *J. Legal Educ.* 307, 310.
33. Arthur Kinoy, "The Present Crisis in American Legal Education" (1969–1970) 24 *Rutgers L. Rev.* 1, 8.
34. Martin Guggenheim, "Fee Generating Clinics: Can We Bear the Costs?" (1994–1995) 1 *Clinical L. Rev.* 677, 679.
35. Barry et al. (n 1) 13.
36. Guggenheim (n 34) 683.
37. See Nina Tarr, "Current Issues in Clinical Legal Education" (1993) 37 *How. L. J.* 31; Jane H. Aiken, "Striving to Teach 'Justice, Fairness and Morality'" (1997) 4 *Clinical L. Rev.* 1.
38. Guggenheim (n 34) 683.

    As we all know, many of the students who come to clinic already embrace a justice mission. That does not mean, however, that they appreciate its implications. There is always room for reflection and the interchange between faculty and student that often result in growth for both. On the other hand, lest we think we will get off too easy in our role as provocateurs, it appears that we are getting more and more students attracted to clinic, not because it is a chance to serve the poor or disadvantaged, but rather because it affords the opportunity to gain the skills needed to be an effective lawyer. See Aiken (n 27).
39. Aiken (n 27).
40. See Jon C. Dubin, "Clinical Design for Social Justice Imperatives" (1997–1998) 51 *S.M.U. L. Rev.* 1461, 1475–1476.
41. Ibid. 1478.
42. Ibid. 1478.
43. "Report of the Committee on the Future of the In-House Clinic" (1992) 42 *J. Legal Educ.* 508, 515.
44. Frank S. Bloch and Iqbal S. Ishar, "Legal Aid, Public Service and Clinical Legal Education: Future Directions from India and the United States" (1990–1991) 12 *Mich. J. Int'l. L.* 108.
45. See generally Gary Bell et al., "Legal Education in Asia" (2006) 1 *Asian J. Comp. L.* 1.
46. Ibid.

47. Carlos Medina, "Law Schools and Legal Aid: The Philippine Experience" unpublished paper presented at the SE Asia CLE Conference, November 26–30, 2005, Phnom Penh, Cambodia.
48. Ibid.
49. Malee Pruekpongsawalee, "Thammasat Clinical Education and the Delivery of Legal Service: A Historical and Personal Perspective" in Louise G. Trubek and Jeremy Cooper (eds.) *Educating for Justice Around the World* (Ashgate, 1999) 127.
50. Pamela Phan, "Clinical Legal Education in China: In Pursuit of a Culture of Law and a Mission of Social Justice" (2005) 8 *Yale Hum. Rts. & Dev. L.J.* 128.
51. As an example, in 2011 Professor Frank Bloch, Vanderbilt University Emeritus, in conjunction with BABSEA CLE, delivered a variety of CLE scholarship academic writing workshops to university personnel engaged in CLE programs throughout Vietnam.
52. See Panarairat Srichaiyarat, "Clinical Legal Education: An Option for Thai Legal Education Reform" (2012) 5 *Naresuan U. L.J.* 80–108; Panarairat Srichaiyarat, "Thai Qualifications Framework for Higher Education and Clinical Legal Education" (2012) 3 *Assumption U. L.J.* 18–31; Bruce Laskyand Norbani M. Nazeri, "The Development and Expansion of University-Based Clinical/Community Legal Education Programs in Malaysia" (2011) 11 *Int'l J. Clin. Legal Educ.* 59–74.
53. Beginning in 2014, the newly formed not-for-profit organization Justice Without Borders (JWB) has made great strides in bridging universities, civil societies, and lawyers to focus on ensuring greater access to justice and legal remedy for migrant workers. Countries of initial engagement include Indonesia, the Philippines, Hong Kong, and Singapore.
54. Christopher Walsh and Nada Chaiyajit, "Sexperts! Disrupting Injustice Through HIV Prevention and Legal Rights Education with Transgenders in Thailand" published paper at the Joint AARE APERA International Conference, 2012, Sydney.
55. In 2011, a Vietnam nationwide CLE project began involving universities in Hanoi, Ho Chi Minh City, and Can Tho, in collaboration with the Vietnamese civil society organization VNP+, and with the support of UNAIDS and BABSEA CLE, to provide legal education, empowerment training, and legal referral services to networks of PLHIV.
56. Since 2009, the National University of Laos Faculty of Law and Political Science Clinical Legal Education program has successfully been running a yearly one to month-long rural community legal education project, which has focused on land law issues.
57. An example of this can be seen in the collaborative cross-border CLE project between Pasundan University, Indonesia, and the University of Malaya, Malaysia Indonesia migrant worker's rights awareness project.
58. Christopher Walsh, Bruce Lasky, Wendy Morrish, and Nada Chaiyajit, "Strengthening Access to Justice Through Clinical Legal Education" (2012) 6 *Transforming Gov't: People, Process and Pol'y* 380–391. Emerald Online Article.
59. Ibid.

CHAPTER 2

Better Lawyers, Better Justice: Introducing Clinical Legal Education in the Maldives

Marium Jabyn and Rogena Sterling

Introduction

The practice of law is a fledging field in the Maldives. The demand for trained law professionals has never been so high. This major shift in career choices can be attributed to the fast developing legal and political institutions in the Maldives and an ongoing goal of integrating democracy into a fundamentally Islamic system. These issues are particularly critical and complex for the Maldives justice system because it is a mixture of Shari'ah and multiple other principles and legal concepts, including English common law. The present system of legal education, however, which offers limited opportunities for applying law school theory to real-life cases, is hugely deficient in terms of preparing students for a legal career in the Maldives or elsewhere. This chapter examines many of these contemporary disparities between legal education and law practice in the Maldives. It explores the effect of introducing clinical legal education (CLE) into law schools by exploring the potential impact on the quality of the graduates and also on legal aid, human rights, and access to justice for vulnerable groups. It is hoped that this appraisal will spotlight some of the most important questions and problems faced by those engaged in legal education, law reform, and the administration of justice in the Maldives.

Legal Pedagogy and the Practice of Law in the Maldives

At present, there is no scope of CLE in the Maldives. When students graduate, they can practice immediately. There is no appetite for a postdegree admission qualifications that include clinical education. Formal legal education in the

Maldives itself dates back to not more than 20 years, and prior to 1995, no postsecondary institutions offered legal education.[1] There are reports, however, that Islamic Shari'ah law was being taught in some parts of the Maldives as early as 1125 AD.[2] Prior to the country's official conversion to Islam in 1153 AD, Arab travelers had arrived at Addu Atoll Meedhoo and started teaching Islamic Shari'ah to students from all over the Maldives.[3] Meedhoo then went on to produce many scholars who served as judicial officers in the Maldives for many years to come.[4]

Legal Education: An Overview

The first official training course for judges was launched in the late 1960s, to address an acute shortage of judicial officers.[5] This course was a prerequisite for all judicial appointments and covered only Shari'ah law subjects such as Islamic family law, criminal law, and law of succession.[6] In 1981, this course was transferred to the Institute of Islamic Studies, where it was revised as a two-year judicial training course, but continued to be fundamentally based on Islamic Shari'ah.[7] In 1988, this institute introduced the first specific course aimed at training lawyers.[8] Titled the Muhaamee course, anyone who had completed grade seven or a secondary-level examination offered by the Ministry of Education was qualified to enroll in this two-year program.[9] In 1995, the Muhaamee course and the judges' course were combined into a three-year Diploma in Shari'ah and Law course to train both judges and lawyers.[10] The three-year Diploma in Shari'ah and Law course was soon revised as an Advanced Diploma in Shari'ah and Law course in 2004 and was first offered as a law degree in 2006.[11]

The late 1990s witnessed the first national efforts to establish a law school in the Maldives. By then, the fast developing economy of the country had started a debate about the system of law and justice in the Maldives and the need for qualified human resources. The primary idea behind starting a law school was to respond to the great shortage of qualified legal personnel in the country, including legal and judicial officials. Introduced as the Institute of Shari'ah and Law, the school initially offered a Certificate of Law, a Diploma of Law, a Higher Diploma of Law, and a Certificate in Justice Studies. In 2001, the Institute of Shari'ah and Law, now renamed the Faculty of Shari'ah and Law at the Maldives College of Higher Education, offered an Advanced Diploma in Shari'ah and Law course, which was equivalent to the first two years of a law degree.[12] A third year was added to this program in 2004, making it a complete law degree, and the first law degree to be offered in the Maldives. The students who completed the Advanced Diploma Course and some students who had completed the Diploma in Shari'ah and Law the previous year enrolled in this additional year to attain their LLB degrees.

Students in the Bachelor of Laws program study both common law and Shari'ah subjects to complete the degree. The program was extended to four years recently. Normal degree programs leading to a bachelor's degree in the Maldives typically require three years of full-time study (or 360 credits).[13] The four-year program is structured in semesters and can be completed in eight years part-time and four years full-time. This law school currently offers a Master's in Shari'ah, Bachelor of Laws, Diploma in Shari'ah and Law, Advanced Certificate in Shari'ah and Law, Graduate Certificate in Law, and Graduate Certificate in Shari'ah.[14]

Three other private institutions—Mandhu College, Villa College, and Maldives Law Institute—have recently introduced legal education. Mandhu College and Villa College offered their first law degree programs in 2013 and 2014, respectively. Maldives Law Institute is more focused on "improv[ing] and strengthen[ing] the legal system by conducting legal research, publication of research journals and conducting continuing legal education programmes for legal practitioners, judges, legal academics and law enforcement officers."[15] Law is offered as an undergraduate degree in all these institutions, and admission to these programs is based on "A level" scores or foundational courses of the same level.

The Profession of Law

In the present system, any Maldivian who has completed a law degree may apply for a license to practice law.[16] Students who complete law as part of another degree may also apply to practice law provided they have completed core modules, including constitutional law, criminal law, contract law, law of trusts and equity, and property law.[17] Unlike in many other jurisdictions,[18] there are neither exams testing the applicant's knowledge on the broad rules of law nor internships prior to one's becoming fully licensed to practice in the Maldives. There is no requirement for professional experience or continuing legal education. Moreover, foreign-trained lawyers are not required to undergo local training to acquire knowledge of the local system.[19] All law graduates, once licensed to practice, are known as "lawyers"[20] and may advise clients, undertake negotiations, draft legal documents, and represent clients in legal hearings.

The first formal lawyers in the Maldives appeared in the late 1950s after passing a law exam offered by the Ministry of Education.[21] No prior qualifications were required to take this exam.[22] The requirement of some legal qualification was introduced in 1996. However, a certificate of law was sufficient to get a license.[23] Practicing licenses were issued to persons who passed the law examination conducted by the Ministry of Education.[24] Foreigners were permitted to practice law in the Maldives, provided they were Muslim and married to a Maldivian.[25] Under these regulations, persons without a basic law degree could still become a practicing lawyer. In 2010, new regulations made a bachelor of law degree a prerequisite to a practicing license.[26]

In the present system, two regulations: the Attorney General's Regulation (Licensing Regulations 2010) and a Supreme Court Regulation, govern the legal profession. The Attorney General's Regulation does not purport to regulate the ethical conduct of lawyers, fees, or the handling of clients, among other things. But the Supreme Court Regulations include fees for services rendered by lawyers, a code of ethics for lawyers, and disciplinary actions that may be taken against lawyers.[27] The Attorney General's Regulations do not cover the entire legal profession. It is still unclear as to when a lawyer can be deemed to be in contempt of court and wide discretion has been placed with judges.[28]

Ideally, neither the Supreme Court nor the Attorney General, as part of the executive, should have such powers over the legal profession,[29] which should be vested with an independent uniform body such as a bar association. There is little recourse for the victimized parties because there is no authoritative figure regulating the ethics of the legal profession, even in circumstances in which lawyers have acted in fraudulent ways. There needs to be a system to ensure that legal professionals behave ethically but that also ensures that new entrants into the field are adequately trained and prepared for the profession. However, these matters are beyond the scope of this chapter.

Law and Social Justice: Growing Disjunctions and the Possibilities for Clinical Legal Education

In 2010, the UNDP conducted a baseline perception survey of the judicial system.[30] The study found that 52 percent of the respondents from the public believed that criminals go unpunished and that 54 percent believed that victims do not receive justice.[31] These factors appear to have contributed greatly to public perceptions of "corruption in the justice system, delays, disinterest and discrimination."[32]

The legal profession is remarkably young, and many judges still possess only basic qualifications.[33] The entire legal sector is emerging from decades of chronic neglect in terms of capacity building, and is now met with an enormous challenge to remain conscious of its new responsibilities, particularly overseeing a new and fragile sociolegal transition engendered by the Constitution. With all of this, combined with the continuing deficiency of qualified legal personnel across the board,[34] the system is faced with multiple challenges. Among the most acute of these issues are the management of caseloads in both the courts[35] and also the State law offices.[36] Many of these cases lodged at the superior courts could have potentially been settled out of court. Family Court uses counseling and reconciliation in limited cases. However, alternate dispute resolution mechanisms are yet to be established.

The independence of the judiciary is also a new concept for the Maldives. In the previous systems, the head of state was the supreme authority of justice.[37] In these systems, if a party was unhappy with the outcome of a decision of the highest court, such a person had a right to appeal to the president, who could reverse the court judgment on the matter. It has been difficult for the public to understand the separation of the judiciary from the executive. Weak institutional structures, a lack of procedural guidelines, and poorly qualified legal professionals also intensify access to justice issues in the Maldives.[38]

> [T]here is a lack of training on international principles, the nature of judicial independence, responsibility and integrity, international human rights law, the

> Constitution and new legislation passed . . . professional trainings . . . access to a wide-range of legal literature in the official language, Dhivehi, and quality continuing education, including specialized training on gender equality and women's rights, international human rights law, and the human rights mechanism.

Legal aid is provided only to those accused of serious crimes, provided they cannot afford private legal representation.[39] There are few nongovernmental organizations (NGOs) that provide free legal services in specialized areas such as corruption.[40] The current legal aid system is underfunded and underresourced, and the State struggles in providing legal aid to persons who qualify. Most lawyers refuse to work within the limited legal aid budget granted to the attorney general's office simply because criminal defense lawyers are highly paid in comparison.

Many people who face losses related to employment, custody cases, or separation from abusive partners are suffering because they do not have the necessary representation. The system therefore puts these groups at an extreme disadvantage. Although the Constitution gives every person a right to a lawyer to represent them in a trial, not many people actually have this basic human right. People are often forced to represent themselves, and this leads to an unfair advantage for those who can afford lawyers compared to those who cannot. There are no legal requirements for pro bono services, and the local civil society is largely underdeveloped, especially in the area of human rights.

The most striking feature of the justice system is that all the superior courts, the High Court, and the Supreme Court is based in Malé, the capital city.[41]The islands have only magistrate-level courts, with very limited jurisdiction. Approximately 66 percent of the population[42] lives outside Malé.[43] These people are separated from the central institutions, government offices, and courthouses by the sea. The 195,275 residents of these outer islands are also separated by extra costs, time, culture, and a lack of public transportation to travel to the capital city.[44] Providing access to justice is therefore of critical concern and a major challenge for the government.

Many people do not have access to justice because they are unaware of the procedures, cannot afford lawyers, and do not trust the judges. In the absence of any requirements for lawyers to provide pro bono services, it is unlikely that any government will be able to fully fund a legal aid scheme for an entire population. Thus, in effect, there is no legal protection for many people. Access to better legal aid and more support through law clinics may be a starting point for improving human rights and justice in the future and enabling lawyers to better serve their community.[45]

Building Professional Legal Skills in the Law School

The purpose of legal education is obtaining knowledge, acquiring skills, and understanding the processes in which lawyers participate.[46] All law schools aim to prepare students for the practice of law.[47] The reality, however, is that most law graduates are not adequately prepared to practice law.[48] Law schools fail to produce ready-to-practice lawyers[49] because they fail to appreciate their responsibilities[50] and fail to adopt the appropriate mode of instruction[51] for training legal professionals.[52]

Historically, in other parts of the world, law was learned through apprenticeship.[53] This took place through students' reading the law in cases and texts and observing real-life lawyering through practitioners who served as teachers.[54] This approach provided with hands-on learning, while at the same time allowing students to gain knowledge of the legal system. But these forms of legal training were self-contained and divorced from reality.[55] There was an increasing call for students both to comprehend the social setting in which law functions and at the same time expose them to practice.[56] It became clear that legal education should be about "law in action."[57] Law schools, then, became more practice oriented,[58] preparing students with skills and professional responsibility.[59]

Legal clinics, as Yale professor Jerome Franks called them, were "legal dispensaries" that offered law students experiential learning opportunities similar to those offered to medical students at medical schools. Such clinics were proposed as early as 1901 by Professor Alexander Lyublinsky.[60] The purpose of clinical education was to acquire the skills needed for competent law practice utilizing the medical model.[61] This method engages students in a meaningful relationship with their clients, legal institutions, and the community around them.[62]

In countries such as the United States, clinical education has become an integral component of law school.[63] Students who work in clinics earn credits[64] and receive feedback and the opportunity for self-reflection, as with other courses.[65] Such a scheme enables them to be placed at an in-house or external institution.

For credit-based courses, there has been a gradual movement toward introducing professional skills or the mechanics of lawyering: skills training, the providing of service, influencing policy, and developing future legal aid and civil rights lawyers.[66] Law clinics were also used to aid legal reform.[67] These modern clinics handle cases, not only for legal aid groups but also for government agencies and "quasi-public bodies."[68]

Commonwealth countries have been slow to develop institution-based clinics. In some places, such as Australia and New Zealand, there are partnerships between law schools and community law centers. Students volunteer to gain experience in interviewing and advice stages of the clinics, thereby reducing some of the burden on practicing lawyers. Other students apply for internships at law firms. In South Africa, law clinics are based on developing and fostering "a culture of democracy and respect for human rights as an integral part of common values and universal heritage of humanity."[69] This is not formally a part of any course and is voluntary.

In various countries, student activism has been an important factor in the growth of legal clinics. This involvement increased during the era of civil rights activism inspired by numerous human rights events, involving police brutality, forced removals, detention without trial, and other breaches of fundamental human rights. They aided in providing access to justice through rights-based legal education programs. These clinics were voluntary and inspired by a desire to serve the poor. Some clinics were either initiated or strongly supported by students in a nonacademic way, inculcating a sense of social justice.[70] They were supported by both academics and practicing lawyers, who did not offer comprehensive services but tended to refer most matters to be litigated to the state-funded legal aid system.

Fostering Social Justice

In critiquing law schools, Debroah Rhode saw that they failed to embrace a social justice mission and instill in students the professional value of providing pro bono service.[71] Wizner and Aiken quote Rhode regarding this socializing role:[72]

> Legal education plays an important role in socialising the next generation of lawyers, judges, and public policy makers. As gatekeepers to the profession, law schools have a unique opportunity and obligation to make access to justice a more central social priority.

Legal education should nurture students' capacity for moral indignation at injustice, equal justice for all, and provide skills and a spirit for social justice.[73] Rhode challenged law schools to do better in socializing law students to make access to justice a more central social priority.[74]

Social justice can be defined as referring to the fair distribution of legal resources in society to aid in access to justice. There is a need for legal representation for the poor in both criminal and civil cases.[75] Although the state may have the primary obligation to provide legal services to the poor,[76] legal clinics support the state at large. The clinic promotes social justice in three ways: first, it promotes access to justice for the underprivileged by representing them at different forums; second, it introduces students to the idea of public service responsibility; and finally, it creates an understanding of law and social justice among law students.[77]

Another important aspect of social justice is related to the use of class action and law reform, which is useful in assisting more people at the same time.[78] It can provide broad access to justice and judicial relief to all persons who are poor, vulnerable, and disabled.[79] Strategic human rights litigation seeks to use the law to advocate for social change on behalf of individuals whose voices are otherwise not heard.[80] This litigation is an essential tool to make government policy more comprehensive so as to alleviate poverty and other social exclusions.[81]

Legal representation has been criticized for the ways in which we lose clients' stories when we repackage them to fit legal categories that are recognized in the court.[82] Thus, a student who is taught in a specialized clinic begins by editing out a client's story that is not relevant to the speciality, and the student thereby misses learning about the client's experience and client's life.[83] Clinicians have argued that narrative theory can help give a client a voice in the courtroom when used as a technique of advocacy, in client interviewing and counseling and in problem solving.[84]

The Proposed Law Clinic Design

Laws in the Maldives are derived from different sources, with family law and criminal law largely taken from Shari'ah law, and civil law mostly derived from common law. According to the Constitution, no law in the Maldives can contradict Shari'ah law. Islamic Shari'ah therefore, is the most influential basis of Maldivian law. In case of a lacuna in the law, lawyers and judges are required to look at the provisions in Islamic Shari'ah. For the legal profession, this means that lawyers in the Maldives need to be trained in both common law and Shari'ah law to effectively understand and apply the law in the Maldives.

Law school clinics in the Maldives thus could be ideally established around these central ideas: (a) building skills; (b) exposing students to real-life cases; (c) familiarizing students with legal procedures; (d) teaching students how Shari'ah and other legal systems are practically integrated into the Maldivian legal system; and (e) helping students understand the broader sociolegal issues around social justice in the Maldives.

The proposed design is modest for a law clinic that is based on the courses offered at the Faculty of Shari'ah and Law, Maldives National University. This program could be tailored to fit into the other law schools in the Maldives. The program design takes into account all challenges, including the needs of the institution, that could provide potential obstacles to the successful launching and running of a law clinic. Ideally, all fourth-year students must complete the clinical experience. However, the law school can choose the 20 highest-performing students from the third year to do a pilot phase.

Clinical Education: An Overview

Unlike in the Maldives, for much of the history of the legal profession's, there has been some form of clinical training requirement for new graduates in many parts of the world. In some jurisdictions, the apprenticeship system still exists in at least a minor way, but for many regions, the requirement for legal office training as an apprenticeship style has either been reduced or eliminated altogether.[85] The inclusion of clinical education as part of a course-based aspect of the university system is new. This has only occurred within the last 100 years, and in some places in a much shorter time than that, especially those under the British-based common law system.

Given the history of social justice on which clinical education is based, the methods and systems of such education are neither uniform nor universal, but are, rather, contextual and politically dependent. Models can be single focused or mixed. The four models of CLE include the service model, the reform model, the participant-observer model, and the teaching model.[86] When we evaluate systems around the world, clinical education can be broken down into a system that uses at least one of the models, or that integrates more than one of them.

The service model was one of the early models of clinical education. It began by serving[87] those who underserved or did not have access to the justice system, and not as a system for students to earn academic credits.[88] It emphasized the public service elements of professional responsibility, and not the operational aspects of legal ethics. It is implemented by either farming out students as additional manpower to community legal aid and public defender offices,[89] or as in-house clinics that enable the earning of credits under the supervision of a law school faculty member.[90] It is cost intensive, but provides a closer and more critical oversight than external placements and is easier to manage.[91]

Some law schools moved away from the service model to focus on preparation for the students' professional career, that is, preparation for tasks actually performed in professional life. This approach is supported by academics such as Arch M. Centrall and Jerome Frank.[92] This model encouraged both the learning of legal professional skills[93] and processes, and the understanding of professional ethics and responsibility, and the future lawyer's role in the legal process.[94] These clinics prepared students for the socialization into their professional life, including interaction with juries, witnesses, and judges.[95] However, some argue that solely focusing clinical education on producing craftsmen able to manipulate the system does not support the community it wishes to serve.[96]

The teaching model[97] was created to overcome the lack of training students received before entering the profession and to protect the law school's reputation and prestige.[98] The origins of this model are in "simulated practice" such as moots and so on.[99] It further developed to include classes, supervision, skills training, simulations, journal writing, guided reflection, and other explicitly pedagogical activities.[100] This model has led to inefficiencies and additional costs as compared to Western Europe, for example, where the traditional lecture method and postgraduate apprenticeships continue to dominate legal training.[101]

Models of clinical education are purposive, and may be designed around the community or student needs or both. A competent model(s) of clinical education requires understanding, imagination, and ethics.[102] Moreover, there should be careful consideration about focusing clinics on specialities that may not meet the needs of the community it wishes to serve[103] and whether they may limit students' experiences to within the particular speciality.[104] When clinics do not limit themselves to a single subject matter, the diversity of cases enriches the students' learning experience, offering both the ease of a single subject and the richness of diverse legal issues.[105]

Component I—Developing Legal Skills and Exposure to Legal Practice

The proposed law clinic will have two compulsory components. The attachment phase of the clinic will be completed in semester A of the fourth year. For this component, students will be attached to a practicing lawyer to gain practical experience in any major practicing area in the Maldives, which could include (1) civil disputes (leases, division of properties, contracts); (2) employment rights; (3) criminal defense and prosecution; (4) legal aid (for those accused of serious crimes) and victim protection for vulnerable groups such as women, migrant workers and so forth; (5) marital and family issues; and (6) tourism issues, to name a few.

During this semester, students will attend court hearings with the supervising lawyer and get hands-on experience and training on the ethical and competent practice of law.[106] This may include attending client meetings, developing case theories, and preparing court documents with the supervising lawyer. The faculty will organize mandatory conferences and seminar programs for the students to attend and learn about the practice of law.[107] These seminars should be included as a compulsory component of the law degree as there is no postdegree system in which the students can acquire these experiences from working judges and lawyers. Such workshops could focus on advocacy, ethics, and legal practice.[108]

Another way of achieve this objective is to redevelop the alternate dispute resolution (ADR) course to include the practical aspects of lawyering. Students will then participate in role-play and simulation exercises throughout the ADR course. Simulation exercises could be an alien method to the faculty and students at the law school, and to be effective, require organization and support from the law faculty, supervising lawyers, and the students. A moot court will then be organized so that the students can role-play their part in a simulated criminal or civil matter. A negative aspect of the simulated moot court experience is that it takes away from the students the flavor of real-life case experiences and gives the idea that there is only one right way of arguing a case.[109] Attending court hearings will enable students to understand how real-life cases evolve and work within the legal system.

The success of this program could be highly dependent on the tasks assigned and on the effective supervision of the students.[110] The faculty needs to carefully organize and monitor student learning during their attachment with the lawyer. It is critically important for the law school to identify qualified and highly regarded practicing lawyers in the Maldives,[111] as student experience and learning will much depend on the ethics and practice of the supervising lawyer. Effective collaboration between the law schools, legal aid programs run by the government, and civil society, and any proper assessments of what the public needs has the potential to "enhance student education by exposing students to other actors and experiences and better prepare them for their professional lives after graduation."[112] Students will also take other values from these collaborations in terms of behavior, changes in ideology, and ideas about the justice system of the Maldives.

Component II—Human Rights, Law Reform, and Social Justice

The second segment of the clinic will ideally give students a flavor of the link between law and justice. This segment will have to be completed during semester B of the fourth year. In semester B, students will compile a research report aimed at law reform, based on an ongoing human rights or social justice issue. This paper can be based on a court case or an important legal or social justice issue that has not been adequately dealt with by the government or the parliament. Students may also do papers targeted at judicial reform. This component of the clinic prepares students and helps them develop the skills necessary to foster and create social change. Students will gain critical exposure to real-life cases and issues related to the system of law and justice in the Maldives, understanding and learning about equality, discrimination, rights, law, and justice.

During this semester, students can volunteer and work with an NGO, which will give then hands-on experience with the issues in the Maldives. Students will be immersed in micro and macro issues of social justice faced in the 21st century. The law school will teach key courses in the legal history of the Maldives; however, it does not in any way teach any courses that allow students to think more broadly about the social justice and legal issues faced by most Maldivians today. Introducing elective courses such human rights, strategic media studies, civil society studies, community studies, global development, legislative reform, and legislative advocacy will be ideal and will assist students in the development of their final research paper in the second semester of the clinic. Building skills and learning the theoretical bases of the law will prepare students to apply the skills necessary to identify key issues regarding the law's inability to provide protection and justice in the context of the Maldives and the critical role a lawyer can play in the life of a client. This approach will encourage students to ask questions and understand the application of law to the real-life cases, and force them to think in terms of the community, human rights, and social justice.

At the end of the semester, students will submit either a research paper or a research project on any issue concerning human rights and social justice. The research paper will be an ideal foundation for further academic study, for a research master's or other postgraduate qualification. This research paper should identify a question or problem of particular relevance within the field of human rights and social justice. The paper should include a literature review of scholarship on the topic of the research, a research methodology, presentation of the data, discussion and analysis of the data to support the research argument, and also a discussion of the larger issues or questions around the key issue. A paper proposal must be submitted at the end of the first month of the B semester to the clinic facilitator at the law school.

The research project option allows students to choose to develop and design a social justice movement project, such as a project for grass-roots community development, a nonprofit, fundraising, campaign development, legislative advocacy, or another area of interest. In this option, students will need to design an original project that is based on an identified need by an existing organization, such as an NGO, or any other developmental organization, such as the United Nations, in the Maldives. Students will then work with those organizations and submit the research project to the clinic facilitator at the end of the B semester. The student will be responsible for contacting these developmental organizations and arranging to do volunteer work and be involved with these projects. The project report, similar to the research paper, must contain a literature review that leads to the identification of the problem that will be addressed by a social justice project.

Limitations and Other Critical Considerations

While law clinics have the potential to create some change, law clinics can at first expect to encounter resistance and multiple challenges in making the leap from the current system in legal education to a more holistic approach to training legal professionals and facilitating human rights and justice via legal aid. The resistance and challenges could potentially come from practicing lawyers, law firms, and students who are not willing to take on the extra workload, or be due to a lack of training expertise within the law schools to teach and conduct clinical programs. As such, the current fraternity of lawyers, law schools, students, and the public all pose challenges to the effective functioning of a clinical program.[113]

Existing Teaching Methodologies

In the Maldives, law teaching is focused on teaching the substantive law and is mostly carried out through delivering lectures. A case method of teaching is adopted at times to teach common law subjects. In deep contrast, most foreign law schools utilize a case method of study together with the Socratic style of classroom teaching,[114] which remains the preferred method of teaching even today.[115] The Socratic method is effective in developing legal analysis skills in students,[116] but is rarely employed in the Maldives as it is alien to both students and most lecturers.

The teaching of common law subjects highly relies on the case method because key skills for a lawyer are spotting an issue and providing arguments on both sides of a case. However, case methods do not teach students to "think like lawyers."[117] The major limitations of this method are that these cases are "static situations with determinate facts," when in reality, lawyers every day have to work with clients' affairs that are dynamically changing, "where the facts as well as the law, are anything but determinate."[118] Focusing only on students' ability to spot issues and develop case theories by applying the law to the facts does not provide the students with a holistic experience on the functions of a lawyer.[119]

These methods of teaching fail to provide students with the necessary legal skills to become a good lawyer. Most graduates therefore lack key skills such as negotiating, interviewing, problem solving, and giving presentations. Students who participated in the law attachment (short term affiliations with courts, attorney general's office, prosecutor general's office and law firms) and mooting programs at the Faculty of Shari'ah and Law in the past have complained about the noncredit nature of these programs and how they increase workloads and add no benefits. The lack of proper exposure to legal practice adds to the growing disjunction between what is taught in law school and what happens in the practice of law.

CLE can compensate for these deficiencies in the current system of educating future lawyers. A clinical experience would provide students with the opportunity to build their legal skills, engage in cooperation,[120] and assume responsibility, thus building their confidence,[121] a necessary facet of the profession. This is crucial to learning the law in the Maldives, where students are required to learn English common law subjects in combination with Maldivian and Shari'ah subjects, and need to be made aware of how that actually works in practice in a court of law. Special importance could be given to subjects such as land law, which can be highly fine-tuned to local contexts, and law school knowledge must be applied to the types of cases students will be handling once in the profession. Introducing law clinics can therefore be a nascent concept for the Maldives.

Current Course Outline and Student Workloads

The current law school program, which is comprised of over 30 modules, covers common law and Shari'ah law subjects, as well as subjects concerned with legal procedures in the Maldives. The courses are preapproved by the University Council, and the lecturers do not have discretion to alter the course outline in any manner. The current framework of the law school curriculum will not be a problem in the introduction of law clinics, because the program already has procedure courses and an ADR course. Students therefore are already learning the theory behind lawyering skills. As such, the faculty will not have to create a separate course outline to teach theory related to topics such as negotiation and legal analysis, and theory development.

Given the number of fourth-year law students, faculty-student ratios could be an issue at the beginning. This may, however, be overcome through coteaching[122] and by having separate staff to organize and conduct the law clinic. Students will be taking ADR and other theory and procedure courses as part of the regular LLB program, and will be supervised by a practicing lawyer for the practical aspects related to the law clinic. To accommodate the entire group, clinics can be run throughout the semester and take a different group of students every semester. At the end of the semester, students will hand over their work to the next group of students at the clinic. In this manner, faculty members will not have to allocate extra time or take on extra responsibilities, except for a clinical supervisor who will have to organize and manage the lawyers who are acting as supervisors.

Participating in a clinic is added work for students, and there may be some resistance from them if participation in the clinical program is not made a compulsory requirement of the law degree. Student maturity also poses significant problems to the success of law clinics, because as undergraduates, they may be not mature enough to handle live client affairs.[123] Some resistance may also come from faculty, who may not have had the necessary experience in clinical education and will pose potential problems in terms of understanding the value of introducing law clinics.[124] Running a law clinic will also be a significant addition to the current workload for faculty. Some of this resistance can arise from unfamiliarity with such clinics, while a lot can arise from the refusal to take on more work.[125] Finding volunteers to work in the law clinic may be an added challenge in the context of the Maldives. Information on clinical programs can be obtained from neighboring countries and also by inviting experts from abroad to visit and stay in the country to establish a clinic.

Infrastructure and Expenses

A major challenge to establishing a law clinic will be obtaining adequate funding and resources. Funding does not necessarily need to translate into the actual salaries paid to clinic staff. However, equipment such as a photocopying machine, a phone, and a computer, trained staff and funding to conduct seminars and workshops, transportation costs and administrative costs related to keeping and managing paper files[126] all cost money. Expenses are also the prime reason why, despite a high need, supervised outreach clinics based on geographic location have not been suggested in this chapter, because this option may not be sustainable in the long run given the high cost of travel and accommodations and also the geographical distribution of the courts and law offices in the Maldives.

The law school will have to come up with some way of raising the funds to pay the supervising lawyers. This can be largely minimized by introducing a system of compulsory pro bono hours for practicing lawyers. Within the present system, the funding issue can also be minimized by the attorney general's office providing experienced lawyers to act as supervising lawyers at the law clinic. In this way, students can do all the desk work for the supervising lawyer, who will represent the client in the court. This may also be an alternative way of fulfilling the government's commitment under the new Constitution and of finding more lawyers to work within the budgetary constraints of the government.

Funding for clinics may also be available from international organizations interested in developing the justice system of the Maldives. The interest of these parties can be increased by focusing on areas of critical need, such as children, women, and migrant workers. The university could also budget to acquire funding from the government. Proper research and documents must be prepared in order to identify the needs and the scope of the legal services that the law clinic will provide support.

Recommendations and Conclusions

This chapter gives a simple glimpse into how law clinics could be introduced in the Maldives. The previous sections have generally outlined the benefits of a clinical pedagogy and how it assists in the exploration of the interface between theory and practice. In doing so, it has shown that a university law clinic can become a substantial provider of legal services; however, given the context of the Maldives, a humble start could be a better approach to introducing law clinics into law schools. The establishment of law clinics is critical to producing lawyers with the necessary skills for legal practice, but it is also a first step toward broadening legal services and justice because it will assist in highlighting the issues of legal representation and access to justice in the Maldives in a unique way. These law clinics are, however, just one single aspect in creating better lawyers for better justice for the people of the Maldives.

In terms of regulatory frameworks, practicing licenses should require prior practical experience. Policies and programs as part of continuing legal education must be introduced in order to ensure that lawyers stay abreast of the most recent local and international developments, which could be made specific to their areas of expertise. Needless to say, a proper and effective regulatory framework for the regulation of the legal profession also needs to be in place in order to ensure legal professionals maintain a code of ethics and professionalism within their practices and jobs.

The proposals offered here for a law clinic are therefore suggestions that could work within the current design of law schools and the system of justice. The proposed design has taken into consideration that the law schools in the Maldives are different and that a proper clinic for a law school will need to be tailor-made based on proper research to see how it can be of use to the law school, to students, and to the broader community. The intention here is to inspire persons within the legal profession in the Maldives to explore and test these ideas to build the skills of the local graduates, prepare them for the practice of law, and make them aware of the more complex issues they will face once in the profession.

Notes

1. Husnu Al Suood, *The Maldivian Legal System* (Maldives Law Institute, 2014) 185–193.
2. H. C. P. Bell, *The Máldive Islands: Monograph on the History, Archaeology, and Epigraphy* (Ceylon Government Press, 1940) 116.
3. Suood (n 1) 185.
4. Ibid.
5. *Vihivana Qarunuge Thereygai Dhivehi Raajje (20th Century Maldives)*, Volume 3 (Malé, Maldives: Centre for Linguistic and Historical Research, 2006) 36; Ibid 187.
6. Suood (n 1) 187.
7. Ibid.
8. Ibid. 188.
9. Ibid. 188.
10. Report of the Asian Development Bank, "Technical Assistance to the Republic of Maldives for Strengthening Legal Education and Judicial Training" (TAR-MDL 32270), December 2, 1999.
11. Suood (n 1) 191.
12. Ibid. 189.
13. UNESCO, *World Data on Education*, 7th ed, 2010/2011 (July 2011).
14. Suood (n 1) 190–191.
15. Ibid. 192.
16. Ibid. 185.
17. Annex 3, Section 2, *Dhivehi Raajjeygai Qaanoonee Vakeelegge Haisiyyathun Masakkaikurumuge Huddha Dhinumuge Qawaidh* (Regulations Governing Legal Licenses) (August 4, 2014).
18. Roy T. Stuckey, "Preparing Students to Practice Law: A Global Problem in Need of Global Solutions" (2001) 43 *S. Tex. L. Rev.* 649, 655.
19. Suood (n 1) 185.
20. Ibid. 185.
21. Ibid. 187.
22. Ibid. (n 1).
23. Section 231 of the Rules of the Court (5) published by the Ministry of Justice in 1996, as quoted by Suood (n 1).
24. Suood (n 1) 179.
25. Ibid.
26. "Licensing Regulations" (2010).
27. Suood (n 1) 182.
28. Daniel Bosley, "Attorney General Resumes Issuing Lawyers Permits" *Minivan News – Independent News for the Maldives* (September 4, 2014) http://minivannews.com/

politics/attorney-general-resumes-issuing-lawyers-permits-82153, accessed May 22, 2014.

29. Gabriela Knaul, "Report of the Special Rapporteur on the Independence of Judges and Lawyers, A/hrc/23/43/Add.3" (2013).
30. United Nations Development Programme, *Access to Justice Assessments in the Asia Pacific: A Review of Experiences and Tools From the Region* (Asia-Pacific Regional Centre, 2012) 50.
31. Ibid. 51.
32. Ibid.
33. Hon. Justice Marcus R. Einfeld, "Strengthening the Maldivian Judicial System" (Draft Discussion Paper, June 2005) 11.
34. United Nations Development Programme (n 30) 51.
35. Ibid.
36. See United Nations Development Programme, "Capacity Development Needs Assessment of the Prosecutor General's Office of the Republic of Maldives" (2008).
37. Art 39, Constitution of Maldives (1998).
38. UN Office of the High Commissioner for Human Rights, "Preliminary Observations of the UN Special Rapporteur on the Independence of Judges and Lawyers on her Official Visit to the Republic of Maldives (February 17–24, 2013)" (United Nations Human Rights, February 24, 2013) http://www.ohchr.org, accessed January 4, 2014.
39. Art 53 (b), Constitution of Maldives (2008); also see Suood (n 1) 169.
40. Musliha Hassan, "Transparency Maldives Launches Free Legal Assistance for Victims of Corruption" *Minivan News –Independent News for the Maldives* (Malé, November 6, 2012). http://minivannews.com/society/transparency-maldives-launches-free-legal-assistance-for-victims-of-corruption-38854, accessed June 11, 2014.
41. United Nations Development Programme (n 30) 51.
42. Statistics Division, *Statistical Yearbook of Maldives 2013* (Department of National Planning, Ministry of Finance and Treasury, 2013) Table 3.4.
43. Ibid Table 3.3.
44. People from the islands have to travel to the capital city even to secure legal representation or information on finding lawyers, or information on how to proceed with a case.
45. See Juliet M. Brodie, "Little Cases on the Middle Ground: Teaching Social Justice Lawyering in Neighborhood-Based Community Lawyering Clinics" (2009) 15 *Clinical L. Rev.* 333.
46. Lon L. Fuller, "What the Law Schools can Contribute to the Making of Lawyers" in Martin L. Levine (ed.) *Legal Education: The International Library of Essays in Law & Legal Theory* (Dartmouth Publishing Company Limited, 1993) 189.
47. Stuckey (n 18) 649, 650; also see Roy T. Stuckey, "Best Practices or Not, itis Time to Re-Think Legal Education" (2009) 16 *Clinical L. Rev.* 307; Roy T. Stuckey, "Teaching with Purpose: Defining and Achieving Desired Outcomes in Clinical Law Courses" (2006) 13 *Clinical L. Rev.* 807.
48. Stuckey (n 18) 650; also see Harry T. Edwards, "Growing Disjunction Between Legal Education and the Legal Profession" (1992) 91 *Mich. L. Rev.* 34.
49. Stuckey (n 18) 660.
50. Ibid. 667.

51. Stuckey (n 18) 656; Jerry R. Foxhoven, "Beyond Grading: Assessing Student Readiness to Practice Law" (2009) 16 *Clinical L. Rev.* 335, 339.
52. Law schools must train students in three critical aspects: legal analysis, skills development, and professional responsibility. See Foxhoven (n 51) 338; Roy T. Stuckey et al., *Best Practices for Legal Education: A Vision and a Roadmap* (CLEA, 2007) 62; William M. Sullivan, Anne Colby, Judith W. Wegner, Lloyd Bond, and Lee S. Shulman, *Educating Lawyers: Preparation for the Profession of Law* (Jossey-Bass, 2007) 27.
53. Suzanne V. Carey, "Essay on the Evolution of Clinical Legal Education and its Impact on Student Trial Practice" (2002) 51 *U. Kan. L. Rev.* 509, 510–511; George S. Grossman, "Clinical Legal Education: History and Diagnosis" (1973) 26 *J. Legal Educ.* 162, 163.
54. Carey (n 53) 510.
55. Ibid. 171.
56. Ibid. 168, 172; Stuckey (n 18) 807.
57. Grossman (n 53) 171.
58. Ibid. 509.
59. Ibid. 172.
60. Richard J. Wilson, "Training for Justice: The Global Reach of Clinical Legal Education" (2003) 22 *Penn St. Int'l L. Rev.* 421.
61. Stuckey (n 18) 816.
62. Wilson (n 60) 431.
63. Carey (n 53) 509.
64. Ibid. 512.
65. Stuckey (n 18) 818.
66. Stephen Wizner and Jane Aiken, "Teaching and Doing: The Role of Law School Clinics in Enhancing Access to Justice" (2004) 73 *Fordham L. Rev.* 997, 998; Shuvro P. Sarker, "Empowering the Underprivileged: The Social Justice Mission for Clinical Legal Education in India" (2013) 19 *Int'l J. Clinical Legal Educ.* 321, 331.
67. Sarker (n 66) 328.
68. Grossman (n 53) 169.
69. Philip F. Iya, "Legal Education for Democracy and Human Rights in the New South Africa with Lessons from the American Legal Aid Movement" (1994) 12 *J. Prof. Legal Educ.* 211.
70. Sarker (n 66) 330.
71. Wizner and Aiken (n 66) 997.
72. Ibid. 997.
73. Ibid. (n 66)1009; Sarker (n 66) 322; Wilson (n 60) 431.
74. Wizner and Aiken (n 66) 1002.
75. Wilson (n 60) 431; Wizner and Aiken (n 66) 997–998; Antoinette S. Lopez, "Learning Through Service in a Clinical Setting: The Effect of Specialization on Social Justice and Skills Training" (2000) 7 *Clinical L. Rev.* 307, 317; Sarker (n 66) 333.
76. Wizner and Aiken (n 66) 997.
77. Sarker (n 66) 324.
78. Wizner and Aiken (n 66) 1006.
79. Sarker (n 66) 334–335.
80. Ibid. 334.
81. Ibid. 334–335.

82. Lopez (n 75) 321.
83. Ibid. 322.
84. Ibid. (n 75).
85. Grossman (n 53) 164.
86. Carey (n 53) 519.
87. Some of these were initiated by the students themselves, while in other cases, they were created through the law school in partnership with community law centers, or others held them in-house.
88. Carey (n 53) 520–521.
89. Ibid. 520.
90. Ibid. (n 53).
91. Ibid. 520–521.
92. Grossman (n 53) 170.
93. These skills included appreciation of the "uncertainty of facts" in litigation and development of the skills of negotiation, problem solving, drafting, trial advocacy, and planning.
94. Grossman (n 53) 169; Stuckey (n 18); Carey (n 53) 509, 518.
95. Grossman (n 53) 169.
96. Lopez (n 75) 311.
97. The teaching model includes a link to the academic program of the institution, inclusive of the theory and the practice of law, such as substantive doctrine, skills, ethics, and values of law practice; placement, predominantly in the final year, supervised by practicing lawyers with no or minimal cost; the issuing of credits or some form of acknowledgment of the placement.
98. Wilson (n 60) 422–423.
99. Grossman (n 53) 171.
100. Wizner and Aiken (n 66) 1005
101. Wilson (n 60) 422.
102. Sarker (n 66) 323.
103. Lopez (n 75) 325.
104. Ibid. 317–318.
105. Lopez (n 75) 325.
106. Haider A. Hamoudi, "Toward a Rule of Law Society in Iraq: Introducing Clinical Legal Education into Iraqi Law Schools" (2005) 23 *Berkeley J. Int'l L.* 112, 125.
107. Ibid 125–127, 128.
108. Ibid 127.
109. Ibid 126.
110. Ibid.
111. Ibid.
112. Kimberly A. Thomas and Nisreen Mahasneh, "Learning from the Unique and Common Challenges: Clinical Legal Education in Jordon" (2012) 5 *Berkeley J. Middle E. & Islamic L.* 1, 17.
113. Ibid.
114. Carey (n 53) 511; Grossman (n 53) 163.
115. Grossman (n 53) 165.
116. See Section of Legal Education and Admissions to the Bar American Bar Association, "Legal Education and Professional Development—An Educational Continuum: Report of the Task Force on Law Schools and the Profession: Narrowing the Gap"(July 1992); Stuckey (n 18); see in general Sullivan et al. (n 52).

117. Stuckey (n 18) 668.
118. Paul Brest, "The Responsibility of Law Schools: Educating Lawyers as Counselors and Problem Solvers" (1995) 58 *Law &Contemp. Probs.* 5, 7.
119. James E. Moliterno, "Legal Education, Experimental Education, and Professional Responsibility" (1996) 38 *Wm.& Mary L. Rev.* 71, 81–82.
120. Catherine G. O'Grady, "Preparing Students for the Profession: Clinical Education, Collaborative Pedagogy, and the Realities of Practice for the New Lawyer" (1997) 4 *Clinical L. Rev.* 485.
121. Angela McCaffrey, "Hamline University School of Law Clinics: Teaching Students to Become Ethical and Competent Lawyers for Twenty-Five Years" (2002) 24 *Hamline J. Pub. L. &Pol'y* 44.
122. Thomas and Mahasneh (n 112) 29.
123. Hamoudi (n 106) 124.
124. Thomas and Mahasneh(n 112) 29.
125. Ibid. 30.
126. Ibid. 31.

CHAPTER 3

Chinese Clinical Legal Education: Globalizing and Localizing

Cecily E. Baskir, Ma Liqun, and Li Ao

Introduction

With its roots in voluntary legal aid associations and with the support of international organizations, clinical legal education (CLE) emerged in China in 2000. Two years later, the first 11 institutions with clinical programs together formed a national academic organization, the Committee on Chinese Clinical Legal Education (CCCLE), affiliated with the China Association for Legal Education. Since then, dozens of additional Chinese law clinics have opened, often alongside the voluntary legal aid associations. Moreover, membership in the CCCLE has expanded dramatically. The new CLE programs offer students the chance to develop professional lawyering skills and provide legal assistance to poor and disadvantaged members of Chinese society. Despite encountering some resistance to its nontraditional approach to legal training, the important role of CLE is increasingly being recognized within the legal academy and the judicial system.

After tracing the origins of Chinese CLE, this chapter explores recent trends in Chinese law clinics, including efforts to expand beyond litigation-focused programs, to develop innovative specialties in response to societal needs, and to work cooperatively with governmental organizations and NGOs to create externship opportunities for law students. It depicts both the diversity of specialized clinical programs and the room that remains for more innovation and diversification. The chapter also examines challenges that confront CLE as it seeks to become further embedded in China as a globally inspired yet locally adapted form of legal study.

A Brief History of Chinese Clinical Legal Education

Legal education in China, essentially nonexistent for over a decade, began its rebirth in 1978 with the end of the Cultural Revolution. Significant reforms in law and legal education followed over the next several years. In 1988, for instance, the *Lawyer's Law*, governing legal practice in China, was revised to permit lawyers for the first time to practice without direct state supervision—no longer were all lawyers considered state legal workers.[1] Cooperative law firms and then later partnership law firms were authorized, opening up new professional opportunities for lawyers.[2] Alongside the new forms of practice, other reforms in the 1990s gave law schools greater autonomy, while tying increased funding to specific targets, and by the end of that decade, legal education was becoming more standardized along a model that focused primarily on legal theory.

Amid these changes, volunteer student legal aid organizations started to grow at some schools in the 1990s. The acknowledged pioneer and most prominent of these legal aid organizations was the Wuhan Center for Protection of Rights of Disadvantaged Citizens ("Wuhan Center"), founded in 1992 with financial support from the Ford Foundation.[3] At the Wuhan Center, student volunteers worked alongside paid staff members to assist members of the community with legal problems, occasionally turning to faculty or lawyers for help.[4] Held in high regard locally, the Wuhan Center particularly attracted cases involving grievances against government entities and was very popular with students.[5]

A few years later, the Center for Women's Law Studies and Legal Services of Peking University was created following a similar model, also with funding from the Ford Foundation.[6] Relying on a staff of students, faculty, and lawyers, the Center for Women's Law Studies sought especially to engage in impact litigation and to advocate for legislative change on behalf of women.[7] At other institutions, students also created legal aid organizations to provide legal information to clients without legal representation.[8] At the time, all of these organizations were outside the regular law curriculum, and students received no course credit and relatively little supervision for their activities. Today, most law schools in China have voluntary student legal aid associations that continue to provide legal information and assistance to their local communities.

In the late 1990s, the Ford Foundation collaborated with Chinese and American faculty to experiment with formalizing CLE to a greater extent in China.[9] In preparation, the Ford Foundation worked with student legal aid organizations to link them with interested law faculty and strengthen their programs, and US clinical teachers provided training for new Chinese clinicians both in China and in the United States.[10] In the fall of 2000, with grants from the Ford Foundation, seven Chinese schools started the country's first curricular law clinics, which (unlike legal aid associations) provided course credit for participating students and supervision by faculty and legal professionals.[11] These pioneers included three schools in Beijing: Peking University, Tsinghua University, and Renmin University; two in Wuhan: Wuhan University and South Central University of Politics and Law (now South Central University of Economics, Politics and Law); and two in Shanghai: Fudan University and East China University of Political Science and Law.[12]

Two years later, four more schools—Sun Yat-Sen University in Guangzhou, Northwest University of Political Science and Law in Xi'an, Sichuan University in Chengdu, and Yunnan University in Kunming—followed suit by starting clinical programs of their own, and in that year, with support from the influential China Law Society, these 11 institutions together formed a national academic organization, the CCCLE.[13]

In the more than a dozen years since the CCCLE's creation, the total number of Chinese law schools has increased, and the number of them expressing interest in CLE has multiplied many times. Of the over 600 higher education institutions in China now offering law degrees, the CCCLE included 177 member schools as of May 2014.[14] As of November 2013, China had 187 different law clinics, with over 800 clinical teachers.

Characteristics of Chinese Clinical Legal Education

As in other parts of the world, the primary stated goals for CLE in China include building practical skills, providing needed legal assistance, and instilling a commitment to public interest in students.[15] From the beginning, international clinicians and lawyers have assisted in the effort to build clinical programs in China through workshops, exchange programs, and fellowships funded by the Ford Foundation, the US Agency for International Development, and others.[16] At the same time, Chinese and international clinicians alike have recognized the need for China to develop its own indigenous model of CLE—that is, CLE "with Chinese characteristics."[17] Since 2002, the CCCLE has played the leading role in the development of CLE in China.[18] With its mission to "launch all possible initiatives to promote the spread and development of CLE in China," the CCCLE engages in both domestic and international projects that balance the internal development of Chinese clinics with the benefits of learning from international colleagues.[19]

Among other things, the CCCLE has issued extensive guidelines for Chinese clinical programs, setting forth norms for the content, structure, and management of legal clinics and clinical courses.[20] The guidelines address issues such as clinic structure, course preparation, credits, student and teacher selection, student and teacher roles, and operations (including funding, file management, and more). According to the CCCLE guidelines on the operation and management of legal clinics, there are five models of clinics: (1) simulation-based legal clinics, (2) legal clinics relying on the student-run legal aid centers, (3) legal clinics combining both simulation and work in student legal aid centers, (4) legal clinics established in cooperation with partner institutions, and (5) independent legal clinics.[21] In its guidelines, the CCCLE recommends that simulation clinics, while the easiest to start, should transition into handling real cases as they mature. It notes that legal aid center-based clinics, in which the legal aid center provides the cases for students in the clinical course, are particularly suitable for programs with little or no separate funding. Partnerships with other institutions such as law firms or community groups have the advantage of providing office space and administrative personnel. Independent legal clinics are organized by clinical teachers and taught as specialized courses, with the advantage of permitting greater synchronization of clinical teaching objectives and activities. In general, the CCCLE advises clinics to establish stable and effective working relationships with relevant outside institutions, such as trade unions, consumer associations, the judiciary, law firms, arbitration institutions, and others, to ensure adequate and appropriate sources of cases.

The CCCLE basic guidelines and classroom teaching and management standards advise that a legal clinical course should combine a classroom component of lectures and class discussion with the opportunity for students to engage in legal practice, thereby combining theoretical and practical training. Professors should strive to make the classroom more interactive and participatory, using teaching methods such as role-play, videos, working in teams, moot courts, and other appropriate methods. The legal practice component should ideally take place in the context of a real case and should include individual supervision of students by professors outside of class.[22] Teachers, who may be either full-time professional teachers or a mix of professional teachers and other outside legal professionals, should establish clear and specific teaching plans. Courses with more than 30 students should be co-taught by several teachers to ensure quality, and co-teachers should strive to be collaborative and consistent. Clinical courses should be incorporated permanently into the formal curriculum of the institution of higher learning and provide at least two credits per semester. Clinics should also establish assessment systems to ensure that students receive proper evaluation.

The pedagogical vision set forth by the CCCLE is notably different from the lecture-based pedagogy of traditional legal education in China, which—in favor of legal theory—has historically paid relatively little attention to professional skills training. In traditional lecture courses, in distinct contrast to clinical methodology, students learn by memorizing the material and imitating the teacher as much as possible, a technique sometimes known as "stuffing the duck."[23] In class, the students are largely passive, and their grades are based mainly on their ability to memorize and reproduce on exams the large quantities of information presented in the lectures.[24] The more interactive approach of CLE requires more faculty training and resources than the traditional, nationally standardized law curriculum.

Noting that clinic topics may evolve over time, the CCCLE recommends that the focus for a clinic be determined by considering the needs of the community, the clinical teacher's professional background and experience, teaching objectives, the school's situation, and feasibility in general. Reflecting these considerations, Chinese clinics today cover a wide range of themes.[25] Some focus on substantive areas such as "women's rights, labor rights, civil rights, rights of the disadvantaged, rural or farmer's justice, environmental protection, and criminal (including juvenile) justice."[26] Others emphasize particular approaches to problem solving, such as litigation, legislation, alternative dispute resolution, or law translation for minority people.[27] Regardless of theme, they share a focus on Chinese domestic issues, with one exception: the Center for Cross-Border Advocacy, a clinic founded in 2010 at the Peking University School of Transnational Law that focused on immigration litigation in the United States (discussed in more detail below).[28]

Consistent with the range of clinical models set forth by the CCCLE, the type of legal practice experience afforded to students varies across clinics. Some clinical programs, such as the simulation-based clinics, do not involve any live-client representation at all. Among those that do, most clinics are oriented toward litigation and consultation, although some engage in more policy-oriented projects. Statistics gathered by the CCCLE and supported by anecdotal evidence indicate that the vast majority of clinical student activity outside the classroom takes the form of legal advice and consultation.[29]

Development and Trends

It appears that some of the earliest clinical programs in China are now well established and well regarded both domestically and internationally. The Wuhan Center, for example, has evolved from a volunteer student organization with paid staff lawyers into a robust clinical program with six divisions and an explicit social justice mission.[30] Renamed the Legal Aid Center of Wuhan University in October 2013, it includes departments focusing on women's rights, juvenile rights, disabled people's rights, elder people's rights, labor rights, and administrative litigation.[31] Law school teachers serve as director and executive secretary for each of the Wuhan Center's various departments, each of which also employs full-time lawyers. Law school students, both undergraduate and graduate, continue to provide most of the legal aid. Due to a lack of systematic legal practice lectures and training before the clinical program was established, student volunteers used to learn as apprentices, acquiring skills from more experienced volunteers or instructors and through their own experiences. Students now have the opportunity to train in the clinic with faculty guidance, get course credit for their work, and then can continue to provide legal services as volunteers in the Wuhan Center in their spare time.

In another example, Northwest University of Politics and Law in Xi'an ("Xibei") now has seven different clinics with broad student, faculty, and local participation. The clinics include a civil law clinic, a public interest law clinic, a rural community clinic, an administrative law clinic, and a labor law clinic, open to undergraduate students, as well as a legislation clinic and a criminal defense clinic, open to graduate students.[32] The legislation clinic at Xibei, for example, works with "government agencies and civic organizations to propose and craft legislation that affects socially disadvantaged groups."[33] Over time, Xibei has developed its own model of CLE, which includes three parts: "focusing on the cultivation of lawyers and promoting the growth of legal community; learning and reforming education theory and methodology through real experience; [and]

providing legal aid so to promote the development of [the] legal profession and justice."[34]

Among the other early pioneers, Sun Yat-Sen University, located in the factory-rich (and pollution-rich) Pearl River Delta of Guangdong Province, now has two vibrant clinics. The labor law clinic, founded first, provides representation to workers, particularly migrant workers, in disputes with employers, often going as far as administrative proceedings to resolve disputes.[35] The environmental law clinic, founded in late 2003, was the first clinic of its kind in China. Focusing primarily on policy research and analysis, it has worked, for example, to survey various stakeholders about issues relating to air and water pollution and awareness of environmental rights.[36] It has also analyzed ways of pursuing water pollution-related litigation in provincial courts. Since 2006, Sun Yat-Sen University and Vermont Law School in the United States have partnered together to work on environmental issues, with Vermont Law School faculty teaching at times in the clinic at Sun Yat-Sen University.[37] In 2011, the two clinics at Sun Yat-Sen collaborated to create an Environmental and Water Health and Safety Advocacy Center, designed "to provide legal advocacy for communities and workers, especially migrant workers, in pollution cases and cases involving environmental health and safety issues."[38]

Renmin University, another leader, established the first law school clinic in China dedicated exclusively to legal services for persons with disabilities.[39] In another example of international partnership, Renmin Law School partnered in 2006 with the Harvard Law School Project on Disability, a team of scholars and advocates who work globally to promote disability human rights through law and policy, to establish the Center for Persons with Disabilities Law and Legal Service and the Law Clinic of the Protection of the Rights of the Disabled.[40] The disability law clinic, designed as part of Renmin's graduate-level Comparative Law Program, is open to students who have completed courses in international human rights, disability law, and advocacy, and is taught by an international collaboration of Chinese and American faculty in Chinese and English.[41] Students enrolled in the clinic participate in classroom activities, training sessions on the international Convention on the Rights of Persons with Disabilities, and other conferences; design curricula for use by teachers throughout China; research comparative laws and practices related to disability around the world to assist in the revision of government regulations; and work with NGOs for disabled persons.[42] Through this diverse range of activities, the clinic "empowers students, faculty, and volunteer lawyers to work with persons with disabilities and their organizations to provide quality legal services, promote the reform and development of laws and policies on the protection of rights and interests for persons with disabilities, as well as increase rights awareness within China's persons with disabilities community."[43]

At Sichuan University, with another long-standing clinical program, approximately 60 students a year participate in the criminal justice clinic, while additional students continue to participate in legal aid cases outside of the formal clinical program.[44] And as of December 2013, Peking University Law School in Beijing had trained approximately 800 students over 27 semesters of CLE courses, providing legal advice in one form or another in over 10,000 situations and representing clients in over 260 legal aid cases.

At the same time, clinical programs at these institutions have not remained static once established. Peking University Law School, for instance, began with a civil law clinic in 2000, followed by a community clinic in 2001. In partnership with the more rural town of Qianxi in Hebei province outside Beijing, students in the Qianxi community law clinic provided legal services, proposed legislative and judicial reforms, and publicized laws in an effort to further grass-roots community law development.[45] In addition, Peking University ran a legal aid clinic in the Haidian District of Beijing, as well as a clinic focusing on student claims against universities.[46] More recently, however, the law school ended its Qianxi program and reorganized its campus-based clinical program, establishing the Center for Clinical Legal Education of Peking University in May 2010. The current program enrolls 30 students in a civil and administrative litigation clinic, 8 to 12 students in a legislative clinic, and about 12 students in an externship clinic. Preparation for a new community legal clinic is underway. In another shift, Peking University also rescinded its affiliation with the Center for Women's Law Studies and Legal Services in spring 2010, after 15 years.[47]

As some of these programs suggest, the expansion of formal CLE programs in China over the last several years has been marked by increasing innovation and diversification. More clinics are venturing into new types of legal practice, areas of law, and organizational structures. Some of the current trends include shifts away from litigation-based clinics and toward specialization and externship programs.

Nonlitigation Clinics

Initially, clinics in China focused on providing unpaid legal assistance in litigation, including negotiations, mediations, and in-court litigation, following the examples set by the early years of CLE in the United States. Time and experience have brought greater diversification. Now, increasing numbers of nonlitigation clinics are being established. These nonlitigation clinics include, for example, civil or judicial mediation clinics. In a civil mediation clinic, students assist two parties, such as neighbors or spouses, to work out legal issues. The Yangzhou University marriage and family law clinic, established in 2006, provides free mediation and legal advice. In a judicial mediation clinic, such as the one in Wuhan University, students—under the guidance of actual judges—play the role of judge instead of agent of a party and help parties reach conciliation statements. The court then draws up a formal conciliation statement.

Following the example set by Northwest University of Politics and Law, another area of nonlitigation legal services offered by more clinics now is legislative advocacy. And more clinics are pursuing policy research and analysis, as exemplified by the environmental law clinic at Sun Yat-Sen University and the disability law clinic at Renmin University. Yet another type of clinic is the street law clinic set up by the Jiangsu Police Institute in 2008. The Juvenile Criminal Legal Clinic aims to prevent juvenile crime and provide legal education to juveniles. From 2009 to 2012, it also provided legal aid for 20 juveniles in cases involving intentional destruction or property damage, swindling, theft, and other crimes.[48]

The shift away from litigation is also marked by clinics with a heavier focus on legal advice, such as the Harbin University School of Political Science Citizens Law Clinic. Established in September 2013, teachers and students at the Harbin Citizens Law Clinic provide legal advice and suggestions for citizens through a networking platform.

Specialized Clinics

Another recent trend is toward even more specialized clinics. One novel example is the tobacco control legal clinic, established in 2010 at China University of Political Science and Law. The clinic is the first public legal clinic in China, established by a university, that is aimed at controlling and reducing the dangers of tobacco. With financial and technical support from the Campaign for Tobacco-Free Kids, the postgraduate student clinic aims to control and reduce cigarette hazards, enhance students' sense of social responsibility, and develop students' professional skills, with an emphasis on legislative advocacy. Its curriculum includes special lectures, public interest litigation, moot court, and a simulated hearing on tobacco control legislation. In its first few years, the legal clinic already has a number of achievements, including drafting the *Feasibility Report of Legislation on Prohibiting Smoking in Public Areas*, proposing modifications for the Lanzhou and Guangzhou Tobacco Control Regulations, and drafting the Beijing Tobacco Control Regulation.

A new effort to provide legal services to victims of domestic violence is also underway. Domestic violence affecting women, elders, and children is a widespread issue that garnered little public attention in China until recently. Although the *Chinese Marriage Law* and the *Law on the Protection of the Rights and Interests of Women* prohibit domestic violence, activists and courts have recognized the need for a more formalized approach to address weaknesses and gaps in those laws. Since 2012, the national legislature has been working to draft the first law specifically on domestic violence. Courts have begun issuing greater numbers of civil protection orders, and the Supreme People's Court intends in the near future to issue an interpretation of domestic violence to provide greater guidance.[49]

Recognizing the need for legal services in this growing area of attention, the first domestic violence legal clinic began operating in spring 2014 at Wuhan University. It provides victims of domestic violence with both litigation and nonlitigation legal services, including requests for protection orders, mediation, and negotiation. In December 2013, Wuhan hosted training for more than 35 clinicians on domestic violence, including how to manage and teach a domestic violence-focused legal clinic. More domestic violence clinics are planned at different universities in upcoming years, as are conferences and networks designed to enable domestic violence clinicians to communicate with each other and share the experiences of their clinical programs.

Yet another example of a specialized clinic is the law translation clinic for languages of ethnic minorities, established at South-Central University for Nationalities in Wuhan. This clinic trains students to qualify as translators and assists in translating a variety of legal documents, from court papers and proceedings to evidence.[50]

Externships

At first, there were few externship-based clinics in China, although some institutions, like Peking University Law School in Beijing, set up parallel clinical programs, with an in-house clinic as well as an externship program. More recently, externship numbers have begun to increase, as Chinese governmental agencies, public institutions, and NGOs have set up a large number of legal service platforms that need legal professionals. These platforms include, for example, governmental legal aid centers, community service stations, rescue shelters, non-governmental mediation centers, and more. For instance, Southwest University of Political Science and Law in Chongqing has set up six legal service stations in the community as externship platforms at which clinic students provide free legal consultation each week. Similarly, in 2008, the Dalian University law school established 14 community legal clinics with the subdistrict office of the Dalian economic and technological development zone.

The need for more legal professionals is creating openings for more cooperative arrangements between law schools and outside organizations, leading to the formation of more externship clinics. In addition, some believe that these forms of externship clinics allow students to more deeply immerse themselves in social practice. Moving forward, however, it will be important for academic institutions and their partner organizations to more clearly delineate and define the roles and responsibilities of the different participants in the externship clinics, including who bears legal responsibility for services provided by externship students.

Challenges and Opportunities Facing Clinical Legal Education

Despite these efforts at innovation and trends toward diversification, China still lags behind some other countries in terms of the diversity of clinics and innovative approaches. For instance, at a time when globalization affects many aspects of life and law around the world, China's CLE programs pay scant attention to international or transnational legal issues. In contrast, many law clinics in the United States provide legal services relating to global, international, and cross-border issues, as well as domestic ones. There are numerous US law clinics devoted to international human rights and immigration, for example.

Founded in 2010, the Center for Cross-Border Advocacy at the Peking University School of Transnational Law (STL) was the first live-client CLE program in China to provide transnational—not domestic—legal representation.[51]

Under the supervision of an American clinical law professor licensed to practice law in the United States, Chinese law students represented immigrants in the United States at the administrative appeals stage of their deportation proceedings. In the complementary seminar, the students studied US immigration law and appellate procedure, practiced advanced legal writing and oral advocacy, and explored issues of professional responsibility and cross-cultural lawyering. The entire course was conducted in English. The Center for Cross-Border Advocacy offered its students a unique opportunity to develop familiarity with lawyering across cultural differences and lawyering in a Western legal system, as well as a more global perspective generally. Due to changes in the STL curriculum and faculty, however, the Center for Cross-Border Advocacy lasted only a few semesters, although the law school plans to replace it with new clinics focused on small business entrepreneurs and on local indigent legal aid services.

Although establishing and sustaining similar types of transnational legal clinics in China is fraught with practical challenges, it also offers potential for a beneficial cross-fertilization of ideas if the transnational clinics are integrated into CLE programs focused on Chinese domestic legal issues. Another alternative to fill this international gap in Chinese CLE is to strengthen existing international partnerships, such as the partnerships created at Renmin University and Sun Yat-Sen University, and to establish new ones through student and faculty exchanges and internships. And yet another innovative model that Chinese clinics could adopt is to collaborate with law students in other countries on clinical projects of a transnational nature, taking advantage of constantly improving technology to work together and even possibly traveling to each other's countries or a third country. While any of these approaches could help fill the void surrounding international and transnational issues in Chinese CLE, however, programs should pay particular attention to ways of integrating the transnational legal expertise developed by students with the professional opportunities potentially available to them in their future careers.[52]

As CLE in China approaches its fifteenth birthday, it also continues to face a number of other internal and external challenges. For instance, Chinese law clinics face the challenge of maintaining high-quality standards as they expand in numbers and experiment with different subject matter, curricula, and pedagogical methods. Clinicians are working to address that challenge in part by strengthening networks for sharing and learning, from the CCCLE on a broad level to regional unions to smaller working groups of clinicians focused on specific areas. The CCCLE, for instance, has set up 15 legal clinic resource bases at different institutions to provide regional demonstration lessons and "train the trainer" workshops.[53] The resource bases organize national teacher trainings for clinicians, and they strive to develop long-term relationships with new clinical teachers to enable continued discussions and advice. And clinical leaders in China are encouraging the formation of regional unions of clinicians as well as more groups like the Anti-Domestic Violence Law Clinic Group, consisting of clinics dealing with similar substantive issues.

The CCCLE is also pursuing other approaches for improving the quality of clinical teaching in China. In addition to maintaining its website as a clearinghouse of clinic-related information and resources and as a platform for clinical teacher exchanges, the CCCLE has established a special video production committee. This committee focuses on producing and sharing videos of clinical teaching demonstrations and lectures, so that other clinical teachers can watch and learn from them. And the CCCLE encourages efforts to publish clinical teaching textbooks and research reports in order to preserve and share the experiences accumulated by China's clinical teachers.

Despite these burgeoning efforts to maintain and improve clinic quality, most clinical teachers continue to face heavy work burdens without adequate reward under current academic standards.[54] No independent promotion or assessment mechanisms yet exist for Chinese clinicians, although the CCCLE's guidelines advise that the assessments of clinical teachers should include their efforts in the classroom as well as their practical and supervisory work on cases, and few clinical professors in China have the luxury of teaching solely in the clinical program.[55] On the contrary, professors generally do not get credit or recognition for their clinical work and are therefore expected to teach a full load of nonclinical courses each semester. Simultaneously, they are expected to engage in research and scholarship in their nonclinical specialties.[56]

Compounding this challenge for the faculty is the sheer number of law students participating in clinical programs, particularly compared to the number of faculty available to supervise them. As many as 2,300 (or more) new students participate in clinics each semester.[57] CCCLE guidelines advise that the ratio of students to supervisors should be no more than 30:1 per clinic.[58] In contrast, American guidelines recommend that clinical programs in the United States maintain a ratio of no more than eight or ten students per supervisor,[59] and the results of the Center for Applied Legal Study's 2010–2011 survey of American law schools indicate that "over 75% of law clinics have student-teacher ratios of 8 to 1 or less."[60]

Another challenge facing CLE in China is to clarify its relationship to legal aid centers and voluntary student legal aid associations, many of which are often combined in some way with CLE (as evidenced by the CCCLE guidelines that recognize reliance on legal aid centers as a form for legal clinics to take). Although both share similar educational and legal service goals, they often have different structures and needs. For instance, a university legal aid organization is usually a distinct legal entity, while a legal clinic may not have as clearly defined legal status or organization. CLE courses also require teaching and research space in different ways than legal aid organizations and centers may. Going forward, it will be important to more clearly define the identity of CLE and ensure that its programs have appropriate resources and space to fulfill their mission.

A long-standing challenge confronting Chinese litigation-based clinics is the fact that existing Chinese laws do not permit students in legal clinics the same rights as legal representatives when handling cases.[61] Under China's *Civil Procedure Law*, law students may appear in Chinese court only in the role of citizen representative, recommended by the community, an NGO, or another "relevant social organization."[62] In that role, clinic students have limited access to documents and, sometimes, to their clients. This challenge of limited student rights is particularly acute in criminal cases, where under the *Criminal Procedure Law*, law students may defend a criminal suspect or defendant only if "recommended by a public organization or the unit to which the criminal suspect or the defendant belongs."[63] In addition, even when students are permitted to represent clients in court, concerns remain about how to ensure high-quality representation and how to manage the supervision of students in court.[64] But with the challenge comes opportunity for more innovation, as clinical programs must try to find other ways to engage students meaningfully. For instance, because of these legal restrictions on representation, legal clinics must cooperate with NGOs, the local community, and organizations like the Women's Federation. In other situations, clinics direct their energy toward nonlitigation projects, such as policy analyses, surveys, and reports related to legislative drafting.[65]

CLE in China also continues to face the more general challenge of overcoming a deeply ingrained preference among many faculty, students, and institutions themselves for traditional pedagogy.[66] This preference for traditional education creates obstacles in setting up, funding, and maintaining adequate support for clinics. To date, for instance, clinical programs have failed to muster significant financial support beyond the funds provided by the Ford Foundation, first directly to individual clinical programs and then through the CCCLE.[67] It also perpetuates the perception in many Chinese universities that clinics are much less important than required courses.[68]

As CLE programs spread into more academic institutions and as more Chinese faculty are exposed to techniques of clinical pedagogy, however, more opportunities may arise to gradually erode resistance to CLE and even to incorporate clinical methodologies into nonclinical courses. Moreover, in December 2011, the Ministry of Education of the People's Republic of China and the Commission of Politics and Law of the Communist Party of China's Central Committee jointly released "Some Ideas about Training Outstanding Legal Talent" (关于实施卓越法律人才教育培养计划的若干意见).[69] The plan aims to reform and improve the quality of legal training by establishing national standards, reforming modes of training legal talent, developing law teaching staff, and creating training platforms for legal practice. Notably it identifies CLE as one of the methods for strengthening law practice teaching, thereby elevating its status to a national level. In addition to establishing a new designation for schools focused on improving practical legal skills (and bringing with it resources and privileges), the plan also requires that 15 percent of credit hours in the law curriculum be devoted to practical, experiential education, such as CLE, moot court, and internship programs.[70]

This new national attention to CLE comes at a time when funding, a persistent challenge, may become even more dire. After providing financial support to individual clinical programs and to the CCCLE for many years, the Ford Foundation is reducing its funding for daily operations of legal clinics in China.

For most clinics now, however, the host institutions and their law schools are the most important resources, and the CCCLE intends to help clinics find the necessary financial support. In particular, the CCCLE is focusing on support—both training and financial—to expand CLE in areas with more ethnic minorities and other more remote areas of China. Greater financial resources for CLE from the government may also help compensate for the loss of private foundation funding as well as guide the future of Chinese CLE toward the development of even more particularly Chinese characteristics.

Conclusion

CLE in China has come a long way from the voluntary student legal aid organizations of the 1990s. Rapidly multiplying in numbers in the last several years, university-based legal clinics are diversifying and gaining greater recognition as they adapt in response to China's particular needs and challenges. Yet as CLE enters the second half of its second decade with a more national profile, it remains to be seen how clinics will continue to grow and prosper, and what forms they will take in the absence of the significant international funding that fostered them in the early years.

Notes

1. Benjamin Liebman, "Legal Aid & Public Interest in China" (1999) 34 *Tex. Int'l L.J.* 211, 219.
2. Ibid.
3. Cecily E. Baskir, "Legal Education in China: Globalizing with Chinese Characteristics" in Shuvro P. Sarker (ed.) *Legal Education in Asia* (Eleven, 2014) 42; Cai Yanmin and J. Pottenger, "The 'Chinese Characteristics' of Clinical Legal Education" in Frank S. Bloch (ed.) *The Global Clinical Movement* (Oxford University Press, 2011) 91–92.
4. Ibid.
5. Liebman (n 1) 234.
6. Ibid. 231–232.
7. Ibid. 235.
8. Ibid. 236.
9. Cai and Pottenger (n 3) 92.
10. Ibid. 92–93.
11. Baskir (n 3) 42; Pamela Phan, 'Clinical Legal Education in China: In Pursuit of a Culture of Law and a Mission of Social Justice' (2005) 8 *Yale Hum. Rts. & Dev. L.J.* 117, 128.
12. Cai and Pottenger (n 3) 92.
13. Ibid. 93.
14. CCCLE Announcement, "Warm Congratulations to Langfang Teachers College and Other Institutions to Become CCCLE Three New Members" (CCCLE, May 15, 2014) http://www.cliniclaw.cn/article/?825.html, accessed May 27, 2014. For a list of CCCLE member schools, see CCCLE Website, Member Schools, available in Chinese at http://www.cliniclaw.cn/hyschool.asp, accessed May 27, 2014.

15. Note, "Adopting and Adapting: Clinical Legal Education and Access to Justice in China" (2007) 120 *Harv. L. Rev.* 2134, 2140; Phan (n 11) 129–130, 136; Su Li Zhu, "An Institutional Inquiry into Legal Skills Education in China" (2009) 20 *Pac. McGeorge Global Bus. & Dev. L.J.* 75, 79–80.
16. Brian Landsberg, "Walking on Two Legs in Chinese Law Schools: A China/U.S. Program in Experiential Legal Education" (Summer 2011) 16 *Int'l J. Clin. Educ.* 38; Note (n 15) 2140.
17. Cai and Pottenger (n 3) 94.
18. Baskir (n 3) 43; Margaret M. Barry, Filip Czernicki, Izabela K. Nicka, and Mao Ling, "The Role of National and Regional Clinical Organizations in the Global Clinical Movement" in Frank S. Bloch (ed.) *The Global Clinical Movement* (Oxford University Press, 2011) 286.
19. Ibid.
20. Baskir (n 3) 43; see CCCLE Clinic Guide, available in Chinese at http://www.cliniclaw.cn/more.asp?channel=%C3%D8%CA%E9%B4%A6&type1=%D5%EF%CB%F9%D6%B8%C4%CF, accessed May 27, 2014.
21. Baskir (n 3) 43; CCCLE Guidelines on Operation and Management of Legal Clinics (October 20, 2010) http://www.cliniclaw.cn/article/?219.html, accessed May 27, 2014.
22. Baskir (n 3) 43; CCCLE Basic Guidelines (October 20, 2010) http://www.cliniclaw.cn/article/?214.html, accessed May 27, 2014; CCCLE Classroom Teaching and Management Standards (October 20, 2010) http://www.cliniclaw.cn/article/?218.html, accessed May 27, 2014.
23. Baskir (n 3) 39; Matthew S. Erie, "Legal Education Reform in China through U.S.-Inspired Transplants" (2009) 59 *J. Legal Educ.* 60, 71, 78; see also R. R. Edwards, "An Overview of Chinese Law and Legal Education" (1984) 476 *Ann. Am. Acad. Pol. Soc. Sci.* 54. The "stuffing the duck" style of learning begins at an early age in China. Phan (n 11) 126–127; Zhu (n 15) 76.
24. Baskir (n 3) 39.
25. Ibid. 44.
26. Ibid. (n 3); Cai and Pottenger (n 3) 94.
27. Baskir (n 3) 44.
28. Ibid.; Cecily E. Baskir, "Crossing Borders: Creating an American Law Clinic in China" (2012) 19 *Clinical L. Rev.* 163.
29. Cai and Pottenger (n 3) 94.
30. Ibid. 91–92, 96–97.
31. Wuhan University Central Office, "Social Protection of the Rights of the Weak" http://www.cprdc.org/web/ShowArticle.asp?ArticleID=621, accessed May 27, 2014.
32. Introduction to Clinical Programs of Northwest University of Political Science and Law, http://www.nwcliniclaw.cn/show.asp?id=158, accessed May 27, 2014; see also Northwest University of Political Science and Law Clinic Overview List, http://www.nwcliniclaw.cn/list.asp?id=1, accessed May 27, 2014.
33. Note (n 15) 2151–2152.
34. Introduction to Clinical Programs of Northwest University of Political Science and Law (n 32; see also Cai and Pottenger (n 3) 94–95.
35. Interview with Cai Yanmin, Sun Yat-Sen University (Guangzhou, China, May 12, 2011); *Sun Yat-Sen University Legal Clinic* (October 21, 2009) http://law.sysu.edu.cn/Item/692.aspx, accessed May 27, 2014.
36. Carlos Da Rosa, Ward Kershaw Environmental Law Symposium, "Globalizing Clinical Education to Protect the World's Health and Environment" www.law

.maryland.edu/programs/environment/events/wardkershaw07/darosa.pdf, accessed July 18, 2014; Rockefeller Brothers Fund, Zhongshan University's Environmental Law Clinic, www.rbf.org/close-up/zhongshan-universitys-environmental-law-clinic, accessed July 21, 2014.

37. "New Environmental Advocacy Centers in Guangzhou and Beijing" Greening China, Fall 2011, www.vermontlaw.edu/Documents/China%20Program/VLS.133.11_CHINA_NEWS_PFF.pdf, accessed July 21, 2014.
38. Ibid.
39. Harvard Negotiation & Mediation Clinical Program at Harvard Law School, "Alonzo Emery '10 Joins the Harvard Negotiation & Mediation Clinical Program" (June 18, 2013) http://blogs.law.harvard.edu/hnmcp/newsletters/alonzo-emery-10-joins-the-harvard-negotiation-mediation-clinical-program/, accessed May 27, 2014.
40. Ding Xiangshun, "Building International Collaboration through a Disability Law Clinic: Experiences from Renmin University Disability Law Center" (2012) 15(1) *Inha L. Rev.* 4–5.
41. Ibid. 8.
42. Ibid. 9–14.
43. Ibid. 7–8.
44. Sichuan University, "Legal Clinic Curriculum Development History http://cc.scu.edu.cn/G2S/Template/View.aspx?courseId=27&topMenuId=115094&action=view&type=&name=&menuType=1, accessed May 27, 2014; Kara Abramson, "Paradigms in the Cultivation of China's Future Legal Elite: A Case Study of Legal Education in Western China (2006) 7 *Asian-Pac. L. &Pol'y J.* 302, 324.
45. Peking University Law School, "Legal Clinics at Peking University Law School" (2010) http://student.law.pku.edu.cn:8080/article_one.asp?MID=2010586514334&MenuId=20105865022&menuname=%D5%EF%CB%F9%B8%C5%BF%F6, accessed May 27, 2014.
46. Ibid.
47. NGOs in China blog, Peking University Women's Legal Aid Center loses its affiliation, April 14, 2010, ngochina.blogspot.com/2010/04/peking-university-womens-legal-aid.html.
48. Honghai Du, "Research on the local generalized street legal clinic function and operation" (2012 Asia-Pacific forum on clinical legal education and annual meeting of CCCLE).
49. Supreme People's Court Monitor, "Supreme People's Court Focuses on Domestic Violence" (March 16, 2014) http://supremepeoplescourtmonitor.com/2014/03/16/supreme-peoples-court-focuses-on-domestic-violence/, accessed May 27, 2014; Didi K. Tatlow, "Pushing for a Law Against Domestic Violence in China" *The New York Times Sinosphere* (February 26, 2014), http://mobile.nytimes.com/blogs/sinosphere/2014/02/26/pushing-for-a-law-against-domestic-violence-in-china/?emc=edit_tnt_20140227&tntemail0=y, accessed May 27, 2014.
50. Dou Mei, Lin Lei, and Wu Zhongming, "An Innovation in Clinical Law Education of Nationalities Universities—The Establishment and Operation of Law Translation Clinic for Languages of Ethnic Minorities and the Few" (UCLA/IALS Sixth International Clinical Conference, October 7, 2005) http://cdn.law.ucla.edu/SiteCollectionDocuments/Workshops%20and%20Colloquia/Clinical%20Programs/Dou%20Mei.pdf, accessed May 27, 2014.
51. Baskir (n 28).
52. See Ding (n 40) 17 (discussing challenges facing the Renmin University disability law clinic).

53. CCCLE Announcement on Planned Resource Base Activities (March 6, 2014) http://www.cliniclaw.cn/article/?769.html, accessed May 27, 2014.
54. Yanmin Cai, "Global Clinical Legal Education and International Partnerships: A Chinese Legal Educator's Perspective" (2011) 26 *Md. J. Int'l L.* 159, 171; Baskir (n 3) 47.
55. Baskir (n 3) 47; Zhen Zhen, "The Present Situation and Prosperous Future of China Clinical Legal Education" (UCLA/IALS Sixth International Clinical Conference, October 7, 2005) http://cdn.law.ucla.edu/SiteCollectionDocuments/workshops%20and%20colloquia/clinical%20programs/zhen%20zhen.pdf, accessed September 17, 2011.
56. Baskir (n 3) 47.
57. Ibid. 47; Cai and Pottenger (n 3) 94.
58. Baskir (n 3) 47; CCCLE Classroom Teaching and Management Standards (October 20, 2010) http://www.cliniclaw.cn/article/?218.html, accessed May 27, 2014.
59. Baskir (n 3) 47; AALS Committee on the Future of the In-House Clinic, "Report of the Committee on the Future of the In-House Clinic" (1992) 42 *J. Legal Educ.* 508, 565–568.
60. Baskir (n 3) 47; David A. Santacroce and Robert R. Kuehn, "The 2010–11 Survey of Applied Legal Education" (2012) *Center for the Study of Applied Legal Education* 18, www.csale.org/files/CSALE.Report.on.2010-11.Survey.5.16.12.Revised.pdf, accessed August 14, 2012.
61. Baskir (n 3) 48; Cai and Pottenger (n 3) 98.
62. P.R.C. Civil Procedure Law, article 58 (amended August 31, 2012).
63. P.R.C. Criminal Procedure Law, article 32.
64. Ding (n 40) 15–16.
65. See Ding (n 40) 16; Rosa (n 36); Rockefeller Brothers Fund (n 36).
66. Phan (n 11) 142–143; Baskir (n 3) 48.
67. Cai and Pottenger (n 3) 98; Zhen (n 55) 23–24.
68. Baskir (n 3) 48.
69. For more details about the plan for training outstanding legal talent, see Carl Minzner, "The Rise and Fall of Chinese Legal Education" (2013) 36 *Fordham Int'l L.J.* 334, 371–374. The plan,"Jiaoyubuzhongyangzhengfaweiguanyushishizhuoyuefalürencaipeiyangjihuaruoganyijian" [Relevant Opinions of the Ministry of Education and Central (Party) Political-Legal Committee on Implementing the Plan for Training Outstanding Legal Talent], *Xinhua*, December 23, 2011, is available in Chinese at http://news.xinhuanet.com/edu/2012-04/25/c_123029528.htm, accessed July 26, 2015.
70. Minzner (n 69) 372.

CHAPTER 4

Clinical Education in South Korean Law Schools: Challenges and Hopes

Helen Haekyong Kang and Kyung Sin Park

Introduction

Korean clinical legal education (CLE) is in its infancy. Before the 2007 Act of the Establishment and Management of Professional Law Schools[1] ("Law School Act") took effect, under which newly established, three-year postgraduate law schools opened in March 2009,[2] examples of clinical education were difficult to find. With one notable exception at Korea University, even in a few schools that exposed students to real cases with real clients, clinical education was at best insubstantial.[3] Students in "legal counseling" projects that were most akin to clinics advised clients on simple general civil and criminal matters, and the clients were often fellow students or employees of the school. These efforts were not part of a school curriculum, but rather community service projects for which students did not receive any academic credit. Similarly, supervising professors did not receive any additional remuneration or reduction in teaching load from their schools.

Before the 2007 reforms, students majoring in law in undergraduate institutions were principally driven to curricular content tested on the bar examination known as the National Judicial Examination (*sabeobshiheom*), which required rote memorization of vast amounts of material.[4]This prereform system has been justly criticized for creating several systemic problems.

Most notably, this old system has been blamed for the public's poor access to justice.[5] Since the advent of the bar examination after Korea's adoption of the Western legal system, the number of applicants who could pass the National Judicial Examination was strictly limited by a numerical quota that set the maximum number of bar passers each year.[6] Under this quota system, Korea typically admitted less than 5 percent of bar examinees (1,000 persons under the latest quota).[7] Compared to a ratio of about 1 lawyer per 260 residents in the United States, Korea has about 1 lawyer per 4,400 residents.[8] As another point of comparison, there is 1 doctor for every 500 Koreans, whereas in the United States there are more lawyers than doctors for every person.[9] Access to lawyer services in Korea has thus been limited, with many regions completely unserved by local lawyers and legal needs requiring specialization being unmet.[10]

Moreover, the intense focus on the bar examination is thought to have resulted in the characteristic lack of diversity of the bar: lawyers tended to be homogeneous in educational background because, as students, they focused on subjects tested on the bar to the detriment of their exposure to other subjects.[11]The two-year compulsory postbar training at the Judicial Training and Research Institute further made all the lawyers under the *sabeobshiheom* system even more homogenized.

The focus on the demanding bar studies also provided scant incentive to most law students for little else, including pro bono services.[12] The concept of lawyers as those entrusted with protecting the public interest is also underdeveloped in Korea. The bar admission quota allowed lawyers to accumulate wealth under the resulting monopoly, separating them as a class from the general populace and making most of them insensitive to the sufferings of the poor. Thus, for the disenfranchised and minority populations such as refugees and foreign migrant workers, access to justice has been an even more magnified problem.[13]

Lawyers were also criticized for being inadequately trained under the old system, primarily for lacking practice experience and expertise in specialized fields. Legal education was delivered primarily through large classroom lectures in undergraduate institutions as in Europe.[14] These lectures were mostly conducted without incorporating active learning methods that were used abroad.[15] Their post-bar training at the Judicial Training and Research Institute largely focused on litigation, preparing them primarily for government service as judges and criminal prosecutors.[16] Prominent members of the bar have indeed criticized this focus as ineffective for preparing lawyers for Korea's globalized economy because lawyers, among other things, do not receive adequate training in corporate transactional law. Such deficiency is problematic, given Korea's role in the global market as one of the world's largest economies and the amount of foreign investments flowing into the country after the International Monetary Fund's bailout of Korea in the wake of the 1997 Asian financial crisis.[17]

The implementation of the Law School Act is envisioned to address these systemic problems created by the old system. Legal education at three-year institutions is intended to develop law students' professional identity, ethics, and practical skills and knowledge. The Act thus ambitiously provides reform that is rooted in an educational philosophy of growing lawyers with a deep understanding of social issues and values based on their commitment to justice and equality and specialized knowledge, ability, and ethics necessary to provide competent legal services.[18] This notion of lawyers as public professionals is similar to that espoused in the 2007 Carnegie Foundation report that has reignited curricular reform efforts in law schools in the United States.[19]

The Law School Act intends to achieve these goals through reforming both law schools and the bar examination. The law limits the operation of such schools to only those that have government authorization and regulates various aspects of school operation.[20] Specific provisions of the Act that may affect clinical, or at least practical, education include requirements that at least one-fifth of post-graduate law school faculties be comprised of lawyers with over five years of relevant practical experience; faculty to student ratio be no more than 1 to 15; and that schools "endeavor" to admit students with diverse knowledge and experience, with at least one-third admitted to come from those who did not obtain an undergraduate law degree.[21] The law also provides that violations of some of the reform requirements by law schools may result in criminal sanctions or civil penalties.[22]

Under this new law, the Korean Education Ministry in September 2008 authorized 25 law schools to operate a three-year postgraduate program.[23] Graduates from these schools are eligible to take a newly instituted bar examination, called the *byeonhosasiheom* (which by 2017 will replace the old exams still being administered concurrently with the new exams). Once graduates pass the new bar examination, they are required to register with the Korean Bar Association and undergo six months of practical training before practicing law.[24]

The reforms present an opportunity to implement wide-ranging changes, including the adoption of meaningful clinical education. Law schools theoretically have an opportunity to newly design themselves, incorporating best practices from abroad, including learning from the reform efforts currently taking place in the United States. Indeed, reform appears to be afoot. All of the 25 law schools authorized under the Law School Act to offer postgraduate programs have established clinics and externships.[25] But whether how meaningful these new programs are in implementing the goals of the reform is a question as yet unanswered. When a professor at the nationally prominent Yonsei University Law School reviewed the state of affairs a year after the law schools opened, he was highly critical of the reform efforts, going so far as to conclude that the curricula were so superficially reformed as to be "window-dressing."[26] He concluded that courses that claimed to contain practical content were in fact similar to those previously offered at undergraduate institutions. The practical content again focused mainly on litigation, while there were some exceptions, including those dealing with contract drafting, transactions, and tax planning, as well as clinics.[27] The extent to which Korean legal education has progressed beyond this assessment is difficult to gauge without a systematic study, which does not yet exist.

Precisely because these postgraduate institutions were established as extensions of already existing law schools, innovations to produce practice-ready lawyers may be difficult to implement for some of the same reasons that US law schools are also finding it challenging to institute changes. Those reasons may include the entrenchment of doctrinal faculty in the traditional method, failure to devote resources to the development of clinical education, failure to provide academic incentives for students to choose clinical educational opportunities and take them seriously, and the failure to hire and train a sufficient number of professional clinical faculty.

The newly minted bar examination, administered initially in 2012 to the first class to graduate from postgraduate programs, may also contribute significantly to the continuing entrenchment of the old system. The new exam, too, has a quota but no passing score. This system pushes students into the prisoners' dilemma of spending as much time in their law school years as possible memorizing legal doctrines and cases to get ahead of one another because they are in competition with each other. Despite these challenges, promising clinics exist, including one that serves as a model for what is possible under the new system of legal education and the bar examination.

History of Korean Clinical Legal Education

Even under the old system, many undergraduate colleges of law had legal help desks where students provided counseling services free of charge to fellow students and employees of that school and, at times, local residents. In at least one case, undergraduate students offered extensive and considerable legal services in a large oil spill case, creating a pivotal moment for the development of Korean clinical education.

In December 2007, a barge owned by Samsung Heavy Industries and loaded with a sea crane collided with a foreign-registered supertanker, the *Hebei Spirit*, which was at a standstill at the time, after more than a full hour of advance warning of such collision. The collision caused the *Hebei Spirit* to spill 10,500 to 11,000 tons of oil (a quarter to a third of the infamous 1989 Exxon Valdez spill in the United States) on the 120 miles of scenic seashores of Taean, about 90 miles southwest of Seoul.[28] The spill devastated tourism, fisheries, oyster beds, and the residents' lives.[29] In the wake of the spill, over 280 students, mostly from colleges of law in Seoul, participated in coordinated legal advocacy for the local residents affected by the spill under the supervision of Korea University law professor Kyung Sin Park (coauthor of this chapter), Hyun Woo Nam (a local attorney), and several other volunteer lawyers.[30]

From early on, the damages caused by the spill so close to and broadly affecting the vast Taean Seashore National Park[31] were initially estimated to be close to 1 trillion KRW (approximately $980 million USD), easily exceeding the aggregate compensation limit of about 321.6 billion KRW set by the relevant international conventions and local legislations enforcing them.[32] Especially disturbing was the initially prevailing media report that the total liability of Samsung Heavy Industries, the primary tortfeasor, would be statutorily limited to 5.6 billion KRW. That is, in their news coverage, the mainstream media, dependent on Samsung business groups' advertising, often reported that there was a statutory cap on damages and strongly discounted the possibility that such a cap may be inapplicable where the ship owner commits a tort knowingly and recklessly. Because the total compensation amount was perceived to be capped (aggregating the *Heibei*

Spirit's insurance proceeds and the International Oil Pollution Compensation [IOPC] Fund covering Samsung Heavy Industries' liabilities, the latter of which are set so that the total amount came to 321.6 billion KRW), local residents did not expect full compensation, and thus in some cases were hesitant to seek relief. If the damages were indeed capped, then larger compensation awards to some victims would have meant a smaller recovery for other victims. The groups that suffered economic damages especially were discouraged about pursuing claims because recovery of such damages was again publicized, and therefore perceived, as difficult under the IOPC Fund's rules, which governed the payout scheme for both sources of compensation

The joint Volunteer Corps of professors, lawyers, and students[33] set up an on-site legal clinic for two months,[34] mostly assisting those suffering economic damages in the preparation of applications for compensation. One of the victims of the oil spill was the owner of an ocean view villa. Expecting and actually receiving no guests after the oil spill, he rented the facility to the Volunteer Corps for free during the two months, which the members made judicious and pleasant use of as they came from Seoul in groups of four or five and stayed there for a week at a time. The Volunteer Corps published and distributed biweekly newsletters, which delivered the information about liability and compensation that the mainstream media did not cover, such as the possibility that damages might not be capped. The Volunteer Corps also conducted a relay demonstration for several weeks in front of Samsung's headquarters,[35] urging the global company not to hide behind the treaty-based liability limitation and to offer a fair compensation proposal.[36] The Volunteer Corps members summarized their counseling experience by publishing a manuscript titled "200 Questions and Answers on Oil Pollution Compensation,"[37] which was mass-produced and locally distributed to the broader communities affected by the oil spill. The Corps members also collected and translated into Korean, major overseas precedents interpreting the liability limitation regimes for sea and air carriers, in order to encourage and educate lawyers who might have wanted to eliminate the damages cap by proving that Samsung had been reckless. This collection was officially published many months later in July 2009, as a 529-page volume, *Major Cases on Ship Owner's Liability Limitation*, and included Professor Park's preface analyzing the significance of these precedents.[38]

The Volunteer Corps was successful in turning the public's attention to the possibility of "unlimited liability," a term first used by the Corps, which then gained wide acceptance among the general public as a normative standard to be applied. Moreover, group of law firms came forth to represent economic damages victims on a pro bono basis, taking on the task of attempting to prove Samsung's recklessness in an effort to eliminate the liability cap. After five months of operation, the Volunteer Corps dissolved itself and turned over all the intake documents to a public interest litigation group, including the law firms providing pro bono assistance. Litigation against Samsung on the limitation cap issue lasted for more than four years, until the Supreme Court's decision on April 17, 2012 that did not eliminate the cap.[39]

What was significant for clinical education was that the Volunteer Corps' efforts became widely known in college circles and raised the awareness of such education among officials at Korea University, who were at the time planning for the opening of a three-year law school in 2009. They commissioned Professor Park to create a pilot project with undergraduate law students in June 2008. The newly created Global Legal Clinic was the first attempt at clinical education in Korea, and it was to be later transplanted once Korea University established a new law school under the new system.

The pilot Global Legal Clinic soon grew from 10 to more than 20 students who worked at three clinics: the Oil Spill Compensation, Foreign Workers' Rights, and Blind's Web Accessibility Clinics, all of which had very narrowly tailored goals. The Oil Spill Compensation Clinic was to be a policy clinic, the goal of which was lobbying the government to ratify the protocols governing the IOPC Supplementary Fund. Korea's ratification would result in increasing the amount available for compensation, from about 360 billion KRW to about 1 trillion KRW. The Foreign Workers' Rights Clinic was also to be a "policy clinic," the goal of which was to repeal the law requiring public employees to report any undocumented alien to the immigration authorities, most of the time, for deportation. The Web Accessibility Clinic was to be a "litigation clinic" aimed at filing civil rights suits against companies and agencies for failing to configure their websites for accessibility to the blind.

When the new law school opened at Korea University in March 2009, the Global Legal Clinic became the country's first clinical center that offered a course that could be taken for academic credit at a law school, and in 2010 it changed its name to the Clinical Legal Education Center (CLEC). The three earlier pilot clinics continued to be offered to law school students and resulted in tangible achievements in 2010 and 2013, which are discussed below.

Also, several college law students who participated and played leadership roles in the Volunteer Corps and the Global Legal Clinic enrolled in the new law schools in 2009 or 2010 and became active in or otherwise contributed to the formal clinics established there.[40] The student leadership was very important for the early phases of the law school clinics because there was barely a professor with any clinical education experience either as a student or as a professor.

Current Status of Korean Clinical Legal Education

As envisioned in the Law School Act, law school education is intended to be consonant with the ideals of clinical education as globally practiced. Similar to the ideal of clinical education, as "hands-on, professional skills training coupled with instruction in—and initiation into—lawyers' public and professional responsibilities,"[41] the reform law is commendably aimed at producing lawyers who are worldly, with knowledge and understanding of the larger society and values based on concepts of equality and justice, and who also possess the skills necessary to serve the public.[42] Indeed, in the competitive process established for the selection of institutions that could operate postgraduate law schools, schools were awarded points for courses that combined practice with theory.[43]

While experiential learning opportunities might appear to be an inevitable component of this aim, lawmakers did not consider clinics specifically as an essential element of the reform. Since the law schools opened in March 2009, externships and skills courses such as legal writing and drafting, litigation skills training, moot court, legal ethics, and problem solving have comprised the primary means of delivering practical education.[44] Of these courses, five are mandatory under the reform law: professional responsibility or ethics, legal research, legal document drafting, moot court, and an externship.[45]

Programs that are considered "clinical" vary, consisting of on-campus clinics under the supervision of faculty; off-campus placements at law offices, NGOs or government offices, which are also commonly referred to as internships in Korea (referred to in the United States as externships); and hybrid models of collaboration between government agencies, law school faculty, and students, in which faculty provides on-campus supervision.[46] Most students consider clinical courses only after fulfilling their practical course requirement though an externship or internship.

Some Numbers on Korean Legal Clinics[47]

In the first year of the newly established law schools, only Korea University had a legal clinic. Clinical programs at that school began in the inaugurating year of 2009 because it was able to build on its previous undergraduate clinical program. A year after the schools opened, only six law schools had adopted clinical courses.[48] Although all 25 law schools had built clinical programs by 2011, that is, when the first admitted class became third-year law students, the reality is that, oppressed by the bar examination pressure, students have rarely enrolled in clinical courses.

Overall, the law schools have not considered clinics an indispensable part of the new establishments. Only three law schools require a clinical course as a graduation requirement.[49] Yet even the graduation requirement at those schools is not very substantial. For instance, one of the three schools requires only one clinical unit, which corresponds to only 20 hours per semester, meaning barely a little more than one hour each week.[50] In addition, all 25 schools grant credits on a pass/fail basis.[51] The clinical courses are expected to lose many students if they are competitively graded.

What is promising—and perhaps this is due to the few demands of clinical courses, including the hours requirement and the pass/fail grading—the number of students who participated in clinical programs is substantial. At least at five schools, more than 100 students per school participated in 2012.[52] There are 14 schools at which fewer than 40 students participated, but that is because 8 schools received an admission quota of fewer than 50 from the educational ministry, and it is likely that these schools are in the group of 14.[53] Actually, given that only eight schools have quotas of 100 or more students per class and that the students are not likely to participate in the clinical program for more than one year,[54] that five schools registered annual student participation of more than 100 is phenomenal. One can say that at those schools nearly every eligible student participated.

However, the depth and limitations of the current design of clinical education needs be considered. Although all 25 schools deal with real cases,[55] at least five schools do not engage in litigation and do not file lawsuits.[56] Such schools do not offer any alternative experience to real litigation to supplement the weak experiential component. As a result, 13 schools did not have any experience of delivering successful relief to their clients through litigation.[57] Indeed, it is rare to hear about a clinical lawsuit that led to a victory. The rarity of such victories is unsurprising: 11 schools allocate only one credit to all clinical courses, 10 schools assign two credits, and only 3 schools assign three credits.[58] Given the few credits, it is difficult to expect a clinical semester to accommodate the successful prosecution of a formal suit.

Twelve schools restrict the timing of enrollment in clinical programs to the upper years of the three-year program.[59] The cold reality is that the pressure to pass the attorney examination is so overwhelming, and more so toward the third year, that only students in their first years or the first semester of their second years have the mental leeway to enroll in a clinical course not related to the bar examination. It would appear that the rule that exists at 12 schools, limiting clinical enrollment to the upper years, results in the overall lack or shallowness of student participation.

Another salient point is that only five schools have a standard for client selection,[60] out of which only one school, Korea University, applies a financial means test. The remaining four schools limit the intake to only certain subject matters, kinds of clients (e.g., the school's employees and students), or to cases sourced from local welfare offices. Out of 25 law schools, only 12 have specialized clinics, with the rest being general civil and criminal clinics.[61]

At most schools, case administration proceeds as follows: (1) intake; (2) first draft opinion by students; (3) professor review and suggestions for revision; and (4) student delivery of final opinion to clients.[62] Only two schools seem to have extra steps between (3) and (4) whereby professors give students the opportunity to improve upon their first draft opinions and, through dialogue with the advising professor, to have the experience of taking responsibility for the Final Opinion themselves.

Ironically, the students' satisfaction with clinical programs is generally very high: fourteen schools and six schools reported "high satisfaction" and "very high satisfaction," respectively, among clinical students.[63] Some students participate in the clinics as volunteers without credit during the summer or winter recesses.

The self-assessment of the clinical programs,[64] as shown through the survey, confirm some of the critique here, namely the following:

1. The pressure from the bar examination chills student participation throughout the three years, and especially participation of third-year students, who

are best positioned to benefit from clinical courses, having received sufficient theoretical training in substantive laws.

2. The utter lack of full-time clinical staff and the poor funding to clinical programs limit the efficiency with which cases are handled. None of the clinical programs has a full-time staff person. Even the largest clinical program in the country, at Korea University, is run on a budget of less than USD 70,000 and with part-time fellows. SNU School of Law, with the largest student body, does not even have an organization responsible for administering clinical education, such as Korea University's CLEC.[65]
3. The lack of full-time staff also has other repercussions. It often leads to the clinic's inability to engage in effective publicity, which makes fundraising difficult. More importantly, without full-time staff, it is difficult to engage in effective case intake to obtain a stream of educationally appropriate cases. The government provides a subsidy of about 1 million USD that is distributed to 25 schools for their clinical programs in amounts set according to each clinic's performance, as evaluated by the Ministry of Education. The funding can be used only for clinical curriculum development and outside lawyers' fees. Critically, payment to outside lawyers is essential since law school faculties are not allowed to practice law.
4. Because even licensed professors are not allowed to practice law, most practical instruction is done by outside lawyers, who have not been trained in clinical pedagogy.

Selected Clinics of Korea

There are Korean clinics that are successful at both educating future lawyers and providing socially valuable services, although educational success is difficult to measure. Yonsei University and Ehwa University have eight clinics and nine clinic courses, respectively. Ehwa opened its Gender Law Clinic in accordance with the school's identity as an all-women law school.[66] Kangwon, Konkuk, and Youngnam do outreach by visiting villages that lack lawyers.[67] Aju works closely with local agencies supporting small-to-medium-sized enterprises, and filed and won a customs tax reimbursement suit for an exporter at the appellate court in December 2012 and at the Supreme Court in June 2013.[68] Joongang has filed constitutional challenges in free speech and communication cases in which students actively participated.[69] We chose to focus on clinical programs at two law schools about which we have firsthand knowledge or obtained sufficient information to be able to assess current operations.[70]

Korea University[71]

Korea University, in Seoul, was founded as the Private Bosung Professional College, established on April 3, 1905, by Lee Yong-Ik, a minister of the last Joseon crown. Its College of Law, originating from the Department of Law of Bosung

College, has been part of Korea University's centennial history. During the modernization period, Bosung College's Department of Law was the only private legal education institution. Korea University's College of Law since then has led the private schools, while Seoul National University (SNU) has led the public schools, in the number of bar passers under the National Judicial Examination system. Out of 3,330 bar passers produced over the span of five years up to 2012, SNU produced 26.4 percent of them, while Korea University produced 16 percent (Yonsei 12.6%, and Sungkyunkwan 7.4%).[72] The Ministry of Education, in distributing the 2,000 law school admissions quota among the 25 law schools, took into account bar passage and gave SNU an admissions quota of 150, while giving Korea, Yonsei, and Sungkyunkwan 120 each year.

As described, Korea University's clinical education began even before the law school opened, with the United States-trained Professor Park working with students on the *Heibei Spirit* case. Close to two-thirds of the first entering class were law students who had sufficient knowledge to receive clinical training right away.

Since then, Korea University's CLEC has led the country in depth and breadth of clinical activities, resulting in a special mention by and financial support from the Ministry of Education in 2012. In each of the graduating classes of about 120, more than half have volunteered or taken credit courses offered by CLEC.

CLEC's major victories include the country's ratification of the protocols leading to Korea's enrollment in the International Oil Pollution Compensation's Supplementary Fund (April 2010)[73] and the settlement of the web accessibility lawsuit on behalf of the blind against Korean Air Line (October 2013),[74] both of which originated from the work of the pilot projects begun in 2008. With those achievements, the Oil Spill Clinic and the Blinds' Web Accessibility Clinic closed.

As of June 2014, there are 15 clinics at Korea University: General Civil and Criminal, International Human Rights, International Humanitarian Law, Public Interest, Social Enterprise, Internet Law, Mediation, Criminal Law, North Korea Human Rights, Legislation, Maritime Insurance, Patent, Tax Law, Competition Law, and Family Law. Below, we will cover the activities up to 2013 of only the most active clinics.

The General Civil and Criminal Clinic, mostly supervised by Professors Young-Hwan Chung and Jewan Kim, Director and Assistant Director of CLEC, respectively, began with the distribution of clinic brochures by students to passersby on one Saturday in March 2009. Since then, more than 100 clients concerned about a broad range of issues have come annually to the clinic after having read the brochures. Several professors, mostly former judges or licensed attorneys, from different fields of concentration have participated in advising 50 or so students each year. Early on, CLEC first adopted "Case Rounds," in which students present the diagnosis and prognosis of the cases to a panel of professors and all the other students in the clinic. Each Case Round can easily last longer than three hours due to the high volume of cases. Some of the cases led to actual lawsuits. In one case, a low-income tenant in public housing faced eviction because he had inherited 2/7 of a house upon his parents' death, which, however, was of no value to him because the house was fully leveraged.[75] The clinic defended the tenant and had the eviction suit dismissed.

The International Human Rights Clinic, supervised by Professor Park, has administered projects related to Myanmar. Over the span of four years, the clinic's most important project has been developing a *Doe v. Unocal*[76]-type legal remedy for the damages that local people suffered under the Shwe Gas project, in which a Korean company, Daewoo International, invested and participated. In 2010–2012, the supervising professor and the students collected information about Daewoo's Onshore Gas Terminal on Kyauk Phyu Island indirectly through expatriates in Mae Sot, Chiang Mai, and Yangoon. In 2013, when the political rule became somewhat liberalized, the clinic finally paid a visit directly to the affected areas to interview local farmers who had sold their land rights to Daewoo in 2010 under unfavorable terms dictated by local military leaders. For instance, Daewoo compensated for only 3–5 years of land use, even though its occupation was planned for more than 30 years. While the clinic made fact-finding visits, it also conducted capacity-building workshops several times on the rule of law and democracy for local lawyers and law students. At the same time, the clinic participated in the international extractive industry transparency movement by working with a legislator to submit to the Korean National Assembly an extractor transparency bill similar to Section 1504 of the American Dodd-Frank Act[77] or the European Parliament's 2013 amendment of the Accounting (and Transparency) Directive.[78]

The Internet Law Clinic, also supervised by Professor Park, runs a counseling-only cyberclinic at www.internetlawclinic.org in the area of communications law, where clients and students exchange questions and advice entirely through the website. Each piece of advice typically goes through the cycle of supervisors' review and the student's revisions 1–3 times. This innovative clinic took advantage of the fact that advising on media and communications law, such as defamation, insult, privacy, data protection, copyright, fair use, trademark, and unfair competition, can be done efficiently through cyberspace as long as the students are allowed to review the "full contents," for example, actual photographs that allegedly infringe upon the copyrights of the original, and the original work itself. The Clinic has advised on 230 cases over the span of 2.5 years since its founding in November 2011. Supervision is augmented by several outside lawyers.

The Public Interest Clinic, supervised by Professor Zoonil Yi, adopted and expanded on the tradition of the Blinds' Web Accessibility Clinic to first operate as a disability rights clinic in 2010. It advised the National Human Rights Commission of Korea on the human rights review of the government's 2010 Plan for Guaranteeing Basic Life and 2010 Plan for Providing Attendants to People with Disabilities. In 2013, at a summer camp operated on the west coast of the country, several students drowned when they were ordered to jump off a boat without life jackets. The Public Interest Clinic intervened to represent the victims' families in the civil and criminal proceeding against the camp operators and obtained an indictment and a subsequent guilty judgment against the CEO of the boot camp in December 2013.

The Social Enterprise Clinic, supervised by Professor Jewan Kim, has provided legal services to WOOZOO, a company working to provide affordable housing to college students, and Enactus Korea, a company conducting various self-help income-generating projects for multiracial families, the elderly, and social activists.

The Mediation Clinic, supervised by Professor Young Hwan Chung, has trained students by requiring them to write memos to be read by mediation judges of the Seoul District Court under an agreement with Korea University to supply real cases. Students who author the mediation memos are also allowed to sit in on the mediation proceeding at the court. In 2013 alone, 41 cases were handled by 25 students.

Sungkyunkwan University School of Law

Founded in 1398 during the Joseon Dynasty, Sungkyunkwan University, in Seoul, is the oldest university in East Asia and one of Korea's elite institutions.[79] The law school is authorized to admit a class of 120 each year.[80] As of May 2014, four clinical programs are in operation: three clinics conceived by the school and directed by Professor He Wan Lee, who served as an appellate judge (and is thus a licensed lawyer) and then as CEO of an Internet-based legal information provider; and a refugee law clinic conceived by Professor Patricia Goedde, a United States-trained and licensed JD/PhD with a particular interest in refugees and with prior practice experience in a South Korean law firm.[81] Launched in 2011 with advance planning, the clinics give students hands-on, practical experience, and participation is quite robust.[82] Students enrolled in the clinics have numbered between 47 and 78 in the last three semesters. According to Professor Lee, nearly all of the students appear to be partaking in the clinical opportunities even though they are not mandatory. Student feedback also has been extremely positive and has even suggested that the clinics be mandatory and permitted to be retaken.

The three clinics that are generally under Professor Lee's direction expressly operate with the dual mission commonly found in foreign clinics—training effective would-be lawyers and providing needed social services—and address civil and criminal, public interest, and nonprofit business (or social enterprise) matters.[83] All three have a common Internet intake procedure. The civil and criminal clinic students are directly supervised by Professor Lee, and those of the other two, by outside lawyers. As to the civil and criminal clinic, with limited exceptions, a graduate fellow makes decisions on case selection according to preestablished guidelines. Generally, the clinic does not handle serious criminal cases and cases that are not amenable to a positive outcome through a legal process or cases that are definitively meritless, while the educational value of a case is considered, and whether it can be resolved within a semester. In between semesters, a formal program comprised of volunteer student teams performs case work. Most cases are resolved at the advice stage, while some cases proceed to litigation. Of the cases that do go forward, some proceed pro se and, in exceptional cases, with a lawyer hired by the clinic (currently, one case). Both types of cases proceed with student participation. Students actively take part in all stages as the cases develop and receive thorough supervision. Supervision entails review of written work product before it leaves the clinic and receiving feedback in prepararing for outside interviews and meetings. However, without student practice rules, any participation in court is reduced to observation of the proceedings and postproceeding debriefings with the lawyers in charge.

Students in the civil and criminal clinic have an opportunity to learn the same skills that their counterparts abroad do with real cases, such as interviewing, fact gathering, collaboration, research, and writing skills. Students also have an opportunity to learn professional values and judgment through case rounds. In case rounds, students are guided by material developed by Professor Lee based on principles espoused in a comprehensive 2011 Korean book covering practicum fundamentals such as necessary skills and values.[84] Participation in rounds is not mandatory, but the participation rate is high.

Typically a team of three students is assigned two cases: a case that is accepted through the intake process and a case assigned through the court-sponsored "early mediation" project (the same one in which the Mediation Clinic at Korea University participates, along with the law school at Jungang, and is described above). Begun in 2013, the mediation project introduces students to Korea's relatively new alternative dispute resolution procedures and to experiential learning, through fact investigation, writing, and meetings with litigants, court personnel, and the professor in charge.

As for the refugee law clinic, it did not at first represent refugees because Professor Goedde believed, based on accepted international principles, that students should not do any casework before being trained. Students instead interacted with stakeholders, including asylum seekers, developed relationships with key players, and, in conjunction with paid researchers, developed a bilingual how-to manual for training future law students and prepared country of origin information used in asylum cases. At the request of a public interest law foundation, students also prepared a report intended for the Ministry of Justice on refugee case law developments in five foreign jurisdictions.[85] The clinic also assisted an NGO in representing an asylum seeker from Afghanistan with research and writing. The clinic is now working with the Korean Bar Association's taskforce on matters related to asylum seekers held in detention facilities and preparing a comparative law report on border asylum procedures in other countries, which will be submitted to the NGO and the taskforce.[86]

Given that Professor Goedde supervises the clinic part-time and that there are no students during breaks and no other staff attorneys, a docket comparable to some of the human rights clinics (with full-time staff) in the United States, where students undertake litigation, appears unrealistic and undesirable. The arrangement that the clinic has with an NGO, which handles casework, however, provides students with indirect casework experience. In addition, students appear to have a rich opportunity to deeply engage in reflection about and to be exposed to the implementation of Korea's newly enacted asylum law, the policies and practices of a complex area of the law, and professional reasoning, judgment and values involved in representing socially vulnerable populations. Students are also learning that developing a presence through relationship building is a core element in representing vulnerable groups and that these efforts necessarily take time. Significantly, students in the clinic, who grew up in a period of relative political stability, and some with many privileges and possibly no past work experience, may be being exposed for the first time to the importance of lawyering as part of a sociopolitical movement.

Critical Evaluation

Even though Korean legal clinics have a short history, their founding is introducing experiential education where little existed before in the education of lawyers. Some clinics are preparing law students for real practice, and most are creating links among alumni and other practicing lawyers, academics, and classrooms. The burgeoning movement is also bringing about interactions among Korean professors with those abroad.[87] Effectuating meaningful clinical education, however, must move beyond simply creating clinics or inserting students into settings with real clients and practicing lawyers.

To be successful in achieving the goals of the 2007 reform law, more should be done by the law schools themselves. Efforts at creating clinical programs must be made with intention, considering the educational goals of the clinic, teaching methodology, and social benefit. Administrators must provide due academic credit to clinical offerings and offer fair treatment between course offerings to ensure that students do not neglect clinical experiences or relegate them to volunteer opportunities with little feedback or accountability. Creating additional clinics also may require consideration of the school's academic focus, the resources that existing faculty can offer as well as other resources at the school, and the school's proximity to institutions that may be critical community partners in the clinical program. Law schools should also secure the resources necessary for ensuring that students are properly supervised and that the work students perform delivers educational benefits.

In this regard, the government and the bar also have a responsibility to do more because achieving the goals of the reform is ultimately about enhancing access to justice and professionalism. Institutions such as the Korean Law School Association must take a leadership role, for example, in formulating guidelines for success. Such efforts could take the form of adopting educational goals of clinical education and would not need to be crafted anew, but could look to articulations found abroad that could be adapted for the Korean context. Some useful exemplars are found in the Carnegie report and the Best Practices Project from the Clinical Legal Education Association (US CLEA).[88] The Carnegie report speaks of three aspects of professional education that are important to preparing students for the profession of law, called "apprenticeships": "intellectual or cognitive, [focusing] the student on the knowledge and way of thinking about the profession," which may be best achieved in academic classes (but in its absence

Korean clinical professors may have to integrate this cognitive aspect into their teaching); "expert practice shared by competent practitioners," to be able to act as professionals in the field do; and introducing students to the values and "the purposes and attitudes that are guided by the values for which the professional community is responsible."[89] The US CLEA project identifies best practices for experiential courses, and, for example, suggests that clinical courses articulate educational goals, provide a model of law office management, and adopt specific supervision models and co-curricular components such as rounds.[90]

Indeed, the formation of an organization like the US CLEA that is purposefully focused on CLE would be a helpful step. Japan, which jump-started its experiment with law school reform before Korea, changed in 2004 from a system similar to Korea's pre-2007 reforms to an American-styled professional school system and introduced a new bar examination for graduates of the newly established law programs.[91] Japan established the Japan Clinical Legal Education Association (Japan CLEA) in 2008, which boasted 236 members in 2011, with the purpose of exchanging information among members, as well as learning from other professionals in Japan and professionals from abroad.[92]

Information exchange with Japan CLEA might be particularly relevant because of similarities in the two countries' legal systems, history of legal education, bar examination quota, licensing requirements, and the absence of rules allowing student practice in the courts.[93] The impetus of the reform, too, was similar: the reforms were meant to increase access to justice, particularly in rural areas, by licensing more lawyers and better educating lawyers for practice.[94] Also similar to Korea, the reform saw the founding of clinics, admission of a more diverse pool of candidates, including those with professional work experience, and faculty members who included practitioners.[95] As of 2008, half of Japan's 74 new postgraduate programs had clinical courses in which students directly served clients, but some of the clinics were in fact more like externships supervised by lawyers off campus.[96] In addition, clinical faculty had lower status, little guarantee of continued employment, were underpaid for the amount of work they did, and did not receive institutional support for professional development.[97] Similarly, in Korea, clinical education is mostly done by practicing lawyers who have little time to devote to teaching students while handling cases. There is no genuine clinical faculty, but between these outside lawyers and theoretical professors moonlighting in the clinical programs, the country's clinical education survives. Given some of these similarities, exchanges between clinical professors of both countries could prove fruitful, and some exchanges are already beginning to occur.[98] Exchanges with longstanding programs outside of Asia could also be beneficial.[99]

Meaningful change will also involve exploring student practice rules. Experienced clinicians abroad believe that, without student rules, students are relegated to thinking like a student rather than a practitioner: "Responsibility for clients and accountability for one's own actions are at the center of clinical experiences."[100] "[T]he learning is deeper and more meaningful when a student is participating as a lawyer, rather than as an observer or assistant."[101] Japanese clinical professors have had preliminary discussions about student practice rules with stakeholders,[102] and lessons learned from the effort could inform the Korean bar and academia. Since lawyers in both countries share pervasively negative perceptions that students are unready to practice, exchanging information on this effort and on the history of practice rules abroad could be helpful to the debate.

However, the most determinative factor in any aspect of Korean legal education is still the strict annual bar admission quota of about 1,500[103] set against 2,000 graduates, which has distorted legal education into something similar to the former system, which was dominated by the 5 percent passing rate under the National Judicial Examination system: that of intense and largely memory-driven exam preparation. Given that 2,000 new examinees graduate every year and that at least 500 of them come back to retake the exam a second or third time, students are under intense pressure to study for the bar examination all through school. Because there is no passing score for the exam, they must study to compete with one another to qualify among the 1,500 without knowing how much better prepared the others might be. All of them end up pushing themselves to their physical limit to prepare for the bar examination, leaving only a small amount of time for clinical training or community service. This pressure was in no small part responsible for the painful experience of SNU, which, with the largest class size of 150, nevertheless enrolled fewer than 10 students in its first and only clinic course in 2011, and then had to shut it down in 2012 for lack of student interest.[104] The school, however, did come back successfully in Spring 2013 with the opening of its Occupational Safety/Workers' Compensation Clinic,[105] whose litigation and policy work contributed to Samsung's partial admission of responsibility in May 2014 in the 50 or so deaths of its employees.[106]

Because of the pressure to pass the bar examination, even if the law schools increase the currently small number of credits given for clinical courses (one to three credits), it is unlikely that many students will take advantage of them. To be sure, on-campus clinical courses are not the only way to effect experiential training, and students can receive one to two externship credits for working full-time at law firms for two weeks, which are usually allotted to summer or winter recesses. Indeed, almost all law students complete at least one externship before they graduate, but less than half participate in clinics. Putting aside the theoretical debate on the relative values of on-campus clinics and off-campus externships, problems with the current externship practices abound as they operate more as opportunities for obtaining a job after graduation than as education. It is not clear whether students obtain educationally meaningful experiences since feedback is not guaranteed.[107]

Conclusion

Korea's legal education reforms could provide an impetus for a grand experiment in designing clinical programs anew, based on best practices from abroad and within Korea from clinical models in practice in other professions such as medicine.

However, only very few graduate law schools have taken on the challenge as an opportunity to map out a new landscape in clinical education, largely restricted by the hostile educational environment that is due to the bar examination system that mandatorily fails a number equivalent to 25 percent of each year's graduating class. The lack of full-time clinical faculty, the rule against faculty practice, and the absence of a clinical education association are also noteworthy.

CLE, however, exists irrevocably in Korea. A few clinics are succeeding in producing impressive results, and students are at the center of critical aspects of these projects. As students with clinical experience move into leadership positions, and as the public reaps concrete benefits through free representation, clinical education may garner advocates even among skeptics.

Notes

1. "*Beophakjeonmundaehakwonseolchiunyeong e gwanhanbeopryul*" [The Act on the Establishment and Management of Professional Law Schools], Law No. 8544 of 2007, http://elaw.klri.re.kr/kor_service/lawView.do?hseq=25756&lang=ENG, accessed June 6, 2014. This chapter uses the Revised Romanization of Korean system of transliteration. As the system allows, personal names are denoted as used by the person, except that given names are provided first.
2. In Korea, almost all schools have their academic years begin with the spring semester.
3. See generally Young-Cheol K. Jeong, "Korean Legal Education for the Age of Professionalism" (2010) 5 *East Asia L. Rev.* 155.
4. Matthew J. Wilson, "U.S. Legal Education Methods and Ideals: Application to the Japanese and Korean Systems" (2010) 18 *Cardozo J. Int'l. & Comp. L.* 295, 335.
5. Jeong (n 3) 158–159.
6. Ibid 335; Rosa Kim, "The 'Americanization' of Legal Education in South Korea: Challenges and Opportunities" (2012) 38 *Brook. J. Int'l L.* 49, 52. Although some refer to the examination as the National Judiciary Examination, the Ministry of Justice itself calls it the National Judicial Examination.
7. Wilson (n 4) 336; Kim (n 6) 49; Jeong (n 3) 158; Korean Bar Association, *byeonhosajedo*, http://www.koreanbar.or.kr/info/info03.asp, accessed June 9, 2014. The quota under the prereform bar examination has annually decreased the number of examinees permitted to pass. Jeong (n 3) 158.
8. The latest reliable statistics for the number of Korean practicing lawyers is from the Korean Ministry of Justice and relate to 2009. According to that information, there were 2,468 judges, 1,699 prosecutors, and 11,016 private attorneys in Korea. Ministry of Justice, Justice System, Overview, http://www.moj.go.kr/HP/ENG/eng_02/eng_2040.jsp, accessed May 22, 2014; the population data come from Country Statistical Profiles: Korea 2009, OECD, http://www.oecd-ilibrary.org/economics/country-statistical-profile-korea-2009_20752288-2009-table-kor, accessed May 22, 2014. Comparing data from the same general period, the United States had 1,180,386 lawyers for 307,006,550 residents, resulting in a ratio of 1 lawyer for about 260 residents. US Census Bureau, Vintage 2009: National Tables, Annual Estimates of the Population for the United States, Regions, States, and Puerto Rico: April 1, 2000 to July 1, 2009, http://www.census.gov/popest/data/historical/2000s/vintage_2009/index.html, accessed May 22,2014; American Bar Association (ABA) National Lawyer Population by State 2003–2013, http://www

.americanbar.org/content/dam/aba/administrative/market_research/2013natl_lawyer10_year_trends.authcheckdam.pdf, accessed May 22, 2014. The current ratio for the United States is not significantly different, at about 1 lawyer for about 250 residents. Ibid. (ABA); US Census Bureau, Annual Estimates of the Population for the United States, Regions, States, and Puerto Rico: April 1, 2010 to July 1, 2013, http://census.hawaii.gov/home/population-estimate/, accessed May 22, 2014.

9. OECD Health Data 2013, How Does Korea Compare, http://www.oecd.org/els/health-systems/Briefing-Note-KOREA-2013.pdf, accessed May 22, 2014; William M. Sullivan, Anne Colby, Judith W. Wegner, Lloyd Bond, and Lee S. Shulman, *Educating Lawyers: Preparation for the Profession of Law* (The Carnegie Foundation for the Advancement of Teaching, Jossey-Bass, 2007) 1.
10. Kim (n 5) 55 (citing Dae-Kyu Yoon, *Law and Democracy in South Korea: Democratic Development since 1987* [Institute for Far Eastern Studies, Kyungnam University, 2010] 136); Editorial, "Too Many Lawyers?" *Korea Herald* (Seoul, December 9, 2010) http://www.koreaherald.com/opinion/Detail.jsp?newsMLId=20101209000705, accessed May 23, 2014 (noting that one-third of municipalities lack resident lawyers); Jeong (n 3) 180.
11. Wilson (n 4) 335; Jeong (n 3) 157.
12. Patricia Goedde, "Globalized Legal Education, Human Rights Lawyering, and Institutional Reform: the Case of a Refugee Law Clinic in South Korea" (2014) 20 *Clinical L. Rev.* 355, 374 (even under the new system, students focus on bar examination preparation in their third year).
13. See, for example, ibid. 359 (noting the existence of only a handful of experts on refugee law); International Bar Association, *Korean Times* (February 2010) http://www.ibanet.org/Article/Detail.aspx?ArticleUid=b4dacd34-e9a2-4a88-a6c2-01c51890bf2a (then president of the South Korea's Bar Association discussing the bar's underpreparedness to meet the challenge of the Korean legal market as one of the fastest growing for commercial law).
14. Wilson (n 4) 335.
15. Ibid. Compare with active learning and problem solving methods used in doctrinal classes, Myron Moskovitz, "From Case Method to Problem Method: The Evolution of a Teacher" (2004) 48 *St. Louis U. L.J.* 1205; Sarah E. Ricks, "Some Strategies to Teach Reluctant Talkers to Talk About Law" (2004) 54 *J. Legal Educ.* 570, 572.
16. Jeong (n 3) 162, 175.
17. Korean Times (n 13).
18. The Act on the Establishment and Operation of Professional Law Schools ("Law School Act," hereinafter) (n 1) ch. 1, arts 1 & 2.
19. Sullivan et al. (n 9) 1, 21–23. This Carnegie report called for reforms of American legal education to change its overreliance on the case-dialogue method (also known as the lecture and Socratic method), underdevelopment of mechanisms for providing feedback and assessment of student learning, and the failure to integrate teachings of doctrine, skills, and professional identity.
20. The Law School Act (n 1) ch 1, art 5, ch 3.
21. Ibid. ch 3, arts 16 & 26.
22. Ibid. ch 6.
23. Jeong (n 3) 157.
24. Korean Bar Association (n 7).
25. Goedde (n 13) 356.

26. Jeong (n 3) 161, 163; Some of the programs, however, may have needed some incubation time, and as of that criticism made in 2010, positive changes have been made at some schools.
27. Jeong (n 3) 163.
28. John M. Glionna, "South Korean Oil Spill Victims Cautionary Tale" *Los Angeles Times* (July 17, 2010); Sang-Hun Choe, "South Korea Cleans Up Big Oil Spill" *The New York Times* (New York, December 9, 2007).
29. Ibid.
30. *Seohaeangireumyuchulsagobeobryulbongsajiwondan* [West Seashore Oil Spill Accident Legal Services Volunteer Corps], http://club.cyworld.com/taeanlegalservice, accessed June 12, 2014. The number of student volunteers can be found at this social media site used by the volunteers.
31. Official website of Taeanhaean Korea National Park Service, National Parks of Korea, Taeanhaean, http://english.knps.or.kr/Knp/Taeanhaean/Intro/Introduction.aspx?MenuNum=1&Submenu=Npp, accessed June 16, 2014.
32. Facts about the case are known to coauthor Park from his work on the case.
33. *Seohaegireumyuchulsagoui "wanjeonbokgu.wanjeonbosang, gahaejamuhanchaegim* [Full Restoration, Full Compensation, No Liability Limitation on Wrongdoers], *Beobryul Journal*, January 7, 2008 http://news.lec.co.kr/gnuboard4/bbs/board.php?bo_table=pass&wr_id=36158>, accessed June 12, 2014. The social media site through which the volunteers communicated was opened at http://club.cyworld.com/taeanlegalservice, accessed June 12, 2014.
34. "*Chamyeoyeondae, taeanheonjibeobryulsangdamsogaesomitbongyeokjeoginbeobryuljiwonhwaldongsijak*" [On-site Legal Clinic Opens for Oil Spill Victims], *Yonhap News* (Seoul, January 7, 2008) http://app.yonhapnews.co.kr/YNA/Basic/article/Press/YIBW_showPress.aspx?contents_id=RPR20080107025200353, accessed June 12, 2014.
35. http://www.ingopress.com/CSOScheduleRead.aspx?idx=626. http://www.ingopress.com/CSOScheduleRead.aspx?idx=626.
36. Mainly due to similar protests from the victims, Samsung agreed in November 2013 to make a regional development grant of about 360 million USD to be distributed over the affected region. For related news report, see below. http://www.yonhapnews.co.kr/bulletin/2013/11/28/0200000000AKR20131128084100063.HTML, accessed June 12, 2014. The individual victims cannot receive cash under this arrangement. http://www.yonhapnews.co.kr/bulletin/2013/11/28/0200000000AKR20131128084100063.HTML, accessed June 12, 2014.
37. Text of the questionnaire available at http://www.korealawschool.com/_data/bbs//notice/2008/bbs7.1.20080929142117.pdf, accessed June 12, 2014.
38. The book is being commercially sold. http://www.kyobobook.co.kr/product/detailViewKor.laf?ejkGb=KOR&mallGb=KOR&barcode=9788976416957&orderClick=LAG&Kc=, accessed June 12, 2014.
39. Supreme Court Judgment 2010 ma 222. The Supreme Court unfortunately did not find the requisite recklessness and knowledge of probable damage on the part of Samsung. It was interesting that the Supreme Court used the complete lack of any direction from the land crew as evidence negating the ship owner's "personal knowledge," but did not choose to allow the same to be the basis for attributing the captain's conduct to the ship owner under the theory of blanket entrustment.
40. Just to name a few, Mi Ro Kang and Ik-Chan Sohn went on to Seoul National University and led in the creation of and participated in a newly created workers'

compensation clinic there, which delved into the leukemia cases that Samsung Semiconductors refused to recognize as work related. Ji-Heon Oh and Woo-Koo Choi went to the graduate law program of their alma mater, Korea University, and continued on with their respective clinical tasks to remarkable success, i.e., the IOPC Supplementary Fund advocacy and publication of the translation of *Major Cases on Ship Owner's Liability Limitation*. Jong Yeon Choi and Kelly Kha-Yeun Kim joined in the first field trip to the Burma-Thai border in February 2010 in an effort that was later formalized into the International Human Rights Clinic of Korea University Law School. Choi also coauthored the first published paper on the feasibility of a *Doe v. Unocal*-type remedy for Daewoo International, which provided a blue print for the subsequent actions of Korea University's International Human Rights Clinic. Jong Yeon Choi, Mi Ro Kang, and Soo Jin Kong, "A Forlorn Garden—Human Rights Abuse in Shwe Gas Development and Feasibility of Legal Action in Korea" (2010) 8 *Gong-ik-gwa In-gwon* 4, http://www.papersearch.net/view/detail.asp?detail_key=2y800094, accessed June 12, 2014. Kim, who led the Global Legal Clinic as a student, also coauthored the first published paper on the issue of web accessibility for the blind, which was submitted to court in a lawsuit against Korean Airline in 2011. Kyung Sin Park, Kelly Kha-yeun Kim, Seong-hun Kim, Son-hee Yang, and Pil-kyuChae, "The Blind's Web Accessibility: A Comparative-Legal Analysis with a Focus on the U.S., the U.K., and Australia" (2011) 61 *Goryeo Beobhak* 131, www.papersearch.net/view/detail.asp?detail_key=1f501080, accessed June 12, 2014.

41. Frank S. Bloch (ed.), "Introduction" in *The Global Clinical Movement: Educating Lawyers for Social Justice* (Oxford University Press, 2011) 22.
42. The Law School Act (n 1) ch 1, arts 1 & 2.
43. Jeong (n 3) 162.
44. Goedde (n 13) 356.
45. Jeong (n 3) 167.
46. Yonsei operates externship (called internships) and clinic programs. http://law.yonsei.ac.kr/curriculum/curri01_01_2.php
47. Data presented here are sourced from Chung Young-Hwan, Choi Won, and Moon Jae-Wan, *Current Status of Korean Legal Clinics and Proposals for Improvement*, Korean Association of Law Schools (January 2013) (Korean).
48. Ibid. 60.
49. Ibid. 63.
50. Ibid. 64.
51. Ibid. 81.
52. Ibid. 65.
53. Ibid. 65.
54. http://ko.wikipedia.org/wiki/%EB%B2%95%ED%95%99%EC%A0%84%EB%AC%B8%EB%8C%80%ED%95%99%EC%9B%90, accessed June 12, 2014.
55. Chung (n 50) 77.
56. Ibid. 80.
57. Ibid. 67.
58. Ibid. 69.
59. Ibid. 73.
60. Ibid. 89.
61. Ibid. 91.
62. Ibid. 94–95.
63. Ibid. 112.

64. Ibid. 113–116.
65. Ibid. 9.
66. Ibid. 8.
67. Ibid.
68. Ibid. 17; http://article.joins.com/news/article/article.asp?total_id=10545282&ctg=1213
69. Chung (n 50) 17.
70. Information gathered is current as of June 2014.
71. All the facts stated in this section originate from the author's memory and the following two useful compendiums: First CLEC Year Book: July 2008–November 2010, Volume 1, and Fourth CLEC Year Book (2013), Volume 1. The Second and Third Year Books were not consulted.
72. Statistics available here: http://www.veritas-a.com/news/articleView.html?idxno=19806,accessed June 12, 2014.
73. Ministry of Land, Transportation, and Seas, Ocean Policy Division, "Ocean Oil Pollution Compensation Limit Increased to 1.2 Trillion Won—Due to Korea Joining the IOPC Supplementary Fund" Blog, http://blog.naver.com/PostView.nhn?blogId=mltm_ocean&logNo=60106721950&viewDate=&currentPage=1&listtype=0, accessed June 12, 2014.
74. PSPD Homepage, "Korean Airline Settles on Blind's Web Accessibility—Due to Fix by May 31, 2014" (October 12, 2013) http://www.peoplepower21.org/PublicLaw/1079578, accessed June 12, 2014.
75. "Korea University Students' Rule of Loving Others: Rescuing a Tenant on Eviction Proceeding" (SegyeIlbo, December 18, 2010).
76. http://en.wikipedia.org/wiki/Doe_v._Unocal; http://www.earthrights.org/legal/doe-v-unocal, accessed June 12, 2014.
77. See http://www.kpmg.com/us/en/issuesandinsights/articlespublications/dodd-frank-series/pages/financial-transparency-extractive-dodd-frank.aspx, accessed June 12, 2014.
78. See http://europa.eu/rapid/press-release_MEMO-13-541_en.htm, accessed June 12, 2014.
79. 2013. World University Rankings, Times Higher Education, Thomson Reuters, http://www.timeshighereducation.co.uk/world-university-rankings/2012-13/world-ranking/institution/sungkyunkwan-university-skku, accessed May 26, 2014; 2013 Asia University Rankings, Times Higher Education, Thomson Reuters, http://www.timeshighereducation.co.uk/world-university-rankings/2012-13/regional-ranking/region/asia, accessed May 26, 2014; 2013 Jungangilbodaehakpyung-gasunui, *Jungangilbo news*, "2013 daehakpyungga" (October 7,2013) http://article.joins.com/news/article/article.asp?ctg=12&Total_ID=12783624, accessed May 26, 2014.
80. Jeong (n 3) 163, Table 1.
81. Goedde (n 13) 366–367; e-mail communications (May and June 2014) between on file with author Kang, Goedde, and Lee.
82. Goedde (n 13) 367; communications with Lee (n 85).
83. E-mail communications (May and June 2014 on file between author Kang and Lee (n 85). This chapter focuses on the civil and criminal clinic as the information received addresses that clinic more specifically.
84. Jaewan Moon, Hanjung Jeong, and Inhoe Kim, Law School *Silseubgwajeong* (Hanguk Haksuljeongbo, 2010).

85. Goedde (n 13), 367–371.
86. Communications with Goedde (n 85).
87. For example, Miyagawa was invited to speak at a symposium in Korea. Shigeo Miyagawa, "Developments and Challenges of Clinical Legal Education in Japan" (March 2012) 15 *Inha L. Rev.* 21.
88. Sullivan et al. (n 10); Roy Stuckey et al., *Best Practices for Legal Education: A Vision and a Road Map* (CLEA, 2007).
89. Sullivan et al. (n 10) 25, 28.
90. Stuckey et al. (n 92) 189–197.
91. Shigeo Miyagawa, Takao Suami, Peter A. Joy, and Charles D. Weisselberg, "Japan's New Clinical Programs: A Study of Light and Shadows," in Frank S. Bloch (ed.), *The Global Clinical Movement: Educating Lawyers for Social Justice* (OUP, 2011) 106–107.
92. Miyagawa (n 91) 32.
93. Miyagawa et al. (n 95); Bloch (n 42) 105–107, 114; see generally Miyagawa (n 877).
94. Miyagawa et al. (n 95) 105.
95. Ibid. 107–108, 110.
96. Ibid. 110–111.
97. Ibid. 112. Like Korea, Japan's continued low bar passage rate (24% in 2011, for example) has had a pervasive influence in what students find important in legal education, with clinical education taking a backseat to their effort to pass the examination. Miyagawa (n 91) 26; Miyagawa (n 95) 113, 113.
98. Miyagawa (n 91) 21.
99. A Japanese professor was present at the April 2014 Conference on Clinical Legal Education of the American Association of Law Schools, which Kang attended.
100. Stuckey et al. (n 92) 191.
101. Ibid 190.
102. Miyagawa (n 91) 23.
103. Miae Kim, http://info.leet.or.kr/board/board.htm?bbsid=job&ctg_cd=&page=1&skey=&keyword=&mode=view&bltn_seq=387, accessed June 12, 2014.
104. Chung (n 50) 8.
105. Ik-Chan Sohn, a graduate of Korea University College of Law who participated in the Global Legal Clinic, went on to Seoul National University and is said to have contributed greatly to the success of this clinic.
106. Seehttp://www.electronicstakeback.com/2014/05/27/samsung-apologizes-to-semiconductor-workers-who-contracted-cancer-promises-compensation/, accessed June 12, 2014.
107. Hankuk University of Foreign Studies (HUFS) has supervising lawyers interact closely with the clinical faculty to control the quality of education for "clinical courses run on externship," but it is not known whether HUFS does that also for the 2-week externship programs as well. Chung (n 50) 16.

CHAPTER 5

Clinical Education in Taiwanese Law Schools

Thomas Chih-hsiung Chen

Introduction

This chapter begins by analyzing the persistent gap between theoretical teaching and practice training in the Taiwanese legal education. Although many other countries have experienced similar problems, the unique political and economic factors in the evolution of legal education in Taiwan make change difficult. Proposals to change curricula have been periodically raised by reformers, but few law schools have been successful in building up clinical courses. The reform from 2005 to 2007 carried the idea of clinical education, but the reform ultimately failed for the immaturity of its considerations. In the second part, this chapter discusses the current types of courses that contain practical elements, particularly legal aid clinics, moot courts, courses on legal ethics, and judicial court externships. In the final part, the chapter discusses the current obstacles to promoting clinical education, including financial difficulties in higher education, the shortage of professional visions and values among legal educators, and students' unwillingness to take clinical courses because of the pressure of low pass rates on the bar exam and the lawyer bubble.

The Long-standing Gap between Academia and Practice

The Paths to Becoming a Lawyer

Most countries grant only one type of legal license to law school graduates, but Taiwan offers numerous approaches to becoming a lawyer, which has impeded the development of the profession. Generally, two major paths can be taken to become a lawyer.[1] The first is to pass the national bar exam. The second is to become a judge or prosecutor first, and then become a lawyer after practicing for several years.[2] It might be unthinkable for people in the Anglo-American tradition that a judge would change his or her career path to that of a lawyer, because career changes in the Anglo-American tradition are typically the reverse. However, because most new judges and prosecutors in Taiwan, who have constitutional tenure protection and enjoy much better prepractice training,[3] are selected from young graduates of law schools, until recently it has been common that young people chose to become a judge or prosecutor first, after graduating from law school, and then become practicing lawyers after several years of practice in the judicial system.[4] In addition, according to the law during the martial law period, people who had served as judges of court martial (trained by a military school) in law schools for a certain period can qualify as lawyers, and numerous lawyers obtained their licenses by taking these steps.[5]

Like most countries, the basic law degree programs in Taiwan are mainly established at the undergraduate level;[6] however, although the majority of lawyers obtain their first law degrees in undergraduate programs, an increasing number of lawyers have earned their first law degree in graduate programs since the 1990s, which are similar to the American Juris Doctor programs.[7] Once a student receives a basic law degree, either in an undergraduate or graduate program, he or she is eligible to take the national bar exam.[8]

The subjects of the bar examination are theoretically oriented and do not include practical skills or professional values. The exam is divided into two stages. The first stage is multiple-choice tests for general subjects, including Civil Law, Civil Procedure, Criminal Law, Criminal Procedure, Legal Ethics, Administrative Law and Compulsory Execution Law, Commercial Laws, Conflict of Laws, Security Law, and Legal English. The top 33 percent of examinees can take the second part of the bar exam, which is an essay. The subjects of the second part include Constitutional Law, Administrative Law, Criminal Law, Criminal Procedure, Commercial Laws, Civil Law, and Civil Procedure. The top 33 percent of examinees can pass the second part.[9] Therefore, the annual pass rate on the bar exam is approximately 10.89 percent.[10] In 2014, 915 out of 8,994 attendees passed the bar exam.[11]

After passing the bar exam, a lawyer must complete preservice training before practicing law. This training consists of two parts.[12] The first part is a one-month program that contains courses on practical skills and ethics. Although the Ministry of Justice administers this training program, in practice, it authorizes the Taiwan Bar Association, which is organized by local bars, to execute this task.[13]

The second part is a five-month apprenticeship. Any lawyer with at least five years of practical experience and without any disciplinary record can supervise apprentices.[14] An apprentice must find his or her own supervisor; however, the increasing number of new lawyers has made it difficult for them to find apprenticeship opportunities.

As mentioned, the second path to becoming a lawyer is passing the national judicial officer examination and becoming a judge or prosecutor before becoming a lawyer. Once a person passes the national judicial officer examination, which is separate from the bar exam, he or she must enter the Judges and Prosecutors Training Institute to be trained for 18 months to two years. The institute is administered by the Ministry of Justice. The training program is divided into classroom courses and on-site apprenticeship training (typically conducted in courts, prosecutors' offices, law firms, or administrative departments).[15]

The aforementioned approaches do not require students in law schools to receive any practical training. The pass rates for the bar exam were extremely low throughout the twentieth century, which led to most law school graduates being unable to get a legal license. Therefore, law schools generally did not consider providing courses on lawyering as one of their missions because too few students would need them. In addition, numerous professors at law schools had never obtained qualifications as lawyers or law officers and had never practiced law, even if they were responsible for examination questions on national bar exams and had the power to determine who could become a lawyer.

The Evolution of Legal Education

Modern legal education was established in Taiwan before World War II under Japanese colonial rule, but it changed significantly after 1949.[16] Curriculum committees at law schools in Taiwan came to determine the proportion of mandatory versus elective courses. From 1949 to 2000, approximately 85 percent of an undergraduate law school curriculum was mandatory, and most of the mandatory courses were related to the six basic fields of law, comprising constitutional law, administrative law, civil law, civil procedure, criminal law, and criminal procedure.[17] In recent years, many schools have changed their graduation policies to allow a larger portion of optional elective courses in graduate requirements; however, mandatory courses still make up the majority of graduate requirements.[18] In most basic graduate law programs, approximately only half of the curriculum is mandatory; therefore, students have more flexibility in these programs. Graduate program policies on curricula differ considerably from those of undergraduate programs.

Universities have discretion in determining how many credits are needed for graduation; therefore, the requirements for graduation vary by school. Most undergraduate law programs require more than 120 credits for graduation. The majority of undergraduate law students can fulfill the graduation requirements in four years (two schools require five years of study).[19] A high school degree is required to be admitted to an undergraduate law department. Basic graduate law programs typically require only 80 to 90 credits for graduation, and students need three to five years to graduate because writing a master's thesis is time consuming.[20] An undergraduate degree in another discipline is required for entering graduate law programs.

Universities in Taiwan are strictly regulated. According to the University Act, the Ministry of Education is responsible for licensing law schools.[21] Sufficient numbers of faculty members, space, and facilities are the most crucial factors for being licensed. In the 1990s, the requirements for these factors were high. Since the early 2000s, however, the government's higher education policy has relaxed the requirements and encouraged the establishment of additional universities and schools.[22] Because establishing a law program is less costly for universities than setting up a department in many other disciplines such as science or engineering, the number of universities with law programs in Taiwan dramatically increased from 8 in the 1990s to 36 in the early 2000s.[23] As of 2014, 34 undergraduate law programs and 41 master's degree law programs were offered by 17 public universities and 19 private universities.[24]

It should be emphasized that most of these 36 universities do not have independent law colleges; instead, their law departments or institutes of law are parts of colleges in other disciplines, such as social science, business and management, or public policy.[25] Some universities have fewer than 15 law professors. They recruit adjunct faculty in order to provide sufficient courses for students.[26]

After the number of universities in Taiwan increased beyond the demands of the society, the Ministry of Education became concerned about the quality of higher education because of the increasing unemployment rates of university graduates.[27] In 2005, the Higher Education Evaluation & Accreditation Council of Taiwan was established, the objective of which is to evaluate the teaching performance of universities. The five major fields for evaluation are (1) curriculum objectives, characteristics, and self-improvement mechanisms; (2) curriculum design and teaching performance; (3) outcome of student learning and extracurricular affairs; (4) academic research and professional performance; and (5) employment performance of graduates.[28]

The limited financial and manpower resources of law school make it difficult to build up clinical programs. The government has traditionally restricted university tuition rates and required that full-time professors must hold a PhD, thereby causing difficulty for institutions in obtaining funding and recruiting teachers for clinical education in Taiwan.[29] Because of these low tuition fees, law schools cannot use high salaries as incentives to recruit as professors excellent senior lawyers with extensive practical experience. Although law professors' salary generally is sufficient for making a living, it is far inferior to the income earned by their peers who are working as lawyers or judges. Therefore, numerous professors hold other part-time jobs or pursue research projects to increase their income. As a result, the amount of time professors spend on teaching decreases, and there are fewer incentives to engage professors in time-consuming and low-pay clinical education. A law professor must hold a PhD, and thus most lawyers with long-term practical experience but without a doctorate degree are not qualified to become professors. Although a few law professors are qualified as lawyers, they have practiced law for only a short period and, therefore, their experiences are insufficient for instructing students in clinical practice.

Because the tuition of private universities is as highly restricted as that of public universities, and public universities have much more government funding, public law schools are typically more prestigious than private law schools and attract better students.[30] However, although some professors provide counsel for private law firms, or are arbitrators in court cases, full-time professors at public law schools cannot register as practicing lawyers. According to Article 31 of the Attorney Regulation Act, lawyers cannot work as civil servants. Because professors at a public university are civil servants, they cannot practice law even if they hold legal licenses. This further hinders the development of clinical education in public universities. Some full-time professors at private law schools have their own law firms, but this situation is rare because the salary and teaching load at private law schools are not attractive enough for senior lawyers to maintain the two positions simultaneously.

Resistance Inside and Outside Law Schools

Although the clinical legal education (CLE) movement has spread worldwide, the value of clinical education is underestimated and even rejected by most law faculties in Taiwan. Most law professors do not value clinical education because of their own lack of practical experience.[31] Although law schools have gradually recognized the necessity of curriculum reform under the pressure of globalization and the lawyer bubble, they do not possess the necessary resources to resolve this problem.

Because legal scholars must hold a PhD, most are enthusiastic about theoretical research, but uninterested in the practice of law. As mentioned, the training of law officers and lawyers is conducted in specialized training institutions after law school graduates pass national exams. Law schools in Taiwan have considered their responsibility to be only that of developing students' ability to pass the national judicial examination, rather than developing students' expertise in the practice of law. In other words, law school provides only the theory of law to students, rather than a clinical education.[32]

Some teachers attempt to implement clinical education in their universities. Reasons for this include the teachers' own interests or teaching philosophy, their experience practicing law before they joined academia, and subjects of instruction that are related to practical legal training (e.g., procedural law). The major mode of implementation clinic courses is assisting law students in organizing a legal aid society to provide free legal advice to the public (not limited to low-income households). Some law schools have awarded credits to students to encourage them to participate in these legal consultation services.[33] However, nearly all law schools consider this type of course to be marginal and optional and that they are not required to provide considerable resources to promote it.

The Failed Reform of 2005 to 2007

Due to the influence of the legal education reforms in Japan and South Korea,[34] Taiwan attempted to promote similar postgraduate legal education from 2005 to 2007 that required that only those who held postgraduate professional degrees could participate in national judicial examinations.[35] In this proposal, law colleges offering postgraduate professional degrees were required to employ a certain number of full-time teachers with more than ten years of practical experience and to provide related practical training courses.[36] However, unlike in Japan and South Korea, this proposal did not consider two fundamental issues. One issue was whether the tuition fees for postgraduate programs could be flexible, and the other was whether teachers with extensive practice experience could be exempted from the requirement of holding a PhD and whether academic publications can be considered less crucial for promotion.[37] In Japan and South Korea, these two critical conditions enabled new professional schools to employ a sufficient number of teachers with extensive practical experience.[38] However, Taiwan's proposal did not emphasize the importance of these two conditions and only proposed requirements for legal experts, without suggesting methods to meet them. Therefore, nearly all leading legal experts objected to this proposal, which was therefore never approved or implemented.[39]

Although this reform was unsuccessful, law schools in Taiwan frequently held conferences on law education during this period of time and, therefore, further came to understand the development of clinical education in other countries.[40] Accordingly, some law schools in Taiwan developed other types of clinical courses, providing a certain degree of diversity to clinical education.

Model Courses with Practical Elements

Law schools are not required to offer any courses containing practical elements. Some schools, however, provide optional practical courses on lawyer skills. Because law schools are typically unwilling to provide extra funding to recruit adjunct instructors for clinical courses, nearly all faculty members who teach practical courses are full-time professors, some of whom have practiced law only for a short time before going into academia. Only a few law schools employ practicing lawyers or judges as adjuncts. The models of practical courses are described in the following sections.

Legal Aid Clinics

Legal aid clinics have been popular in undergraduate law programs for over 30 years and were likely the only type of clinical course available before 2005.[41] At least 19 schools now offer optional legal aid courses.[42] The courses are typically offered for junior or senior undergraduate students only, because students begin to learn civil procedure and criminal procedure in the third year of their undergraduate study. Students can provide legal counsel, but do not draft documents or advocate for people who require legal assistance but are unable to afford counsel. Clinics cannot recommend lawyers for clients.[43] Most legal aid courses are supervised by full-time faculty members.[44] The procedure is such that students are divided into groups, and each group interviews clients, discusses issues, and forms analysis and suggestions. Professors might observe the process, correct a wrong analysis, or answer students' questions when they cannot find a solution.[45]

Because students cannot draft documents or appear in court, teachers do not accompany students to court for court appearances or filings. The courses usually offer two to four semester credits.[46] Many law schools that provide legal aid courses typically have student societies called legal aid societies. Students can join the societies to provide legal aid services without obtaining credits.[47]

The College of Law at National Chengchi University built up the first legal aid clinic in universities. Similar to numerous other schools, students from the College of Law organize a student society and provide free legal advice to the public under the teachers' instruction.[48] First- and second-year university students who do not have sufficient knowledge mainly provide labor such as collating information and recording interviews. Third- and fourth-year students who have learned civil and criminal procedure law participate in formulating legal advice. Master's students are the leaders of various student groups. All legal advice must be approved by public-interest lawyers who assist with this service before the advice is provided. The unpaid lawyers who enthusiastically provide support for this service are typically alumni of the college, who themselves benefited from this type of training. This type of training was once a compulsory course in the College of Law at National Chengchi University; however, this course did not produce satisfactory results because students who were not public minded did not provide an excellent quality of service, which affected the teamwork. Therefore, this course is no longer a compulsory course, but rather is an option for third- and fourth-year university students. Other students cannot enroll in this course, but can only participate in the form of a student society activity. According to the instructor of this course, because students choose this course voluntarily for pro bono service, now enrolled students provide an excellent quality of service and no manpower shortage occurs. Generally, at least five volunteer lawyers, 12 master's students, and a total of approximately 80 people participate in this service every semester.[49]

Moot Courts

This type of course is used to prepare students for specific moot court competitions. For example, National Chiao Tung University has a course called the "International Moot Court Competition," which prepares students for participating in the European Law Students' Association Moot Court Competition on World Trade Organization Law. The course includes analysis of issues, the drafting litigation documents, and oral statements.[50] National Chengchi University has a course called "Case Study on International Law," which prepares undergraduate students for participating in the Jessup International Law Moot Court Competition.

In addition to courses on moot court competitions, several departments of law often organize teams to participate in moot court competitions, such as the Philip C. Jessup International Law Moot Court Competition and a local moot court competition sponsored by the law firm Lee and Li Attorneys-at-Law.[51] The teams are selected from student societies. Law schools provide funding or teacher instruction to support the teams or societies, but not in the form of a course.

Legal Ethics and Professional Responsibility

Since 2011, legal ethics and professional responsibility has been a compulsory subject on the bar exam.[52] Although the exam includes only a few simple multiple-choice questions on this subject, most law schools now have provided at least one course in this field. Accordingly, the number of teachers of and studies on this subject has substantially increased. However, most of those who teach this subject do not focus their research on related topics, and some of them have never practiced law. Therefore, the number of related textbooks and treatises in this field is limited. Because the number of people who pass the bar exam has substantially increased in recent years, lawyers must compete in a highly competitive market. Legal ethics violations have increased as a consequence. Still, numerous lawyers have focused on research regarding legal ethics and professional responsibility. From a long-term perspective, the knowledge development regarding this subject is promising.

Judicial Court Externships

In 2006, National Chiao Tung University innovated the first course to let students learning in courts. The school selects graduate students to clerk in district courts under senior judges' one-to-one instruction. Students spend at least 160 hours in court to obtain three credits. The content of externships includes reading the documents of ongoing cases, observing the trial process, discussing issues related to cases with supervising judges, researching precedents and statutes, and writing memoranda.[53] A preliminary survey showed that about 88 percent of students are satisfied with the course.[54] At least five schools now offer such courses.[55]

Initially, the legitimacy of this type of course was unclear. Allowing clerking students access to confidential documents in ongoing cases raised concerns about courts' confidentiality duty. Some leaders in the judiciary (particularly those who had studied in the United States), however, supported the notion that courts can be a forum for educating future lawyers. In 2008, the Judicial Yuan (the head of the judicial branch of the government) promulgated an administrative rule that permits and encourages courts to collaborate with law schools to organize courses on practical skills. Courts can offer four types of plans to law schools. The first type is a judicial court externship, as previously described, which is available to graduate students only, whereas the other three types are available to undergraduate students. The second type is litigation aid, whereby students get intern jobs in a courthouse to counsel people in need of litigation assistance to help them understand the process. Students serve over 150 hours during one year receive a court service certificate. The third type involves providing space in courthouses for the legal aid societies of law schools to counsel people. The fourth type involves offering tour guides for law students to observe trials.[56] This rule legitimates judicial externship and encourages more law schools to offer this type of courses.

Externships in Collaboration with Prosecutors Offices

Because prosecutors are under a confidentiality obligation during case investigations, they cannot let nonlawyer students participate as an extern. However, not all prosecutorial work requires confidentiality, and thus students can be allowed to take part on some occasions. In 2012, National Chiao Tung University and the Hsinchu District Prosecutors Office signed a collaboration agreement whereby students can participate in general affairs that do not require confidentiality. For example, students can help victims of crime understand their legal rights, help prosecutors litigate, or issue autopsy certificates. For students, criminal procedure is a distinct field that requires expertise; therefore, doing externships at the Prosecutor's Office is extremely beneficial for students' who may take future jobs related to criminal law suits. Students can also support the manpower requirements of the Prosecutor's Office. This course might be an effective way to attract talented students to pursue a career in prosecution.[57] Presently, only National Chiao Tung University provides this type of practical training, but other universities might initiate similar programs in the future.

Government Lawyering Externship

In 2014, National Chiao Tung University School of Law signed a collaborative agreement with the Office of Trade Negotiations, Ministry of Economic Affairs, allowing students to participate in the negotiation process about trade agreements between Taiwan and other countries.[58] Students need to write memorandum about ongoing negotiation under the supervision of professors teaching the course and instructors from the office. This is the only government lawyering externship course in Taiwan.

Law Firm Observations

The College of Law at National Taiwan University has a long history and a large alumni population. Therefore, an honorary mentor program has been established in which some prestigious senior lawyers who are alumni of the College of Law offered some places to third- and fourth-year university students to participate in legal cases in their law firms (including some of the top law firms in Taiwan) and to observe the operating procedures in the law firms.[59] In addition, some law firms provide on-site prepractice training for prospective judges. Because these law firms have experience in instructing prospective judges, they might be willing to provide training opportunities to master's students at law schools or upper-level undergraduate law students.

Mandatory Pro Bono Work

Lack of practical training is a problem in numerous disciplines in higher education in addition to law. Therefore, the Ministry of Education in Taiwan encourages all universities to provide opportunities for undergraduate students to participate in functions within the society and in charitable activities. Circa 2000, many universities required undergraduate students to participate in charitable activities (which were worth at least two credits), including serving as volunteers in non-profit organizations.[60] However, successful pro bono activities requires teachers' active participation, practical training planning, and frequent communication with internship units; otherwise, practical training can easily become a mere formality without substantive content.

Trial Practice and Litigation Document Drafting

This type of trial practice courses introduces ongoing trial processes. Some courses use documents in real cases for analyzing and explanation. Some courses ask students to draft litigation documents, as a legal writing course. At least four schools offer these types of courses.[61]

To enroll in judicial court externship courses, a graduate student must have completed criminal procedure and civil procedure courses. However, additional training is needed to bridge the gap between the theory of litigation procedure courses and court practice. Therefore, in 2008, National Chiao Tung University implemented a new three-credit course called "Litigation Document Drafting." The purpose of this course is to prepare students to clerk effectively in judicial court externship courses. In the course, senior judges, prosecutors, and practicing lawyers explain the meaning of trial documents to students, and teach them how to write an effective complaint. Most reading assignments are actual trial documents, including evidence and proceeding records. Students must finish all the writing assignments and obtain high scores to enroll in judicial court externships. Although some other schools offer courses on litigation documents drafting, legal counseling and negotiation, contract drafting, and moot courts, these courses are not prerequisite or corequisite courses before enrollment in a clinical program.

Challenges in Clinical Education

During the reform from 2005 to 2007, law schools were forced to consider clinical education seriously because it was contained in the reform proposal.[62] Because the pressure from the reform has since been removed, however, practical courses are now not an important concern for most administrators of law schools. Consequently, the number of clinical educators in Taiwan is low, and the number is unlikely to increase in the foreseeable future. No community or group exists for clinical educators; therefore, these instructors rarely have the opportunity to exchange ideas or collaborate. Although some instructors are ardently promoting clinical education in their own schools, they generally face the following challenges.

Staffing Clinical Courses

Because full-time instructors are typically professors who do not hold a legal license or do not have long practice experience, collaboration with lawyers with sufficient experience is essential to protect clients' interests and prevent malpractice. Schools with long histories as institutions typically ask alumni lawyers to assist in these courses at no charge; however, not all alumni are willing to offer this pro bono work, and it is not foreseeable whether sufficient lawyers will be available to take part in such courses. In addition, students in master's programs require more advanced instruction because they are likely to practice law soon, but few law schools employ the necessary staff.

Evaluating the Outcomes of Clinical Education

Although each school has its own standards of grading students, no study has been conducted on the outcome of clinical education, and clinical educators in various schools almost never exchange ideas. For the judicial court externship course at National Chiao Tung University, students in judicial court externships are graded based on the supervising judges' evaluation and the instructors' evaluation of essays the students write describing every 40 hours of their courtroom experiences. Because each judge has his or her own subjective standards, it is difficult to make a fair score judgment among students. Other schools face similar problems.

Skills Training with no Professional Application

Because numerous paths exist to become a lawyer, the background of members of the legal profession is diverse, and it is difficult to develop professional identity awareness even among lawyers. Although clinical instructors typically wish to help people in difficulty obtain justice, their beliefs are not necessarily related to professional value or professional responsibility. Few courses are well designed in a way that enhances students' practical skills. Even moot court courses might not include the element of professional value because many law students in Taiwan will ultimately not become members of the legal profession.

Students' Incentives under Bar Exam Pressure

Although Taiwan has not implemented similar reforms to those in Japan and South Korea, the number of new lawyers passing the bar exam has increased to similar standards as those in Japan and South Korea, in relation to the population.[63] Competition among lawyers is increasing, and young lawyers face greater difficulty in finding apprenticeship opportunities or employment in law firms. Theoretically, law firms should prefer young lawyers who have taken clinical courses in schools. However, because the pass rate of the bar exam has been raised, but is not high (approximately 10%),[64] many students prefer to prepare for the bar exam first, instead of taking time-consuming clinical courses. In addition, the benefit of taking clinical courses might not be substantial enough to attract students because of the aforementioned problems of staffing and evaluation. Consequently, although law schools realize the importance of practice-oriented courses, the progress toward establishing clinical education is slow in Taiwan.

Conclusion

Because of recent reforms in Japan and South Korea, debates were held in Taiwan regarding whether it should establish a new law school system that includes more practical elements. Most law professors, however, rejected this option, believing that law schools should be a place for academic study only. Law professors, like professors in other fields of the social sciences and literature, should focus on research, in their view. Students can learn how to practice law after they pass the bar exam and become apprentices in law firms. Consequently, although clinical education has been thoroughly discussed in other countries, it has drawn little attention in Taiwan.

According to the practical course models currently taught in law schools, law schools in Taiwan should provide more practice-related components. First, such courses do not cost law schools too much. Judicial court externships in several schools have proven that it is possible for courts to assist law schools in training future lawyers. Second, it is unethical to use clients' cases as a means of training newly licensed lawyers. Although young apprentices will practice law under the supervision of senior lawyers, these lawyers might not be effective teachers, despite being effective in practice. Law schools can and should select talented practical instructors for students because law professors should know what constitutes good teaching and have more time than lawyers to observe the reactions of students in skills courses. Third, in the previous decade, criminal procedure in Taiwan has been amended to add more elements of cross examination. The purpose of this change is to protect defendants' procedural rights, but because many lawyers are not well trained in the skill of cross-examination, defendants might be in a more disadvantageous position than before. Lawyers should be more effectively trained before they take criminal cases. This training cannot be accomplished solely by the bar. Fourth, if law schools refuse to adopt this role, this objective must be carried out by public organizations. Because public funding is limited, it will not be possible to increase the bar exam pass rate without lowering the quality of lawyers. Adding more practice-related components to law school curricula is the only method of simultaneously increasing the bar exam pass rate and improving the quality of lawyers.

Notes

1. Chang-fa Lo, "Driving an Ox Cart to Catch Up with the Space Shuttle: The Need for and Prospects of Legal Education Reform in Taiwan"(2006) 24 *Wis. Int'l L.J.* 41, 64; Joseph L. Pratt, "The Two Gates of National Taiwan University School of Law"(2001) 19 *UCLA Pac. Basin L.J.* 131, 153–156.
2. Thomas Chih-hsiung Chen, "Legal Education Reform in Taiwan: Are Japan and Korea the Models?" (2012) 62 *J. Legal Educ.* 32, 39–40.
3. Constitutional Law 1947 (TW), Art. 81: "Judges shall hold office for life. No judge shall be removed from office unless he has been found guilty of a criminal offense or subjected to disciplinary measure, or declared to be under interdiction. No judge shall, except in accordance with law, be suspended or transferred or have his salary reduced."

4. Heng-Wen Liu, "Cong zhishijishouyuxuekedingweilunbainianlai Taiwan faxuejiaoyuzhibianqian" [From the Perspective of Knowledge Transplant and Disciple Deposition to See the Transformation of Legal Education in Taiwan in the Past Century] (PhD thesis, Graduate Institute of National Taiwan University College of Law, 2005) 266–267, http://www.airitilibrary.com/searchdetail.aspx?DocIDs=U0001-2407200521003900.
5. The Attorney Regulation Act 1962 (TW), Art. 1.
6. Lo (n 1) 50–55.
7. Liu (n 4) 201–206.
8. Chen (n 2) 44–46.
9. Ibid. 58–59.
10. Lo (n 1) 66–68.
11. Ministry of Examination, "Updated News" (December 23, 2014) http://wwwc.moex.gov.tw/main/news/wfrmNews.aspx?kind=3&menu_id=42&news_id=1996, accessed June 7, 2015.
12. Chen (n 2) 37–38.
13. Ibid. 37.
14. Ibid. 38.
15. Ibid. 37–38.
16. For a more detailed description of the development of legal education in Taiwan, please see Thomas Chih-hsiung Chen, "Legal Education in Taiwan: A Plural System in Transition," in Shuvro P. Sarker (ed.) *Legal Education in Asia* (Eleven International Publishing, 2014) 155–173.
17. Lo (n 1) 57–60.
18. Chen (n 16) 157–158.
19. The two schools are Soochow University School of Law and Chung Yuan Christian University Department of Financial and Economic Law.
20. Tay-sheng Wang, "The Development of Legal Education in Taiwan: An Analysis of the History of Law and Society," in Stacey Steele and Kathryn Taylor (eds.) *Legal Education in Asia: Globalization, Change and Contexts* (Routledge, 2011) 142.
21. The University Act 2011 (TW), Art. 4.
22. Chen (n 16) 158–159.
23. Liu (n 4) 191.
24. The data can be found at the website of Ministry of Education "Yibailingyi Xueniandu Daxue Yuanxiao Yilanbiao" [The List of Universities in the 2013 AcademicYear] http://ulist.moe.gov.tw/Query/DISCIPLINE?DISCIPLINE_ID=38&DISCIPLINE_NAME=%E6%B3%95%E5%BE%8B%E5%AD%B8%E9%96%80&pageSize=10&page=1, accessed July 25, 2014.
25. Chen (n 16) 159–160.
26. Ibid.
27. Higher Education Evaluation and Accreditation Council of Taiwan, "Brief History" http://www.heeact.edu.tw/ct.asp?xItem=1092&CtNode=444&mp=4, accessed July 25, 2014.
28. Higher Education Evaluation and Accreditation Council of Taiwan, "The Fields for Evaluating Law Schools" http://www.heeact.edu.tw/public/Data/931111272471.doc, accessed July 25, 2014.
29. Chen (n 2) 55–56.
30. Taiwan Law Resources, "2008 Taiwan Law School Rankings" (December 22, 2008) http://www.taiwanlawresources.com/index.php?option=com_content&task=view&

id=238&Itemid=31, accessed July 25, 2014. Unfortunately there is no more updated law school ranking after 2008.
31. Chen (n 16) 158.
32. Lo (n 1) 58–62.
33. For details of the reform, please see Chen (n 2) 48–51.
34. Regarding the legal education reforms in Japan and Korea, see Mayumi Saegusa, "Why the Japanese Law School System was Established: Co-optation as a Defensive Tactic in the Face of Global Pressures" (2009) 34 *Law & Soc. Inquiry* 365, 382–384; Annelise Riles and Takashi Uchida, "Reforming Knowledge? A Socio-legal Critique of the Legal Education Reforms in Japan" (2009) 1 *Drexel L. Rev.* 3, 11–20; Matthew J. Wilson, "U.S. Legal Education Methods and Ideas: Application to the Japanese and Korean Systems" (2010) 18 *Cardozo J. Int'l & Comp. L.* 295, 318–322 & 338–339.
35. Chen (n 2) 49.
36. Lo (n 1) 61.
37. Chen (n 2) 55–56.
38. Saegusa (n 34) 167–168; Jasper Kim, "Socrates v. Confucius: An Analysis of South Korea's Implementation of the American Law School Model" (2009) 10 *Asian-Pac. L. & Pol'y* 322, 332; It appears that the new Korean law schools are still underfunded. See Kyong-Whan Ahn, "International Conference on Legal Education Reform: Law Reform in Korea and the Agenda of Graduate Law Schools" (2006) 24 *Wis. Int'l L.J.* 223, 233–234.
39. Chen (n 2) 50–51.
40. Ibid. 50.
41. Lo (n 1) 61.
42. Ministry of Justice, "Resources for Free Legal Counsels," http://www.moj.gov.tw/ct.asp?xItem=29350&ctNode=27961, accessed July 25, 2014.
43. See, for example, Legal Aid Society of National Taiwan University, "The Process of Legal Aid Cases"http://www.law.ntu.edu.tw/legalservice/index.files/Page486.htm, accessed July 25, 2014.
44. According to the curriculum websites of all law schools in Taiwan that were analyzed by the author. In 19 law schools that offer clinics, 12 schools list only full-time faculty members as instructors.
45. Interview with Professor Hung-En Liu, College of Law, National Chengchi University (Taipei, May 1, 2014).
46. According to the curriculum websites of all law schools in Taiwan analyzed by the author.
47. National Chengchi University College of Law, "History of Legal Aid Society," http://www.law.nccu.edu.tw/service/super_pages.php?ID=service1, accessed July 25, 2014.
48. Ibid.
49. Interview with Professor Hung-En Liu, College of Law, National Chengchi University (Taipei, May 1, 2014).
50. Tsai-fang Chen, "The New Direction of Moot Court" (National Chiao Tung University Institute of Technology Law, Leading Technology Law Newsletter, Vol. 28, July 1, 2013) http://140.113.31.141:8092/28/, accessed July 25, 2014.
51. Lee and Li Foundation, "About Lee and Li Moot Court Competition," http://www.leeandli.org.tw/cup.html, accessed July 25, 2014.
52. Taiwan's Bar Exam Regulations 2013 (TW), Art. 12, S. 2.

53. Cui-Ping Weng, "An Innovation in Legal Education: NCTU Law Students Attend Judicial Court Externship" (Dajiyuan, April 26, 2006) http://www.epochtimes.com/b5/6/4/26/n1299510.htm, accessed July 25, 2014.
54. Chih-hsiung Chen, Ruo-ting Fu, and Yun-rong Huang, "The Theory and Practice of the Judicial Court Externship: The Experience of Chiao Tung University Institute of Technology Law" (2010) 12 *Mag. Judges Ass'n Repub. China* 187–212.
55. The five law schools are National Taipei University College of Law, Master's Program Graduate Institute of Financial and Economic Law, Kainan University Department of Law, National Chung Cheng University College of Law, and National Dong Hwa University Graduate Institute of Financial and Economic Law.
56. "Sifayuan Suoshu Gejiguan Banli Sifashiwuyu Faxuejiaoyu Zhengheyaodian" [Notes for the Organizations Supervised by the Judicial Yuan to Arrange the Integration of Judicial Practice and Legal Education] 2008 (TW).
57. UDN, "Graduate Law School Externship Listening to the Voice of Criminal Victims" (Udn.com, September 9, 2012) http://www.pac.nctu.edu.tw/Report/report_more.php?id=23292, accessed July 25, 2014.
58. National Chiao Tung University, "Syllabus of International Trade Externship," https://course.nctu.edu.tw/Course/CrsOutline/show.asp?Acy=103&Sem=2&CrsNo=5536&lang=zh-tw, accessed June 8, 2015.
59. National Taiwan University College of Law, "Honors Mentor Program," http://www.law.ntu.edu.tw/main.php?mod=custom_page&site_id=0&page_id=18, accessed July 25, 2014.
60. see, for example, National Chiao Tung University, "Understand Service Learning" http://service-learning.nctu.edu.tw/about.php,accessed July 25, 2014.
61. The four schools are National Chiao Tung University Institute of Technology Law, National Taipei University College of Law, National University of Kaohsiung College of Law, and National Taiwan University College of Law.
62. Chen (n 16) 166.
63. Ibid. 59–60.
64. Ibid. 159.

CHAPTER 6

Clinical Legal Education in Israel

Yael Efron

Introduction

The story of Israeli clinical legal education (CLE) is related to developments in the legal profession in Israel. As such, one must view this story in light of the circumstances surrounding the establishment and development of the State of Israel. In a country born from the roots of ancient peoples and the ashes of abolished communities, Israelis continuously struggled to find their distinct legal identity throughout the years. Israel's 66 years of societal deliberations have left their mark on the legal profession and, foreseeable, on legal education as well. This chapter describes CLE's introduction into Israeli law schools and illustrates the forces affecting its development.

The legal culture predominant in prestate Israel was formalistic and private, taking after the British Mandatory system,[1] which governed the region known as Palestine from 1922 until Israel's independence in 1948. This chapter of history had significant and lasting effects on Israeli law and legal culture. During the British Mandate period, Jewish lawyers mainly took on work that was Zionist in nature. They worked on supporting Jewish social establishments and on institution building. Of course, lawyers sometimes compromised these priorities at the expense of professional goals.[2] However, it appeared that achieving and maintaining the exclusivity of the legal profession comprised an even more pressing goal for lawyers in Palestine (the pre-Israel state).[3] The exclusivity of the profession remained a pressing issue and an ethical concern in student clinics, as discussed in this chapter.

This legacy from the period of the British Mandate combined with the nation-building ethos and financial concerns characterizing pre- and early poststate Israel, dictated the professional ideology of the Israeli Bar. This sometimes caused tension between lawyers' social and professional responsibilities. For instance, the rules of the Israeli Bar Association Act required lawyers to be loyal to clients while preserving the dignity of the profession and of the court.[4] However, such devotion sometimes conflicted with notions of collectivism and national solidarity, as lawyers were expected to represent the client as an individual beyond (even, against) the interests of the state or nation.[5] The primary goal of the Israel Bar Association Act was ensuring the profession's autonomy, not maintaining the public interest in a broad sense. Indeed, minimal attention was devoted, in the legislative hearings on this Act, to the role of lawyers in the preservation of justice.[6] This tension between the private and public goals of the legal profession remains palpable to this day.

The Israeli Bar Association dominated the representation of legal professional ideology until the 1990s.[7] However, since then it has lost some of its influence due to the entry of new social groups to the bar,[8] changes in legal education,[9] the increase in competition between lawyers,[10] the rise of public interest and community lawyering,[11] and the Supreme Court's increasing tendency to scrutinize the bar's practices under Israel's new constitutional framework. Over the course of the past two decades, public interest in Israeli legal practice has been on the rise, additional law school clinics have opened, and "cause lawyering" has become an accepted form of practice.[12] These developments have allowed CLE to gain a foothold in Israeli law schools during this period. Now incorporated into every law school in the country, both in-house clinics and externships are recognized as a legitimate part of the legal curriculum.

Although flourishing today, CLE has only recently come to enjoy this positive status. Furthermore, although appreciated today by the legal academy, CLE remains an elective study element in the process of gaining a law degree, demonstrating its lack of centrality. Much of this has to do with an ongoing debate regarding the purpose of the legal academy in Israel. The institutional and ethical complexities involved in setting up and running a legal clinic within a law school present Israeli CLE with additional obstacles. This chapter addresses one possible underlying rationale (both social and pedagogical in nature) for these impediments as well as for the growing development of legal clinics in Israel. Next, it reviews the scope—both in numbers and in content—of clinics currently active in Israeli law schools. Finally, this chapter discusses the challenges—institutional, social, and ethical—that clinical education in Israel faces today.

This introduction cannot be complete without a definitional comment: what *is* a legal clinic? Israeli legal education has not yet formed unified terminology to govern the field of clinical work in law.[13] Though CLE is, in essence, experiential learning, not all experiential learning is clinical (e.g., moot courts, simulation-based courses, etc.). While some CLE is clearly "fieldwork," other forms of CLE reside far from "the field"—based in in-house clinics, housed on campus. CLE is always supervised, but this supervision might vary in form, in the supervisor's role and identity (e.g., law professors, lawyers, law professors who are lawyers, etc.). Some, but not all, clinics, serve real, live clients, while other clinics focus on policymaking and not client service. When we discuss CLE in Israel, different models of practice (elaborated in the next section) come to mind. To clarify the concept for the purposes of this chapter, then, the term CLE will be used to connote a CLE that consists of supervised experiential learning and teaching of law, which bears real-life consequences.

Developments of CLE in Israel

Early Initiatives

The very first attempts to include experiential aspects within the legal academy took place in the 1980s, in the form of civil legal aid services that operated under the auspices of the Hebrew University Law Faculty (HU) and the Bar Ilan University Law Faculty (BIU).[14] These early initiatives took the form of a law *office* rather than a law *course*. A more organized movement of CLE, combining experiential and theoretical studies, developed in Israel's law faculties in the 1990s. The first of these more advanced models included a criminal law clinic at HU (which has operated almost continuously from 1989 to the present day), and a criminal law clinic and a human and civil rights clinic at Tel Aviv University Law Faculty (TAU), established in 1991. Haifa University's Faculty of Law opened its clinics right at its inception in the early '90s, and most of the new private law schools in Israeli colleges[15] have followed. Today, all Israeli law schools include experiential studies as part of the curriculum, with legal clinics being at the forefront of this trend.

The establishment of clinics in the legal academy over the years represents a paradigm shift in legal education in Israel. Some have suggested that this trend demonstrates a new maturity in the understanding of the role of a law school.[16] This transformation has resulted from an ongoing tension between the bar and the legal academy, and from internal tensions between and inside law schools themselves as well, regarding the purpose of academic legal education in Israel. This debate, as discussed here, has focused on two different themes: the private versus public interest debate, and the skills versus theory debate. Both of these debates have greatly evolved since the early initiatives in CLE were set in motion, and help explain the evolution of law school clinics to this day.

Further Developments: The Private versus Public Interest Debate in Israeli Law Schools

For many years, the curriculum design prevalent in Israeli law schools highlighted the Israeli legal culture's private interest focus.[17] For instance, the basic legal concepts introduced to students in the first-year curriculum (such as the right to private property, the freedom of contract, and the duty of care) were grounded in a liberal-capitalist worldview and assumed autonomous and rational actors in a free market. Very few courses discussed issues such as public housing, social rights, and welfare policies.[18] The "hidden curriculum"[19] of legal education in Israel seemed to be in line with the legal culture that was predominant until the 1990s.

However, some legal scholars and educators objected to this curricular norm. Regarding the law as a public resource and believing in equal accessibility to all,[20] they held that the bar had a duty to promote public welfare owing to its monopoly—de facto and de jure—on legal services in Israel.[21] According to this view, the legal community in general, as a profession (rather than merely an occupation), holds a firm responsibility to the public interest.[22] Stephen Wizner, a patriarchal figure in the field of CLE in Israel, illustrates the vital connection between legal education and public interest through several arguments.[23] First of all, lawyers use their education in the real world, with real people. Second, the public interest requires law students to learn about their social and professional responsibility, to challenge injustice and pursue social justice in society. NetaZiv, another leader of socially oriented legal scholarship and education, discusses the monopoly on legal education given to law schools by the state. She advocates that this imbalance requires them to keep social responsibility in mind when designing the Israeli legal curriculum.[24] In her view, the absence of an alternative to legal representation, other than that provided by licensed lawyers educated through this monopolistic system, requires the system to emphasize public interest in its curriculum.

From these ideals to advocacy for CLE, the road for socially oriented educators is short and clear. The law school clinic, they so stress, exists as the primary place in law school in which students learn to be competent, ethical, socially responsible lawyers. It plays a unique role in exposing students to social and economic injustice in society, and challenges the message presented in legal education that everyone receives equal access to legal help.[25] In the 1990s, conceptual changes to the bar's and the judiciary's priorities transformed the legal culture and encouraged educators to instill in students the value and duty of public service.[26] These teachers assumed that through the experience of assisting needy clients and the student's seeing results from those efforts, the student would feel more motivated and responsible toward helping these clients.[27]

Wizner claims that through CLE, law students gain the opportunity to learn (1) that social issues can be resolved through law, (2) that poor people need legal representation just as much as the rich, (3) about the development and application of legal theory, (4) how the legal system can be used to seek social change, and (5) the limits of law in solving individual and social problems.[28] Wizner's vision seems to fit well in the general developments in legal education in Israel today, which has embraced CLE in the last two decades. However, research points to a developed sense of public interest in most students at the beginning of their legal education, while this social call erodes through the course of their studies.[29] Students report a sense of disillusion regarding their ability to affect society as novice lawyers, and attribute these qualities to experienced practitioners who are financially well enough to afford pro bono services.[30] This phenomenon can be explained by the emphasis on private and business law in the curriculum.[31]

The Skills versus Theory Debate in Israeli Law Schools

Licensed lawyers in Israel must all graduate from law school. As a stepping-stone each lawyer must pass through, law schools expect their faculties to prepare the students for practice. This expectation, noted in the scholarship,[32] also dominates most of the marketing statements used by law schools to attract potential students.[33] However, a close examination of law school curricula reveals a gap between these statements and the actual curricular design in most institutions. The curriculum of most law schools indeed includes doctrinal courses[34] alongside more theoretical ones,[35] but these doctrinal courses teach very little practical skills. Most law school curricula offer skill-oriented courses as elective courses for advanced students, and most of these courses hold fewer credit hours and are taught by adjunct teachers.[36]

Due to the legal academy's more widely associated role of reviewing, challenging, and criticizing the law and legal culture,[37] skill-oriented teaching received a reputation of irrelevance to academic studies.[38] This academic and less practical role is, of course, an important role of the academy. Academia is one of the few institutions able to voice contradictory and perhaps even provocative views, thus promoting change in social orders.[39] It seems that Israeli law school curricula are closer to this more theoretical approach.[40]

Criticized both by supporters of such an approach as well as their adversaries, many prefer to see a different legal curriculum. The supporters of the theoretical approach, who claim that not enough emphasis has been put on these aspects of the curriculum, advocate the introduction of a wider scope of disciplines to law students, such as philosophy, culture, economics, and so forth.[41] These educators claim the law reflects these components and should be studied as such.[42] The critique by those who advocate for a more skill-oriented curriculum is that law schools do not focus on adequate preparation for practice as part of their social responsibilities.[43]

With that said, it is quite uncommon today to view the practice versus theory divide as a dichotomy.[44] The well-accepted view of legal education today, as reflected by the current curricular design of the legal academy, advocates that "good theory is practical and that good practice is informed by theory."[45] Although the review presented in the next segment indicates changes in the legal academy's perspective regarding the importance of practical teaching and experiential learning, the current place of clinical programs in law schools still resides far from the ideal. Jerome N. Frank, one of the forefathers of the legal realist movement, had a vision. He initiated the CLE movement in the United States and advocated for the transformation of law schools into "clinical lawyer schools," in which students would learn the interaction of legal theory and legal practice.[46]

Current Clinical Programs in Israeli Law Schools and Faculties

General Review

The foundation of the Board of Clinicians in Law Schools and Faculties in 2011 signifies maturity of the field and one of the most important developments in CLE in Israel.[47] This volunteer-based initiative invites representatives from all academic institutions teaching law to send a representative to the Board and puts forth the need to rethink legal education in Israeli academy. Its activities, run by devoted volunteer clinicians, involve providing support in academic research, developing a lively peer network, providing a platform for consulting in administrative as well as professional exertions, liaising with experts, and more.

From 2012–2013, the Board conducted a survey on the function of legal clinics in Israel. The results were presented in the annual clinicians' meeting organized by the Board in February 2014.[48] The Board sent out and collected the data from questionnaires, distributed to all clinics, addressing four sets of questions:[49] the academic institution; the students in the clinics; the teaching staff; and the clinical program itself. Since not everyone answered all the questions, and due to the dynamic nature of CLE in Israel and the lack of a unified terminology, not all answers to the questionnaires produced worthwhile information. The significant data gathered and presented shall be discussed accordingly.

Institutional Aspects of CLE in Israeli Law Schools and Faculties

The survey indicates that all 14 legal education institutions in Israel offer CLE to their students.[50] Over all, the survey reports 116 legal clinics, and the Board's presentation indicates that this number has increased since the data was collected.[51] Since the differences among clinics per law schools are vast, one should not regard these numbers as average at each institution. While Ono Academic College Law School (Ono) offers 19 clinics in AY 2014–15, Zefat Academic College School of Law (ZAC) holds only 3.[52]

The number of clinics per institution does not indicate the type of institution either. These differences are not indicative of the difference between colleges and universities, as both Ono and ZAC are colleges, meaning the difference shows no indication of college versus university. It is also not indicative of the differences between private and public institutions, as both ZAC, and Bar Ilan University (offering 14 clinics)[53] are public institutions. The size of the institution, rather, offers a more compelling explanation for these differences. ZAC, being the smallest law school in Israel (of approximately 150 students),[54] holds the least number of clinics, while Ono (of approximately 1,200 law students)[55] holds the most.

Most institutes, approximately 65 percent of them, reportedly designate space for the clinical work, studies, and staff meetings. Some institutes, approximately 18 percent, partially provide a designated compound for the clinics. The rest, 18 percent of Israeli law schools, report not having such designated space at all.[56] This data is not necessarily indicative of how "seriously" a law school regards its clinics. Although physical space generally costs significant amounts, the university may then utilize it for a variety of purposes. This concern rings especially true in Israel since its law schools usually choose urban locations, limiting their options for expansion.[57] Unlike other curricular changes, not entailing physical adaptation, the rise of CLE challenges the institutions in a unique manner. In this situation students must share their learning space with clients and organizational partners. This challenge is sure to be met over time, as CLE continues to gain its weight in Israeli legal education.

The Students of the Legal Clinics in Israel

On average, 40 percent of the students in a law school or faculty participate in legal clinics.[58] Generally open for enrollment in later stages of the students' course of studies, the minority of clinics are open to first-year graduates (4%) or only second-year students (2%). Clinics open for third- and fourth-year students make up only 3 percent. More frequently, second- and third-year students may enroll in the clinics (35%).Twenty-two percent of the clinics include third-year enrollment, while clinics enrolling students from years second through fourth make up 32 percent.[59] The data suggests that clinical work in law schools takes place in mixed classes, comprised of students from the second year to the third or fourth year.

Whether elective or required, participation in legal clinics receives credit in all law schools. The range of credit hours allotted to clinical work varies from four to eight credit hours.[60] This information may also assist in explaining the above data. In a common curriculum, the first year of law school focuses on the basic foundations of the law and of legal doctrine.[61] Therefore, the first year of law school is considered to be less suitable for experiential learning. It is also less common to offer elective courses during the first year of law school, and most law schools offer clinics on an elective basis.[62] Usually, the fourth year of law school lasts only one semester.[63] At this time, most law students have covered most of their credit requirements to graduate, and probably feel less inclined to add any surplus to their study load. This short period is also considered less suitable for long-term, legal representation-type processes.

The Teaching Staff in Israeli Legal Clinics

The survey revealed vast differences in the status of clinicians in Israeli law schools. When asked to describe the employment modality of the clinician, law schools' replies varied immensely.[64] This variety raises fundamental questions regarding the definition of clinicians, their status in the institution, and the institutional concerns regarding their employment.[65] The survey reveals that universities only permanently employ 12 percent of the staff in legal clinics, while they periodically renew 88 percent of the clinicians' contracts. Eighty percent of the periodically renewed contracts do so on a full-year cycle, while 20 percent of the contracts are renewed on a part-year basis.[66] This data suggests that the employment status of clinicians in Israeli law schools is less secure than those of more "traditional" doctrinal affiliation, who usually enjoy tenured positions. By the time the survey was conducted, a significant advancement occurred at HU, where a clinical tenure track was introduced for university approval.

Clinicians work with real live clients and personally take responsibility for their students' work with those clients.[67] This status puts clinicians in a vulnerable place, subjecting them to professional liability lawsuits. Institutions provide their clinics with professional liability insurance in 35 percent of law schools, and 20 percent of law schools provide insurance to clinicians without personal insurance, while 10 percent of Israeli law schools leave their clinicians without insurance. In 10 percent of law schools, the clinicians are active lawyers, who already have professional liability insurance policies of their own.[68] For a quarter of the law schools, the data on this issue is missing or inconclusive.

In most institutes, the clinicians hold regular staff meetings. These meetings, held with diverging frequency, can take place from every other week (during school time) or "rarely," as reported, and concern a specific issue.[69] One might expect such disparity in light of the huge differences in employment practices.

The Clinical Programs in Israeli Law Schools and Faculties

Most clinical programs in Israeli law schools are elective, with only a quarter of the programs required for graduation.[70] This means that a law student in 75 percent of law schools in Israel may graduate from law school without ever meeting a real-life client, or dealing with an actual case. In light of the Israeli Bar Act, law graduates still receive their license to practice law with real-life experience, since admittance to the bar requires a mandatory internship from each law graduate.[71] The internship is not a part of academic legal education. The bar itself takes responsibility for this internship. During this period, they supervise the graduate's experiential learning.

With this experiential "back-up plan," one gains a better understanding of both why a debate over the place of legal clinics existed in Israeli academia for many years[72] and why there is such diversity in the legal clinical programs in Israeli law schools.[73] Many of the questions regarding the actual clinical work conducted in law schools[74] in this survey went unanswered or did not produce sufficient comparable information. However, a complementing study conducted by the author in 2013 and described below, highlights several models of supervision strategies used in CLE and helps fill in some of the informational gaps.

Models of Clinical Legal Practice

As discussed above, the definition of clinical legal study is a supervised experiential learning and teaching of law, bearing real-life consequences. Clinicians provide supervision not only to protect clients but also to ensure meaningful learning by the students. The ethical code assigns the clinician the responsibility of effectively supervising the students, and details the actions required for such supervision: meeting with them, providing feedback, reviewing documents, being available for their queries, and generally overseeing their work.[75]

The experience of the students in CLE varies according to the institution, the teaching staff, and the learning content. Hereafter specific examples of legal clinics in Israel will discuss and demonstrate this variety. These specific examples were chosen for this demonstration for two main reasons, first, due to the frequency of the supervision model practiced within Israeli CLE. Only commonly used models were chosen for this discussion, bearing in mind that the list is not, by any means, exhaustive. Other forms of supervision, if not discussed hereafter, are unique, and, although they deserve discussion, fall beyond the scope of this chapter. The second reason for choosing these specific examples is the availability of the information.[76]

In-house Clinics

An in-house clinic is fundamentally a law office on the premises of the law school. The students gather the relevant information from the clients and provide them with initial information regarding the process of counseling or representation. The client then receives and signs proxies, wavers, and other relevant legal documents. The supervisor, usually a licensed lawyer, drafts and signs these documents if necessary,[77] and assists the students in assessing the information and deciding on a course of action. The clinician, responsible both professionally and ethically for this course of action,[78] occasionally assigns research tasks to the students to explore the best possible path. The students then report the action chosen to their client and begin carrying it out.

Several institutions hold such in-house clinics. The CLE Centre at the Hebrew University Law Faculty (HU Clinics) houses Israel's most veteran clinic. This pioneering first clinic in Israel[79] represents a very established and well-accomplished institution. The newly renovated premises of the HU Clinics host seven types of legal clinics: Criminal Justice, International Human Rights, Rights of People of Disabilities, Youth Rights, Community Lawyering, Aiding People in the Periphery, and Economic and Social Development.[80] These rich and diverse learning opportunities for the students of the HU Clinics offer supervision conducted by experienced and accomplished practitioners. Interestingly, the HU Clinics focus on more than law studies. The students and teaching staff all report great personal satisfaction from making a social difference, assisting the less privileged, and contributing to social justice.[81]

Externships

Externships involve experiential learning and the teaching of law conducted outside the classroom, such as in courts, governmental agencies, prisons, and other facilities outside the law school.[82] Essentially, students are placed at the side of experienced practitioners, while they observe and take part in the real-life work performed by these practitioners.[83] These experienced lawyers are sometimes, but not always, members of the clinic's teaching staff. Clinical faculty hold responsibility for providing feedback and supervision to the students. When meeting with clients in the practitioner's real-life law practice, student supervision remains just as intense as in the in-house clinics, and occasionally even more so.

ZAC's criminal law clinic exemplifies this model of supervision. The clinician assigns each student a specific practicing lawyer from the State's Public Defender Office. Throughout the school year, the students regularly accompany the lawyers in their daily work—in courts, at their office, in prison, police stations, and so forth. They take part in consult meetings with their accused clients, participate in investigation file assessments by the defense teams, and review documents prepared by the practitioner. The students then report to their classmates on their experience, and the supervising clinician, a faculty member who is an experienced criminal lawyer,[84] analyses the professional course of action taken by the practitioner with the class. The practitioners also report to the clinic supervisor on the students assigned to them, providing the supervisor with information required for delivering feedback to the students. The students in this clinic report on the meaningful learning experience, connecting the lessons taught in criminal law classes in their first year and criminal procedure classes in their second year, with the real-life experience they receive in their third year of school. In interviews conducted by the author, the students in this clinic all point out the importance of their participation in the clinic in bridging the gap between the theoretical knowledge they have accumulated and real-life practice.[85]

Clinical Partnerships with Nonacademic Organizations

Many legal clinics partner with NGOs or other cause organizations, which share common social goals. The organization, often basing its activities on a roster of volunteers, benefits from the contribution of the law students, who dedicate their time, legal skills, and knowledge to the cause. The students in turn gain familiarity with a social cause close to their heart, benefit from the experiential learning, and enjoy personal gratification from their contribution to the cause.[86] In these partnerships, the students are placed "in the field." Under the auspices of the partner organization, they observe and participate in its activities and report on their experience in class and to the supervising clinician, who may or may not be present with the students during their experience. The supervisor, always an experienced lawyer in the relevant field of law, analyzes the legal and social lessons that can be learned from the students' experience. The supervisor also provides personal feedback based on his or her own observation, on the students' reports, and on reports received from the clinic's liaison at the organization.

The clinic for Patient's Rights at ZAC, partnered with Rivka Ziv Medical Center in the city of Zefat, serves as a good example of this supervision model. In this clinic, the students meet weekly at the Ziv hospital with its medical and social work staff. They discuss cases of real patients with the students, contemplating ethical and legal dilemmas that arise during the patients' treatment. The supervisor, a law faculty teacher and experienced lawyer specializing in biomedical law and bioethics,[87] facilitates the discussion. The students receive guidance and feedback from their supervisor while applying their knowledge in biomedical law to the dilemmas presented to them by the hospital staff.

In one of the most touching examples of a case dealt with at this clinic, ZAC students faced the case of Syrian citizens. These clients, wounded in the crossfire of their internal war, fled the border to Israel to seek medical treatment.[88] Ziv, the hospital closest to the Syrian border, faced (and still faces) the obligation to save their lives, but with the lack of funding to do so. The treating staff had to deal with daily dilemmas regarding these patients—some of them children—regarding questions such as the fine line between emergency life-saving treatment and essential life-improving (but not saving) treatment. Other concerns arose as well regarding these patients' rights as nonresidents, isolated and detached from their homes and families. Students participating in this clinic reported on their sense of duty and personal stake in this experience as unequivalent to any other they have had in law school.[89]

Another example of such a partnership can be found in the Clinic for Legal Aid in ZAC, supervised by the author. The students at this clinic volunteer in two cause organizations, providing legal consult to underprivileged residents in the periphery of Israel.[90] The students' work in these organizations relates closely to the projects conducted in in-house clinics, as described above, with the exception that it is held at the premises of the partner organization. Similar to externships, the students report in class on their experience. Then, in class, the supervisor (an experienced lawyer) analyzes the legal and social lessons drawn from these experiences with the students. The professional responsibility lies jointly with the partner organization and the supervisor, providing students with detailed instructions for conduct with clients.[91] The students in this clinic report, almost unanimously, on how law classes complemented their clinical experience on the one hand, but how this experience highlighted the gap between the theory and the practice of law on the other hand.[92]

Challenges Facing Clinical Education in Israel

Institutional Concerns

An efficient and responsible clinical course requires the close accompaniment and the monitoring and mentoring of the students by their instructor. This makes clinical courses expensive in terms of teacher/student ratio, classroom premises, teaching hours, and so on.[93] Experiential courses also require the mastering of diverse pedagogical skills, in which law schools have yet to train their teachers. Law schools thus rarely train clinical teachers within the law school, and therefore require special resources. All of these factors put a serious financial strain on the academic institution hosting a clinical course.[94]

The launch of CLE in the United States came from generous donations to law schools. In fact, it was not until the late 1960s that the Ford Foundation and its antipoverty initiatives provided CLE with financial support and advocated for it in the United States. The foundation established funding that provided grants to law schools to found legal clinics serving the poor. The schools that received the grants agreed to continue the clinical program after the funding ran out. Most of them indeed did so, and today, clinical programs are included in the permanent law school budgets in the United States.[95] In Israel, however, budgeting clinics presents a challenge. Only a few of the legal clinics rely on private donations for funding.[96] Most use the general institutional budget for their operation, and none receive funding specifically from the Council of Higher Education (CHE).[97]

The Planning and Budgeting Committee (PBC) of the CHE has responsibility for imposing strict and uniform budgeting standards in Israel. They also fund the country's universities and public colleges. These standards do not differentiate the budget according to pedagogy but rather according to the academic discipline and the enrollment rate per capita. Thus, clinical courses are subject to special budgetary needs, not specifically funded by the PBC, which again use up more of the institution's administrative resources. In private colleges, in which the budget relies on tuition alone, these concerns increase since keeping a balanced budget remains a crucial focus. For these corporations, measuring the investment in clinical courses vis-à-vis their academic benefits is a challenge.[98]

Israeli scholars researching clinics debate the concept of a student as a client. Those who regard this concept as a blessing state that the paying costumer (the student) enjoys a variety of services for purchase (academic education), and thus the suppliers of these services (the academic institutions) constantly strive to improve their quality, making themselves attractive to the client.[99] Other scholars who oppose this concept emphasize the nonprofit nature of education. They point out that academia as a market entails an inherent market failure, because the best product—meaningful learning—is achieved at the smallest teacher/student ratio.[100]

However, others disprove the claim that budgetary constraints make curricular reform by enhancement of CLE impossible.[101] A detailed financial analysis undertaken in 2007 shows that experiential pedagogy does not necessarily entail budgetary additions, but only requires changes in the current budget itself.[102] Furthermore, research finds that revisions in the current budget could provide 1,280 additional teaching hours a year in an even more modest budget.[103]

Another institutional concern inhibiting the development of CLE in Israel includes the teaching faculty's background. Clinical teaching staff should have a practical legal background for numerous reasons. First, the teacher introduces the profession to the students and provides them with professional skills and knowledge.[104] Second, the Bar Act and its rules govern the standards of legal ethics and professional conduct.[105] Generally speaking, only Bar members are bound by these standards, as discussed below. This rule presents a challenge for law schools hosting clinics. One possible solution to this problem includes appointing a member of the bar as a teacher and supervisor of the clinic. But since law teachers in Israel are not necessarily members of the bar, placing law faculty in this position adds to the challenge.

Hiring adjunct teachers to supervise the clinics provides another option. However, since no real avenue for tenure or promotion for adjuncts exists, this method suggests the "adjunct" value of the clinics themselves. Here they seem supplementary, and not an inherent part of the law school and its curriculum. The more substantial solution to this challenge would require recognition and advancement of the practical background of law school faculty, which is rarely the case in Israel. In most academic institutions, the hiring, promoting, and acknowledging of faculty achievements replace focus on scholarship rather than on practical or teaching skills.[106] This, of course, creates a negative incentive for young faculty to invest time and energy in clinical training.[107] The academic institute itself presents little incentive to invest in clinical training, as long as theoretical scholarship remains the only parameter of law school prestige.[108] For any change to occur in law school's attitude toward clinical education, the values of legal education in Israel would have to be revisited:

> Education institutions must determine the appropriate role of faculty, while taking into account . . . the established educational objectives, the necessary balance

between the faculty's role in education and scholarship, and the extent to which a particular faculty structure requires students to find crucial training outside the law school.[109]

Social Implications

Academia in Israel, as in other countries, struggles with the notion of shifting the focus from theory to practice. Sociologists such as Young and Goodson explain this phenomenon by pointing out the hegemony's fear of losing its prestige. Law schools' concern for their social status reflects any changes in legal education generally and, especially, the introduction of experiential learning. Such changes threaten the four elements recognized by Young as indicators of social prestige:[110] abstractedness (practical and applicable knowledge is less prestigious than the abstract and theoretical kind); literacy (written knowledge enjoys a higher prestige than the orally transferred kind); individualism (acquiring and transferring knowledge individually is more prestigious than teamwork or the accumulated knowledge of the group); and relatedness (interdisciplinary knowledge enjoys less prestige than "pure" specialized knowledge within a discipline).

Young's argument that curricular changes affect social attitudes may explain law schools' reluctance to promote clinical education as opposed to theoretical, literacy-based, individually measured, and legally "pure" education. Not with ease, the legal academy adapts to the demands of students, the community, the bench, and the bar to enhance clinical education, since by essence, CLE is practical, oral, teamwork-based, and interdisciplinary.

Psychiatry observed similar processes with its introduction into medicine,[111] and environmental studies into geography.[112] The initiation of "academization" for these areas of study occurred outside of the faculty. They then gained legitimacy within the academy by establishing their theoretical basis and disseminating it through scholarship. The foundation of an Israeli law review for social change at Tel Aviv University in 2008 indicates a step in the same direction. The journal, titled *Ma'asei Mishpat*,[113] translated from Hebrew as "Practices of Law," serves as the young academic sibling of the most prestigious law journal, titled *Theoretical Inquiries in Law*, published by the same university.[114] In addition, a Code of Ethics for Law School Clinics, drafted in 2011, describes the clinic as a "laboratory for the research of law."[115] These developments hold a promise for change in the social status of CLE in Israel.

Ethical Considerations

The Bar Act states that only lawyers may perform the unique duties of the profession, such as representation and the drafting of legal documents, and clearly forbids nonlawyers from doing so.[116] Thus, this restriction inhibits law students, who are not yet members of the bar, from representing clients and providing them with legal services. The introduction of clinics into law schools creates prima facie, a breach of this section of the Bar Act. Therefore, the Ethics Committee of the Bar confronts the need to decide to what extent and capacity legal clinics can provide legal services; supervise of the quality of these services; address issues of conflict of interest between the university and the represented clients, and so forth. Since the ethics rules of the Bar Act and its bylaws bind only members of the bar, the committee must specifically regulate the clinics' activities that are not performed by lawyers. Law school clinics status received a definition in a decision issued by the head of the Ethics Committee of the Bar in 2009.[117]

This decision of the bar's Ethics Committee stated that the clinics should be organized as a law office, headed and managed by a licensed lawyer, who closely supervises the work done by students. The lawyers managing these clinics remain bound by the rules of the bar. They themselves maintain representation of the clients, and not the host institution, so the clinic must clearly differentiate itself from the university. Under these rules, the loyalty of the clinician Should be focused towards the client and not to the institution under whose auspices the clinic functions. Furthermore, the lawyer may not collect fees from clinic clients.

The flourishing of law school clinics on the one hand, and the lack of unified form of their governance on the other hand, calls for a thorough rethinking regarding their function. In 2011, the David Weiner Center for Lawyers' Ethics and Professional Responsibility in the School of Law at The Academic College of Management[118] took on the important task of drafting an ethical code for the law school clinics.[119] Not mandatory, unlike the ethical rules of the bar, this code lacks methods of enforcement. Its contribution to the field includes guidance and direction, rather than discipline and sanctions. Law school clinics may turn to it for assistance when setting up a new clinic or when an ethical dilemma arises during the course of their work.

The Ethical Code for Legal Clinics in Israel describes the essence of clinical education[120] and the purposes of legal clinics.[121] The code regards the clinics as an inherent part of the students' academic and practical legal education, and calls for special attention to the teaching of professional ethics.[122] According to the code and in coherence with the decision of the Ethics committee of the bar, a lawyer should head each clinic. This lawyer's role is to bear all legal responsibilities; to train, supervise, and mentor the students; and to sign all legal documents.[123] The code addresses the relationship between the clinic and its host institution, stating that a clear differentiation must be made.[124] Without obligations toward the rules of ethics in the Bar Act, the code clarifies the rules applying to students' work, such as informed consent, conflict of interest, confidentiality, and so on.[125] Additionally, the limitations on the collection of fees from clinic clients are articulated in this code of ethics, in accordance with the decision of the Ethics Committee of the Bar.[126] Finally, the code establishes a consulting committee for the ethical concerns of legal clinics. This committee, comprised of both academics and clinicians, takes charge of consultations, liaisons with the Ethics Committee of the bar, and revisions to the code itself.[127]

Every so often, ethical concerns merge with institutional concerns. While the students in the clinics take on advocacy for their community, such advocacy sometimes promotes the interests of their clients against the university hosting the clinic. The university might find itself between a rock and a hard place when allowing the clinical studies to criticize its own managerial decisions. One such example case occurred in Tel Aviv University in 2008.

The students in the legal clinic for employees' rights at Tel Aviv University took on representation of the teaching staff of another university (the Open University). In this conflict the Open University staff engaged in a dispute with its management. The university tried to prevent their workers from establishing a workers' union, and the students in the clinic assisted the staff with their efforts to resist.[128] Out of collegiality and solidarity, probably, with the management of the Open University, the law students received instruction from the Rector of Tel Aviv University to cease their representation of the workers at the Open University.

The bar supported the students against the Rector's instruction, and pleaded with him to reconsider his order. In a letter sent to the Rector of Tel Aviv University by the Chair of the Ethics Committee,[129] the bar's predominance of loyalty for the client was zealously stressed. The bar urged the Rector to refrain from interfering with the professional decision of the students in the clinic, and indeed their representation was not interrupted.[130]

Conclusion and Thoughts for the Future

This chapter discusses the growth of CLE in Israel as walking in the path of the development of legal education in Israel. This topic, in turn, tells the story of the Israeli legal profession's evolution, which closely follows the story of establishment of the State and its institutions. As the State struggled to create its distinct identity while at the same time heavily relying on a British heritage and painful memories, so did the legal profession. The struggle between two poles pulling in different directions—public causes and private interests—influenced the legal academy when shaping Israeli legal education. With time, cause lawyering, although still not dominant in the profession presently, gradually gained weight. The worldwide and internal criticism of legal education drew more and more attention to the benefits of experiential learning. Along with the growing accessibility of legal education in Israel, the legal academy's role has shifted. The debate over this role—whether it should focus on the theoretical devolvement of the law or on the training of future lawyers—is becoming obsolete.

Today, Israel boasts CLE's definite presence in its law schools. All 14 legal education institutions in the country offer legal clinics as an inherent part of their curricula. Many of them offer multiple opportunities combined with social causes and legal training. Twenty-five years ago, Wizner asked, "What is a Law school?"[131] He claimed that if we only knew "what lawyers do—or ought to do—we should be able to design a curriculum that would prepare law students to carry out that professional role in a competent, ethical, socially responsible manner."[132] Perhaps he envisioned a dynamic much like the one taking place in Israel today.

Clinical education continually gains recognition and acknowledgment from both the legal profession and the academic community. The notion of a lawyer as a scientist whose laboratory is the library gives way to a different perception. The Israeli Code of Ethics for Legal Clinics clearly crowns the legal clinic as a laboratory for the research of law.[133]

However, it would be naive to consider the CLE forefathers' vision[134] a dream fulfilled in Israel. Many concerns still obscure the path to true reform. Changes in general are costly, and experiential learning seemingly demands even more. These progressions require the forfeit of deeply rooted beliefs regarding educational goals, the pedagogy derived from them, and the teaching staff performing them. Socially, it is difficult to expect the academic hegemony to step aside from a hierarchical position. Although it is unlikely that these changes would occur by a mere decision or a regulatory action, they lose viability without such official legitimization. Changes in curriculum design, staff recruitment, and promotion habits must embed themselves alongside old beliefs, allowing gentle growth alongside the carefully selected preservation of respected traditions.

As any reform, changes bring about both constructive and destructive effects. The line between meaningful learning and socially irresponsible service to the public can run thin at times. As Israeli legal education continues to cultivate CLE, institutions, clinicians, and students must remain closely monitored under ethical lenses. The doors to change are wide open, but the path must be walked with caution. Enriching Israeli scholarship and pedagogy in CLE innovations holds a key ingredient in promoting true reform in Israeli legal education. From here begins an essential step toward fulfilling CLE's social and educational goals.

Notes

1. Neta Ziv, "Combining Professionalism, Nation Building and Public Service: The Professional Project of the Israeli Bar 1928–2002" (2003) 71 *Fordham L. Rev.*1621, 1622; Assaf Likhovsky, *Law and Identity in Mandate Palestine* (The University of North Carolina Press, 2006).
2. Ziv, ibid. 1628.
3. Ibid. 1631.
4. Section 53, Israeli Bar Act, 1961; Section 2, Rules of the Bar (Professional Ethics), 1986.
5. Ziv (n 1) 1637.
6. Ibid. 1644–1646.
7. Ibid. 1623.
8. Ibid. 1662.
9. Yael Efron and Noam Ebner, "Legal Education in Israel: Developments and Challenges," in Shuvro P. Sarker (ed.) *Legal Education in Asia* (Eleven, 2014) 99, 103.
10. Ziv (n 1) 1650.
11. Ibid. 1665.
12. Ibid. 1666.
13. This is, of course, not unique to Israel, and has been a topic of debate wherever CLE is practiced. See, for example, discussion of the same issues with regard to law schools in the United States: http://bestpracticeslegaled.albanylawblogs.org/2014/02/12/building-on-best-practices-and-the-clinical-theory-workshop/

14. Noya Rimalt, "Legal Education: Between Theory and Practice" (2001) 24 *Tel Aviv U. L. Rev.* 81, 82 (Hebrew).
15. Ibid. 82.
16. Ibid. 129; Efron and Ebner (n 9) 116.
17. Yuval Elbashan, "On the Absence of Social Justice from the Legal Education in Israel" (2003) 3 *The Law Review of the Academic Center of Law & Business* 5 (Hebrew); Yaron Silverstein and Yael Efron, "Law Students as Agents of Social Change—Moral Values and Attitudes in Zefat College School of Law" (2014) 6 *TAU J. Law & Social Change* (Ma'asei Mishpat) 105 (Hebrew).
18. Elbashan, ibid. 8.
19. A term coined by Bowels and Gintis (1976) to describe the values underlying the curricular rationale without explicitly admitting to them.
20. Neta Ziv, "Two Decades of Cause Lawyering in Israel: Where Do We Go from Here?" (2008) 1 *TAU J. Law & Social Change* (Ma'asei Mishpat) 19 (Hebrew).
21. Ibid. 21.
22. Ibid. 19; Neta Ziv, "Legal Education and Social Responsibility: On the Link Between the Law Faculty and the Community in Which it is Placed" (2001) 25(2) *Theoretical Inquiries in Law* 385, 388 (Hebrew).
23. Stephen Wizner, "The Law School Clinic: Legal Education in the Interests of Justice" (2002) 70 *Fordham L. Rev.* 1929–1930.
24. Ziv (n 20) 388.
25. Wizner (n 23) 1935.
26. Ibid. 1634.
27. Ibid. (n 23).
28. Ibid. 1635.
29. Rimalt (n 14) 127; Silverstein and Efron (n 17) 22.
30. Ibid. (n 17) 22–23.
31. Elbashan (n 17) 8.
32. Menachem Mautner, *On Legal Education* (Tel-Aviv: Ramot Publishing House, 2002) 14 (Hebrew).
33. See, for example, the institutions with which the author is affiliated. The Hebrew University Faculty of Law: http://law.huji.ac.il/eng/about.asp?cat=2771 and Zefat Academic College School of Law: http://www.zefat.ac.il/?CategoryID=467&ArticleID=537&dbsAuthToken=
34. Such as contract law, torts, criminal law, and constitutional law.
35. Jurisprudence, law and economics, legal history, etc.
36. Yael Efron, "Legal Education in Israel: Where is it Headed?" (2011) 9 *Aley Mishpat* 45, 66 (Hebrew).
37. Mautner (n 32) 12.
38. This was the legacy of Harvard's legendary Dean from 1870 to 1895, Christopher Columbus Langdell. See Robert Stevens, *Law School: Legal Education in America from the 1850s to the 1980s* (The University of North Carolina Press, 1983) 36. The same notion was common in Europe as well around this time. The philosopher Wilhelm von Humboldt, who is considered the forefather of the new German university system in the 1900s, identified practical training as one of the excluding elements in the definition of a university, thus differentiating between a university and a vocational school. See Itzhak Englard, "Thoughts on Legal Education" (1982) 12 *Mishpatim* 217, 221 (Hebrew).
39. Mautner (n 32) 61.

40. This observation is discussed in Efron (n 36) 64–68.
41. Mautner (n 32) 30.
42. Uriel Procaccia, "Bubbles of Law: A Lecture for the School Year Opening" (1990) 20(1) *Hebrew U. L. Rev.* 9 (Hebrew).
43. Ziv (n 1), Wizner (n 23), and Efron (n 36).
44. Rimalt (n 14) 129.
45. Wizner (n 23).
46. Ibid.
47. The Board's activities are conducted by dedicated individuals, with no official title or regular budget. The information described hereafter was provided via e-mail correspondence by one of these devoted volunteers, Adv. Debby Sadeh, who presented it in the annual clinicians' meeting held in February 2014.
48. Summarized outcomes of this survey are on file with author. The Board wishes to issue the following disclaimer: the clinical field in Israeli legal education is rapidly changing, so differences from the time the information was gathered to the present day are expected. Furthermore, the lack of a unified terminology may also cause inaccuracy in the data, and should be taken into consideration.
49. The questionnaire is on file with author.
50. (n 48).
51. Ibid.
52. This information was also cross-checked and confirmed with the information gathered by a committee in the Israeli Bar Association, headed by former Justice Dan Bein, endowed with the mandate to grade law schools and faculties in Israel. The committee's report was published by the Bar in 1.12.2011. Israeli Bar Association, "Interim Report of the Bein Committee for Grading Legal Education Institutions" 10 (Hebrew) http://www.israelbar.org.il/article_inner.asp?pgId=122575&catId=156
53. Ibid.
54. Data with the author.
55. Grading of Colleges and Universities in Israel (Hebrew) http://www.campus-il.info/law/ono
56. (n 48).
57. For example, teaching, staff meetings, client counselling, and even for publicity purposes.
58. (n 48).
59. Ibid.
60. Ibid.
61. Efron and Ebner (n 9) 107.
62. See section 3.
63. Efron and Ebner (n 9) 104.
64. The descriptions used in the replies to the relevant question of the survey in supra note 47 included adjunct teacher, interior staff, external staff, teaching assistant, clinical staff, project employee, research employee, personal contract, special contract, doctoral fellowship stipend, volunteer, nonstaff, NGO employee, administrative contract, administrative staff, hourly employed, and research authority personnel.
65. More on these questions in section 4.1.
66. Ibid.
67. David Weiner Center for Professional Ethics of Lawyer, *Ethical Code for Legal Clinics* (2011) 9 (Hebrew).
68. (n 48).

69. Ibid.
70. Ibid.
71. Israeli Bar Act (n 4) Section 24.
72. See more on this debate in section 4.
73. See more on this in the next section 3.
74. (n 49).
75. (n 67).
76. The author of this chapter is a clinician at ZAC, and personally familiar with the legal clinics there. Complementary information was gathered with the assistance of clinicians at other institutions and the websites of the institutions.
77. This is the ethical requirement in the *Ethical Code for Legal Clinics* (n 67) 7, 9.
78. *Ethical Code for Legal Clinics* (n 67) 7, 9.
79. Rimalt (n 14).
80. See detailed information on the website of the Clinical Legal Education Centre at the Hebrew University Law Faculty at: http://law.huji.ac.il/merkazim.asp?cat=1946&in=475&ini=1
81. Ibid.
82. The American Bar Association included a standard for the study outside the classroom in the ABA Standards for Approval of Law Schools 2013–2014 (Standard 305). See http://www.americanbar.org/content/dam/aba/publications/misc/legal_education/Standards/2013_2014_standards_chapter3.authcheckdam.pdf. In Israel it is not the Bar that accredits law schools and no equivalent standard exists. However, even without the regulation requiring that it should be done, the practice of externships is quite common in Israeli legal clinics.
83. The terminology used in the United States for this type of learning is "field placement programs." Ibid. In this chapter, the term "externship" was chosen to differentiate the auspices of practicing lawyers from other nonacademic organizations, discussed in the next section, and also involving "field placement."
84. Dr. Mohammed S. Wattad: http://www.carmel.ac.il/?categoryid=1263&articleid=782
85. Yael Efron, "What Can be Taught by Clinical Teaching? Students' Experiences in an Israeli Legal Clinic" (work in progress). Recordings and transcripts of the interviews with students at ZAC's clinics, conducted for a study partly funded by the Galilee Research Center at ZAC, are on file with author.
86. Ibid.
87. Dr. Oren Asman: http://en.califtax-law.com/attorneys/oren-asman/
88. See an example report on this issue: Ashley Gallagher, "Some Wounded Syrians Seek Treatment from Israeli Hospitals" *Al-Jazeera America* (March 18, 2014). http://america.aljazeera.com/articles/2014/3/18/some-syrian-woundedseektreatment fromisraelihospitals.html.
89. (n 85).
90. One of these organizations is Schar Mitzvah, the pro bono service of the Israeli Bar (see http://www.israelbar.org.il/english_inner.asp?pgId=75176&catId=372). The other is the NGO Yedid, an association for community empowerment (see http://www.iataskforce.org/yedid-%E2%80%93-association-community-empowerment).
91. Students at this clinic undergo specific training at the partner organization before beginning their experience.
92. (n 85).
93. Jennifer S. Bard, "Practicing Medicine and Studying Law: How Medical Schools Used to have the Same Problems We Do and What We Can Learn from Their Efforts to Solve Them" (2011) 10 *Seattle J. for Soc. Just.* 135, 188.

94. Ibid. 189.
95. Wizner (n 23) 1933.
96. For example, Tel Aviv University benefited from the generous donation of the Ford Foundation as well.
97. Although colleges and universities may apply for special budgets for "community activities," and if granted may use these funds to operate the legal clinics.
98. In fairness, it should be stated that many of these corporations in Israel are NPOs, and not businesses that are concerned with shareholders' profits.
99. Yossi Melamed, "The Concept of Quality in Higher Education" (2003) *Derby University Newsletter* 2 (Hebrew) http://213.8.137.125/press/yosi.pdf.
100. Niva Elkin-Koren, "On the Colleges Revolution," a presentation at a Conference on Legal Education in the College of Management, Israel (October 21, 2010).
101. Bard (n 93) 160 details the manners in which medical schools are able to fund skills teaching and suggests that law schools adopt them as well.
102. John O. Sonsteng, Donna Ward, Colleen Bruce, and Michael Petersen, "A Legal Education Renaissance: A Practical Approach for the Twenty-First Century" (2007) 34(1) *Wm. Mitchell L. Rev.* 303,471–472.
103. Ibid. 469–471.
104. Bard (n 93) 184 observes law professors —for the most part—as ones who do not know, have, or value practical skills. On p. 198, she calls for skilled faculty to take a more significant role in law schools. This is specifically discussed concerning clinical faculty, 201–203.
105. (n 4).
106. Bard (n 93) 30 and 34; See also Brent E. Newton, "Preaching What They don't Practice: Why Law Faculties' Preoccupation with Impractical Scholarship and Devaluation of Practical Competencies Obstruct Reform in the Legal Academy" 62*S.C. L. Rev.* 105, 131–132.
107. From a symposium on "Teaching in a Transformative Era: The Law School of the Future" (December 2010) "information on how skills training was currently marginalized in law schools in that it was taught through the low status legal writing and research faculty rather than the more prestigious and scholarly doctrinal or casebook faculty . . . they showed how the task of teaching skills had been delegated to primarily female faculty members who held non-tenured positions and were almost always paid considerably less." Bard (n 93) 3–4. Her findings are detailed on p. 40.
108. Newton (n 106) 107.
109. Sonsteng et al. (n 102)467
110. Michael F. D. Young, "An Approach to the Study of Curricula as Socially Organized Knowledge," in Richard Brown (ed.) *Knowledge Education and Cultural Change* (Tavistock Publications, 1973).
111. Ivor Goodson and Ian Dowbiggin, "Docile Bodies: Commonalities in the History of Psychiatry and Schooling," in *The Changing Curriculum: Studies in Social Construction* (Peter Lang Publishing, 1997).
112. Ibid.
113. See http://www.law.tau.ac.il/Eng/?CategoryID=289
114. *Theoretical Inquiries in Law* was ranked first in impact factor ranking outside the United States in the Washington and Lee index for 2013. http://www.clb.ac.il/uploads/WL%20RANKING%202013.pdf
115. (n 67) 5.
116. Section 20, Israeli Bar Act, 1961.

117. Dror Arad-Eylon, "A Decision Regarding Associations, Non-profit Organizations and Legal Clinics" (2009)29 *Prof. Ethics* 1 (Hebrew).
118. See http://www.colman.ac.il/English/TeachingResearch/research_institutes/DavidWeinerCenterLaws_ProfessResp/Pages/default.aspx
119. (n 67).
120. Ibid 3.
121. Ibid 5.
122. Ibid 6.
123. Ibid 7.
124. Ibid 8.
125. Ibid 9.
126. Ibid 12.
127. Ibid 14.
128. The actions taken by the clinic in their advocacy are described in their annual report, seehttp://www.law.tau.ac.il/heb/?CategoryID=756 (Hebrew).
129. The letter from the Chair of the Bar's Ethics Committee to the Rector of Tel Aviv University was posted on the internet and became public knowledge. www.tau.ac.il/law/clinics/files-for-clinikan/200812emdalishka.doc (Hebrew).
130. See the clinic's report (n 128).
131. Stephen Wizner, "What is a Law School?" (1989) 38 *Emory L.J.* 701.
132. Ibid.
133. (n 67) 5.
134. Wizner (n 131) 709–712.

CHAPTER 7

Clinical Legal Education in Palestine: A Clinical Case under Military Occupation

Mutaz M. Qafisheh

Introduction

The legal clinic (hereafter "clinic") has expanded nationally, regionally, and internationally. This clinic may offer yet a further demonstration that, in the words of Frank Bloch, "clinical legal education has gone global."[1] The legal clinic of Hebron University represents an example of the ability of such clinics to start from scratch and gradually develop a system that suits a particular context. The clinic has played the key role in establishing the law school within two years. It has not only led the overall legal education process in campus but it also became a model for legal clinics in Palestine and the Middle East region.[2] The clinic, which was originally set up to provide pro bono services to marginalized groups and for students to practice law before graduation, now constitutes a hub of rights activism, policymaking, curricular development, practical training, conferencing, and networking with governmental bodies and civil society, as well as with international organizations well beyond the campus. This model proves that the capacity for law clinics to advance legal education is unbounded. Educators are still moving toward discovering the range of actions that young lawyers may afford to their local communities and to the world. However, the institutionalization of this clinic, as is the case with other legal clinics in Palestine and many Middle Eastern universities, is an issue that only the future can tell.

Hebron is the largest district in Palestine, with approximately 15 percent of the country's population.[3] Hebron University began with a single college in 1971. It now hosts ten colleges, over forty bachelor programs and seven master's programs, and has approximately 8,000 students, of whom about 70 percent are females.[4] The university established the Department of Law and Jurisprudence as part of the College of Islamic Law in September 2008, offering a Bachelor of Laws (LLB). It catered to the growing need for the study of law in Palestine in general and the Hebron district in particular. This led to the opening of the College of Law at Hebron University in August 2013.[5] The College has incorporated the existing Department of Law and Jurisprudence, in addition to two additional departments: the Department of Public Law and the Department of Private Law. The College will be the first law school in Palestine that grants three distinct undergraduate degrees in law.[6]

Due to the occupation, Palestinian universities were for some time prevented by Israel from initiating law programs. In 1986, Hebron University was the first Palestinian university to start teaching law.[7] However, implementation was blocked when Israel threatened to shut down the university if the teaching of law continued. It seemed that the Israelis feared the potential use of the vehicle of law and courts to resist their military actions.[8] The situation eased with the establishment of the Palestinian Authority after signing the Oslo interim agreement with Israel on September 13, 1993.[9] In 1995, Al-Quds became the first Palestinian university to start teaching an ongoing law program.[10] Ten years later, Al-Quds also became the first institution to set up a law clinic.[11]

This chapter is divided into three sections. Section 1 explores the Hebron University legal clinic itself: its context, location, governance and management, partnerships, and external relationships. Section 2 details the programs of the clinic, including its pro bono legal services, curricula development, formal and practical training, law profession and public awareness workshops, and academic activities. Section 3 highlights obstacles that clinical education faces in Palestine and proposes some ways to address them.

The Clinic

Context

In 2009, with the purpose of strengthening access to justice by low-income groups in Palestine, the UNDP supported the establishment of legal aid clinics in six Palestinian universities.[12] Hebron was one of them.[13] Of the schools that received funding, a few ceased operating the clinical programs after the funding ran out."[14] Clinical operations commenced in September 2011.[15] The university administration realized the significance of having a clinic, and now currently enjoys a strong reputation not only in the Hebron district but also at the national level. There are now established relations in place at the regional and global levels.[16]

The clinic seeks to encourage its students to practice law by applying their knowledge of legal theory in the provision of legal aid to community members.[17] Law students give pro bono legal assistance to certain marginalized groups. "The provision of legal aid services has been integral to many clinical legal education programs around the world."[18] The clinic has become the hub for legal information, training, and rights activism, and has given law students the opportunity to extend the application of their legal skills to law reform, research and advocacy, and public speaking skills through community legal education.[19]

On-Campus Clinic

The clinic operates from the campus of Hebron University because accessibility to the population is the primary consideration."[20] University students come from all over the city of Hebron and the surrounding countryside. Since it is located on campus, the clinic allows law students to work or volunteer between classes, conduct competitions in the moot court hall, and use the various meeting rooms, conference venues, libraries, and computer labs that are available.[21] It also allows the clinic to have easy access to the university's logistical and administrative support, including electronic and human resources support.

Governance

As with other colleges and research centers within the university with mandates exceeding any single department or college, the clinic falls within the administrative responsibility of the Vice President for Academic Affairs. The rationale is that, while the content of the clinic's work is legal, its services are provided to all university divisions, students, faculty members, and staff. The governance of the clinic is thus a departure from the standard approach in most universities around the world whereby legal clinics are placed within law schools. However, with the establishment of the College of Law in 2013 (above), the clinic is expected to be incorporated into the College.[22]

The clinic is supervised by an in-house board of directors composed of three to five full-time law faculty members and headed by the clinic's director. The board is in charge of supervising the ongoing work of the clinic. It assists in developing policies and strategies, and monitors the overall activities. It meets monthly to examine the clinic's plans, identify gaps, and recommend ways of resolving difficulties.[23] However, as in settings elsewhere in the world, there is a need for "demarcation between the governance of the clinic and daily operational management."[24] Indeed, "a board of directors needs to come to grips with its policy deliberation role alone and entirely opt out of management, which is the exclusive province of the clinical director(s)."[25] This situation is not confined to Hebron University. Legal clinics in most Palestinian universities are not completely free to set their own programs due to bureaucracy and the politics of university administrations that are often motivated by personal conflicts and funding constraints.[26]

Management

The day-to-day work of the clinic is conducted by its core administrative staff: the director, coordinator, and researcher.[27] The director is normally a professor of law who dedicates half of his time to clinical work. He determines the strategic goals of the clinic, designs its plans, represents it within the university's administration and beyond, conducts fundraising activities, and ensures proper implementation of the work plan. The coordinator and the researcher work on a full-time basis and are responsible for executing the work plan. Students volunteer in the clinic on a part-time basis.

The clinic has relationships with various departments and divisions of Hebron University. The senior management of the university provides overall policy guidance to the clinic, participates in the opening ceremonies of key activities, meets with senior partners, and officially signs the clinic's correspondence with heads of international organizations, ministers, governors, and the like. The clinic is supported by the university's Public Relations Division as its media office. The division publicizes clinical activities via the Internet and newspapers, and invites the media to cover events. On media issues, the clinic works with the university radio station (*Radio Alam*).[28]

Relationship with the College of Law

The relationship between the clinic and the College of Law is characterized by a certain amount of tension and interfaculty conflict. The positioning of the clinic within the office of the Vice-President for Academic Affairs gives it a position superior to that of the College. Due to the range of activities undertaken by the clinic with students from the College, some see the clinic as having overshadowed the College. The College has been left with the limited functions of in-class instruction, development of curricula and teaching materials, and evaluation of teaching staff. While at other universities the traditional "academic-professional divide in legal education"[29] has resulted in "the marginalisation of clinical academics,"[30] at Hebron University the clinical academics are placed in a superior position to the general academic faculty. The clinical faculty works theoretically (through classroom instruction in the same way as their academic peers) as well as practically in the clinic.

Within the previous Department of Law and Jurisprudence, the clinic successfully submitted proposals for reforming a number of courses that had been adopted as part of the department's curricula. The clinic introduced the Contract Law Course, which was in the past part of the general course on Civil Obligations. It suggested the adoption of the Principles of Criminal Law as a compulsory course, which did not exist in the previous curriculum, thus leaving students without such a significant framework. Similarly, the course Principles of Commercial Law, which did not exist before, has become part of the course Principles of Commercial Law and Companies Law. The course Enforcement of Court Judgments has been incorporated as an elective course. In fact, the clinic has been mandated to teach clinical education under the formal name Applied Training Course, which exists in the curriculum, de facto turning it into a clinical course.

External Relationships

Nothing can be more effective than the Hebron University clinic's relations with external partners. The clinic has managed to forge professional ties and implement joint programs with a number of local, regional, global governmental and nongovernmental institutions, other universities, and international organizations.

The clinic has worked with various ministers and departments of the Palestinian government at the local and national levels. Locally, the clinic has worked with the Hebron Governor, including participating in workshops related to security and crime revenge in the district,[31] and with municipalities by conducting field research on municipality services. At the national level, the clinic cooperated with the Palestinian Negotiations Affairs Department in developing policy papers[32] and participating in conferences,[33] with the Ministry of Justice,[34] the High Judicial Council,[35] the Ministry of Information,[36] the Civil Police,[37] the Ministry of Social Affairs,[38] the Office of Islamic (Family Law) Chief Justice,[39] and the Ministry of Economy.[40] The clinic implemented projects in partnership with the Independent Human Rights Commission, the official national human rights institution/ombudsperson of Palestine, by referring cases and conducting joint training courses (examples below). Such partnerships give the clinic staff and students the opportunity to network with official bodies, advocate policy reform ideas, and handle individual cases requiring formal intervention.[41]

In addition to the UNDP (the main clinic donor), international governmental and intergovernmental partners of the Hebron University clinic include the United Nations Office of the High Commissioner for Human Rights (organizing joint training courses and providing human rights publications), the United States Agency for International Development (supporting the establishment of the clinic's computer lab and renovation of the moot court hall), and the Temporary International Presence in Hebron (offering joint workshops and training).[42] Examples of activities that the clinic has undertaken with these organizations are below.

The clinic has established ongoing linkages with a number of international NGOs operating in Palestine, including the International Committee of the Red Cross, Terre des Hommes Foundation Lausanne, International Centre for Transitional Justice New York, Tiri-London, International Legal Foundation New York, and Defence for Children International. The activities the clinic takes part in with these NGOs range from participation in workshops, conferences, and training courses, to the development of joint projects. Local NGO partners include the Palestinian Centre for Development and Media Freedoms, Human Rights and Democracy Media Centre, Hebron Rehabilitation Committee, Hebron Defence Committee, Palestinian Institute for Human Rights, Women's Legal Aid and Counselling, and Palestinian Centre for the Independence of Judges and Lawyers. The following are examples of activities the clinic has implemented with NGOs.

The clinic has been involved in the organizing conferences, workshops, and joint training sessions with eight Palestinian universities: Al-Quds, Al-Najah, Al-Istiqlal, American Arab, Al-Azhar, Al-Ahliya, Birzeit, and Palestine Polytechnic. It has initiated contacts with 13 new legal clinics in the Arab world, including in Bahrain, Egypt, Iraq, Lebanon, Jordan, and the United Arab Emirates. The clinic has established institutional ties with the Washington College of Law at the American University in the United States. It has academic contacts with the following universities in the United States: Boston, Catawba, Fordham, Gonzaga, Cornell, Florida, Georgetown, Johns Hopkins, Ohio State University, Washington and Lee, Vanderbilt, and University of Virginia; in the United Kingdom: Cambridge, London, Oxford, Queen's(North Ireland), Northumbria, and York; in France: Aix-en-Provence, Aix-Marseille, Caen Basse-Normandie; in India: Gauhati,

Raksha Shakti, and West Bengal National University of Juridical Sciences; in Canada: Toronto and Western Ontario in Canada; and the following universities: Geneva (Switzerland), KwaZulu-Natal (South Africa), Monash (Australia), and Osijek (Croatia), as well as the International Judicial Academy, the World Academy of Art and Science, and the Global Alliance for Justice Education.

The clinic has similarly developed relationships with various media outlets, including newspapers, television stations, electronic media, and radio stations. Clinic activities are reported by a number of daily newspapers: *Al-Quds*, *Al-Ayam*, *Al-Hayat*, and *Hebron Times*. Its activities are also covered by a number of satellite television stations: Palestine TV, Al-Quds, Mix-Maan, and Palestine Today. Well-known electronic media sites report the clinic's activities, including Maan News Network, Al-Jazeera, Palestine News Network, and Qantara, Shasha, in addition to social media networks and the Hebron University website. Radio stations that broadcast clinic news include the Voice of Palestine Radio, Huriya Radio, Rabia Radio, and Ajyal Radio.

In a place relatively distant from the country's center, as is Hebron, external partnerships are crucial for law students. Students, who largely come from the countryside, have the opportunity to initiate contacts with prominent institutions and learn from their expertise.[43] In the words of one law student at Hebron University, "As we cannot travel abroad, the clinic has brought the world home. With the clinic we now know how official institutions, courts, NGOs, and international organizations interact. By learning about programs of other universities from clinic's visiting professors and practitioners, we realize who we are. We know that we are also as good as them."[44]

The Clinic Actions

The clinic of Hebron University was initially set up to provide free legal assistance to enlarge access to justice for marginalized groups within the local community and to equip law students with practical skills that enable them to transition smoothly into the legal profession.[45] The role of the clinic has, however, expanded considerably. It now contributes to curriculum development within the university. Through its symposia, the clinic brings together lawyers, judges, prosecutors, professors, and students. Academic conferences organized by the clinic demonstrate that clinics can contribute to the research and theoretical life of universities, while at the same time focusing on legal practice and student careers.

A Generalist Clinic

Unlike other legal clinics that have a specialized focus on, for example, labor law,[46] women's rights,[47] refugees,[48] or people with disabilities,[49] Hebron University's clinic adopts a general multidisciplinary mandate.[50] The clinic deals with a wide range of matters, including human rights, criminal law, health law, juvenile justice, family law, and landlord and tenant law. One reason for adopting a general mandate was the perceived lack of specialized students or lawyers who could work exclusively on a particular area of focus.[51] It was also felt that, given the absence of any other legal aid clinic at the university or within the local area, the clinic should not turn clients away on the basis that their matter did not fall within a specialist mandate.

The clinic does already appear to be moving toward a form of de facto specialization. Most of the cases received by the clinic to date have concerned landlord and tenant law, labor law, family law, and criminal law. Given the specific context of the military occupation in Palestine, and precisely due to the presence of armed Israeli settlers in the Hebron city center, as indicated above, the clinic has dealt with a number of human rights and humanitarian law abuses through the United Nations Human Rights Special Procedures. It took a role in documenting human rights violations by participating in campaigns in partnership with NGOs. Indeed, human rights cases often lead to disappointing outcomes as a result of a lack of governmental collaboration.[52]

Pro Bono Legal Aid

The provision of pro bono legal assistance is the traditional task of legal clinics around the world,[53] and is a core function of the clinic. Clients are offered legal advice directly by the law students who enroll in the clinical course or by volunteers under the clinic staff's supervision. Clients are sometimes referred by the clinic to relevant government institutions, civil society bodies, or international organizations, such as the United Nations Human Rights Special Procedures, or private lawyers.[54]

In the year 2012–2013, as a typical instance, the Hebron University clinic handled some 50 cases on various legal matters. These cases included topics relating to the right of blind people to education, landlords and tenants, medical malpractice, inheritance, divorce disputes, road accidents, health insurance, arbitrary arrest, extradition, and theft. In effect, the clinic now acts as on-campus law firm.[55]

As a step toward financial sustainability, the clinic is considering reaching agreements with private lawyers to refer certain cases to them. Such cases normally relate to civil/money-generating matters such as labor law, landlord and tenant law, and medical malpractice. The lawyers to whom the matters are referred usually deduct a percentage (normally 10 percent to 15 percent) from the compensation that the client receives from the other side. It has been suggested that the clinic should receive 50 percent of the lawyer's revenue.[56] However, lawyers sometimes refer cases to the clinic, normally small-scale disputes, matters from low-income clients, or issues related to conflict with the government in which NGO intervention is needed.[57]

Interactive Teaching

When the clinic opened in September 2011, there was no clinical course delivered by the Department of Law and Jurisprudence. There was, however, a course named Applied Training Course (above). The clinic assumed responsibility for teaching this course, which was converted, in practice, into a clinical course. This was similar to other practices in some Middle Eastern countries, such as in Jordanian and Iraqi universities.[58] All graduating students were required to enroll in this course.[59]

The approach taken to the teaching of law at Hebron University is similar to that of other Arab universities:[60] a theoretical approach following the Continental model.[61] The clinic, however, takes a more practical method by focusing on case analysis, field research, presentations by students, group work, court visits, and invitations to external experts to come in and train students on selected topics.[62] These methods were used in the teaching of a number of courses: Public Administration Law, Public International Law, Constitutional Law, and Criminal Law. Students are organized into working groups, and each group conducts fieldwork. Each group studies a given government department at the district level and reviews the legal basis of the department under consideration in order to conduct brainstorming discussions, prepare questions, distribute tasks among its members, interview government officers, and make assessments of the department's mandate, functions, staffing, policies, relation with the central government and with other departments, resources, transparency, corruption, and reform plans.[63]

Through this process, students develop relationships with government offices and learn about the interaction between law and the bureaucracy.[64] This, in turn, has the potential to contribute in the long term to administrative, policy, financial, and legal reform.[65] As Clapman observes, "clinics have the potential to dramatically effect evolving legal systems in transitional democracies; by improving general access to justice; by directly exposing law students . . . to the legal needs and problems of the poor; and by calling attention to shortcomings in these legal systems."[66]

Formal Training

Practical legal training sessions are an integral part of the Hebron clinic. The objective of these sessions is to prepare law students for postgraduation careers. Such courses address issues that are not incorporated into the regular law curriculum. Through such trainings, students deal with fields of law in which they have "had no previous classroom instruction. In such work the seamless web quality of the law is brought forcibly to mind. Resourcefulness is at a premium."[67] Half of the marks are allocated for attendance and the other half for a short report in which each student explains what he or she learned, skills gained, and recommendations for improvement.

The clinical course can consist of different training modalities that may vary from one semester to the next. The 2012 clinical course comprised four training modules: legal writing, lawyering skills, procedural law, and study visits. The 2013 course consisted of a series of targeted training sessions on selected practical topics.[68] The following is some elaboration of these two modalities.

Model Course I: Four Modules

Legal Drafting

The clinic organizes training modules on the skill of legal drafting. In the 2012 semester, this module lasted for five intensive days, eight hours per day. The course was given one week before the beginning of the semester in which the students take the clinical course. The course aims to enhance students' skills in various types of legal writing, including legislative drafting, writing of contracts, formulating legal opinions, designing complaints, and documenting human rights violations. Topics also included the making of legislative policy and its translation into law or regulation, crafting petitions, writing legal letters, and writing oral pleadings and court decisions. The trainers were exclusively practitioners: judges, lawyers, advisers, and experts from different organizations.[69]

Lawyering Skills

With the objective of enhancing the capacity of students to provide legal advice at the clinic and to gain the practical skills necessary for any practicing lawyer, the clinic organized an intensive training course on lawyering skills. The course included topics on client-lawyer theory, client interviewing techniques, and alternative dispute resolution, with a focus on mediation and negotiation.[70] In the spring semester of 2012, for example, the training was led by Professor David Chavkin of the Washington Legal Clinic at the American University's College of Law. This training included students and staff from various Palestinian clinics.[71]

Procedural Law

Realizing that no curriculum of any law school can cover all legal matters even for a given jurisdiction, the clinic complemented the law curriculum of Hebron University by delivering a skill-oriented training module, focusing on procedural law as it is applied by courts and law enforcement officials. For example, a course called Enforcement Court Judgments was not included in the Department of Law and Jurisprudence curriculum, and thus the clinic filled this gap by offering a training on the enforcement of court judgments. Trainers in such modules have included judges and court staff working exclusively in executing court judgments. The clinic provided sessions on criminal investigation techniques and family procedures law. These sessions were based on actual cases rather than on textbooks.

Study Visits

To ensure that students are exposed to actual life, the clinic organizes visits for students to the magistrates' courts, family courts, courts of first instance, and the Supreme Court. Attendance at a minimum number of court sessions was a requirement for students to pass the course. The clinic also organized study visits to the Forensic Medicine Institute to observe the autopsy of the body of a crime victim, and study tours to the police academy to observe a moot investigation process at the "criminal scene." Students met with police investigators and prosecutors.[72]

Model Course II: Targeted Sessions

In 2013, the clinical course was implemented through a series of training sessions on selected topics relevant to the practice of law. Such sessions were provided by practitioners based on actual cases. Some of the sessions that were held in 2013 were as follows: Techniques of Advice at the legal clinicdelivered as an orientation by the clinic staff; Practical Cases on Labour Law; Legal Professional Responsibility;Registration of Real Estate Contracts; The United Nations Special Rapporteurs; Skills on Traffic Insurance Law; Civil Procedures That Lawyers Tend to Miss; Cases on Criminal Investigations; Selected Cases and Procedure on Guardianship and Alimony; Cases on Arbitration Law; Starting as a Trainee Lawyer; Land Lord and Tenant Law, and Practice and Procedures before the Palestinian High Court of Justice.

Extracurricular Training

Moot Court

The clinic conducts regular sessions on moot court competitions. Law students learn about moot pleadings and hearings: preparing memorials and counter-memorials and playing the roles of judges, lawyers, prosecutors, plaintiffs, and defendants. In 2013, the clinic trained 12 law students on international humanitarian law and international criminal law for one full semester as part of a program facilitated by Al-Quds University. The Hebron University team won the national competition that took place in Ramallah, Palestine, July 1, 2013. The Hebron University's team was ranked first among the five competing Palestinian universities; it won the three awards available within the competition: Best Team, Best Prosecution Verbal Pleading, and Best Defence Verbal Pleading.[73] Earlier, in April 2012, the clinic organized an international law competition, and five students won it.[74] Then these five students participated in a national competition among four Palestinian universities in July 2012 in Nablus, Palestine, as part of the Jessup International Law Moot Court Competition.[75] Selected students emerging from such processes are normally nominated to take part in international competitions abroad.[76]

Human Rights Training

With the objective of improving the international legal skills of law students, and taking into account the particular context of the occupied Palestinian territory, the clinic organizes training courses on selected international law issues.

In May 2012, the clinic organized a training course on Humanitarian Law and the United Nations Human Rights Mechanisms in cooperation with the United Nations Office of the High Commissioner for Human Rights and the Temporary International Presence in Hebron. The course consisted of two parts. The first was open to the general public and students. The second part was confined to law students and focused on reporting techniques and the documentation of human rights violations.[77] In December 2012, the clinic organized a workshop on juvenile justice in Palestine in collaboration with the Swiss Terre des Hommes Foundation and Defence for Children International. The event incorporated stakeholders working in the field of juvenile justice: prosecutors, lawyers, social workers, and law students. It aimed to contribute to Palestinian juvenile justice reform to serve the child's best interests and sought to promote specialization of the judiciary, prosecution, the police, and probation officers.[78] Moreover, the clinic organized two training courses on the Prohibition of Torture in International and Domestic Law in partnership with the Palestinian Human Rights Commission and the Office of the Attorney General in June and July 2013.[79]

Language Training

Although operating at the local level, the clinic views itself as part of the global movement of clinical legal education (CLE). To this end, it organizes training courses on English and French languages. For instance in June and July 2012, during the summer holiday in which standard university courses are less demanding, the clinic conducted an intensive training course on the French language for law students. A follow-up plan would include a selected number of students to pursue specialized juridical French language courses. Likewise, the clinic is planning to organize a series of general English and legal English courses to enhance its students' skills in this language, with focus on legal writing. Multilanguage skills would enlarge students' potential to find better jobs and scholarships in various countries worldwide.[80]

Internship

The clinic opens the door for regular internship programs, which enable new law graduates or soon-to-be-graduated students to work in the clinic. Examples of internships include a program on juvenile justice funded by the Terre des Hommes Foundation Lausanne.[81] The project has been jointly implemented by the Ministry of Social Affairs with the involvement of judges, prosecutors, police, probation officers, the Ministry of Education, and NGOs. As part of the project, two law students affiliated with the clinic were hired for a paid externship funded by NGOs. Another internship program on criminal justice aid is projected to be initiated in partnership with the International Legal Foundation, a New York-based organization, in partnership with Washington and Lee University, Virginia, in the United States.[82]

Practical Symposia

The clinic engages the legal community through a series of lectures and symposia. In the beginning of its operation, the clinic desired to disseminate the clinical concept outside the campus. To this end, in December 2011, the clinic hosted David Chavkin, professor of Clinical Legal Education at American University in Washington, DC, who delivered a public lecture on "Legal Clinics: Concept, History, and Functions." Chavkin hinted at the significance of having a clinic at the university and pointed out that the Hebron Clinic has become "part of the global movement of legal clinics in the United States, Canada, Latin America, Europe, Asia and Africa."[83] The clinic also seeks to expand lawyers' knowledge beyond local cases. Hence, in April 2012, it hosted Chavkin again to talk, this time about the "Jury System in the United States." The level of attendance and discussion at this session showed the enthusiasm of Palestinian students and jurists for learning from others' experiences.[84]

Events that target the general public, particularly university students other than those studying law, are part of the clinic's agenda as well. Such activities address issues existing in the community or relating to the general interest of law students. Specialists (e.g., jurists, government officials, journalists, civil society) are invited as resource persons. In February 2012, the clinic, in partnership with the College of Shari'ah and the Human Rights and Democracy Media Centre, held a seminar on death penalty in international law and Islamic law.[85] Also in February 2012, the clinic conducted a seminar on media freedoms in Palestine in cooperation with the Ministry of Information and the Centre for Development and Media Freedoms.[86] In May 2012, the clinic and the Hebron Defence Committee showed a movie called *Roadmap to Apartheid* that compares the systematic human rights violations that Israel is committing in Palestine with the policies that were practiced by South Africa.[87] Also in May 2012, the clinic, in cooperation with the Temporary International Presence in Hebron and the UN Office of the High Commissioner for Human Rights, organized a seminar on the applicability of humanitarian law and human rights in Palestine[88] (above). In December 2012, in partnership with Hebron University's Department of Political Science, the clinic held a seminar on the "Egyptian Political Scene" with the purpose of raising awareness on the constitution-making process in neighboring countries, particularly in the context of the "Arab Spring" and the revolutions sweeping the region.[89] In February 2013, the clinic organized a seminar on "Israeli Elections and the Prospects for Palestinian Elections," with the objective of assessing the impact of the latest election in Israel on the question of Palestine and the possibility of holding Palestinian elections as a step toward political conciliation in light of the American foreign policy. Speakers came from American, Israeli, and Palestinian universities.[90]

Through such activities in which law students and faculty members participate in the discussions, the connection is established between the university and its educational and social justice mission.[91]

Regional and Global Events

To enlarge its reach beyond Palestine and to learn from developments in the world, the clinic takes part in regional and international events.[92]

The clinic was invited to the United Nations conference on the "Question of Palestine" that took place in April 2012 at the United Nations Office in Geneva. The meeting discussed the "question of Palestinian political prisoners in Israeli prisons and detention facilities: legal and political implications." The clinic was represented by its director, who presented a paper entitled "Political Prisoners in Peace Processes and Peace Agreements: The Case of Palestine/Israel *vs.* Namibia/South Africa." The meeting was attended by a Palestinian delegation that included the Minister of Prisoners Affairs, Prisoners Club, law professors, and representatives of human rights NGOs, in addition to representatives of various United Nations member states. The meeting addressed the rights of Palestinian prisoners in light of the Geneva Conventions, human rights, and ways to bring an end to the suffering of Palestinian prisoners, inhumane treatment, torture, and maltreatment.[93]

The clinic participated in and presented a paper at the Tenth Annual Conference of the *International Journal of Clinical Legal Education* held at Northumbria University in Durham, United Kingdom, in July 2012. This conference serves as forum in which clinical educators from various jurisdictions come together to discuss clinical education in order to share best practices. It brought together academics, lawyers, students, and social activists with a mix of keynote speeches, panel discussion, formal presentation, and interactive workshop sessions. The conference themes include trends in international clinical education, internationalizing clinics, clinic twinning projects, assessment/grading of clinical education, evidencing best practices, new clinics and new clinicians, review of clinical operations, and student and faculty attitudes toward clinical learning.[94]

In March 2013, the clinic attended and delivered a paper at the First International Conference on Legislative Drafting and Law Reform in Washington, DC. The event, which was organized by the US Federal Bar Association, the International Judicial Academy, and the International Journal of Legislative Drafting and Law Reform, was attended by experts on legislative drafting and legal reform from various parts of the world. The event discussed a number of topics, including statutory interpretation, the role of Islamic law in the interpretation of constitutions, a comparison of legislative drafting in the United States and Europe, teaching skills and techniques of legislative drafting in legal clinics and law schools, technology and legislative drafting, and the role of legislative drafting in law reform with special reference to transitional states.[95]

In May 2013, the clinic represented Palestine at an international law conference on "Legal Tradition in a Diverse World" hosted by the *Cambridge Journal of International and Comparative Law* at the University of Cambridge, United Kingdom. The conference was attended by academics from all continents and some 50 papers were discussed. The clinic presented a paper entitled "The Coexistence of Diverse Legal Traditions in a Single Territory: The Case of the Freedom of Expression in Palestine." The paper explored the freedom of press, freedom of assembly, freedom of association, freedom of religion, and privacy, within the legal system of Palestine.[96]

In June 2013, the clinic chaired a session at the think-tank expert meeting on "Search for an Alternative Paradigm to address the Multi-dimensional Global Crisis," which was organized by the World Academy of Art and Science at the Library of Alexandria, Egypt. The clinic director joined 20 thinkers from selected institutions around the world, who discussed multidisciplinary issues, including security, economy, education, law, technology, global warming, financial instability, pollution, unemployment, inequality, arms proliferation, and social unrest. The participants found that, while the world is facing an unprecedented dilemma, expanding opportunities are emerging side by side with intensifying problems.[97]

Also in June 2013, the clinic director acted as an expert at a regional workshop initiated by the American Bar Association in Amman, Jordan. The purpose of the event was to train newly established legal clinics in Jordan on the methods of work at legal clinics. In addition to the legal clinic of Hebron University, training at the workshop was delivered by clinicians from the United States, Lebanon, Jordan, and Bahrain. The experts presented steps toward setting up new clinics and furthering the advancement of existing clinics. A group of law professors from the University of Jordan, Yarmouk University, Al-Israa University, Al-Albayt University, the Middle East University, Philadelphia University, and other institutions attended the workshop.[98]

Academic Programs

With a view to encouraging Palestinian scholars to address legal issues relating to the applicable law in the country using comparative and global approaches, the clinic organizes national and international conferences. It also initiated the launching of a refereed law journal and formulated a master's program on international law.

To support the legislator in drafting modern legislation, the clinic held a national conference in March 2012 on family law in the context of the decree signed by the Palestinian president on March 8, 2009, declaring that the International Convention of the Elimination of All Forms of Discrimination of Women is part of Palestinian law. While the *Jordanian Personal Status Law* of 1976 in the West Bank differs from the Egypt-enacted family law of 1954 in the Gaza Strip, both contradict international standards.[99] Fifteen papers were presented that dealt with issues ranging from marriage age to polygamy, divorce, alimony, guardianship, wills, and inherence.[100]

To be part of recent legal issues that have strategic impact, the clinic held an international conference on the legal and political implications of the membership of Palestine in the United Nations in April 2012.[101] Twenty-six papers were presented by professors of international law, political science, history, and economics from various Palestinian universities and from Oxford, Ohio, Geneva, Georgetown, Florida, London, and American University, Washington, DC. The outcome of this conference was a volume of collected essays published in 2013 by the Cambridge Scholars Publishing, United Kingdom.

The clinic is initiating a master's in international law and human rights as a multidisciplinary program that will be open to students from various backgrounds: law, political science, history, media, and economics. The program will be the first of its type in Palestine. The two-year program includes compulsory courses on human rights, humanitarian law, international relations, refugee law, and international organizations; and elective courses on issues such as human rights documentation, the United Nations system, the Palestinian-Israel conflict, settlements of disputes, and the environment.

Conclusions: Challenges and Promises

Financing is expected to remain the main obstacle, casting doubt on the very existence of the clinics.[102] At present, all Palestinian legal clinics are funded by external donors. Universities still view clinics as new and untested, and it may take some time for universities to realize the relevance of clinics to academic programs. In the short term, it is unlikely that universities will allocate funds for clinics. Clinics are still perceived, as in other countries, as "a relatively expensive form of legal education,"[103] and legal clinics do not generate direct revenues to universities.[104] International donors are increasingly interested in promoting legal clinics, but most clinics are funded on an annual basis, with no assurances regarding the continuation of funding (or even the existence of some clinics) in the following year.

If well funded, clinics offer a treasure to universities.[105] Clinics can conduct practical research, facilitate policy forums, and form training centers on the rule of law, human rights, judicial reform, access to justice, and by becoming recognized specialists in these areas they might attract project funding. A clinic can generate funds by representing certain clients and deducting a percentage from their successful claims. Or clinics can refer cases to practicing lawyers in return for a share of any successful outcome. The courses delivered by the clinics may attract tuition fees.

In order to maintain clinics with or without having external donors, universities need to parentally link the clinics' management with existing administrative structures. For example, a clinic's director could be the director of another department and be assisted by other colleagues assigned with clinical tasks either as part of their academic instruction or as part of their administrative responsibilities. One secretary in the department or college could simultaneously serve as secretary of the clinic. The staff of the clinic could be assisted or supplemented by law students who enroll in the clinical course for credits and grades, or who volunteer for the purpose of an internship or of acquiring practical experience needed for their curriculum vitae.

Clinics in Palestine, particularly in Hebron, need to more clearly define their relations with colleges of law. Clinics are still viewed as "projects," temporary programs seen by most universities as a means of generating money. In certain universities, clinics are established for cosmetic reasons or as a public relations exercise to show that the university has embraced modern trends in legal education. Universities must be encouraged to integrate clinics into the administrative structures of the colleges of law, giving clinics a status similar to research centers, laboratories, or other academic programs or departments.

In Palestine, as elsewhere in the Middle East, the typical approach to teaching law is the traditional one: "lecture and leave." Professors tend to have their own law offices, provide freelance consultancies, or spend most time on their own academic research. Such attitudes need to be changed. Universities must assign to clinics lawyers willing to teach on a full-time basis. Professors should also be trained to use clinical methods in various doctrinal classes. A number of them do use such methods already, but many others still prefer a purely theoretical approach. Such changes would gradually create a generation of law professors specialized in clinical education.[106]

According to Law Profession No. 3 of 1999,[107] only lawyers who register with the Palestine Bar Association after passing the two-year apprenticeship may appear before courts (Article 3). Neither law students nor legal clinics, as legal entities, are permitted to represent clients in courts. Clinics, however, may represent clients by hiring lawyers to work on a full- or part-time basis. The students can in reality do much of the work associated with a legal matter, including preparing memorials and counter-memorials, conducting legal research, and drafting letters, notifications, oral pleadings, and the like, while the formal appearance is made by the clinic's lawyer.

Concern might be raised about the ability of law students to provide meaningful legal opinions, let alone be capable of representing clients before courts. This concern is legitimate because law is still taught theoretically.[108] Students are sometimes out of touch with procedures and would usually only become familiar with the reality of legal practice after completing the postgraduation apprenticeship.[109] Students in Palestine, as in Middle Eastern and European countries, go directly from high school to study law, typically at 18 years of age, unlike those in North America, where students come to law school equipped with an undergraduate degree in another field. While the question of age and experience would be overcome by allowing students to work in clinics only during the final year of their study, such concerns will continue to be an obstacle facing clinics if the current teaching methods persist.[110]

The final factor influencing the future of legal clinics is the attitude of practicing individual lawyers toward clinics. Some lawyers perceive clinics as a threat and a source of competition, since clinics provide a free service that might turn clients away from law offices and toward universities. This has also occurred in other countries at the initial stages of clinical education. In Canada, for example, "Canadian clinics faced early opposition from the practicing profession."[111] In England, "self-interested local solicitors were concerned that 'some of their potential clients were obtaining free legal services at the clinics.'"[112] Such an attitude is expected to diminish when a number of points are clarified: that clinics normally handle small-scale cases that lawyers would not benefit from; that clinics assist low-income people who could not get legal services elsewhere; and that clinics may even benefit lawyers by referring cases to them. Clinics need to raise the awareness of lawyers on such points.

The journey of the Hebron University legal clinic over the past two years shows that clinics can play a far greater role than we might anticipate. It could rise out of its contextual local space (although fully engaged with local community matters) and reach out regionally and globally. It may offer a model for what Bloch once called "the global reach of clinical legal education."[113] The clinic has learned, and is still learning, from the experiences of others, while maintaining its own characteristics and develop its own program of actions as a response to the needs of its students and community. The unprecedented collaboration among clinicians in various counties of the world is expected to change the entire notion of locality. What is local in a certain place will affect other locations with rapid communication and exchange facilities. Thus in order for any legal clinic to have a global reach, it should develop its own programs and services based on the needs of its local context. That is what may turn the clinic, if successful, into a model that can be replicated and followed elsewhere.

In an ever-competing world, the necessity of having a legal clinic in each law school should be beyond question. I cannot imagine how our students would enter the market should they have no past clinical exploration. In the clinic, students not only provide legal advice and serve their communities but they also learn how to deal with each other, with practitioners, with governments, with NGOs, with judges, lawyers, business people, and so forth. They can realize that the law is a social animal that is beyond formal texts. We should stop thinking that clinics represent a certain culture or pedagogical approach. We should cease to develop clinics to satisfy donors or attract funds. Legal clinics are not public relations fabrics or tactical cosmetics. I believe that these clinics offer a way of life and that once we enter it, we cannot leave it.

Despite the existence of six legal clinics in Palestine and the plans to open more in other universities, the country's CLE system remains in transition. Notwithstanding the clinical achievements over the past few years, the future of clinical pedagogy remains uncertain. It may take many years for clinics to take a firm root in the frameworks of legal education, professional training, bar associations' rules and policies, and legal aid modalities. Thus far, law schools have not formulated a clear or uniform system for clinics within the academic curricula. After obtaining their degree, graduated law students spend two years practicing law before being qualified as lawyers, regardless of the time that they might have spent in clinics. The bar has recently reformed the apprenticeship system by requiring trainee lawyers to attend a number of practical training classes, to write a research paper, and to sit for preadmission and final bar exams. The bar, however, has ignored the linkages between the apprenticeship and clinics or legal aid. The recently (2012) bar-led Legal Aid draft law has similarly failed to recognize clinics as a means for providing aid.

In this chapter we argued, by using the model of the Hebron University legal clinic as a case in point, that the capacity of university clinics to advance legal education, to complement the apprenticeship stage, to strengthen the legal profession, and to become a primary legal aid provider, is unbounded. We elaborated on certain areas that should be reformed in order to develop a coherent clinical system that goes in parallel with the systems of professional training, practice, and legal aid. The chapter pursued a comparative approach by looking at models of successful clinical programs in various countries, using available scholarship, and drawing on the personal experience of the writer as the director of the said clinic.[114]

Despite being at the beginning stage, Palestine's CLE has not achieved any less than other clinics in many countries of the world over the past few years. Many legal clinics could achieve, by dwelling on the experiences of others, what others have developed over decades. Yet the uncertainty that surrounds the future of clinical legal pedagogy is attributable to the fact that we, the educators, still think in old ways. In order for clinics to take a firm root in the framework of legal education and professional training, we need to change our perception of teaching and learning. We need to change the legal profession law. We need to change the apprenticeship system and the concept of legal aid.

Notes

1. Frank S. Bloch (ed.) *The Global Clinical Movement: Educating Lawyers for Social Justice* (Oxford University Press, 2011).
2. This article builds upon a shorter article by Mutaz Qafisheh, "The Role of Legal Clinics in Leading Legal Education: A Model from the Middle East" (2012) 22 *Legal Educ. Rev.* 177.
3. In July 2013, the inhabitants of Hebron were estimated at 662,454, while Palestine's population was 4.42 million. Palestinian Central Bureau of Statistics, Press Release (Ramallah, July 11, 2013).
4. Hebron University Brochure, Hebron, Palestine, September 2012.
5. *Al-Quds*, 15807 (Jerusalem, August 14, 2013) 9.
6. A fourth undergraduate degree in Islamic Law (called "Jurisprudence and Legislation") is granted by the College of Islamic Law. This is a separate degree from those degrees offered at the College of Law.
7. A copy of the Department of Law profile exists in Hebron University archives.
8. Meeting with Dr. Othman Takrouri, Former President of Hebron University; currently Judge at the Palestine Supreme Court (Ramallah, March 29, 2012).
9. Declaration of Principles on Interim Self-government Arrangements (Washington, DC, September 13, 1993).
10. Munir Nuseibah, "Clinical Legal Education in an Occupied Territory: Attempting to Bridge the Human Rights Standards Gap" presentation delivered at the *Tenth Conference of the International Journal of Clinical Legal Education*, July 11–13, 2012.
11. David Chavkin, "Thinking/Practicing Clinical Legal Education from within the Palestinian-Israeli Conflict: Lessons from the Al-Quds Human Rights Clinic" (2010) 18 *Hum. Rts .Brief* 14.
12. UNDP, "Supporting the Rule of Law and Access to Justice for the Palestinian People," agreement signed by the Palestinian Minister of Justice and Minister of

Planning and Administrative Development with UNDP Special Representative in Palestine (Ramallah, September 2009) 13.

13. The other UNDP-supported clinics are Al-Najah and Al-Quds universities in the West Bank; and Al-Azhar, Islamic, and Palestine universities in the Gaza Strip.
14. Jeff Giddings, Roger Burridge, Shelley Gavigan, and Catherine Klein, "The First Wave of Modern Clinical Legal Education: The United States, Britain, Canada and Australia," in Frank S. Bloch (ed.) *The Global Clinical Movement: Educating Lawyers for Social Justice* (Oxford University Press, 2011).
15. *Al-Hayat*, 5717 (Ramallah, October 3, 2011) 15.
16. On May 28, 2012, the Hebron Clinic and 14 other clinics established the Middle East and North Africa Legal Clinics Alliance at the Middle East Regional Colloquium on Clinical Legal Education, organized by the Johns Hopkins University School of Advanced International Studies, United States, in cooperation with the Global Alliance for Justice Education. On November 6, 2012, six legal clinics in Palestinian universities from the West Bank and Gaza agreed to form the "Palestinian Union of Legal Clinics (PULC)." Edward Santow and George Wachira, "The Global Alliance for Justice Education," in Frank S. Bloch (ed.) *The Global Clinical Movement: Educating Lawyers for Social Justice* (Oxford University Press, 2011);Ibid 371.
17. Frank Dignan, "Bridging the Academic/Vocational Divide: The Creation of a Law Clinic in an Academic Law School" (2011) 16 *Int'l J. Clin. Legal Educ.* 75.
18. Frank S. Bloch and Mary A. Noone, "Legal Aid Origins of Clinical Legal Education," in Frank S. Bloch (ed.) *The Global Clinical Movement: Educating Lawyers for Social Justice* (Oxford University Press, 2011) 153, 164.
19. See the website of Hebron University Legal Clinic at www.hebron.edu/LegalClinic.
20. Margaret M. Barry, "Clinical Legal Education in the Law University: Goals and Challenges"(2007) 12 *Int'l J. Clin. Legal Educ.* 27, 46.
21. Kathryn Munn, "Clinical Legal Education Through the Looking-Glass" (1989) 12 *Dalhousie L.J.* 505, 521.
22. Meeting between the author and the president of Hebron University, August 11, 2013.
23. Margaret M. Barry, "Clinical Supervision: Walking that Fine Line" (1995) 2 *Clinical L. Rev.* 137.
24. Adrian Evans and Ross Hyams, "Independent Evaluations of Clinical Legal Education Programs—Appropriate Objectives and Processes in an Australian Setting" (2008) 17 *Griffith L. Rev.* 52, 76.
25. Ibid.
26. The same has been the case in legal clinics in Jordan, as has been observed by the present writer during a workshop that incorporated a number of Jordanian legal clinics and law professors, which were organized by the American Bar Association, Rule of Law Initiative in Jordan (Amman, June 27, 2013). See Peter Joy, "Political Interference in Clinical Programs: Lessons from the US Experience" (2005) 8 *Int'l J. Clin. Legal Educ.* 83.
27. Frederick Zemans, "The Community Legal Clinic Quality Assurance Program: An Innovative Experience in Quality Assurance in Legal Aid" (2000) 33*UBC L. Rev.* 243, 246.
28. Jane Aiken and Stephen Wizner, "Promoting Justice Through Interdisciplinary Teaching, Practice, and Scholarship Law as Social Work" (2003) 11 *Wash. U. J.L. & Pol'y* 63.
29. Giddings et al. (n 14).

30. Ibid. 16.
31. Sulaiman Jaradat, "The Relationship Between the Governor Office and Security Forces with Law Schools: The Model of Hebron University Legal Clinic," paper presented at the International Conference on Global Legal Education Approaches: Experiences for Palestine, Hebron University, October 1–3, 2013 (forthcoming).
32. The clinic developed the Palestinian Nationality Draft Law that determines the legal status of the Palestinian citizens in the future State of Palestine (Ramallah, January 2012).
33. The Head of the Negotiations Office, Dr. Saeb Erakat, participated in the opening session of the International Conference on Palestine Membership in the United Nations held on April 18–19, 2012.
34. The Minister of Justice headed one session in the conference on Palestine membership in the United Nations.
35. The High Judicial Council is the official partner through which the clinic invites judges to participate in the clinic's public lectures, training courses, and seminars.
36. The clinic organized a seminar on media freedoms on February 23, 2012 (below) in partnership with the Ministry of Information.
37. Police officers often accept the clinic's invitations to events on human rights, forensic medicine, and juvenile justice. For example, the clinic organized training sessions in collaboration with three police officers on investigation and the role of police in domestic violence in March 2013. *Maan News*, Bethlehem, March 28, 2013.
38. For instance, the clinic trained probation officers from the Ministry of Social Affairs on international standards and Palestinian law relating to juvenile justice in Hebron on June 12, 2012.
39. The clinic organized its conference on family law in Palestine in March 2012 jointly with the Office of Islamic Chief Justice.
40. The clinic attended a workshop on intellectual property draft law (trademarks, commercial names, patents) organized by the Ministry of Economy on June 20, 2012 at the Hebron Chamber of Commerce.
41. Mutaz Qafisheh, "The International Status of National Human Rights Institutions: A Comparison with NGOs" (2013) 31 *Nordic J. Hum. Rts.* 5.
42. Justus Weiner, "The Temporary International Presence in the City of Hebron (TIPH): A Unique Approach to Peacekeeping" (1998) 16 *Wis. Int'l L.J.* 281.
43. Arturo Carrillo, "Bringing International Law Home: The Innovative Role of Human Rights Clinics in the Transnational Legal Process" (2004) 35 *Colum. Hum. Rts. L. Rev.* 527.
44. Michael Cozens, "Clinical Legal Education: A Student Perspective" (1993) 2 *Dalhousie J Legal Stud.* 201.
45. Hebron University Legal Clinic, Brochure (Hebron, September 2011).
46. Rachel Micah-Jones, "From Pedagogy to Partnership: Leveraging the Law Clinic to Institutionalize Cutting Edge Strategies in Transnational Labor Advocacy: The Centro de los Derechos del Migrante, Inc.—University of Maryland School of Law Clinical Partnership" (2011) 26 *Md. J. Int'l L.* 113.
47. Kevwe Omoragon, "Interface of Law and Medicine in Clinical Legal Education: Success Story of the Women's Law Clinic is Improving the Health of Women and Ensuring Women's Access to Justice in Nigeria" (2002) 17 *Int'l J. Clin. Legal Educ.* 49.
48. Stephan Anagnost, "Promoting Refugee Law as a Means of Challenging the Status Quo at University Level Education in Europe: The Role of the Refugee Law Clinic" (2002) 2 *Int'l J. Clin .Legal Educ.* 38.

49. Frances Gibson, "The Convention on the Rights of Persons with Disabilities: The Response of the Clinic" (2011) 16 *Int'l J. Clin. Legal Educ.* 11.
50. Ross Hyams and Faye Gertner, "Multidisciplinary Clinics—Broadening the Outlook of Clinical Learning" (2012) 17 *Int'l J. Clin. Legal Educ.* 23.
51. Susan Campbell and Alan Ray, "Specialist Clinical Legal Education: An Australian Model" (2003) 3 *Int'l J. Clin. Legal Educ.* 67.
52. Jocelyn Kestenbaum, Esteban Hoyos-Ceballos, and Melissa Talvadkar, "Catalysts for Change: A Proposed Framework for Human Rights Clinical Teaching and Advocacy" (2012) 18 *Clinical L. Rev.* 459; Arturo Carrillo and Nicolas Yaksic, "Reimaging the Human Rights Law Clinic" (2011) 26 *Md. J. Int'l L.* 80.
53. John Bradway, "Some Distinctive Features of a Legal Aid Clinic Course" (1934) 1 *U. Chi. L. Rev.* 469.
54. Cath Sylvester, "Bridging the Gap—The Effect of Pro Bono Initiatives on Clinical Legal Education in the UK" (2003) 3 *Int'l J. Clin. Legal Educ.* 29; Frank S. Bloch and Iqbal Ishar, "Legal Aid, Public Service and Clinical Legal Education: Future Directions from India and the United States" (1990) 12 *Mich. J. Int'l L.* 92.
55. Kelly Behre, "Motivations for Law Student for Pro Bono: Lessons Learned from the Tuscaloosa Tornado," paper presented at Durham Conference in July 2012.
56. Patricia Pierce and Kathleen Ridolfi, "The Santa Clara Experiment: A New Fee-Generating Model for Clinical Legal Education" (1997) 3 *Clinical L. Rev.* 439.
57. Kimberly O'Leary, "Clinical Law Offices and Local Social Justice Strategies: Case Selection and Quality Assessment as an Integral Part of the Social Justice Agenda of Clinics" (2005) 11 *Clinical L. Rev.* 335.
58. Nisreen Mahasneh, "Applied Training Course: Legal Clinic" (College of Law, Yarmouk University, 2013), paper presented at a workshop on Law Schools Legal Clinics in Amman.
59. Barry Metzger, "Clinical Legal Education and Curriculum Reform: Humanizing the Law School of the Future" (1972) 3 *Singapore L. Rev.* 118.
60. Fayez Mohammed, "Legal Clinic," paper presented to American Bar Association, Rule of Law Initiative in Cairo, Egypt, October 22, 2011.
61. Hector Olasolo, "Legal Clinics in Continental Western Europe: The Approach of the Utrecht Legal Clinic on Conflict, Human Rights, and International Justice" (2010) 194 *American Society of International Law Proceedings* 98; Richard Wilson, "Western Europe: Last Holdout in the Worldwide Acceptance of Clinical Legal Education" (2009) 10 *German L.J.* 823.
62. Deborah Maranville, "Passion, Context, and Lawyering Skills: Choosing Among Simulated and Real Clinical Experiences" (2000) 7 *Clinical L. Rev.* 123; Jose Fuentes, "Reflections on Lawyering and Clinical Methodology" (1991) 60 *Revista Juridica Universidad de Puerto Rico* 40.
63. Paranto Wignjowidolo, "Purpose of Setting up a Legal Aid Clinic—Social Service or Legal-Reform?" (1972) 3 *Singapore L. Rev.* 114.
64. William Patton, "Getting Back to the Sandbox: Designing a Legal Policy Clinic" (2001) 16 *Int'l J. Clin. Legal Educ.* 96.
65. Les McCrimmon and Edward Santow, "Justice Education, Law Reform, and the Clinical Method," in Frank S. Bloch (ed.) *The Global Clinical Movement: Educating Lawyers for Social Justice* (Oxford University Press, 2011).
66. Alice Clapman, "The Clinical Revolution: How Asylum Law Clinics can Influence National Policy and Practices in Transitional Democracies" (2001) 3 *Eur. J.L. Reform* 67.

67. Bradway (n 53).
68. Richard Wilson, "Practical Training in Law in the Netherlands: Big Law Model or Clinical Model, and the Call of Public Interest Law" (2012) 8 *Utrecht L. Rev.* 170; Frank Dignan, "Bridging the Academic/Vocational Divide: The Creation of a Law Clinic in an Academic Law School" (2011) 16 *Int'l J. Clin. Legal Educ.* 75.
69. *Al-Hayat*, 5833 (Ramallah, January 30, 2012) 13.
70. Ross Hyams, "On Teaching Students to Act Like a Lawyer: What Sort of Lawyer?" (2008) 13 *Int'l J. Clin. Legal Educ.* 21; John Boersig, James Marshall, and Georgia Seaton, "Teaching Law and Legal Practice in a Live Client Clinic" (2002) 6 *Newcastle L. Rev.* 51.
71. *Al-Hayat*, 5918 (Ramallah, April 24, 2012).
72. *Palestine News Network* (Ramallah, March 19, 2012).
73. "Hebron University Won the National Moot Court Competition on International Law" *Al-Hayat*, 6347 (Ramallah, July 3, 2013).
74. "Moot Court Competition Takes Place at Hebron University" *Monthly Newsletter*, Public Relations Department, Hebron University (Hebron, April 11, 2012).
75. *Al-Hayat*, 5998 (Ramallah, July 13, 2012), 5. See Harry Almond, "Strengthening the Philip C. Jessup International Law Moot Court Competition" (1998) 4 *ILSA J. Int'l & Comp. L.* 668.
76. Abdul H. Ansari, "Clinical Legal Education: Benefitting from the Banaras Experience" (2011) 7 *J. Appl. Sci. Res.* 2162.
77. *Al-Hayat*, 5949 (Ramallah, May 10, 2012).
78. *Maan News* (Bethlehem, December 4, 2012).
79. *Al-Ayyam*, 6269 (Ramallah, June 21, 2013).
80. "Hebron University Legal Clinic Concludes an Intensive Course on French Language for Law Students" *Hebron Times* (Hebron, August 15, 2012) 51.
81. "Hebron University Signs Partnership Agreement with Terre des Hommes Foundation, Switzerland" *Al-Hayat*, 5974 (Ramallah, June 19, 2012) 14.
82. Meeting with Nicole Taylor, Program Director, International Legal Foundation, July 25, 2013.
83. *Maan News* (Bethlehem, December 29, 2012).
84. *Al-Ayyam*, 5852 (Ramallah, April 25, 2012), 13.
85. *Maan News* (Bethlehem, February 14, 2012).
86. *Al-Hayat*, 5859 (Ramallah, February 25, 2012).
87. *Al-Quds*, 15350 (Jerusalem, May 7, 2012) 11.
88. *Al-Quds*, 15353 (Jerusalem, May 10, 2012) 7.
89. *Maan News* (Bethlehem, December 12, 2012).
90. *Al-Hayat*, 6200 (Ramallah, February 6, 2013).
91. Philip Iya, "Fostering a Better Interaction Between Academics and Practitioners to Promote Quality Clinical Legal Education with High Ethical Values"(2003) 3 *Int'l J. Clin. Legal Educ.* 41.
92. Richard Wilson, "Training for Justice: The Global Reach of Clinical Legal Education" (2004) 22 *Penn St. Int'l L. Rev.* 421.
93. Mutaz Qafisheh, "Political Prisoners in Peace Processes: Palestine/Israel vs. Namibia/South Africa" (2012) United Nations, New York, UN Doc. CPR/IMQP/2012/11.
94. *Al-Quds*, 15428 (Ramallah, July 24, 2012) 6.
95. *Al-Hayat*, 6236 (Ramallah, March 14, 2013).
96. *Monthly Newsletter*, Public Relations Department, Hebron University (Hebron, May 22, 2012).

97. World Academy of Art and Science, "Search for an Alternative Paradigm to Address the Multi-dimensional Global Crisis" (June 18, 2013).
98. *Maan News* (Bethlehem, July 4, 2013).
99. Mutaz Qafisheh, "The Dilemma of Legislative Reform in Line with International Standards on Gender Equality in the Islamic World: The Case of Palestine" (2013) 1 *Int. J. for Legislative Drafting and Law Reform* 219.
100. *Al-Hayat*, 5892 (Ramallah, March 29, 2012).
101. *Al-Quds*, 15332 (Jerusalem, April 19, 2012) 10.
102. Peter Joy, "The Cost of Clinical Legal Education" (2012) 32 *B.C. J.L. & Soc. Just.* 309.
103. Giddings et al. (n 14), 15.
104. Lee Stuesser, "Skills for the Masses: Brining Clinical Skills to More Students at Less Cost" (1992) 10 *J. of Prof Legal Ed* 119.
105. Phyllis Goldfarb, "Back to the Future of Clinical Legal Education" (2012) 32 *B.C. J.L .& Soc. Just.* 279.
106. Justine Dunlap and Peter Joy, "Reflection-in-Action: Designing New Clinical Teacher Training by Using Lessons Learned from New Clinicians" (2004) 11 *Clinical L. Rev.* 49; Kimberly O'Leary, "Evaluating Clinical Law Teaching—Suggestions for Law Professors Who have Never Used the Clinical Teaching Method" (2002) 29 *N. Ky. L. Rev.* 491.
107. *Palestine Gazette*, No. 30, October 10, 1999, 5.
108. Beverly Balos, "The Bounds of Professionalism: Challenging Our Students; Challenging Ourselves" (1997) 4 *Clinical L. Rev.* 129.
109. Graeme Coss, "Field Placement (Externship)—A Valuable Application of Clinical Education"(1993) 4 *Legal Educ. Rev.* 29.
110. Claire Sparrow, "Reflective Student Practitioner—An Example Integrating Clinical Experience into the Curriculum" (2009) 14 *Int'l J. Clin. Legal Educ.* 70.
111. Giddings et al. (n 14), 4, 10.
112. Ibid 11.
113. Bloch (n 1).
114. David Chavkin, "Palestine Membership in the United Nations: Opportunities to Create a Justice System that Never was," in Mutaz Qafisheh (ed.) *Palestine Membership in the United Nations* (Cambridge Scholar Publishing, 2011).

CHAPTER 8

Clinical Legal Education in Singapore

Rathna N. Koman and Helena Whalen-Bridge

Introduction

Law schools have traditionally confined themselves to the academic instruction of law, but recent curriculum development, around the world and in Singapore, represents a paradigm shift in goals and methods of instruction. Clinical legal education (CLE) programs have become an established feature of the Singapore law school curriculum, in order to, inter alia, instill legal professionalism in students and fulfill an institutional responsibility toward indigent needs.

This chapter considers the two Singapore law schools' alternative approaches to CLEs, molded and dictated by their respective university core values and pedagogy. First, the provision of funded legal services to indigent persons is considered. Second, the development of legal education and its historical origins are discussed. Third, CLEs and relevant case studies are considered. Fourth, the question of whether these programs have importance beyond pedagogical value, and the potential impact of programs on the profession, students, and the community regarding issues of social justice, are considered.

Provision of Legal Aid and/or Representation to Indigent Persons in Singapore

Singapore is not a welfare state. Funded legal aid, state or otherwise, is available only under limited circumstances.

State-Funded Legal Aid and/or Representation

For civil cases, state-funded legal aid is governed by the Legal Aid and Advice Act (LAAA). Indigents qualify if the threshold disposable income and capital are that of $10,000 each per annum[1] (the means test), and if they have shown 'reasonable grounds' for taking or defending the action[2] (the merits test). Applicants are required to pay a contribution toward the costs of work done, usually not exceeding $1,000.[3] Amendments were made to the means test in 2013 that expanded existing income limitations and added new deductibles,[4] thereby increasing coverage to a wider section of the population and/or offsetting higher costs of living.[5] LAAA does not provide for criminal legal aid.[6] Generally, there is no generic state-funded criminal legal aid. State-funded counsel is provided when an accused is facing a capital charge in the Supreme Court,[7] or when the Chief Justice considers it to be in the "interests of justice" in noncapital criminal appeal cases,[8] although government contributions to criminal legal aid have been expanded recently.[9] In summary, the granting of legal aid to indigent persons in Singapore, notwithstanding recent expansions, is circumscribed.

Non-State-Funded Legal Aid or Representation

Legal advice to indigent persons is supplemented by community legal clinics run by the Singapore Law Society Pro Bono Office (PBSO), the Singapore Management University Pro Bono Centre (SMU Pro Bono Centre),[10] private practitioners, and various private organizations.[11]

In community legal clinics, volunteer lawyers render legal advice without undertaking full legal representation. These clinics aim to assist indigent persons by dispensing legal advice. If private practitioners decide to take up these cases pro bono, disbursements, including court fees, remain the liability of the indigent.[12] Disbursements so paid can be substantial in amount and may not be within the reach of an impecunious individual.

Additionally, Criminal Legal Aid Scheme (CLAS), a pro bono initiative set up by the Singapore Law Society in 1985,[13] renders legal advice and representation[14] to all impecunious defendants regardless of nationality.[15] Applicants are subjected to a means test. The scheme was historically sourced by volunteer lawyers and assisted by student volunteers from law schools of both universities. Recently expanded government contributions mean that lawyers will receive modest honorariums, and law firms will second or sponsor lawyers to work full-time at the Pro Bono Services Office.[16] The efforts of CLAS are also supplemented by the Association of Criminal Lawyers, an organization registered under the Societies Act, whose members provide pro bono assistance for criminal cases.[17]

Indigents who are not covered by state-funded legal aid but who present exceptional circumstances[18] also qualify for legal representation under the PBSO Ad Hoc Pro Bono Referral Scheme. These indigents are referred by the Court or volunteer lawyers who render legal advice at community legal clinics.[19]

Challenges to Access to Justice in the Singapore Context

Individuals who require more than just the free legal advice provided in legal clinics or who are within the "sandwich class"[20] are entirely dependent on pro bono lawyers. This raises the issue of the sufficiency of pro bono lawyers in society and whether law students are sufficiently sensitized to social justice issues to carry on the pro bono tradition upon graduation. Accordingly, curriculum development in Singapore law schools reflects this sentiment and goes beyond the academic instruction of the law. CLEs promoting access to justice are becoming part and parcel of our legal curriculum, inter alia, to inculcate social and professional responsibility in law students.[21]

CLE in Singapore

Introduction: Traditional Methods of Instruction Make Room for Legal Skills and Clinic Legal Education

Many strands of legal education are necessary in order for CLE to develop, including acceptance of a variety of teaching and assessment techniques and expanded notions of professional identity that include access to justice. Law schools in Singapore now incorporate CLE into the law curriculum, but the foundations for CLE developed slowly over time. The LLB degree, the main route into legal practice in Singapore,[22] is currently offered by two universities, the National University of Singapore Faculty of Law (NUS)[23] and the SMU School of Law.[24] The different paths taken by these universities toward CLE are addressed below.

Traditional Academic Instruction of the Law

Law teaching in Singapore began in 1957 with the setting up of the Department of Law within the then-University of Malaya,[25] renamed the University of Singapore in 1962 and the National University of Singapore in 1981.[26] SMU received official approval for its School of Law in 2007. Until 2007, when SMU welcomed its first LLB cohort,[27] NUS was the sole university awarding an LLB in Singapore, and so for decades it represented the state of law teaching in Singapore.

As the only law school in the country for many years, NUS had to ensure that its graduates had the knowledge and skills to supply the needs of the legal fraternity.[28] In 1999, NUS law professor Alexander Loke noted the common understanding that the end of legal education was the promise of professional pecuniary rewards, with the consequence that undue emphasis was placed on black-letter law, particularly in commercial fields.[29]

In addition to an emphasis on black-letter law, the NUS Faculty of Law also traditionally relied on a combination of larger lectures and tutorials for the teaching of core subjects.[30] While some lectures used a more interactive Socratic method, the traditional, one-way transmission of information in lecture delivery is not suitable for CLE. The tutorials, in which smaller groups of students tackle hypothetical and critical questions with a teacher, allow for more interaction, but more focused teaching and feedback techniques are required in CLE.[31] In terms of assessment, a final examination was still a common method of assessment in 2006, although it was increasingly used together with other forms such as group work, class participation, class presentations, and assignments.[32] More recently, increased receptiveness to a variety of teaching and assessment methods has greatly expanded the possibilities of experiential teaching in general and CLE in particular.

The Legal Skills Precursor to CLE and Access to Justice

Expansion into legal skills courses arguably helped established the basis for current offerings in CLE. For "generations" at NUS, legal research and analysis skills were taught through the first-year "Legal Method" module, a one-semester course that taught students how to read cases, identify ratio, research issues, and write legal memoranda and letters.[33] Informal feedback to NUS from legal practitioners in 2001 prompted a study on the need for an enhanced legal skills curriculum, which in turn prompted curriculum reform and produced compulsory courses in legal skills, comparative law, and legal theory.[34] After the curriculum reform was fully implemented, LLB students at NUS were required to take two years of skills courses: a year-long course in the first year, Legal Analysis, Writing and Research (LAWR), which developed fundamental objective and argumentation skills,[35] and two semester-long courses in the second year,[36] Legal Case Studies[37] and Introduction to Trial Advocacy.[38] NUS had undertaken a substantial commitment to skills training, but skills courses do not only serve the limited purpose of professional preparation. As noted by former Faculty of Law Dean Tan Cheng Han, skills courses should "attempt to place the subject matter within the wider fabric of the legal system."[39]

Instruction of Law Demonstrating Professional and Community Relevance and Sensitizing Students to Social Justice Issues

Charting a law school's support for the commitment of lawyers to the community and access to justice is trickier than noting changes in courses and curriculum. In Singapore, professional obligations have historically been taught at the postgraduate stage[40] and integrated into the LLB curriculum using a pervasion approach[41] and electives.[42] More recently, students have been exposed to legal ethics in the first-semester course Singapore Legal System since 2008, and since 2012 the Singapore Legal System syllabus has included professional obligations to access to justice.

The SMU School of Law has taken a different approach to legal ethics. Consistent with the university's mission, SMU's LLB curriculum aims to mold students into excellent holistic lawyers who will contribute significantly to society.[43] Both law and nonlaw students at SMU take a compulsory course in Ethics and Social Responsibility as part of their overall university requirements.

Both law schools have also supported student pro bono, and students from both universities participate every year in activities that support access to justice.[44] NUS students have undertaken voluntary pro bono for many years, prompting students to organize the Pro Bono Group in 2005[45] and the Criminal Justice Club in 2009,[46] groups that function with faculty supervision. At SMU, student pro bono activities are organized via the Pro Bono Centre.[47]

The Impact of Stakeholders and Developments in the Wider Legal Community on Legal Education in Singapore

Other stakeholders in Singapore have also participated in educational developments that support access to justice. The Singapore Institute of Legal Education established a mandatory pro bono requirement for students in LLB programs at Singapore's two law schools.[48] The requirement applies to students commencing their degree in 2013 and requires students to perform 20 hours of pro bono work at any time after their first year of study.[49] There is also a concern that areas of community law, such as family and criminal law, will not be adequately served by the current number of law graduates, so the Report of the 4th Committee on the Supply of Lawyers recommended the establishment of a third law school in Singapore, with a specific focus on community law, including civil, criminal, family, and juvenile law.[50]

Developments within the university take place in the context of the legal system as a whole, and awareness of access to justice and the need for indigent legal services has experienced a renaissance in Singapore. In recent years Singapore has seen expanded pro bono services, the establishing an aspirational target of 25 hours per lawyer per year in 2006,[51] and the launching the Office of Pro Bono Services in 2007,[52] which manages and develops all of the Law Society of Singapore's pro bono programs. The mandatory provision of pro bono services by lawyers has also been explored.[53]

Finally, in a major departure from its long-held stance toward legal aid for criminal defendants, the government will play a larger role in funding direct legal assistance to defendants in noncapital criminal cases.[54] In summary, the development of CLE that promotes awareness of the needs of indigent persons has proceeded together with parallel developments in pedagogical flexibility and access to justice in the Singapore legal community.

System Restrictions on CLE Programs

In general, restrictions on legal practice and law firm structure have presented challenges to the development of CLE in Singapore.

Legal Profession Act

The main law governing the lawyer's profession in Singapore is the Legal Profession Act.[55] Lawyers practicing Singapore law are for the most part required to hold a practicing certificate.[56] There are no exceptions for faculty members in a clinical setting, although there is a limited exception for academic staff in law departments acting in an advisory capacity.[57] Students may not give legal advice or represent a party in court, even when acting in a supervised capacity.

Required practice structures present another challenge to CLE in Singapore. Currently, advocates and solicitors in Singapore practice in one of four main legal structures, that of sole proprietorship, general partnership, limited liability law partnership, and limited law corporation,[58] and none of these structures lends itself well to CLE in the university setting. Alternative business structures, such as multidisciplinary practices, are not currently allowed in Singapore. Lawyers cannot share premises jointly with[59] or share fees for legal work with an unauthorized person,[60] and law firms in Singapore provide purely legal services and are managed and owned only by lawyers.[61] A legal practice owned by an educational institution would therefore require regulatory change. CLE, to the extent it provides legal services to live clients, must contend with these practice restrictions.

In this regulatory context, two models have developed in Singapore. At NUS, a course entitled The Law Clinic is held outside the university at the Legal Aid Bureau. At SMU, legal clinics for indigent clients are conducted on campus. The legal clinics are staffed by volunteer lawyers from the Pro Bono Services Office's volunteer list, and the lawyers are assisted by SMU law students.

Mushrooming of CLE Programs Promoting Access to Justice in Singapore

NUS: The Law Clinic

The first CLE program in Singapore was The Law Clinic, formally launched in Semester 1 of AY 2010–11 under then Dean Tan Cheng Han.[62] The Law Clinic works exclusively with Legal Aid Bureau (LAB) matters and is essentially a classroom within the LAB.[63] A Memorandum of Understanding was entered into between the NUS Faculty of Law and the LAB to facilitate the setting up of the program.[64] The LAB can appoint lawyers without practicing certificates as Volunteer Assistant Directors of Legal Aid, and does so in order to promote pro bono.[65] The professors who supervise The Law Clinic, Associate Professors Lim Lei Theng (Course Supervisor) and Ruby Lee, are also Volunteer Assistant Directors at the Legal Aid Bureau.[66] This arrangement allows law professors to give advice to LAB clients and represent them in court without a Practicing Certificate, as well as engage in this limited type of law practice outside of the law firm structure. It also brings the legal representation within LAB insurance coverage.

The Law Clinic is an elective course open to third- and fourth-year NUS law students. Students apply for the course and are required to submit a curriculum vitae, and prior experience serving access to justice or community legal needs can be a factor in student selection.[67] In The Law Clinic, students work with clinical instructors on live files involving LAB clients, and assist the instructors in taking statements from clients, preparing affidavits, doing legal research, and preparing for court.[68] LAB handles only civil matters, but students are exposed to a variety of cases, including matrimonial matters and torts. In addition to case files, students assist clinical instructors when the instructors give legal advice prior to the issuance of a certificate of LAB eligibility. Students also support clinical instructors in case conferences with judges via video conference in the program JusticeOnLine.[69]

In preparation for the work in The Law Clinic, students are familiarized with protocols on how to conduct themselves in a law practice setting; how to compile, maintain, and follow up on matters in a client file; how to draft documents such as affidavits and court pleadings; and how to interact with clients and support personnel. Clinical training stresses the subtleties of client interaction, including how to interview clients and get relevant information, as well as how to effectively convey legal information to clients with a view toward their life circumstances. Students also become familiar with and use LAB manuals and materials.

Initial training is followed quickly by training on actual client matters, in which students have supervised responsibility for live cases. In this environment, students learn that "precedents" do not provide the answer to legal problems and that they must think creatively to meet client needs. The challenges posed by having students work on live client cases also means that students receive extremely close supervision. Students must take the initiative by identifying what is required by the client matter and how best to accomplish it, but their activities are scrutinized at every turn. Students are only allowed to work in LAB if an instructor is there, which is usually most days of the week. The required level of supervision is made possible in part by the class size at The Law Clinic, which is limited to eight students at a time. The course requires that students engage in 80 hours of work, and after they complete that requirement students are allowed to continue working if they desire. The hourly requirement allows The Law Clinic to keep numbers small but to offer two tranches in one semester, thereby opening up more spaces for students.

In terms of skill goals, The Law Clinic pedagogy emphasizes professional attitudes of self-learning and initiative, and respectful interactions with colleagues and clients, as well as high-quality work on files, including legal research, document production, timely and appropriate follow-up, proper documentation of client meetings, and accurate closing and handing off of completed matters.

The Law Clinic is an upper-class elective module at NUS. The course awards academic credit, and students are evaluated on several criteria, including the quality of the legal work they produce, the initiative and energy they display in LAB matters, and the quality of the self-reflections they submit. At the end of the program, clinical instructors sit down with students and review their experience, giving feedback about their performance and discussing future plans. Students also complete an exit survey, which includes queries on student attitudes toward pro bono and whether students have been inspired to do pro bono in their professional careers.

A law school legal clinic that assists indigent persons serves both access to justice and educational goals. When The Law Clinic was launched, Tan Cheng Han, Dean of the NUS Faculty of Law at the time, noted the dual nature of a law school legal clinic, stating that students "see how the law operates in society and this deepens their understanding of the law and legal institutions. At the same time, [clinical legal education] will help to inculcate values that the law school believes is important for our graduates to have."[70] CLE therefore serves two goals, but as the NUS course is offered for course credit in the context of the LLB degree, the primary goal at The Law Clinic is educational. Clinical instructors choose the cases that students will work on to achieve multiple purposes. More ordinary cases develop certain skills, while unusual matters can raise more challenging questions of law and procedure for students to tackle.

Over the course of The Law Clinic, students work with a variety of clients who present different challenges. Students are exposed to the joys and frustrations of working to make justice accessible, and they learn that clients are not always grateful for their considerable efforts. Students in the module have commented on the value of working with actual clients:

> The best feature of the course is the hands on experience—we get to draft court forms, affidavits, and opinions from scratch and in the process, I also gain a better understanding of the civil process.

> The best feature of the course is the court attendances—there are many opportunities to go to court, and I had the privilege of seeing how it is like dealing with a litigant in person, interacting with other counsels, and also compare these scenarios to a mediation setting.

Students also noted the relevance of working with indigent persons:

> My most memorable experience in the course was interacting with the clients as I saw the impact of our work on the lives of those who would otherwise be unable to afford legal service.[71]

Overall, students have found the experience satisfying, from both an educational and inspirational perspective.[72]

The SMU Pro Bono Centre Legal Clinic

At SMU, the SMU Pro Bono Centre is responsible for managing all pro bono activities and placements of SMU students. In August 2013, the Centre started a pilot run of its own legal clinic on campus for indigent persons. Prior to August 2013, and since the inception of the School of Law in 2007, SMU students were actively involved in community legal clinics, assisting lawyers in legal clinics run by the Pro Bono Services Office and other pro bono placements serving social justice issues.[73]

At SMU, student service at legal clinics for indigent persons is born out of a social justice imperative. Students were inculcated into pro bono culture from the inception of the School of Law, through vehicles such as the university wide graduation requirement to serve 80 hours of community service.[74] Given the university's[75] and the School of Law's[76] core values of dedication to the service of humanity, pro bono placements and attendance at the community legal clinics were done with the purpose of filling the "justice gap."[77] Service to humanity and promoting access to justice were ends in themselves. The legal clinics at SMU were primarily born out of the same social justice imperative, to address the issue of the redistribution of essential legal services for indigent persons. The role of clinical teaching therefore assumed a lesser imperative in the genesis of these clinics.

The SMU Pro Bono Centre runs legal clinics for indigent persons at the university on a fortnightly basis. After the pilot run in 2013, the clinics started to run for the whole year since August 2013, except for a "pro bono blackout period" in the months of November and April when law students have their exams.

Student Training and Supervision Given that the purpose of these clinics was to address the redistribution of essential legal services borne out of the recognition of the inability of many to access legal services to enforce their rights, the clinics were modeled differently from the traditional clinical teaching courses offered in American jurisdictions. The SMU Legal Clinic was structured primarily to deal with the exigencies of the Singapore system and its challenges to access to justice, together with the university's core values, and then pedagogical value.

The SMU Legal Clinic is a collaborative effort between the SMU School of Law and the Pro Bono Services Office. The Centre Director,[78] along with student assistants, manages the clinics at the SMU Pro Bono Centre. The Centre engages pro bono lawyers on a roster basis to give legal advice to clients, who are subject to a means and a merit test. It is important to note that the lawyers are volunteer lawyers dedicated to the pro bono cause. The Pro Bono Services Office maintains a list of such lawyers, and Pro Bono Services Office professional indemnity insurance covers the work they do at SMU legal clinics. These lawyers are not per se clinical teachers. Some of them may have some form of training in mentoring students, although this is not a prerequisite. This serves the primary function of the Legal Clinic, which is to provide preliminary legal advice to indigent clients. About 90 percent of the cases with which students assist at the clinics are limited to merely providing legal advice without further representation or continuity to the matter. The training and supervision of the student is geared to this end. The student is paired with a lawyer, and he or she assists with taking instructions from the client, providing research, performing note-taking, and so forth.

In preparation for the Legal Clinics, students are trained in particular legal skills such as fact investigation, client interviewing, negotiation, mediation, problem solving, counseling, ethics, and professional values. This training is done separately by the Centre Director with the assistance of specialist practitioners. Students in the second year of law school receive special online research training in a nutshell from library specialists to deal with exigencies of the legal clinics and internships. Additionally, each student is given separate quality time with the attending clinic lawyer after the client interview to facilitate quality post mortem analysis of the fact investigation and the manner in which the interview was conducted. Given the intensive nature and 1:1 ratio of the lawyer and the student, the roster only allows a maximum of four clients per session with a lawyer. A pedagogical reflection with the student is done by supervising faculty after the clinic in some circumstances.

Limitations It is important to recognize at the outset the limitations of such a clinic model. First, although the student begins to assume a formal role within the legal system with this type of clinic model, the learning outcome is limited. There is no direct responsibility toward indigent clients or decisions made for them.

Secondly, the supervision of students by lawyers is limited to the period spent in the clinics, and often there is no continuity to the matter. The clinic focus is primarily on rendering legal advice; hence, a student does not get to see the whole picture of social justice issues.

Third, the "skills training" of the student by the Centre Director and specialist practitioners is generic and does not refer to the cases seen during clinics. Although references to real cases are made during the training conducted by faculty, such discussion is limited in terms of time and content since the clinics are primarily seen to alleviate reduced access to justice. Additionally, class discussion of specific case content is constrained by confidentiality rules and solicitor client privilege.

The SMU Pro Bono Centre has developed a student training manual in addition to the training described above. The student manual highlights and details the following essentials of the clinic:[79]

- workings of the SMU Pro Bono Centre Legal Clinic, stating learning outcomes, required skills, and so on;
- ethics and legal professional conduct rules;
- imperatives/rules before, during, and after the clinic, that is, not giving legal advice during client interview, making accurate and factual investigation, asking the right questions, and so forth;
- online resource knowledge and research websites;
- the basics of giving advice and the role of the student in the clinics;
- proper record keeping as an essential of legal practice;
- confidentiality issues;
- office facilities and procedures;
- knowledge of forms used at the clinics and procedures;
- indemnity issues; and
- benefits of working at the clinics.

Fourthly, mentioned above, generally lawyers attending to indigent persons at the clinic are not clinic teachers, nor are they trained in mentoring students and learning outcomes. Currently none of the institutions running a legal clinic has an instructional program on effective coaching and mentoring skills for supervising lawyers. Accordingly, only a handful of supervising lawyers are mindful of mentoring the attendant student during the pro bono session in an effective manner. As part of the learning outcome, the supervising mentor lawyer must be able to guide the student in the exigencies of serving indigent needs, sensitize the student to what they are seeing, and raise his or her consciousness to a deeper understanding of the real issues of the distribution of legal services and social justice issues. Most often, there appears to be a lack of knowledge regarding the difference between shadowing and mentoring by the supervising lawyer. Attending lawyers at the clinics can be trained in mentoring skills so as to facilitate the pedagogical aspect and the "practice gap" effect of the clinics. An instructional program focused on

- the professional and business benefits of coaching and mentoring;
- the skills and techniques employed in good coaching;
- an understanding of the relationship between lawyer and learner; and so forth

will facilitate the multiple goals of achieving student learning outcomes at clinics, serving indigent needs, and sensitizing supervising lawyers to coaching and mentoring skills.

However, it is not an easy task to interest a pro bono lawyer in attending a workshop on mentoring skills, given that the lawyer's primary task at the legal clinic is to render pro bono advice. Workshops of this nature are seen as a deviation of valuable resources required to promote access to justice. Therefore, universities using this model must be mindful of the fact that the supervising lawyer is not a faculty member and may not be familiar with ways of imparting clinical teaching and pedagogical relevance in a manner that best promotes learning outcomes. Hence, in these kinds of clinics there is often a gap, fundamental or otherwise, between student learning/desired outcomes and actual outcomes.

These limitations and concerns have also been mirrored by students who assist at the clinics, as explored in the case study presented below.[80]

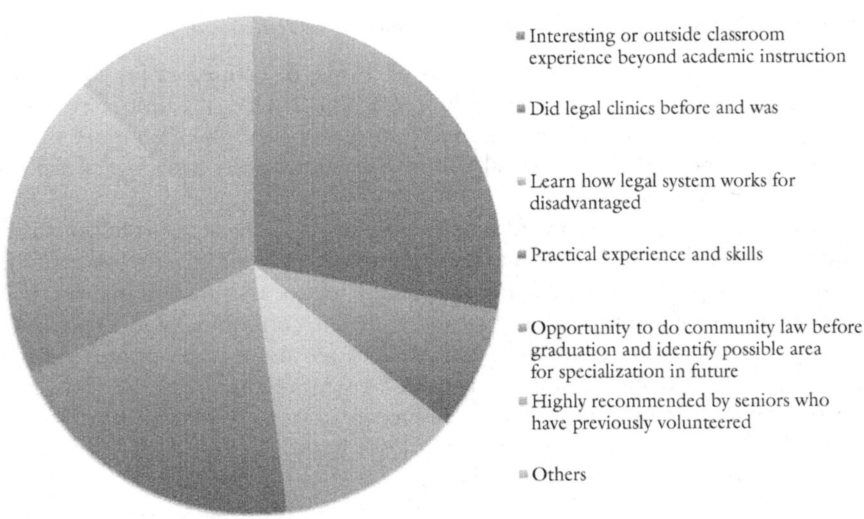

Figure 8.1 Why do you choose to volunteer at the legal clinics?

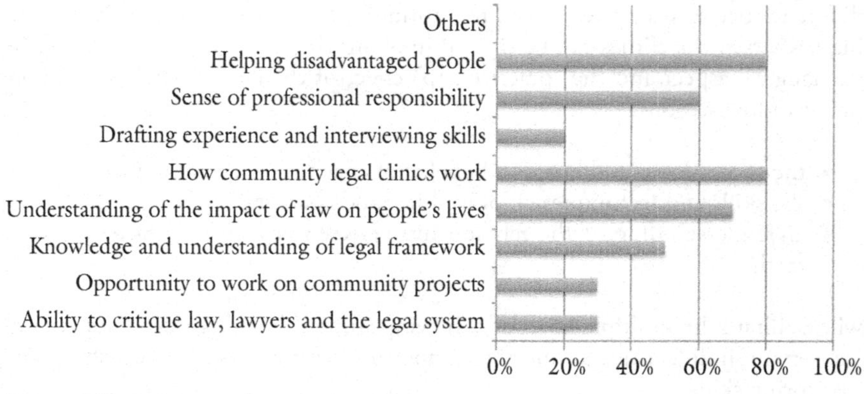

Figure 8.2 Volunteer take-aways from the clinics.

Case Studies In the first quarter of 2014, the SMU Pro Bono Centre conducted a study on all students participating at its legal clinics and various other social justice projects. Case studies over the last academic period rendered the following data.

CLE Programs Run by the Universities in Conjunction with Other Organizations
Student Training and Supervision Students assisting in other community legal clinics do receive skills training, albeit to a limited extent. In the case of clinics run by the Pro Bono Services Office, the Pro Bono Services Office has developed manuals, forms, and training.[81]

Benefits of Incorporating CLE into the Legal Curriculum

Traditionally, CLE that promotes access to justice is justified in the university setting on the basis of pedagogical value. At SMU, The Legal Clinic started as a social justice imperative. Notwithstanding the genesis and the limitations of the legal clinic model, the SMU Legal Clinic does advance the pedagogical aspirations of a law school.

CLEs, inter alia, have tremendous potential to instill the legal professionalism and professional values in students that are fundamental for an effective practice of the law by providing direct training in legal ethics and professional practice skills such as problem solving, factual investigation, communication, techniques of client interviewing, counseling, negotiation, advocacy, observation, and the drafting of legal documents in a supervised environment.[82] Practice skills can be truly mastered only in a clinical environment *via* opportunities presented through real cases. CLEs accordingly reinforce both NUS and SMU's commitment to a strong skill-based curriculum.

Students appreciate and integrate academic work with practical experience in clinics.[83] The experience provides an invaluable opportunity to understand, appreciate, and actualize rules of law in a supervised legal environment.

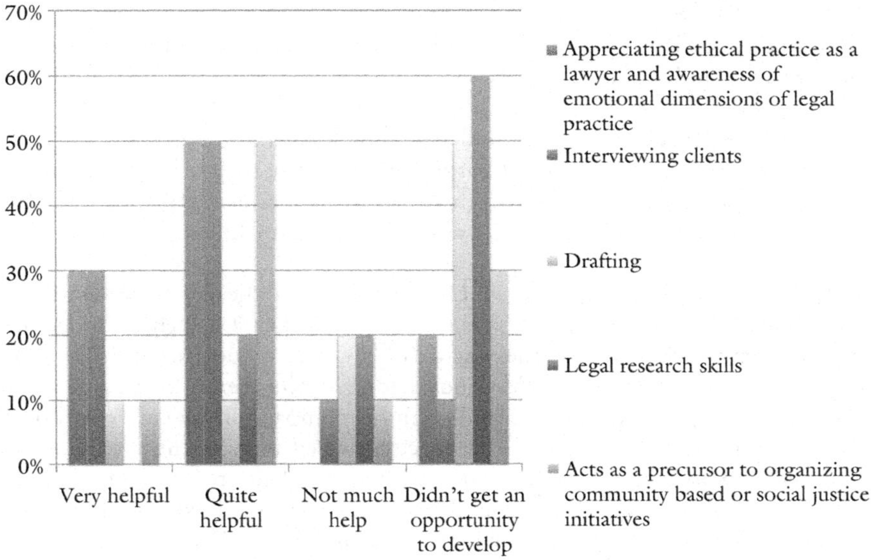

Figure 8.3 Effectiveness of SMU legal clinics in developing below-mentioned skills and interests.

Unlike simulations or hypothetical exercises, community engagement via legal clinics tends to instill a sense of social responsibility via community engagement. Students learn from situations by reflecting on professional responsibilities demanded by the situation and demonstrated by the supervising practitioner or faculty member. It also allows students to reflect on and evaluate the ability of the justice system to provide, respond, and deliver justice. For others, it acts as a catalyst for law reform projects and so forth.

The NUS and SMU legal clinics both focus on indigent persons, thereby heightening student awareness of access to justice and the distribution of legal services in society. It sensitizes students to social justice issues and ethical sensibilities of the law. Ethical sensibilities learned in these programs provide students with a much-needed foundation for cultivating a principled approach in practice.

Legal clinics aspire to instill and nurture and sustain the pro bono commitment in a student, which may otherwise wane due to the lure of the private sector, materialism, the latent curriculum,[84] changes in political viewpoints, and so on. The SMU Legal Clinics promoting access to justice have become the new buzzword in the latent curriculum.

Participation in legal clinics reinforces the four paramount principles of the Legal Profession (Professional Conduct) Rules: providing access to justice; maintaining the rule of law and the administration of justice; ensuring the integrity and independence of the profession; and acting in the best interest of clients.[85] In particular, clinics enable law students to facilitate access to justice and provide supervised assistance to indigents. Essentially, clinics educate law students on the ethics of being a lawyer.

SMU Case Studies

Case studies particularly showed that students who volunteer at these social justice projects, clinics or otherwise (CLE)

- benefited by perceiving and understanding legal education better; and
- were inspired to have an enduring commitment to pro bono culture or public service for an effective practice of the law, as demonstrated by SMU alumni who render legal advice at the SMU Legal Clinics for indigents.

The most beneficial facet of the CLE experience as indicated by students was the filling of the "practice gap." It was indicated that the CLEs helped bridge the gap between study of law and the practice of law. Seventy percent of the respondents, as shown in Figure 8.4 below, indicated that volunteering at the clinics has allowed them apply the law and understand the impact of the law on people's lives. Additionally, the practical experience provided the students with a sense of social responsibility for others, with 80 percent of the respondents indicating satisfaction in being able to help disadvantaged people in society. Particular remarks by students, excerpts of which are reproduced below, clearly reflected the students' mind-set when participating in the study. The first of such remarks is from a third-year law student who indicated that participating in the clinics has *"helped (him) to appreciate the great trust people place in their lawyers and the importance of honoring this trust."*

Indeed, similar sentiments have been highlighted, with 60 percent of respondents saying that they have gained a sense of professional responsibility and seriousness from being exposed to real clients and real-life situations and from observing how their supervising practitioner or faculty approached the clients and conducted themselves during these demanding situations.

It is noted from Figure 8.4 that prima facie, students did not gain much practical skills training. Only 20 percent of respondents indicated a gain in drafting experience and interviewing skills from volunteering at the clinics. As highlighted above, one possible explanation could be the systemic limitations within

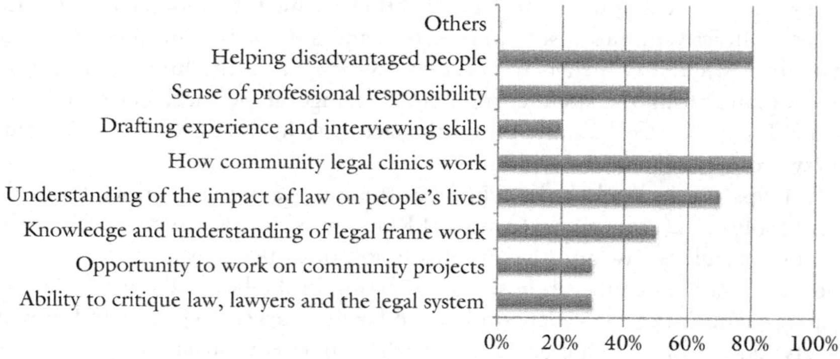

Figure 8.4 What have you gained from the clinics as a volunteer?

the Legal Profession Act that prohibit students from engaging in the practice of law and offering legal advice, while another could be the limitations of the Legal Clinic model adopted by SMU.[86]

A second-year law student indicated that

> Interviewing is an art. I learnt from observing the questions asked of the client by the lawyer to identify details that I could've and should've asked. The lawyer doesn't have time to ask unnecessary questions. From the type of questions asked, I learnt to make my briefs and writing more succinct.

Regular debrief sessions at SMU Legal Clinics appear to be critical in allowing the student and the lawyer to have a postmortem analysis of the case. These provide valuable opportunities for students to reflect on their experiences at the clinics, where supervising practitioners and faculty motivate and help guide them in discovering the skills that they have been taught. This approach also ensures consistency in experience at the clinics for all students.

However, the case study does indicate that that a sizable portion of the students feel that they do not gain much practical skills training from legal clinics generally. Indeed, 70 percent of respondents, as shown in Figure 8.5 below, indicated that they found it hard to contact lawyers to discuss and share what they learned from the cases they handled, and further that feedback given by the lawyers was ad hoc, unstructured, and lacking in content.

The case studies demonstrate that debriefing sessions are fundamental for effective clinic learning given the model used in legal clinics, SMU or otherwise. Second, not all supervising lawyers are able to mentor their students at the clinics for an effective learning outcome. This can be attributed to the lack of a basic instructional coaching and mentoring program for supervising lawyers at legal clinics. Third, there is the attitude of the student. As evidenced in the responses,

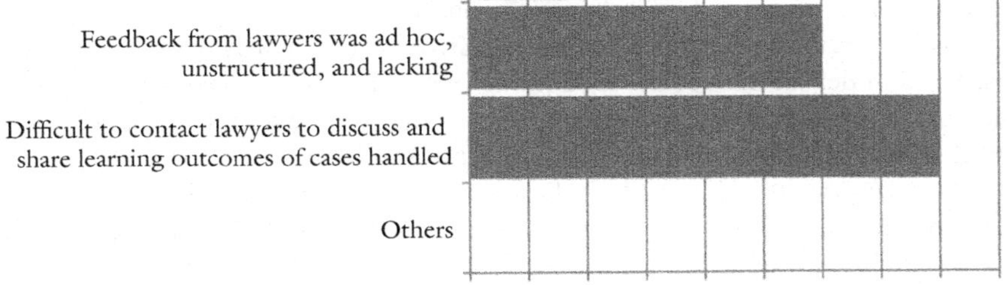

Figure 8.5 How would you describe your experience consulting with lawyers on duty about the client work you handled?

some students merely enrolled in clinics to clock the graduating hours, and hence their attitude was not well suited for a desired learning outcome.

Nonetheless, it is noted that 40 percent of the respondents did indicate a positive experience with the lawyers where an open door policy was adopted and constructive feedback was given based on questions and observations made by the students.

Student attitudes appeared to have a critical effect on learning outcomes at clinics. A graduating law student who volunteered at the clinics to fulfill graduation requirements indicated that

> I was mostly doing mundane activities. I could have taken more initiative.

This is contrasted with a rising third-year law student's remark that

> I started to initiate outreach programs for the Voluntary Welfare Organization [VWO] representing similar clients whom I met at the clinics. We even managed to distribute flyers educating the applicants of their rights under the Work Injury Claims Act through partnering with Khoo Teck Puat Hospital [KTPH] at their specialist outpatient clinics. This was an incredible experience.

It can be seen that students who take the initiative to learn and ask questions gain more from the CLE experience. For such students, the CLE experience was a precursor to organizing community-based social justice initiatives. Where students merely attended the clinic to clock the graduating hours, the learning outcomes were often circumscribed. However, in some cases, even such students had a change of heart after hearing the heartfelt pleas of indigents. As one student remarked, her attitude toward the Legal Clinic "shifted" after the first clinic, when she heard the pleas of an elderly person at the instruction station at her first clinic.

To enhance student learning at a holistic level, supervising practitioners should engage students at a meaningful level to inculcate and nurture the pro bono commitment. The above has proven true at the SMU Legal Clinics, at which, as shown in Figure 8.6 below, 90 percent of respondents felt that, given proper guidance, their experience volunteering at the legal clinics had inspired them to take or maintain an interest in volunteer legal work. Further, 80 percent of respondents said they would promote community legal education, social justice issues, and/or inculcate the pro bono spirit in others.

It is interesting to note that interest in law reform activities is tied to knowledge and understanding of the legal framework, which Figures 8.4 and 8.6 indicate are both at 50 percent. Perhaps, legal training in law and regulation may increase participation and interest in law reform projects.

In conclusion, the case study indicates that the synergy between supervising lawyers, faculty, and students is critical to learning outcomes in a clinical setting. Each plays a significant role in ensuring the smooth and efficient running of CLE/clinics in achieving optimum learning outcomes. Systemic limitations, such as the need for an instruction program in coaching and mentoring skills for supervising lawyers, must be seriously considered to ensure optimum learning in CLE.

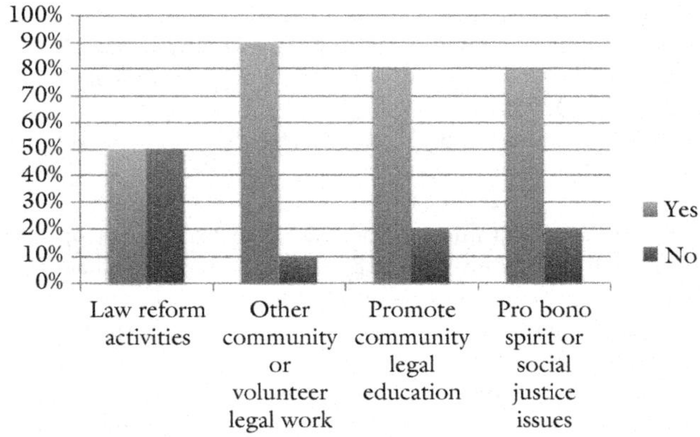

Figure 8.6 Whether experience at the clinics inspired you to take or maintain an interest in volunteer legal work?

Moving Forward

Law schools as well as law students in Singapore have historically displayed a firm commitment to student pro bono over the years, notwithstanding the lack of CLE programs promoting access to justice in formal legal education. The lack of CLE programs has now been remedied, and it is likely that such programs will continue to grow. The ultimate question of whether these educational experiences will result in more lawyers taking up pro bono work to support access to justice is, of course, difficult to predict.[87] Research by Robert Granfield suggests that a failure to integrate lessons learned in pro bono work throughout the curriculum is a source of student dissatisfaction with mandatory pro bono schemes,[88] so to the degree that law schools offer coursework that incorporates access to justice concerns, law schools will have achieved an important goal. Because of its compelling blend of access to justice and key legal skills, CLE offers a particularly powerful method of integrating education and social justice, and after being neglected for many years, is now firmly integrated into the Singapore legal curriculum.

Notes

1. Legal Aid and Advice Act (Cap 160, 1996 *Sing. Rev. Ed.*) s 8(2).
2. The Director of the Legal Aid Bureau can refuse legal aid if it appears that it is unreasonable to give legal aid "*in particular circumstances of the case*"; see LAAA, s 8(3)
3. LAAA, s 9(1) and 13(3).
4. Legal Aid and Advice (Amendment) Act 2013 (No. 6 of 2013), s 21(*h*) and (*i*).
5. See Hansards Singapore (4-02-2013, Vol: 90, Start Col, End Col). See Debate on Legal Aid and Advice (Amendment) Bill in which the proposed amendments to the LAAA expanded the LAAA "means test" and gave the LAB Director discretion to depart from the general means test in exceptional cases. See Hansards Singapore February 4, 2013, vol 90, cols *x-y*.

6. The position taken by the Singapore government, during the Parliamentary debates of LAAA, is that it does not make sense, philosophically, jurisprudentially, or practically for the State to prosecute and then defend, in public interest.(2003) 76 *Singapore Parl. Rep.*(2003), 715.
7. Supreme Court (Criminal Appeals) Rules 1997, R 11(a). This is provided without reference to any eligibility criteria.
8. Ibid. R 11(b).
9. Sara Gross, "Enhanced Criminal Legal Aid Scheme to Benefit up to 6,000 People Yearly," Channel News Asia (May 18, 2015), http://www.channelnewsasia.com/news/singapore/enhanced-criminal-legal/1854588.html,accessed June 8, 2015.
10. See Pro Bono Centre (*Singapore Management University*) http://centres.smu.edu.sg/pbc/, accessed May 18, 2014.
11. Singapore Counsel of Women's Organisation (SCWO), Catholic Lawyers Guild (CLG, Singapore), Association of Women for Action and Research(AWARE), Healthserve Ltd Legal Clinics, Harry Elias Partnership Pro Bono Program, Rotary Club Legal Clinics, Donaldson & Burkinshaw Pro Bono Program, Braddell Heights Legal Clinic, BLC Community Services Legal Clinic, Amarick Gill & Co Pro Bono Program etc.
12. Rathna Koman, "Responsibility of Schools in Dispensing Equal Justice: A Singapore Case Study" (2011) 53(2) *J. Ind. L. Inst.* 312.
13. The Legal Profession Act (Cap 161, 2009 *Sing. Rev. Ed.*), s 38(g) places a statutory obligation on the Law Society of Singapore to "make provision for or assist in the promotion of a scheme whereby impecunious persons on non-capital charges are represented by counsel."
14. However, the accused may be asked to pay for disbursements such as cost of obtaining statements or reports from the police.
15. Koman (n 11).
16. ara Gross, "Enhanced Criminal Legal Aid Scheme to Benefit up to 6,000 People Yearly," Channel News Asia (May 18, 2015), http://www.channelnewsasia.com/news/singapore/enhanced-criminal-legal/1854588.html,accessed June 8, 2015.
17. See Singapore State Courts, "Join us as Court Volunteers!"—Programs Managed by Other Organisations (*Singapore State Courts*) https://app.statecourts.gov.sg/subcourts/page.aspx?pageid=94781, accessed May 20, 2014.
18. See Pro Bono Services Office, "Representation for Individuals" (*Law Society of Singapore*) http://probono.lawsociety.org.sg/volunteer-Schemes/Supportforourvolunteers112/Criminal-Legal-Aid-Scheme/, accessed May 20, 2014.
19. See Legal Profession Act (Cap 161, 2009 *Sing. Rev. Ed.*), s R 13. See also Legal Profession (Publicity) Rules Revised Edition 2010, R 10, "Giving of Free Legal Advice."
20. For more on individuals who do not qualify for the means test for state-funded representation and cannot afford legal representation, see Legal Aid Review Committee of the Law Society of Singapore (2006) Report, 50, 52. A copy of the Report is available from the Law Society of Singapore upon request.
21. Koman (n 11).
22. Tan C. Han, "Challenges to Legal Education in a Changing Landscape—A Singapore Perspective" (2003) *Sing J. Int'l &Comp. L* 545, 556.
23. See NUS Law, Admissions, Undergraduate Programs, http://www.law.nus.edu.sg/admissions/llb_prog.html, accessed May 27, 2014.
24. See SMU School of Law, Programs, Bachelor of Laws, http://law.smu.edu.sg/programs/bachelor-of-laws/rigorous-challenging-curriculum, accessed May 27, 2014; SMU also

offers a Juris Doctor Degree, a basic law degree for students with undergraduate degrees in other disciplines or who have studied law in non-common law countries, that will qualify students for legal practice in Singapore, SMU School of Law, Programs, JD Program, http://law.smu.edu.sg/jd/home, accessed May 27, 2014.

25. Han (n 20).
26. Alexander F. H. Loke, "Educating the Thinking Lawyer," in Kevin Y. L. Tan (ed.) *The Singapore Legal System* 2nd ed.(Singapore University Press, 1999) 327.
27. SMU School of Law, About, Overview, http://law.smu.edu.sg/about/overview, accessed May 27, 2014.
28. Loke (n 24) 326.
29. Loke (n 24) 333.
30. Tan C. Han et al., "Legal Education in Asia" (2006) 1(1) *Asian J. Comp. L.* 1, 19.
31. See, for example, the clinical techniques identified in Susan Bryant and Elliott S. Milstein, "Rounds: A 'Signature Pedagogy' for Clinical Legal Education?" (2007) 14 *Clinical L. Rev.* 195.
32. Han et al. (n 28).
33. Alexander Loke, "Forging a New Equilibrium in Singapore Legal Education" (2006) 24 *Wis. Int'l L.J.* 261, 266.
34. Ibid. 261.
35. Helena Whalen-Bridge, "Towards a Comparative Rhetoric of Argument: Using the Concept of 'Audience' as a Means of Educating Students About Comparative Argument" (2006) 1(1) *Asian J. Comp. L.* 1, 9.
36. Han (n 20)545, 564–565.
37. The NUS course catalogue includes the following description: "This problem-oriented course will be centered on a complex commercial transaction that raises issues in several subject areas, some of which the student will not have studied. It is designed to teach students how to: (a) analyse complex hypothetical problems containing multiple legal issues from different areas of the law; (b) analyse and research issued in areas of law they have not studied; and (c) understand how the legal issues are linked to the transactional goals of the parties. It will also expose students to transactional documentation (drafting and review), client service skills and a basic understanding of business." http://ivle7.nus.edu.sg/lms/Account/NUSBulletin/msearch_view_full.aspx?modeCode=LC2003, accessed May 27, 2014.
38. The NUS course catalogue includes the following description: "The objectives of this course are to: introduce students to basic trial techniques and skills, including the basics of presentations in Court, modes of address, examination in chief and cross examination and submissions on facts. It will also introduce students to witness preparation for trial. The practical skills learned in this will complement those learned in first year Legal Writing. This course will also give students an opportunity to interact with and learn from practicing litigation lawyers, and thereby give them a taste of the 'real world' litigation practice." http://ivle7.nus.edu.sg/lms/Account/NUSBulletin/msearch_view_full.aspx?modeCode=LC2002, accessed May 27, 2014.
39. Han (n 20)545, 563.
40. See Singapore Institute of Legal Education, Admission to the Singapore Bar, http://www.sile.org.sg/part-b, accessed May 27, 2014.
41. Helena Whalen-Bridge, "The Lost Narrative: The Connection Between Legal Narrative and Legal Ethics" (2010) 7 *J. Ass'n Legal Writing Directors* 229, 240.
42. Electives have included "Conflicts and Obligations in Legal Ethics" and "Regulation of Lawyers."

43. See Singapore Management University (SMU) School of Law program description, http://law.smu.edu.sg/programs/bachelor-laws/why-smu-law/overview, accessed May 25, 2014.
44. Data on file with authors.
45. See NUS Pro Bono Group, Previous Excos, http://nusprobono.com/about-us/archive-exco-contacts/, accessed May 27, 2014. Associate Professor Helena Whalen-Bridge, a full-time faculty member and former practitioner, has been the Group's Faculty Advisor since its inception in 2005.
46. See Criminal Justice Club, http://www.nuslawclub.com/sub-clubs/cjc/, accessed May 27, 2014.
47. http://pbc.smu.edu.sg/
48. Singapore Institute of Legal Education, Pro Bono Program, http://www.sile.org.sg/pro-bono-program, accessed May 27, 2014.
49. Ibid.
50. Fourth Committee on the Supply of Lawyers, "Report of the 4th Committee on the Supply of Lawyers"(May 2013) 5–14, http://www.mlaw.gov.sg/content/dam/minlaw/corp/News/4th%20Committee%20Report.pdf, accessed May 27, 2014.
51. See Law Society of Singapore, Office of Pro Bono Services, About Us, http://probono.lawsociety.org.sg/About-Us/, accessed May 27, 2014.
52. Ibid.
53. Committee to Study Community Legal Services Initiatives, "Second Consultation Paper on Community Legal Services" (April 2, 2013) http://www.sal.org.sg/RegistrationForms/CORP%20COMMS/Second%20Consultation%20Paper%20for%20CLS%20020413%20(Annex%20A).pdf, accessed May 27, 2014.
54. Amir Hussain and Amanda Lee, "Govt will Provide Direct Legal Aid to Defendants in Criminal Cases" *Today* (Singapore, December 7, 2013) http://www.todayonline.com/singapore/govt-will-provide-direct--aid-defendants-criminal-cases#inside, accessed May 28, 2014.
55. Legal Profession Act (Cap 161, 2009 *Sing. Rev. Ed.*).
56. Ibid. s 32 and 33.
57. The Legal Profession Act (Cap 161, 2009 *Sing. Rev. Ed.*), s 34(1) h provides that the unauthorized persons prohibitions of s 33 do not apply to "any full-time member of the academic staff of any department of the National University of Singapore or of any department of law in any other institution of higher learning in Singapore who is a qualified person rendering any opinion or acting in an advisory capacity on any matter in which he has been instructed by an advocate and solicitor."
58. See Jeffrey C. W. Teck, "Liberalisation of the Singapore Legal Sector" (2009) Workshop Paper, ASEAN Law Association 10th General Assembly, p. 2, and Legal Profession Act (Cap 161, 2009 *Sing. Rev. Ed.*), Parts VIA and VIB.
59. Without approval from the Council of the Law Society of Singapore, per Legal Profession Act (Cap 161, 2009 *Sing. Rev. Ed.*), R 1, Legal Profession (Professional Conduct Rules) (2010 *Sing .Rev. Ed.*), r 9.
60. Legal Profession Act (Cap 161, 2009 *Sing. Rev. Ed.*), R 1, Legal Profession (Professional Conduct Rules) (2010 *Sing. Rev. Ed.*), r 39.
61. See Legal Profession Act (Cap 161, 2009 *Sing. Rev. Ed.*), Legal Profession (Limited Liability Law Partnership) Rules 2006, r 5, and Legal Profession Act (Cap 161, 2009 *Sing. Rev. Ed.*), Rule 21, Legal Profession (Law Corporation) Rules (2002 *Sing. Rev. Ed.*), The Schedule para 2.

62. K.C. Vijayan, "Law Students get to help as they learn" *The Straits Times* (Singapore, October 7, 2010) D8, http://newshub.nus.edu.sg/news/1010/PDF/LAW-st-7oct-pD8.pdf, accessed May 28, 2014. See also Tan C. Han, "The Goals and Objectives of Law Schools beyond Educating Students: Research, Capacity Building, Community Service—The National University of Singapore School of Law Experience" (2010) 29 *Penn St. Int'l L. Rev.* 67, 74–78.
63. "New NUS Course to Allow Law Students to Work on Real Cases" *Channel New Asia* (Singapore, October 6, 2010);Tan C. Han, "Law School has to Keep up with the Times" *The Straits Times* (Singapore, April 26, 2007).
64. Ibid.
65. Legal Service Commission, "Annual Report 2011"(The Legal Branch, The Legal Aid Bureau, 2011) http://app.lsc.gov.sg/data/AR/2011/html/6-legal_aid_bureau.html, accessed May 29, 2014.
66. Vijayan (n 60).
67. Unless otherwise noted, details regarding The Law Clinic were graciously provided by Associate Professor Ruby Lee, National University of Singapore Faculty of Law.
68. NUS News Portal, "Faculty of Law Launches Singapore's First Clinical Legal Education Program" (Singapore, October 8, 2010) newshub.nus.edu.sg/headlines/1010/law_08Oct10.php, accessed May 29, 2014.
69. Singapore State Courts, JusticeOnLine, http://www.statecourtsvc.com.sg/, accessed June 1, 2014.
70. Ibid.
71. These student comments, as well as other details regarding The Law Clinic, were graciously provided by Associate Professor Ruby Lee, National University of Singapore Faculty of Law.
72. See "Law Students Get to Help as They Learn" *The Straits Times* (Singapore, October 7, 2010) B8.
73. At that time, the SMU students had the added option of clearing the community service requirement by doing pro bono placements and/or service at community legal clinics as legal assistants to pro bono secured and/or approved by the law school. See Koman (n 11).
74. Singapore Management University (SMU) Centre for Social Responsibility states that SMU recognizes the importance of preparing her students to be responsible citizens who give back to society. Students are thus required to complete a minimum of 80 hours in community service as part of their graduation requirement. See Centre for Social Responsibility, "Why Community Service" (SMU) http://centres.smu.edu.sg/c4sr/why-community-service/, accessed May 24, 2014.
75. See Singapore Management University's (SMU) CIRCLE values, which constitute an integral part of SMU's holistic approach to education. At the heart of the SMU Spirit, the CIRCLE values stand for Commitment, Integrity, Responsibility, Collegiality, Leadership, and Excellence. See Vision and Mission (*SMU*), http://www.smu.edu.sg/smu/about/university-information/vision-and-mission, accessed May 24, 2014.
76. The Singapore Management University (SMU) School of Law (SOL) has 3 Core Values—Integrity, Scholarship, and Humanity. See SOL, "Mission Values" (*SMU*) http://law.smu.edu.sg/about/mission-values, accessed May 24, 2014.
77. The essential role of SMU legal clinics is really to act as a provider of legal services to indigent persons and to promote access to justice. This is in line with the university's

and the School of Law's core value to be of service to humanity. A by product of this role was that the clinics provided a source of clinical learning, albeit limited to students when assisting in these clinics.

78. Rathna N. Koman, a full-time law faculty member and a former practitioner, is the Director at the SMU Pro Bono Centre. Prior to the setting up of the Centre, Associate Professor Rathna Koman was the faculty adviser for pro bono from 2007 till 2013. She has been responsible for setting up the various pro bono placements for SMU law students since 2007.
79. A copy of the SMU Pro Bono Centre Student manual can be obtained upon request from the Centre Director at email id, probonocentre@smu.edu.sg.
80. For detailed discussion of case study results, see section 3.4.4.
81. A copy of the manual used at these clinics can be obtained on request from the Pro Bono Services Office, the Law Society of Singapore, at the email address tanguy@lawsociety.org.sg.
82. Koman (n 11).
83. See SMU case study data provided in section 3.4.1.2.3.
84. See Jill Chaifetz, "The Value of Public Service: A Model for Instilling a Pro Bono Ethic in Law School" (1993) 45 *Stan. L. Rev.* 1695, 1699, where the author defines latent curriculum as a "set of values about what 'good' (i.e. smart, efficient, respected) lawyers practice in their professional lives. Latent curriculum is transmitted to students through class content, the emphasis placed on certain skills and areas above others, cues from law faculty, discussions between students, advice from attorneys and the method of job recruitment. It is part of a process of acculturation whereby students shape their legal identities in accordance with majority viewpoint."
85. Legal Profession Act (Cap 161, 2009 *Sing. Rev. Ed.*), s 71, Legal Profession (Professional Conduct) Rules 2010, R 2(2) and R 2(2)(a)–(d).
86. See above section 3.3.2.2.
87. See Robert Granfield, "Institutionalizing Public Service in Law School: Results on the Impact of Mandatory Pro Bono Programs" (2007) 54 (5) *Buff. L. Rev.* 1355.
88. Ibid. 1379–1380.

CHAPTER 9

Clinical Legal Education in Thailand: A Pedagogy Whose Time Has Come

Panarairat Srichaiyarat, Lisa Radtke Bliss, and Withoon Taloodkum

Introduction

As a developing country with a growing economy, Thailand needs lawyers who are equipped to serve the growing needs of the country.[1] Thailand is a member of the Association of Southeast Asian Nations (ASEAN), a coalition of countries in Southeast Asia that have agreed to cooperate in multiple areas, including economic integration. As the country continues to grow, a strong legal system and legal profession are essential to its success. Clinical legal education ("CLE") has long been accepted in other parts of the world as a method for training law students to become competent, ethical professionals. This chapter will describe the implementation of CLE in Thailand. The chapter begins by introducing the Thai legal and legal education systems, and the history of CLE in Thailand. CLE began with the community legal service initiative of a group of Thammasat University female law students in 1949, and continues today through multiple CLE initiatives, many of which are supported through the activities of an NGO, Bridges Across Borders Southeast Asia Community Legal Education Initiative[2] ("BABSEA CLE"), which began working to introduce CLE throughout the region in 2005.

This chapter will describe the multipronged efforts to encourage the development of CLE within Thailand, including clinical teaching workshops, CLE conferences, CLE scholarship, and the hosting of international clinicians in-residence. This chapter also highlights case studies of Thai law clinics and other CLE programs that provide access to justice for the poor, access to lawyering skills training for law students, and that inculcate professional values and ethical standards in law students. Finally, the chapter analyzes factors affecting the sustainable development of CLE in Thailand as well as its effect on legal education reform, justice delivery, and law reform in general. The authors conclude with predictions for the future of CLE in Thailand.

The Thai Legal System

The Thai legal system is a product of the country's origins as a monarchy. In the fourteenth century, the king of Thailand presided over disputes. Legal knowledge was transmitted from person to person. After the fourteenth century, the king passed power to resolve disputes on to royal noble officials known as *purohita*.[3] Royal officials were given the power to draft laws, which were then approved by the king. The king's decrees or rulings on issues served as precedent for others to follow. Thus, law and legal knowledge were restricted to certain officials and members of their families who had access. Others did not have the opportunity to learn about the law until it later became available in written form.[4]

After 1782, all existing Thai laws and regulations were assembled, revised, and rectified.[5] This effort resulted in three written copies of Thai law, which were referred to as the "Three Emblems of State Law," or the "Law of the Three Great Seals."[6]In the nineteenth century, Thailand also promulgated new laws directed toward enhancing trade relations between Thailand and other countries.[7] Laws were also printed in books and thus became more widely available.[8]

In 1891, the royal Thai government established the Ministry of Justice, which developed a civil law system. However, Thailand had a lack of trained personnel to help address legal problems. As a result, the Thai government hired legal experts from foreign countries to assist.[9] Additionally, many Thai officials and members of the royal family studied overseas. This had an influence on the development of Thai law. In 1932, absolute monarchy in Thailand was abolished, and a constitutional form of government was introduced. This new form of government followed a system of rules and laws, and further increased the need for trained, educated persons to assist in its implementation.[10] The reformed "rule of law" system in Thailand is based upon codes, a constitution, legislative enactments, and executive regulations.[11]

The Thai Legal Education System

Thai law schools were initially founded in order to train legal officials to serve in the courts and to apply the law under the reformed legal system.[12] Because law teachers had been trained abroad, particularly in England, the English approach to teaching and curriculum design influenced the development of Thai law schools and their curricula.[13]

Currently, legal education in Thailand is an area of study offered as part of traditional university education.[14] Students may elect to study law as part of a four-year undergraduate course of study, and obtain a Bachelor of Laws (LLB) degree. Students who wish to pursue additional education in law may pursue a Master of Laws (LLM) degree at a Thai university or abroad. Some universities in Thailand also offer postgraduate study in law for those who wish to obtain a Doctor of Laws (PhD) degree.

The Ministry of Education oversees and sets educational standards for all universities in Thailand. These standards set forth requirements that all universities must meet, regardless of the subject area of study. However, the Thai system of education is not completely centralized. Universities have wide latitude and autonomy to create law programs. Universities and their law departments may design their own curricula, so long as they meet the common standards for university education set forth by the Ministry. To date, the Ministry has not established specific standards for either legal education or CLE. Nevertheless, all law curricula must reflect learning outcomes, and schools are required to report those outcomes to the Ministry of Education. This focus on outcomes is based upon the adoption of the Thai Qualifications Framework for Higher Education, known as "TQF."[15] The focus of TQF is to set learning outcomes for students in order to guarantee that graduates meet certain qualifications as the result of their education. Under TQF, students' learning outcomes include the following components: ethics and morals, knowledge, cognitive skills, interpersonal skills and responsibility, and numerical analysis, communication, and information technology skills. These learning outcomes hold the most promise for Thai legal education reform.

CLE methods are uniquely suited to helping students achieve professional competence and to satisfying the outcomes established by TQF.[16] Some Thai law schools are already incorporating CLE into their programs, by developing for-credit CLE courses as a part of the law curriculum and by integrating interactive, reflective teaching methods into existing courses. In order to fully achieve the TQF goals, CLE should be recognized, and required, as a core component of the law curriculum. As a result, developing CLE as a tool for complying with TQF will further reform the Thai legal education system.

The History of CLE in Thailand

The history of law clinics in Thailand can be traced back to 1949 when a group of female law students at Thammasat University voluntarily began an initiative aimed at providing legal consultation and education services to the community.[17] These progressive students also advocated for law reform relating to women's rights. After graduation, they continued to pursue these goals and established the Women Lawyers' Association, designed to provide pro bono legal assistance to the public, especially to women. The Association has provided such services ever since.

Another initiative was started at Thammasat University in 1962 as a community project, with aims similar to the 1949 initiative: to provide legal consultation and education services to underserved communities.[18] In the early 1970s, when the country experienced political difficulty, Thammasat law students formed a study group named Nitisuksa, or "Legal Studies," with the goal of relating their legal studies to social reality. While similar to the 1949 initiative, all of the Nitisuksa founders were men. During the first half of the 1970s, the Nitisuksa group and the Thammasat University Faculty of Law actively provided legal services to farmers and workers. However, after the October 1976 bloody coup, the group was terminated, as were many other student activist groups. Two years later, when Thailand's political atmosphere became more democratic, the legal literacy initiative of the Nitisuksa group resumed[19] and became a part of an official faculty unit under the name of "Law Center."[20] This Law Center continues to exist today and follows a legal services office model, with lawyers providing the primary representation and law students serving in assistant roles.[21]

Understanding and appreciating the benefits of CLE through academic law programs and courses is not new to Thailand. The concept of CLE as a structured academic program and as a part of the legal education curriculum was brought to the attention of Thai legal academia in 1971. In an article titled "A New Approach to Legal Education," Professor Pichaisak Horyangkul, at that time a law professor at Chulalongkorn University, proposed the idea of including CLE in the law curriculum.[22] Around the same time, Thammasat law students presented a similar idea to their faculty, proposing that providing public service should be required for all students. This idea was generated by approximately 70 Thammasat law students and lecturers who participated in a 15-day Legal Literacy Campaign in 1974. This campaign was the product of a law student's plea for legal aid assistance for farmers in his hometown who were losing their land. The students came back from the campaign to their legal studies with an understanding of how the law unfairly affected disadvantaged people.[23] Unfortunately, neither of these early CLE proposals were accepted into the curriculum of any Thai university.

CLE, as a structured academic program that integrates public service and education for academic credit, is currently still new to Thai legal academia. Although many Thai law schools have had community legal service initiatives to provide legal advice and knowledge to the public for decades, most of them have been primarily operated by either professors as pro bono initiatives or by students as extracurricular activities. Some programs are operated by full-time lawyers and allow students to play supportive roles. Very few Thai law schools, however, provide CLE as accredited courses in their law curriculum, thereby balancing universities' public service and educational missions. However, one school that offers such courses and one school that has a strong plan to do so, Chiang Mai University Law School and University of Phayao Law School, are the focus of this chapter.

Strategies to Promote CLE in Thailand

In recent years, there has been a concerted effort to promote CLE as an accredited course throughout Thailand. This has been done in collaboration with universities, NGOs, and other organizations. This effort has had a significant impact on both raising awareness of CLE's potential as an educational enterprise as well as the development of CLE programs. These strategies have included CLE-related workshops, conferences, scholarship and research, and the use of "clinicians-in-residence"—international clinical legal educators who have accepted long-term university placements.

CLE Workshops and Conferences

In November 2010, the first national CLE workshop in Thailand was held at Chiang Mai University. The workshop's aims were to develop a greater understanding of the principles and methodologies of CLE among Thai legal educators and to promote the development of law clinics. The workshop was cohosted by BABSEA CLE and the Chiang Mai University law clinic, described more fully in the section below. Twenty-two law lecturers from 11 Thai law schools participated. Some of them were the key persons in the schools' legal aid initiatives, and some were the deans or the heads of the law departments. The workshop also brought together international clinicians to share their experiences and to present to the Thai participants how CLE functions in their countries. This broad array of international clinicians came from Australia, China, Indonesia, Laos, Malaysia, and Vietnam. Each of these international clinicians were engaged and had expertise in different CLE program models. Participants were thus exposed to a wide, demonstrative scope of CLE program options. Although unique, each CLE program also included a common core component of being educational, student-centered, social justice-related university programs.

Like those on which it was modeled, this national Thailand CLE workshop was an immense success. As planned, it provided the participants a much deeper understanding of the CLE methodologies and their purposes. Bringing in the international scholars also assured the Thai participants that CLE is not limited to any specific country nor to a common law or civil law system or to only a developing or developed country. Rather, the participants were clearly able to see that CLE was a global movement that would apply to Thailand.

Building on this accomplishment, a second national Thailand CLE event, titled "Clinical Legal Education: A Means to Improve Legal Teaching Methods" was held in Chiang Mai, Thailand, in April 2012. This workshop was initiated and organized by the Chiang Mai University law clinic. Many of the goals of this workshop differed from the first one. Although both workshops aimed to promote and develop the understanding of principles and methodologies of CLE among Thai legal educators, the primary aim of the second workshop was to promote the incorporation of CLE teaching methodologies into regular law courses. The second workshop thus shifted the target group of participants from scholars who were directly involved with law clinics or legal aid initiatives to those who took charge of academic affairs or nonclinic law lectures. The workshop drew attention from 40 participants who were from 16 Thai law schools. Some of them were heads of law departments and associate deans. As planned, the workshop provided the participants an understanding of how to change the lecture-based teaching method used predominantly in Thai law schools to an interactive method and how CLE could help them fulfill the requirements of the Thai Qualification Framework for Higher Education of the Ministry of Education. Some law lecturers from the National University of Laos also participated in the workshop. The workshop's main supporters, BABSEA CLE and Professor Katherine Lindsay from Newcastle Law School, Australia, played major roles in making this workshop an immense success.

Continuing from the success of the 2012 workshop, the next significant CLE event occurred in November 2013—the hosting of the first national CLE conference in Thailand. The conference, titled "Clinical Legal Education as a Means to Assist in Reforming the Thailand Legal Education System: Regional and International Experiences and Perspectives," was held at Khon Kaen University Faculty of Law. The conference aimed to raise awareness of the benefits of CLE at the Thailand educational policy level. The UNDP, the Law Reform Commission of Thailand (LRCT), BABSEA CLE, and Khon Kaen University Faculty of Law cohosted the conference.[24] This multifaceted support significantly demonstrated that major stakeholders were convinced of the value of CLE.

Like similar events before, the conference gained ardent support from both regional and international CLE scholars. Fourteen CLE scholars from Australia, China, the United States, and almost all the Southeast Asia countries presented how CLE functions in their legal education systems. Thirty-five legal scholars from 15 Thai law schools participated as well as four representatives from the LRCT, and 25 legal scholars from 9 Myanmar law schools and 4 from Laos law schools.

After years of attempts to introduce CLE to Thai legal academia, these workshops and conference gradually brought the Thai CLE movement to the next level. Many law school deans showed strong intentions to integrate CLE into their curriculum as an accredited course. The workshops and conference made it clear that CLE involved much more than just providing legal services to people. There was an unmistakable demonstration that CLE is an educational program that provides students with practical experience, an understanding of the ramifications of the law, lawyering skills, and other values of the profession.

Among the many achievements resulting from these undertakings, these CLE events helped foster a keen interest among many of the participants in developing a best practice model for their CLE programs. The Khon Kaen conference also initiated the creation of the Southeast Asia Clinical Legal Education Association (SEACLE), a regional CLE alliance formed to give its members the opportunity to share experiences, ideas, and a passion for social justice.

During the years described above, the move to support CLE in Thailand was not solely limited to national events. On the contrary, BABSEA CLE, in conjunction with both Thai and other Southeast Asia regional partners, also designed and held numerous CLE workshops on-site at various Thai university departments. They included multiple workshops at the University of Ubon Ratchathani, University of Phayao, Mae Fah Luang University, Thaksin University, and Prince of Songkla University. These workshops were designed to introduce

CLE concepts and methods to law faculty and students. Many of these institutions' personnel may not have had the opportunity to attend the aforementioned workshops and conference. A primary feature of the workshops was to use and demonstrate interactive, reflective teaching techniques. This included sharing sample teaching manuals that contained contextualized, relevant lesson plans as a means of encouraging and assisting participants in more easily implementing what they learned from the workshop experience.

There is little doubt that these workshops, conferences, and other CLE initiatives have been a successful part of the development of CLE in Thailand. Through these initiatives, Thai legal academia has gained a better understanding of CLE and its values. Many academics have expressed interest in either establishing a structured law clinic at their law school or integrating CLE teaching methodology into their regular law courses. The Law Reform Commission of Thailand has also shown an interest in including CLE in its plans for legal education reform.[25]

CLE Scholarship

CLE scholarship, in addition to using conferences and training workshops, has also served to promote CLE in Thailand. In 2009, Panarairat Srichaiyarat, at that time the director and founder of the CMU law clinic, initiated a research project entitled "Clinical Legal Education: An Option for Thai Legal Education Reform." The project has a number of goals, including seeking to gain a greater understanding about CLE, to determine whether CLE functions well in a civil law country in which legal education starts at the undergraduate level, and to analyze whether CLE can reform legal education in Thailand.[26] Because China is an Asian civil law country like Thailand, and a number of Chinese law schools have implemented CLE programs for more than a decade, CLE in China was selected as a case study.[27] While the research began with very positive prospects, the project's outcomes and its benefits for CLE development in Thailand far exceeded the researcher's expectations.

The project's research was extensive and enveloped a broad scope. Dr. Srichaiyarat interviewed clinic professors, program executives, and law students of three leading Chinese law schools: Peking, Tsinghua, and Renmin University of China. These interviews revealed that CLE in China enhanced students' lawyering skills, knowledge of legal theories and provisions, and awareness of the law's effect on real people and of both the potential and the limitations of the legal system in the real world. One of the most significant findings of this research is that CLE in China instilled legal professional values and ethics in law students. Many of the student interviewees demonstrated both social responsibility and responsibility toward clients.[28] For example, a Renmin Law School student stated, "In other classes, it does not matter if we do not understand the lecture. We could hold it as long as it does not affect our exam. If we pass the exam, that's still fine. But when you study the clinic course, you've got to help people. You can't say that you don't understand and you will hold on your doubtfulness and not clarify it. If we do not understand, we must try to understand."[29] Similarly, another student stated, "When we firstly talked about social responsibility, I felt it was so empty, so ambiguous. However, after I started working with the clinic, I gradually had experience with the poor. People who came to the clinic are poor. They are grass-roots people. University students have no contact with these people . . . Before working with the clinic, social responsibility was nothing, so vacant. But after working with the clinic, I know that it's real. It is true."[30]

These words were quoted in the research report that was submitted to deans of Thai law schools, legal scholars, and Law Reform Commissioners of Thailand, and were presented at the aforementioned CLE workshops and conferences. Perhaps these heartfelt and straightforward answers are the most compelling evidence that will make Thai legal scholars believe that CLE has the potential to be a means of Thai legal education reform.

In addition to interviews, this research studied the accredited CLE curricula of two American law schools,[31] CLE methodologies, and critiques of traditional teaching methods applied in law schools by means of documentary research. The findings revealed the paths to structurally integrating two main basic missions of law schools—legal education and public service, the shortcoming of traditional teaching methods, and a rationale for supporting the acceptance of CLE as an accredited educational program.

The analysis part of this research then drew on the findings of both the interviews and the documentary research, and pointed out that CLE methodologies are in accordance with the goals of the Thai national education reform and have high potential to make the Thai legal education reach all of the learning outcomes required by TQF, including enhancing students' morals and ethics, as well as strengthening of their legal knowledge and necessary professional skills.[32] This research, thus, recommends that CLE should be integrated into the Thai law curriculum as a compulsory comprehensive course and that CLE teaching methodologies should be utilized in every law course.[33]

Dr. Srichaiyarat's analysis was confirmed by a research project of Duangporn Lertjareansamai titled "The Achievement of Learning Administrative Law by Legal Clinic for Academic Activity according to Thailand Qualifications Framework."[34] The researcher was a participant in the 2012 CLE workshop held in Chiang Mai. She brought the idea of incorporating CLE teaching methodologies into her administrative law course. The 26 students of Duangporn Lertjareansamai responded to the questionnaire, saying that CLE teaching methodologies brought about all TQF learning outcomes. They showed their satisfaction at the highest level toward all of the five domains of the TQF learning outcomes.[35]

To more broadly disseminate the findings and recommendations of Dr. Srichaiyarat's research, two journal articles based on her research were also written and published in two Thai law journals.[36] Additionally, other scholarship on CLE in Thailand has focused on how CLE can shape the development of the legal profession and the future of the Thai legal system.[37] Undoubtedly, this CLE research and these articles are going to be merely the first wave of Thai CLE scholarship. Many future studies, articles, and textbooks are confidently anticipated, and this scholarship will become a solid foundation of the sustainable development of CLE in Thailand.

The Use of Law Fellows and Clinicians-in-Residence to Support the Development of CLE in Thailand

In addition to designing multiple workshops to introduce CLE methods and sharing teaching manuals and sample lesson plans, other innovative methods have been designed to support the development of CLE in Thailand. Two initiatives have had the greatest impact: the placement of International Clinicians-in-Residence ("ICIR") within host Thailand universities and the hiring of Thai law fellows.

BABSEA CLE has been a key facilitator in the sourcing and placement of the ICIRs. BABSEA CLEA considers a number of factors in their selection of ICIRs, including any experience they may have had in developing CLE programs both in their own country and elsewhere (preferably countries in transition and, when possible, within Southeast Asia). The ICIRs must be able to commit to a minimum of a one-month placement with the host university, and they must have relevant and applicable working knowledge of CLE programs similar to those established in Thailand with both client, community, and classroom components.

In addition, ICIRs have been sought based on the following requirements:

- They come from institutions demonstrating willingness to support CLE and legal education in Thailand.
- They are associated with associations that adhere to "best practices," such as the Global Alliance for Justice Education,[38] the European Network on Clinical Legal Education, the Southeast Asia Clinical Legal Education Association, and the *International Journal on Clinical Legal Education*.[39]
- They must be prepared to volunteer their time. They are not paid for their services, but reasonable travel and living expenses may be covered.
- They must have their own institution's permission and support to take time from their duties.
- They must come from institutions in which CLE has a social justice focus.

These ICIRs have, through both long-term and shorter-term visits at Thai universities, supported the implementation of clinical teaching methods into the general curriculum and supported law faculty in clinic development and design.[40]

In addition to the placement of ICIRs, BABSEA CLE has hired Thai law fellows, who have assisted in designing and teaching CLE in workshops for law students and faculty as well as legal education workshops in the community, and who are contributing to the development of teaching materials. These law fellows are typically Thai law graduates who have successfully participated in a CLE Thai program. The fellowship program works by placing a law fellow at a Thai law faculty, sometimes in conjunction with an ICIR. Another effective mechanism is the hiring of the law fellows by BABSEA CLE and the primary placement of fellows within the BABSEA CLE office in Chiang Mai. From there, the fellows provide technical support and liaison assistance with partner universities as they initiate or strengthen their CLE programs.

Case Studies of Thai CLE Programs

All of the above CLE program development efforts have proven to be effective in different ways. Such success can be demonstrated through an evaluation of a variety of Thai CLE program case studies, some of which will be discussed below.

Chiang Mai University Law Clinic

The Chiang Mai University Law Clinic, otherwise known as the Legal Community Service Project, was founded in 1994. The clinic was founded based on a proposal initiated by Dr. Panarairat Srichaiyarat when the first group of CMU law students reached their third year. The fundamental objectives of the clinic were to instill in law students the idea of a public service obligation and to provide free legal counseling to the community to fulfill the university's community service commitment. The clinic, operated by the CMU law professors and law student volunteers, mainly provided counseling to walk-in clients.

In 2006, the CMU Law Division was changed to the Faculty of Law by the CMU Council. Around the same time, the law clinic also reached a new phase. With technical assistance and financial support from two international not-for-profit organizations, BABSEA CLE and the Open Society Institute, the clinic extended its services to include community legal education, a for-credit internship program for law students, and more structured training for volunteers and intern students. The newly structured clinic also placed more focus on working with socially vulnerable and marginalized individuals and communities. The clinic's objectives also expanded to include the following aims:

1. instilling in the students an ethical obligation to engage in public service and social justice pursuits while at the university and throughout their lives
2. providing free legal counseling and community service to people of all socio economic statuses, especially to those of limited financial means
3. creating a source for legal counseling and education that guarantees trustworthy, reliable, and quality client-centered services
4. providing law students an arena in which to learn law by working in real-life situations with real people, in order to increase their legal practice skills using interactive, reflective, educational, and student-centered methods
5. creating a positive public perception of the legal education system and the legal profession

The CMU Law Clinic operates differently from other Thai law schools' legal public service initiatives in that it endeavors to be primarily student centered. For example, CMU Law Clinic students take significant roles in providing the clinic services. In the legal consultation section, the students take charge of interviewing the clients, doing factual and legal research and analysis, identifying the case theory, and giving advice to the clients. In the community teaching section, the students take charge of designing the lesson plans, selecting the topics and teaching methods, and being the teachers. CMU law professors take hands-off roles as supervisors through a CLE-structured educational approach.

Since it was started, the CMU Law Clinic has provided students an interactive, hands-on learning opportunity. However, the way in which the clinic trained and prepared students for their tasks in the clinic was very limited. In 2007, based on the technical support from BABSEACLE, the CMU Law Clinic started to provide CLE-structured training to students prior to their work in the clinic. This training curriculum included the following topics: introduction to CLE, teaching methodologies, lesson plan development, lesson plan demonstration, practice teaching, professional ethics and client confidentiality, client communication and interviewing skills, skills related to taking a statement, client counseling skills, and in-house office setup.

In 2011, a research project was conducted to find out whether the CMU law clinic shared any similar outcomes with CLE in China. The same set of questions used in China was asked of 12CMU law school alumni who graduated during 2008 to 2010 about their CLE experiences. Many of these graduates performed legal services through the CMU clinic as volunteers. Some interviewees stated that they performed community teaching around 70 to 80 times.[41] Most of them had two or three years of clinic experience before they graduated.

These alumni had different purposes and motivations for taking part in the clinic—for example, to fulfill the internship requirement of the LLB curriculum,[42] to gain practical skills,[43] and to experiment with an aspect of the legal profession.[44] All of the interviewees expressed a positive attitude toward their clinic experiences. Many of them stated that the experiences surpassed their expectations. Their answers reflected that not only were their practical skills and knowledge of legal provisions and theories enhanced but also their understanding of how the law affects people's lives in the real world. For example, when one student was asked how CLE differed from traditional law courses, he said that in the traditional courses the lecturers hardly talked about the societal reality, and mainly focused on the written law. In contrast, the clinic provided him an arena in which to find out that some legal provisions had loopholes, other provisions were inapplicable in a particular case, and still others were unfair to specific groups of people. The student said he would consider the legal provisions infallible if he only studied in traditional classes.[45] Similarly, another student reflected upon her clinic experience by saying, "I learned that it does not matter for nonlawyers what the law prescribes. What matters for them is how the law affects them. The law we study in the class is very limited. It cannot make us able to deal with real problems of real people."[46] She also stated, "The law we study in class is so dry. There is no life. In the clinic after we put in our heart and our feeling, the law has a life."[47]

Perhaps most significantly, the interviews in Chiang Mai found, similar to those conducted in China, that CLE has succeeded in instilling social justice and human rights values in these alumni. The interviewees stated that their attitude toward prisoners and ethnic minorities was significantly changed by their community teaching clinic experiences. A student reflected upon his experience of visiting a prison by saying, "I had a thought that prisons were overcrowded and dirty. People in there were bad. However, after exposure to them my attitudes towards them are changed. Perhaps they were there just because of one mistake in their life. They are not born to be bad."[48] Similarly, another student stated after the prison visit, "I was afraid of them but I changed my attitude after teaching in there. They are not dreadful. They have kids, have families. They talked to us as if they were our aunts, our sisters."[49]

The values and ethics of the legal profession, for example, principles of being competent, demonstrating loyalty to the client, maintaining confidentiality, and participating in pro bono work, have also been instilled in the Chiang Mai alumni. The two student interviewees affirmed that they approached their clinic work more seriously than their studies in traditional classes. They reasoned that in real situations with real people they had a greater responsibility. They said that in the traditional classes they were responsible just for themselves. If they failed an exam, they could make it up. However, in the clinic, their clients and their learners are people. Once again, the answers from the Thai students are almost identical to an answer from a Renmin Law School Student, who said that in clinics, "You've got to help people."

In addition to the educational value of the CLE program at Chiang Mai University, the clinic has been a resource for access to justice for the underprivileged. Although the clinic had only four faculty members, at its peak, it could provide access to legal consultation services to 154 clients and access to legal knowledge to hundreds of learners through 35 community teachings in various settings, including a juvenile training center and ethnic minority villages. The clinic students were the key factors that made these services possible. Recently, the CMU law clinic had around 40 students, both volunteer and enrolled, who worked for the clinic. They work under the close supervision of the four clinic faculty members and under some strict regulations to assure the service quality.

After the CMU law clinic adopted CLE methodologies into its operation, the clinic also served as a model for the development of CLE both in Thailand and the region. The clinic welcomed vice rectors, deans, and senior law faculty members from leading universities in Laos, Myanmar, Thailand, and Vietnam who were in the emerging stages of developing CLE programs, or who have a strong interest in doing so. Their study visit to the CMU law clinic provided them not only an opportunity to observe the CMU clinical program in action and gain a better understanding of how to develop and implement an accredited CLE courses at the university level but also the inspiration to do so.

Unquestionably, the success of the CMU law clinic was the outcome of the long-term dedication of all the clinic faculty members and students. Perhaps, at present, the greatest challenge for the CMU law clinic is how to keep leading the development of CLE in the country and the region.

University of Phayao, Law Clinic

In 2010, CLE was introduced into the School of Law at the University of Phayao ("UP") as the result of faculty attending one of the CLE workshops described above. After that workshop, the participants from the School of Law at UP began implementing CLE reform into legal teaching, with plans to reorganize the legal aid and training center (law clinic) in order to develop legal teaching and legal aid.

Since its creation, the School of Law at UP, the legal aid and training center has mainly focused on legal aid. This clinic will now provide legal assistance to people, in which law students will play the main roles in the survey and interview processes. The clinic focuses on rural community outreach. Law professors, as center directors, set all the proposals, plans, objectives, and choose target communities. Students involved in the clinic will be exposed to real legal problems in communities, especially those involving the homeless or the stateless in those areas. However, the clinic operation is currently limited by the clinic supervisors' interests and specializations; thus, the provided legal assistance does not cover all legal problems.

CLE gained more support at UP following a CLE workshop held at the School of Law at UP, and presented by BABSEA CLE. The workshop was an introduction to CLE, CLE methodologies, and its importance. The workshop was conducted in English, which helped improve the English skills of the UP students. Nevertheless, the students learned slowly at first because CLE was quite new and because of the language barrier. UP faculty held additional CLE workshops to provide both students and faculty with a better understanding of CLE. UP has also instituted more community outreach through Thai and international students working together. In addition, Thai lecturers exchanged knowledge about CLE and discussed CLE assessment methods with professors who supervised international interns. There was concern about how to assess practical learning, such as CLE, in a system in which assessments are done primarily by examination. Advice from international professors on course curriculum, lesson plans, outcomes, and evaluations has helped UP's CLE program become more systematic.

The collaboration between the School of Law at UP, BABSEA CLE, and the CLE Foundation have fostered CLE programs. BABSEA CLE has provided human resources, including clinicians and international students, training workshops, and technical support. As a result, the School of Law at UP changed the way it provides legal assistance from a passive to an active approach, and students now go out into and learn from the community.

However, there is an obstacle to making CLE mandatory at the School of Law at UP. CLE is still only a part of a community service activity. It lacks sustainability and efficient mechanisms to drive the program forward. Thus, the School of Law at UP needs to change its status from a student activity to an accredited course. This will result in both better legal education and increased access to justice.

Community teaching is a new program of CLE in the School of Law, University of Phayao. The community teaching was developed from a project in which a law lecturer taught students to be more interactive learners who could then go out into the community and teach community members about their legal rights.

Community teaching lessons were chosen based on research and surveys collected by law students and law lecturers. Before undertaking the surveys, law students and lecturers worked together to plan activities. These learning activities improved law students' skills in research and data collection. Most community teaching programs at the School of Law, University of Phayao, focused on nationality law and issues involving legal status of being persons. These issues came from a survey carried out in the districts located near the border between Thailand and Laos. Stateless persons currently lack the knowledge and documents to establish their status. The students study by reading law and providing legal knowledge to these people in the local area. Community teaching is hard for the students because they have never been asked to communicate with local people. The students have often never spoken with a stateless person who has no legal background. However, after teaching small groups of stateless people, the students improved their ability to communicate with others.

The most important aspect of community teaching is the curriculum. The students and the lecturer have to work together to design a curriculum suitable to the learner. One part of this legal education is about raising an awareness of access to justice for the students, but it also helps them understand the relationship between society and law. The students are able to better understand the condition of people with no access to law and justice.

The greatest challenge in CLE is changing legal learning by adding this type of education to traditional legal learning. Traditionally, legal instruction has been done by lecturing, without students practicing their skills and determining value. In particular, this approach never evaluates the student's legal mind. It is usually only evaluates the student's ability to remember the law and Supreme Court decisions. Law students mainly study by listening, reading a legal textbook, and remembering decisions of the Supreme Court.

Most traditional law lecturers only focus on the law on paper, not on the practice and the impact of practicing law. These lecturers are normally satisfied with the learning outcome from students' writing legal essays. However, one small group of lecturers is trying to improve legal education by providing opportunities for students to practice law. Because of their experience students will then better understand the law and its impact in society.

The School of Law, University of Phayao, became one of a few Thai law schools where CLE started taking root in the law curriculum. Many lecturers are strongly interested in implementing CLE teaching methodologies in their teaching and aim to make CLE a mandatory course for their law students. This aim is to fulfill the required learning outcomes by the TQF as well as to help students learn better.

Conclusion: The Future of CLE in Thailand

While CLE has already taken firm root in many Asian countries, in Thailand it is still at an advanced beginning stage. While suggesting that the future of CLE in Thailand is very promising may be too reckless to say, suggesting that CLE has no future in Thailand also underestimates the potential of the CLE movement there. A number of strong factors support the sustainable development of CLE in Thailand. One of the most important factors is the need of Thai law schools to fulfill the requirements of the educational standard or the TQF issued by the Ministry of Education in 2009. The TQF has made many school executives aware that legal education in this era cannot be entirely knowledge based. It requires other dimensions of education, including skills-based and values-based learning. It is quite clear that many of the TQF required learning outcomes cannot be achieved by traditional lecture-based teaching methods. Therefore, the learning-through-doing teaching method and social justice dimensions of CLE have high potential to provide these outcomes. After almost ten years of CLE advocacy in Thailand, the capability of CLE as a means for Thai legal education reform is widely recognized by law lecturers, program executives, and policymakers. As of the writing of this chapter, the Subcommittee on the Legal Education of the Law Reform Commission of Thailand has already started the process of issuing a specific standard for legal education. It is reasonable to believe that this initiative was partially influenced by the recommendations made during one of the major CLE conference in Thailand—the "Clinical Legal Education as a Means to Assist in Reforming the Thailand Legal Education System: Regional and International Experiences and Perspectives" in 2013. Hence, there is a strong possibility that CLE will be included in the standard as a recommended elective course that law schools should provide to their students.

The potential of CLE to produce better law graduates for Thailand is another important factor that will make CLE sustainable. As mentioned earlier, Thailand needs better trained and more ethical lawyers. If Thai law schools implement CLE properly, either as a separate program or as a teaching methodology integrated into traditional law courses, law graduates will be better equipped with legal knowledge, practical skills, and professional values. Additionally, if CLE can be implemented in an environment that focuses on underprivileged communities, it would assist Thai law schools in producing lawyers who have a social justice awareness and a sense of justice, and that is the utmost real need of the country.

Notes

1. Lisa R. Bliss et al., "Moving into the Future: Legal Education in Thailand," in Shuvro P. Sarker (ed.) *Legal Education in Asia* (Eleven International Publishing, 2014) 214.
2. See Bridges Across Borders Southeast Asia Community Legal Education Initiative, http://www.babseacle.org/, accessed June 18, 2014.
3. Bliss et al. (n 1) 218.
4. Ibid.

5. S. Boonchalearmwipas, *The Thai Legal History* 5th ed. (Winyuchon, 2005) 114.
6. P. Boondechet al., *The Judicial System in Thailand: An Outlook for a New Century* (ASEAN Law Association, 2005) 62, www.aseanlawassociation.org/docs/Judicial_System_in_Thailand.pdf.
7. Ibid.
8. Ibid.
9. Ibid.
10. Ibid.
11. Ibid. 106.
12. Ibid. 66; T. Chuerboonchai and P. Srivanit, *Challenges to Legal Education in a Changing Landscape: The Case of Thailand* (ASEAN Law Association, 2003) 1, www.aseanlawassociation.org/docs/w3_thai.pdf.
13. Boondech et al. (n 6) 66.
14. For a more comprehensive explanation of Thai legal education, its historical developments, and its requirements, see *Legal Education in Asia* (Eleven International Publishing, 2014) 217–233.
15. See Legal Education in Asia at 222 fn. 1 .The focus of TQF is to set learning outcomes for students to guarantee the graduate's qualifications under the education. Under TQF, students' learning outcomes comprise of five components: ethics and morals, knowledge, cognitive skills, interpersonal skills and responsibility, and numerical analysis, communication and information technology skills.
16. Panarairat Srichaiyarat, *Clinical Legal Education: An Option for Thai Legal Education Reform* (Winyuchon, 2012) 242–245.
17. Malee Pruekpongsawalee, "Thammasat Clinical Education and the Delivery of Legal Services: A Historical and Personal Perspective," in Louise G. Trubek and Jeremy Cooper (eds.) *Educating for Justice Around the World* (Ashgate, 1999) 127.
18. Lauren Donnison, "Clinical Legal Education in Thai Law Schools and Access to Justice" (Master of Arts thesis, Chulalongkorn University, 2013) 31.
19. Pruekpongsawalee (n 17) 133.
20. Donnison (n 18) 31.
21. Ibid. 36–37.
22. Pichaisak Horyangkul, "A New Approach to Legal Education" (1971) 8 *Soc. Sci. J.* 128–138.
23. Pruekpongsawalee (n 17) 130–131.
24. http://www.lrct.go.th/en/?p=5, accessed June 8, 2014.
25. http://www.babseacle.org/articles/clinical-legal-education-means-assist-reforming-thailand-legal-education-system-regional-international-experiences-perspectives-khon-kaen-conference/, accessed June 8, 2014.
26. Srichaiyarat (n 16) 26.
27. Ibid. 25.
28. Ibid. 238.
29. Interview with Gui Lin (Renmin University Law School, May 18, 2009).
30. Interview with Hu Jia Yi (Renmin University Law School, May 18, 2009).
31. Children's Education Law Clinic, Duke University; and Environmental Law Clinic, Yale Law School.
32. Srichaiyarat (n 16) 242–245.
33. Ibid. 247.
34. Duangporn Lertjareansamai, "The Achievement of Learning Administrative Law by Legal Clinic for Academic Activity according to Thailand Qualifications

Framework" Management Science Academic Conference, Pibulsongkram Jajabhat University, March 2014, http://ms.psru.ac.th/admin/file/8_Research_in_the_classroom.pdf, accessed June 8, 2014.

35. Ibid.
36. Panarairat Srichaiyarat, "Thai Qualifications Framework for Higher Education and Clinical Legal Education" (2012) 3 *Assumption University Law Journal* 18–31; and Panarairat Srichaiyarat, "Clinical Legal Education: An Option for Thai Legal Education Reform" (December, 2012) *Naresuan U.L.J.* 80–108.
37. See, for example, Lisa Bliss, "Lessons Learned from Teaching Clinical Legal Education in Thailand" (February, 2014) 63 (3) *J. Legal Educ.* 524; Lisa R. Bliss and Supamas Chinvinijkul, "Preparing Law Students for Global Practice: An Innovative Model for Teaching Lawyering Skills and Social Justice in a Large Enrolment Law Course" (2014) 1 *Asian J. Legal Educ.* 1.
38. See www.gaje.org.
39. See http://www.northumbriajournals.co.uk/index.php/ijcle.
40. Author Lisa Bliss served in this capacity at Mae Fah Luang University during the summer of 2012, and returned in 2013 to visit Mae Fah Luang again as well as other Thai universities.
41. Interview with Maythavee Lertdethanapong and Soracha Santatirat (Chiang Mai University Law Clinic, April 25, 2011).
42. Interview with Narudol Wannarat (Chiang Mai University Law Clinic, May 21, 2011).
43. Interview with Maythavee Lertdethanapong (Chiang Mai University Law Clinic, April 25, 2011).
44. Interview with Kathaleeya Jaisrithi (Chiang Mai University Law Clinic, May 3, 2011).
45. Soracha Santatirat telephone interview with Wathachana Wongsinnak (July 12, 2011).
46. Interview with Soracha Santatirat (Chiang Mai University Law Clinic, April 25, 2011).
47. Ibid.
48. Interview with Preeda Saisuparat (Chiang Mai University Law Clinic, May 21, 2011).
49. Interview with Thidarat Chompuming (Chiang Mai University Law Clinic, May 3, 2011).

CHAPTER 10

Empowering the Underprivileged: The Social Justice Mission for Clinical Legal Education in India

*Shuvro Prosun Sarker**

Introduction

The 1960s and 1970s were an important time in the history of legal education in India, a time when the legal aid movement and various legal aid committees' reports started to draw attention to the importance of experiential learning, or learning on the job, in legal education. The main aim of involving law students in the national legal aid movement was to make them feel more responsible for the considerable part of the Indian population who, because of their socio-economic status, could not access justice. The history of how India's clinical programs were introduced has a lot in common with the history of clinical programs in other parts of the world. There was a desire to create a pool of lawyers who would serve as soldiers in the fight for social justice for underprivileged groups in the country.

While some prestigious universities started their clinical programs in the 1970s, most of the regulators of legal education took a long time to include clinical papers in the curriculum. In 1997, the Bar Council of India introduced four practical papers into the curriculum. The spirit of public service, and the widespread poverty in a country, has always been central to the push for clinical programs everywhere. But in India, the legal aid committees' and other statutory bodies' reports calling for clinical programs to support social justice, were always ignored. The National Knowledge Commission's working group on legal education specifically mentioned the need to introduce students to issues relating to poverty, social change, and social exclusion, through clinical legal education (CLE).[1]

After the introductory section of this chapter, the second section discusses deliberation by various bodies, commissions, and committees about the need to introduce clinical programs with a social justice perspective in India. The second section tries to search for clinical models best suited to India, with reference to clinical programs in China and South Africa. Several examples of clinical activities in a few Indian law schools have been highlighted in this chapter to explain these models' effectiveness and suitability for Indian circumstances. The third section sets out some suggestions for law schools and stakeholders of legal education in India as to how to further the country's social justice mission of CLE.

Justice Mission of CLE and India

> "What do generations signify? Growth in self-reflection and wisdom and capacity to serve the underprivileged."
>
> —Professor Upendra Baxi[2]

In an interview about legal education reform, Professor Upendra Baxi expressed his concern that there is no new generation of lawyers coming up in India who will work to help the underprivileged access justice. The reason behind this fear might be the failure of the law school curriculum to put the values of public service and social justice at the center of young law students' education, instead encouraging the growth of a corporate culture.[3]

There should be a teaching method within the law school framework that will inculcate a spirit of public service, and help young law "students to confront the uncertainties and challenges of problem solving for clients in fora that often challenge precepts regarding the rule of law and justice."[4] CLE aims at exactly this sort of teaching method and spirit of public service. Professor N. R. Madhava Menon refers to "clinical legal education as a pedagogic technique is its focus on the learner and the process of learning,"[5] not to create future lawyers who are "mere craftsman manipulating advocacy skills in the traditional role of conflict resolution in court."[6] Avrom Sheer emphasizes that understanding, imagination, and the ethics of justice are central to CLE.[7] Accordingly, CLE plays an important role in making access to justice a reality for many low-income people. It does so not only by exposing law students to the legal problems that the poor face but also by allowing students to experience an obligation to find substantive and creative ways to respond to unmet legal needs.[8]

Teaching students that they are responsible for their actions and society has always been at the heart of CLE.[9] In India, recognition of the difficulties that the majority of the population faced when they tried to access justice through legal institutions kick-started the free legal aid movement. The Ministry of Law and Justice formed three committees in the 1970s to come up with solutions to help deal with the struggle that many people faced in trying to access justice. All three committees recommended involving law schools in the country's legal aid mission, but clinical work was only introduced in the curriculum later.

In 1973, the Expert Committee on Legal Aid[10] proposed involving law teachers and students in legal aid programs. They characterized legal aid services as "every step or action by which legal institutions are sensitized to respond to the socio-economic realities" of India.[11] The expert committee's "idea of linking legal aid and law schools had a practical element; given the extent of the need for legal services for the poor and the limited resources available, this made perfect sense."[12]

The Juridicare Committee on Legal Aid[13] submitted its report in 1977, echoing the ideas of the previous expert committee, and formulated more focused recommendations relating to legal aid schemes. These were aimed more at reaching the most helpless members of society and identifying the broadest possible types of assistance that could be made available to them under the law, including education, community development, and community organizing.[14]

Along the same lines, in 1981, the Committee for Implementing Legal Aid Schemes insisted that court-oriented legal aid programs alone cannot provide social justice in India. The committee concentrated more on promoting legal literacy, organizing legal aid camps to carry legal services to people's doorsteps, training paralegals to support legal aid programs, establishing legal aid clinics in law schools and universities, and bringing class actions through public interest litigations.[15]

An important part of the clinical methodology is its emphasis on experimental learning and other interactive teaching techniques that give students a sense of participating in the process as adults and draw them into the role of a lawyer.[16] Thus legal educators in India had a responsibility to improve the quality of legal education through the legal services clinical method of law teaching, which would help encourage a sense of justice, equity, and public service responsibility among young law students. However, they have failed to do so.

CLE in India

The idea of involving law schools in legal aid can be seen as the first attempt to introduce some kind of CLE framework in India. The legal aid movement of the 1960s in India "assumed that law schools would have a significant role in dispensing legal services."[17] This idea has been reflected in various reports relating to legal aid and judicial reform dating back to the 1970s. Reform was considered necessary to foster the country's nascent democracy and help achieve the goals of good governance, expressed in the Constitution of India, by developing competent legal minds.[18] In India, after long deliberations, the Bar Council of India introduced four clinical papers in 1997. The papers introduced are far from comprehensive and do not place much emphasis on the need for young lawyers to struggle for social justice, one of the original aims of CLE.

In 1994, a three-member committee made up of Justice A. M. Ahmadi, Justice B.N. Kirpal, and Justice M. Jaganaddha Rao dealt in detail with law school teaching methods.[19] The committee made important suggestions relating to pedagogy and the more practical side of legal education.

The committee's suggestions marked the starting point for the introduction of a clinical teaching curriculum into the modern Indian legal education system. It was after this committee's report that the Bar Council of India introduced four practical papers into the curriculum, which was viewed at the time as a "big step toward introducing clinical legal education formally into the curriculum and law schools have been required to introduce the four papers since academic year 1998–99."[20] These papers concentrated on specific issues of legal skill training: paper I addressed instruction in litigation skills, including pretrial preparation and trial practice; paper II focused on legal drafting skills and pleading; paper III covered professional ethics and bar-bench relations; and paper IV introduced legal aid work and public interest litigations.

However, most legal educators see the papers as providing only limited support for including instruction in social justice lawyering in the new curriculum or for providing social justice to indigent clients.[21] Finally, the Bar Council of India's mandatory directive to introduce the four practical papers into the curriculum was welcomed only halfheartedly by law school authorities as their staff lacked the skills and experience necessary to teach the course properly or "simply put, law faculty neither had a vision for, nor properly understood, the value of these papers."[22]

Nevertheless, the Law Commission Report of 2002 emphasized further the professional skills and values future lawyers need to develop at law school.[23] Though their central focus was on the Mac-Crate Report[24] to be introduced into the curriculum safely by modifying it as per the India circumstances, some of the legal educators found it unacceptable to start the teaching of skills training in the law schools as India needed more to concentrate on the social justice movement elaborated by the legal aid committees in 1970s.[25]

The Bar Council of India adopted a resolution, based on the recommendations of the Supreme Court's three-member committee, to set up legal aid clinics in every law school to provide inexpensive and speedy service to underprivileged groups in society.[26] This was a mandatory requirement, reflected in the Bar Council of India's *Inspection Manual 2010*.[27] It serves as a starting point for a formal system, giving law schools a very good opportunity to build their legal aid programs in line with the requirements of the local community. It affirmed the need for a multiclient-based legal aid program for every community.[28] The vision statement of the then law minister on legal education reform played an important role in encouraging the Bar Council of India to take this initiative.[29]

Another important authority that bears responsibility for regulating legal aid services nationally, the National Legal Services Authority (NALSA), has come up with an important set of rules in line with the Bar Council of India's mandatory clinic resolution in 2011. NALSA issued the National Legal Services (Legal Aid Clinics) Regulation on August 10, 2011.[30] This regulation in reality serves as the implementation mechanism for legal aid clinics in cooperation with the local authorities.

Another Planning Commission subcommittee, which focused on how to get higher learning institutions involved in community development, came up with effective recommendations for planning and funding.[31]

The subcommittee developed several ways to boost academic institutions' community engagement through networking, funding, and policy change. First, it proposed an Alliance for Community Engagement, an active membership-based network to promote ideas and practices of community engagement throughout India, and a funding and policy committee, the Autonomous Empowered Committee on Community Engagement, to review funding proposals, design schemes to encourage community engagement, and set policy at the level of the Planning Commission and University Grants Commission. Next, it recommended that higher education institutions be given more curricular flexibility in offering programs, courses, and initiatives that are more relevant to the needs of society, and that due recognition for public intellectual engagement be given to faculty, students, and institutions. Lastly, it recommended that a few educational institutions beset up to focus on community-based and common knowledge traditions.[32]

The regulatory authorities overseeing legal education, and other administrative bodies, have taken many initiatives to increase access to justice for the underprivileged. But bureaucratic hassles, and the indifference of almost all of the 950 legal institutions in India, have prevented these initiatives from being properly implemented. The Report of the Law School Based Legal Aid Clinics, 2011, has very effectively pointed to all of the reasons why the legal aid programs at law school clinics have not been running well.[33]

The Indian Model

Legal education in India has been described as a "sea of institutionalized mediocrity with a few islands of excellence."[34] There are often calls for reform of legal education, for a system that is of excellent quality and that can spread its scope to be more sensitive to the underprivileged sections of Indian society. It must be kept in mind that law grows when it engages with society and interacts with other branches of knowledge. Engagement with social problems and movements make legal education relevant and contextual. For this to happen, a liberal, holistic, and decentralized approach to curriculum planning and the development of clinical teaching is necessary, for which each university teaching law should have the primary responsibility.

Law schools should take up the CLE syllabi to implement it in line with local needs through some clinic-based activity. To implement this sort of activity, a meaningful coordination with the local bar and bench, NGOs, and legal services authority is required. This combined effort to set up social justice-based clinical activity will make legal education more socially relevant and meaningful.

This chapter deals with creating a model for law schools' clinical activity that will not only supplement the curricular requirements of CLE but also complement social justice-based CLE and secure the rights of underprivileged groups in India.

Rural Access to Justice

"The soul of India lives in its villages."
—Mohandas Karamchand Gandhi

In the beginning of the twentieth century, Mohandas Karamchand Gandhi, father of the Indian nation, expressed this thought-provoking statement. Even today, the same could be said. Data from the Census of India, 2011, shows us how many people live in rural India: 833,087,662 persons, among them 427,917,052 men and 405,170,610 women.[35]

Most rural Indians do not have in-depth or accurate knowledge about the administration of justice or administration and governance procedures. This lack of knowledge makes it difficult for rural Indians to access the system of justice delivery, administration, and governance. Not only that, the problem of a lack of transparency and accountability in the administration and governance system is, in part, a result of that ignorance.

The focus of this clinic model is on the reform of legal education to accelerate the empowerment[36] of marginalized rural communities in India. This model is primarily inspired by the community lawyering movement of South African CLE. The idea of community lawyering in India as a way to ensure access to justice and legal empowerment for the underprivileged is gaining importance as "advocacy on behalf of a group is seen as more efficient and cost effective, particularly when the group as a whole is at odds with the social, economic, cultural, and political situation."[37]

If we look at Jindal Global Law School (JGLS) and the SM Sehgal Foundation (formerly Institute of Rural Research and Development), we can broadly determine the nature and duties of a clinic for the empowerment of rural Indians. Using CLE methodology, the Sehgal Foundation and JGLS train rural villagers in their locality about government programs enacted to help them.

The training explains the Right to Information Act and the proper channels for following up on applications that become stuck in the system. Armed with the knowledge acquired over the course of the year-long training, villagers monitor the functioning of local government and share their findings at periodic feedback sessions. Residents of over 200 villages have been trained as of December 2011.

To conduct the training, the Sehgal Foundation's staff partner with law students and their teachers at JGLS. JGLS established a Good Governance and Citizen Participation Clinic. For the training, the Sehgal Foundation has published brochures in the local language, Hindi, drafted by law students on government schemes and the Right to Information. The clinic supports the efforts of villagers in several ways in addition to the governance training, including through panel discussions with government officials, policy advocacy based on problems identified in the field, legal aid camps in villages, and responses to bribe seeking and other forms of corruption that villagers encounter. The Sehgal Foundation and JGLS seek to replicate the NGO-law school-community model through conferences, publications, and research on its impact. They host an annual conference on good rural governance and citizen participation, and in 2011–12 held regional conferences across India.[38] To support Good Governance Now partnerships, the Sehgal Foundation and JGLS offer training to interested NGOs and academic institutions to deliver training and support to rural communities. The Sehgal Foundation's Rural Research Center and JGLS' clinical program also host fellowship recipients and other visitors engaged in research or teaching on rural development and governance.

This sort of experiential clinical model can be an inspiration for all law schools in India. The collaboration between a law school clinic and an NGO while working in the rural development sector can bring significant change in that particular area, when it comes to citizen participation in democracy, governance, and administrative procedure.

The students who were involved in this program were required to prepare legal literacy materials in local languages that explain in easy-to-understand terms government schemes, programs, and acts like the public distribution system, the *anganwadi* system, the Right of Children to Free and Compulsory Education Act, the National Rural Employment Guarantee Scheme, the midday meal program, and the Right to Information Act, which rural community members should know about.[39] They also assist community peers in preparing right-to-information applications and write letters to government officials. Students have also undertaken advocacy on behalf of the rural community to various commissions and statutory bodies.[40] The students who work for this sort of clinic have the opportunity to develop skills in interviewing, client representation, fact investigation, report writing and documentation, and emphatic lawyering.[41]

It could be said that this model cannot be followed or implemented by other law school clinics because of a lack of financial resources. But this lack of financial resources can be overcome through collaboration between that particular law school, a local NGO working in the area of that particular law school, and the district or taluka legal services authority. The district or taluka legal services authority can create the platform and take some financial initiative for the combined work with the law schools and NGOs with the help of the National Legal Services Authority (Free and Competent Legal Services) Regulations, 2010; National Legal Services Authority (Legal Aid Clinics) Scheme, 2010; and Para Legal Volunteer Scheme, 2010.

It is now up to law schools to decide whether they are ready to undertake this sort of clinical activity. It will also be up to the law schools to find their local NGO partner and enlist the help of the district ortaluka legal services authority.

Human Rights Litigation and Law Reform

Strategic human rights litigation seeks to use the authority of the law to advocate for social change on behalf of individuals whose voices are otherwise not heard.[42] In India, the use of public interest litigation has the same meaning. Human rights litigation can be a helpful tool to provide relief to a large number of people and to create a policy that state must follow. It can provide "broad access to justice and judicial redress to all persons or class of persons that are in a position of poverty, vulnerability, disability and exclusion in general."[43] Noble Laureate AmartyaSen refers to poverty as not only the lack of resources but also the concept of capability.[44] So it is necessary to provide essential tools to the underprivileged to use their assets to move out of poverty and to change the rule of power in society.

Human rights litigation is an essential tool for making government policy more comprehensive and functional in order to alleviate poverty and other social exclusions. It is through both human rights litigation and law reform clinics that social or economic issue that need to be dealt with can be found.[45] China's legislation clinic, where law students work with civic bodies and grass-roots organizations to find specific issues in legislation for amendment, is the inspiration behind this human rights litigation and law reform clinic.

In India, there are some examples of public interest litigation by law students[46] and also zeal toward law reform activities. The Legal Aid Society of the West Bengal National University of Juridical Sciences (NUJS), Kolkata, has been involved in seeking justice for the scheduled caste population in Puri District, Odisha, since 2010.[47] They have filed specific complaints with the Odisha State Human Rights Commission regarding right to water, right to enter into the temple for the scheduled caste population, and free and compulsory education for the scheduled caste children.

Because of the intervention of the NUJS Legal Aid Society, the District Legal Services Authority has been proactive in engaging legal aid lawyers for the scheduled caste population of Puri. The change in the lives of the scheduled caste population of Puri due to the intervention of the NUJS Legal Aid Society has been discussed in the Seminar on Civil Rights of Scheduled Castes and Scheduled Tribes.[48] In that seminar, leaders of the scheduled caste community and various human rights NGOs presented their views and voiced their appreciation for the work done by the NUJS Legal Aid Society.

The activities of the students in this sort of human rights litigation and law reform activity will help them develop interviewing skills, counseling abilities, and drafting capabilities. As one scholar has put it, "human rights lawyering involves litigation, advocacy, monitoring and reporting, policy and legislative drafting, organizing and lobbying. Human rights clinics aim to acquaint law students with this variety of practice, and to engage them critically and practically in developing one or more of these skills."[49]

It is important that if this sort of clinic is to work, it must be a long-term project. That is the only way to gain people's confidence. The goals of CLE have to be developed in this sort of clinic, and these goals may include advancing human rights and social justice.[50]This human rights litigation and law reform clinic can operate alongside the rural access to justice clinic to ensure community engagement.

For law schools, community engagement for human rights litigation and law reform should occur in three spheres: teaching and learning; community service; and research. Engaging with the community is an important way of making students aware of the society around them, teaching them to apply academic learning to real life, providing material for curriculum and research that is relevant to society, preserving traditional knowledge and culture, and promoting social justice. Proper collaboration and division of work between the two clinics could bring significant change for the underprivileged and fulfill the goals and values of CLE.

These proposed models of clinical activities for Indian law schools focus on fulfilling the curricular objectives of CLE at large and also putting some stake on the Indian socioeconomic structure to meet the millennium development goals. Though it is argued by the Western world that CLE is primarily concerned with skills training for law students, in a world full of poverty and discrimination in the distribution of wealth, we can set an agenda to serve the underprivileged and at the same time develop lawyering skills.

The issue of financial resources to run a clinical program is important in India as most Indian law schools are privately managed. This is also a point that we can learn from clinical programs in China and South Africa. China manages its clinical programs using money from donors through the organized efforts of CCCLE. A developing country like South Africa has also formed a national forum of university-based legal aid institutions, named AULAI, which can then take a more organized approach toward getting funding. In India, many lacunae can be addressed by forming a national legal aid advocacy institution for law schools, to help them set up their clinical programs and get funds from various governmental, nongovernmental, and international organizations.

It is promising that there is a new generation of legal academics and students who have risen in India with a mission to inspire others to action, particularly in the pursuit of justice. The government is also expanding its vision of legal education, working toward systematic reform and listening to ideas about how to make legal education more meaningful and relevant for Indian society. Now, it is only a matter of time until we see law students, under the supervision of their teachers, working closely with underprivileged communities throughout India to make the Preamble of the Indian Constitution a reality for all.

Suggestions and Conclusion

Having looked closely at the nature and status of CLE in India, and in three other countries, it is clear that Indian CLE's primary objective is to secure a social justice mission and work for the empowerment of underprivileged groups in Indian society. The two models put forward in this paper could be of great value, not only helping to empower the underprivileged but also to ensure the goals and values of CLE.

Now all the stakeholders of legal education have to take up certain points, to create a platform for the law schools to introduce these models of clinical teaching, get funds to continue with these models, and train faculty members in clinical teaching. These suggestions can be divided into the following headings:

For Law Schools/Colleges/Universities

The Bar Council of India has made it mandatory for every law school or college to have a functional clinic that should work with the community to provide basic legal services. It is now suggested that each law school or college should establish its clinic in rural or semiurban areas. This kind of clinic may be established in association with any local NGO or municipality or panchayat authority. The office must be easily accessible by the community members. It would be helpful if those behind the institution liaise with the District or Taluka Legal Services Authority, telling them about the clinic. These government bodies could provide some funding.

The community clinic should be open on the weekends, like Saturday evening or Sunday morning, because the prospective client must be free to attend. The ideal student group for a clinic should not exceed 25 for each Saturday evening or Sunday morning. The fourth- and fifth-year (in the case of a five-year LLB course) students or the second- and third-year (in the case of a three-year LLB course) students should be divided into several groups to run the clinic each Saturday evening or Sunday morning, and these groups should rotate as is convenient. One faculty member experienced in clinical teaching must supervise the students. In other cases, lawyers appointed by the District or Taluka Legal Services Authority may also supervise the students in their clinical activities. If there is continuous clinical activity in a village, villagers will be more confident that they are not going to be left alone, and are more likely to come to the clinic for advice. The cases may range from domestic violence, maintenance, land-related disputes, RTI matters, to atrocities toward the SC/ST population.

First, it will be the students who will take care of these cases, interviewing and counseling the client, preparing necessary drafts, and instructing the client to approach the appropriate authority for consideration. For example, if the client is in need of a legal aid lawyer to defend his or her case in a court of law, then the clinic can act as a bridge between the legal services authority and the client.

For the Bar Council of India/State Bar Councils/Bar Associations

The Bar Council of India (BCI) under the Advocates Act, 1961, has the authority to regulate legal education. BCI has framed several rules, curriculum development committees to bring excellence to legal education. Yet despite these efforts, there are areas in which gaps exists, like in CLE. As establishing a clinic is now mandatory under the BCI rules, so the clinical activity of the students in those clinics must be credit based.

It is now urgently required by the BCI to take clinical activity under the credit-based/marks-based system. It is also important to establish a subcommittee on clinical legal education under the Legal Education Committee of BCI, of which trained Indian clinicians will be members. The subcommittee should work to standardize clinical programs and make it a uniform activity, inspecting and monitoring the clinical programs of various law schools, liaising with various authorities to get funding for clinical programs, and arranging workshops and seminars for clinical law teachers or designated clinical faculties once a year.

State bar councils and bar associations should play an active role in implementing the clinical programs in each state. State bar councils, with the help of the local bar association, may provide some mentor lawyers for the students in a particular clinic. The mentor lawyers, in cooperation with the designated clinical faculty, may supervise the works of the clinic students on Saturday evening or Sunday morning. This would not only build a working relationship between the senior lawyers and the future lawyers but also bring a sense of professional ethics and etiquette.

For the National Legal Services Authority (NALSA)

The potential of a law school to reach the community has historically been ignored by the National Legal Services Authority. But recently, some of NALSA's activities have created a light in the middle of the sea. The NALSA Clinic Regulation Rules, 2010, have shown the direction toward collaboration between the legal services authorities and the law schools. Now, NALSA should come up with a resolution for all the District Legal Services Authorities to take appropriate steps to collaborate with law schools in that district to provide legal services at the doorsteps of the people. The model of starting clinics in rural or semiurban areas can be effectively implemented with the help of the District Legal Services Authority or Taluka Legal Services Authority. One legal aid lawyer may be present there to collaborate on behalf of the legal services authority, and if any litigation comes, he may take the matter to the appropriate court of law. The clinic students can work under the legal aid lawyer to prepare the necessary documents. It is also important for NALSA to provide some funds for these collaboration activities with the law schools. NALSA should allocate a separate fund for every District Legal Services Authority depending upon the number of law schools in that district. There must be an equal amount of funds for every law school in each district, and the District Legal Services Authority may distribute the funds to the law schools for running the clinic activities, and at the end of each financial year they may ask for an audited report of the expenditure of funds by the clinic.

For the University Grants Commission (UGC)

Finally, the UGC must take some steps to develop the faculty standard for clinical teaching in law. It should start a faculty development course on CLE for the staff of law schools in charge of teaching practical papers.

First, UGC should look at some model institutions that have exceptionally good clinical activities and that have trained clinical faculty members, and use these models as a basis to develop a curriculum for a faculty development course in CLE. The duration of this sort of course may range from two to four weeks. The model institutions, after preparing the curriculum, will conduct the course in association with UGC. There should be at least four to six model institutions throughout the country to conduct the course. UGC must provide funds for this course and encourage experienced law teachers who have prior experience in conducting large-scale clinical programs in their own university or college to teach this course.

Another faculty improvement activity that can be undertaken by UGC is to start some fellowships for clinical law teachers to undergo special training in CLE at foreign law schools. Previously the United States India Education Foundation (USIEF), New Delhi, in association with the government of India had the Neheru-Vanderbilt Fulbright Scholarship for Indian clinical law teachers to study a one-year specialized LLM in Clinical Legal Education from Vanderbilt University, United States. But this program has been discontinued. Now, there is no opportunity for Indian clinical law teachers to take such courses, mainly due to a lack of funds. However, the UGC may start similar programs with some foreign universities that offer an LLM in Clinical Legal Education, a PG Diploma in Clinical Legal Education, or a Diploma in Clinical Legal Education. Bringing back the fellowships for law teachers in CLE will also encourage them to work hard for their respective law school clinics, and the rigorous training will make them equipped with the art of clinical working and supervising.

New Reforms in Legal Education[51]

It is inappropriate to continue the three year and five year LL.B program together. It is time to consider innovation in curriculum as well as in pedagogy by scraping both these programs. There must be some initiative to consider whether Indian law schools can offer programs like the Juris Doctor (J.D.), which may be a four year, eight semester degree program instead of a five year LL.B.* Courses like legal method, legal ethics, and legal theory must come in the first semester along with courses on legal and constitutional history, political science, and sociology of law. Every semester must have six subjects each; thus there will be 48 subjects in total.

There must be emphasis on clinical legal education. Within these 48 subjects there must be six clinical courses that should be offered by the law school faculty. In other words every law school should operate six clinics on different themes, which may include a human rights litigation clinic, legal literacy clinic, women empowerment clinic, law reform clinic, criminal law clinic, disability law clinic,

*This is now a popular discussion among the visionaries of Indian legal education reform. Professor Ranbir Singh spoke about this opportunity in the National Consultation for Second Generation Reforms in Legal Education, New Delhi, 2010. He has particularly pointed the introduction of J. D. in the Melbourne Law School which scraped its LL.B program in 2008. Professor N. R. Madhava Menon led the Gangtok Declaration of Legal Education reform in 2013 with a similar mission.

public policy clinic, consumer law clinic, intellectual property law clinic, corporate law clinic, arbitration law clinic, competition law clinic, displaced persons and refugee law clinic, and so on. In operating these clinics law schools must prioritize those persons who have experience in clinical education or studied in a setup where clinical legal education is central to the curriculum.

While decreasing the program duration to four years, we have to think about starting a system of pupilage to make the students eligible to appear for the bar examination.* This system of pupilage must be carried out after passing all the 48 course of the program and must be under a district court lawyer over a period of six months. The district court lawyer, that is, the pupil master, should have at least ten years' experience in active practice. To ensure proper supervision of the students, law schools must prepare a database of lawyers with this experience and with the help of the bar association of that district place the students under them. There should be a contract between the law school, pupil master, and pupil regarding the terms and conditions of the pupilage. At the end of six months, the pupil master will issue a certificate of eligibility to the student to appear for the bar exam; it should be endorsed by the law school as well.

A student will be accepted to appear for the bar examination after completion of the 48 courses and the pupilage. The examination should be conducted throughout with multiple choice questions from all the subjects of the program and practical questions relating to legal proceedings. It must be the Bar Council of India who will take care of this examination, as it is now. It is now time to think about allowing full-time clinical law teachers and law students to practice the profession of law in court. There can be a separate practice rule for the full-time faculties who teach clinical courses and law students who undertake clinical courses.†

It is clear that Indian legal education is suffering from multiple controlling authorities. On one side there is the University Grants Commission, and the Bar Council of India in on another side. It is time to re-organize this multiple control. It is obvious that the Bar Council of India must hold control for the bar examination vis-à-vis the admission of advocates in the bar. However, their control over the accreditation of law schools and maintenance of the standard of legal education must be curtailed without fail. Legal education is a professional education and like other types of professional education it's now time to establish a new professional body (it may be All India Council of Legal Education) to look after matters like accreditation of law schools, maintenance of standard of education and research, prescribing syllabi, pedagogy, and teacher appointment.¶ It has

*This practice first started in England and Wales to become a Bar-at-Law. See http://www.tcph.co.uk/. Now it is a practice of so many commonwealth nations. For example see, Pupilage of Malaysian Bar, available at http://www.malaysianbar.org.my/pupillage.html.

†For a comparative view from the United States, see http://www.law.georgetown.edu/library/research/guides/StudentPracti ce.cfm.

¶In India there are separate regulatory bodies for Medical Education, Engineering, Dental Education, and Agricultural Education.

to be kept in mind that while creating such a body, representation from legal academia must be more than half of its required members, and other members should proportionately come from the judiciary and the bar.

After creating such a body like the All India Council of Legal Education, the first thing that should be done by the body is to reduce the number of law schools to 50 percent of its present number. In India, now, there are about 1,000 law colleges and most of them do not fulfil the standard as per the Rules of Legal Education, 2008. Most of these colleges are suffering from little infrastructure, part-time teachers, poor library facilities, and little funding for development. It is true that India as a large country with a large population needs lawyers to cater to the needs of its people; however at the same time India does not need half-educated lawyers who are making the justice delivery process inoperative by various unfair and unethical means. In continuation with these initiatives, it should not be the priority to set up model institutions. The priority should be to make all the institutions at par with regards to infrastructure, libraries, and funding. It should be the priority that the students can get the most possible outcomes from their choice of studying law. Funding to these institutions must be equitable in nature to ensure development at par.

On a final note, the author is of the opinion that Indian CLE's primary objective is to ensure social justice and empower the underprivileged groups in Indian society. This mission cannot be achieved unless there is a combined effort from the law schools, BCI, UGC, and NALSA. The models that have been formulated in this paper and the formality of starting clinical programs like that will be the primary responsibility of the law schools. It is the stakeholders of legal education that must act positively to carry forward with these models.

Notes

* This chapter is a shorter and modified version of the author's article that appeared in the *International Journal of Clinical Legal Education*, Vol. 13, 2013. The permission from the Journal is kindly acknowledged.

1. "Report of the Working Group on Legal Education" National Knowledge Commission, 3.3.2, http://www.knowledgecommission.gov.in/downloads/documents/wg_legal.pdf, accessed September 25, 2012.
2. Interview with MyLaw.Net, YouTube, http://www.youtube.com/watch?v=0y2AT-rk6-E., accessed September 25, 2012.
3. Ibid.
4. Margaret M. Barry, Jon C. Dubin, and Peter A. Joy, "Clinical Education for this Millennium: The Third Wave" (2000)7 *Clinical L. Rev.* 1, 38.
5. N. R. Madhava Menon (ed.) "Clinical Legal Education: Concept and Concerns," in *A Handbook on Clinical Legal Education* (Eastern Book Co., 1998).
6. Ibid.
7. Avrom Sheer, "Clinical Legal Education at Warwick and the Skills Movement: Was Clinic a Creature of its Time?" in Geoffrey Wilson (ed.) *Frontiers of Legal Scholarship* (John Wiley & Sons, 1995) 108, 119.
8. Margaret M. Barry et al. (n 4) 15.

9. Norman Redlich, "The Moral Value of Clinical Legal Education: A Reply" (1983) 33 *J. Legal Educ.* 613, 616.
10. See generally Government of India, Ministry of Law, Justice and Company Affairs, "Processual Justice to the People: Report of the Expert Committee on Legal Aid" (1973).
11. Ibid 180.
12. Frank S. Bloch and M. R. K. Prasad, "Institutionalizing a Social Justice Mission for Clinical Legal Education: Cross-National Currents from India and the United States" (2006–2007)13 *Clinical L. Rev.* 165, 169.
13. See generally Govt. of India, Ministry of Law, Justice and Company Affairs, "Equal Justice-Social Justice: Report of the Juridicare Committee" (1977).
14. Ibid. 52–65.
15. Frank S. Bloch and M. R. K. Prasad (n 12) 175.
16. See Frank S. Bloch, "The Andragogical Basis of Clinical Legal Education" (1982) 35 *Vand. L. Rev.* 321, 322–323; see generally John S. Bradway, "Some Distinctive Features of a Legal Aid Clinic Course" (1934) 1 *U. Chi. L. Rev.* 469, 469–473; Robert A. Gorman, "Clinical Legal Education: A Prospectus" (1971) 44 *S. Cal. L. Rev.* 537, 551–555; Michael Meltsner and Philip G. Schrag, "Report from a CLEPR Colony"(1976) 76 *Colum. L. Rev.* 581, 584–587.
17. Frank S. Bloch (n 16) 96.
18. See generally A. S. Anand, "Legal Education in India —Past, Present and Future" (1998) 3 *S.C.C.*1.
19. Bloch (n 16)179; see also 3-Member Committee Report on Reform of Legal Education, Bar Council of India, 2009, 41.
20. Bar Council of India Resolution No 04/1997; see also Bloch (n 16) 180.
21. Bloch (n 16) 180.
22. Bloch (n 16) 180.
23. The Law Commission of India, 184th Report 50 (2002).
24. American Bar Association, 1992.
25. See Bloch (n 16)187–195.
26. See 3-Member Committee Report on Reform of Legal Education, Bar Council of India 1, 4 (2009).
27. Bar Council of India, *Inspection Manual 2010: Guideline for Inspection of Bar Council of India of University/Institution*, http://www.barcouncilofindia.org/about/legal-education/inspection-manual-2010.
28. Bar Council of India, *Inspection Manual 2010: Guideline for Inspection of Bar Council of India of University/Institution* 36, http://www.barcouncilofindia.org/wp-content/uploads/2010/06/Inspection-Manual.pdf.
29. The Bar Council of India, "The Law Minister Announces Vision for Legal Educational Reform" http://www.barcouncilofindia.org/law-ministers-vision-statement-for-second-generation-reforms-in-legal-education/.
30. National Legal Services Authority, *National Legal Services Authority (Legal Aid Clinics) Regulations, 2011* (The Gazette of India, August 18, 2011) http://www.google.co.in/url?sa=t&rct=j&q=&esrc=s&source=web&cd=1&cad=rja&ved=0CCMQFjAA&url=http%3A%2F%2Fnalsa.gov.in%2FSchemes%2FNALSA%2520LEGAL%2520AID%2520CLINICS%2520REGULATIONS%2C%25202011.doc&ei=KPJmUPzOGIbUrQfm4oHgAQ&usg=AFQjCNH1cGM1l92fOTrCtWRFvcPGd7Binw.
31. Rajesh Tandon, *Re-affirming Civil Engagement of Education* (September 19, 2011) http://priaeducation.org/rajeshtandon-blog/.

32. Ibid.
33. Report of the Law School Based Legal Aid Clinic, 2011.
34. N. R. Madhava Menon, *To Go from Mediocrity to Excellence* (The Hindu, June 18, 2010) http://www.thehindu.com/opinion/lead/article470073.ece?homepage=true.
35. Census of India, http://censusindia.gov.in/2011census/censusinfodashboard/index.html.
36. Access to justice for the rural poor includes not only access to courts and legal redress mechanisms, but also good governance including transparency and accountability in the making of laws and process of their implementation and administration.
37. Sopriyo Routh, "Experiential Learning Through Community Lawyering: A Proposal for Indian Legal Education" (2011) 24 *Pac. Mcgeorge Global Bus. & Dev. L.J.* 1,116.
38. In 2011, Regional Good Governance and Citizen Participation Conferences have been held at Assam University, Silchar; J.S.S. Law College, Mysore, Karnataka and Chanakya National Law University, Patna, Bihar.
39. See Promoting Clinical Legal Education in India: A Case Study of the Citizen Participation Clinic 18–22 (2012) (A Joint Report Prepared by Cornell International Human Rights Clinic and Jindal Good Rural Governance and Citizenship Participation Clinic).
40. Ibid.
41. Ibid. 9–12.
42. "Litigation Report: Global Human Rights Litigation" Open Society Justice Initiative (February 2012) 4, http://www.soros.org/sites/default/files/litigation-report-20120228.pdf.
43. Discrimination on the grounds of poverty often prevents access to the very tools needed to fight this condition. It is important to fight against recognized forms of discrimination, which include race, ethnicity, religion, gender, and others. Poor people are also often discriminated against on the basis of their socioeconomic condition. The challenge is to overcome this major obstacle to their empowerment; otherwise, those trapped in poverty may fall into a vicious circle from which it is hard to break out. See Maritza F. Prada, "Empowering the Poor Through Human Rights Litigation" 28 (2011).
44. Drawn up and expanded in the work of Amartya Sen. See generally Amartya Sen, *Development as Freedom* (1999); Amartya Sen, *Inequality Reexamined* (1995); Amartya Sen, *Commodities and Capabilities* (1987); Amartya Sen, *Poverty and Famines: An Essay on Entitlements and Deprivation* (1982).
45. Law school-based, credit-bearing course or program that combine clinical methodology around skills and values training with live case-project work, all or most of which takes place in the human rights context. See Arturo J. Carrillo, "Bringing International Law Home: The Innovative Role of Human Rights Clinics in the Transnational Legal Process"(2004) 35 *Colum. Hum. Rts. L. Rev.* 527, 533–534 (Here, "human rights context" refers to "a dynamic ecosystem comprised of the formal and informal rules, procedures, mechanisms, and actors that continuously interact at myriad levels to apply, promote, defend, or develop human rights principles").
46. Students of the V. M. Salgaokar College of Law, Goa, have successfully filed 14 public interest litigations before the Mumbai High Court (Panaji Bench) on various issues ranging from the use of helmets to violations of Coastal Regulation Zones. See V. M. Salgaocar College of Law, http://www.vmslaw.edu/
47. Author was a part of the team consisting of Prof. Anirban Chakraborty, Soumyajit Das (LL.M Student), Sabyasachi Chatterjee (LL.M Student), S. Jyotiranjan (LL.M

Student), Amarendra Gogoi (LL.M Student), Niteesh Kumar Upadhyay (LL.M Student), Lokenath Chatterjee (LL.B Student), Puneet Rathsharma (LL.B Student), and Rajesh Kumar Singh (NUJS Staff).

48. The seminar was organized in Puri District, Odisha, jointly by the Legal Aid Society, the West Bengal National University of Juridical Sciences and District Legal Services Authority, Puri, on September 1, 2012.
49. Deena Hurwitz, "Engaging Law School Students through Human Rights Clinics. A Perspective from the United States" (2006) 11 *Austl. J. Hum. Rts.* 37, 38–39.
50. Jocelyn G. Kestenbaum, Esteban Ho Yos Ceballos, and Melissa C. Del Aguila Talvadkar, "Catalysts for Change: A Proposed Framework for Human Rights Clinical Teaching and Advocacy" (2011–2012) 18 *Clinical L. Rev.* 459, 482.
51. For greater discussion, see Shuvro Prosun Sarker (ed.), *Legal Education in Asia* (Eleven International Publishing, The Hague, 2014).

CHAPTER 11

Legal Clinical Education in Japan: A Work in Progress

Matthew J. Wilson

Introduction

Around the turn of the century, Japan embarked on a monumental course of legal reform. Japan had become increasingly concerned about its sluggish economy and mounting debt. It also desired to play a greater role in global affairs. Spurred on by pressure from the business community, Japan's discussions about revitalizing its economy together with an interest in positioning itself internationally for the century to come evolved into a wholesale re-evaluation of its political, economic, and legal structure. Visionary reformers reasoned that the country needed to expand the role of law to resolve its ongoing problems and meet the future challenges associated with globalization.

As part of the reform movement, Japan passed a litany of significant revisions involving its codes, commercial laws, administrative laws, judicial system, legal education system, and alternative dispute approaches. The major reforms revolved around deregulation, reduced government, greater public involvement in the justice system, quality enhancement, and transparency. Repositioning the public "as actors, not bystanders, in governance"[1] and transforming them from "governed objects" to "governing subjects"[2] was key in the reformers' minds.

Judicial reform had been considered as the "final linchpin" in reshaping Japanese society.[3] In June 1999, Japan established the Justice System Reform Council ("JSRC")[4] to study potential legal reforms aimed at enabling the justice system to better support the nation. The reformers sought to fashion a more accessible and user-friendly justice system, redefine the legal profession, ensure public participation in the system, and reinforce the administration of justice. As a key part of these reforms, they also sought to raise the quantity and quality of legal professionals supporting the justice system. In quantitative terms, the JSRC set a goal to triple the number of new bar examination passers in the country to 3,000 per year by 2010.[5] Qualitatively, Japan turned its attention toward its legal education system in anticipation of an even greater need for lawyers who could provide high-level and diverse legal services. Up until this point, the legal system had been hindered not only by the relative scarcity of licensed attorneys but also because many attorneys were not equipped to deal with diverse and sophisticated legal issues that required broader background and experience. Accordingly, Japan decided to reconstruct the legal education system, revamp its bar examination system, and place a greater emphasis on legal clinical education.

This chapter explores Japanese legal education leading up to the recent adoption of legal clinical education by universities. It also examines Japan's efforts to create a practical environment in which law students can acquire lawyering skills, including the introduction of law school clinics and clinical courses. More specifically, this chapter looks at the accomplishments and challenges faced by clinical legal education (CLE) in Japan since its adoption in 2004 as well as several examples of law school clinics. Finally, it explores avenues for improvement and growth.

The Japanese Legal Education System—Generally

Historical Perspective up until Major Reforms in 2004

After World War II, Japan implemented a three-pronged legal education system consisting of undergraduate study at universities, a national bar examination administered by the Ministry of Justice, and practical training under the direction of the Supreme Court for successful bar exam takers. Accordingly, up until 2004, nearly 100 universities delivered legal education exclusively through undergraduate law (*hougakubu*) and graduate law (*hougakuin*) departments. Each year, approximately 45,000 new students around the country would pursue a degree in law.[6] The overwhelming majority of these students never aspired to become or ever became a licensed lawyer (*bengoshi*). As a result, universities did not view their mission as preparing students to practice law. University law professors were academics and not lawyers. Courses did not focus on the practice of law or professional legal education. Rather, university law departments basically functioned as general education programs to train future white-collar workers, business leaders, and bureaucrats.[7] In essence, there was no need for lawyer training or CLE in the university setting because the traditional Japanese university law curriculum was separate from bar exam preparation or lawyering skills training.

Influenced by the German legal education tradition, Japanese universities integrated liberal arts courses with courses on law, political science, and public administration.[8] Undergraduate law courses focused on black-letter law and theory rather than legal analysis, practical training, or preparation for legal practice.[9] Graduate-level legal education was geared toward producing academic scholars. Moreover, traditional Japanese education methods at the university level involved minimal student participation and passive learning attitudes instead of interactive and hands-on learning. As a result, legal education in Japan did not even offer anything close to CLE as it was void of skills training and practical exercises.

Students desiring to become licensed attorneys attended expensive private bar examination preparation or "cram" schools. Due to the extreme difficulties associated with passing the national bar examination, most individuals interested in becoming an attorney often expended more time studying at cram schools than in formal university settings.[10] The cramming system focused on test-taking skills and memorization of the six areas of law tested on the bar examination: constitutional law, civil law, commercial law, criminal law, civil procedure, and criminal procedure. Skills development, theoretical legal education, or techniques of learning beyond memorization did not come into play at the cram schools either. Because very few could pass the bar examination, however, most individuals ended up wasting valuable time and energy that could have been efficiently utilized elsewhere in society.

Before 2004, the likelihood of passing the national bar examination was extremely low. The Ministry of Justice administered the three-stage bar examination only once each year, and the pass rate historically fluctuated between 2 and 5 percent.[11] This exam did not necessarily function as a qualifying examination; rather, it operated as a quota on the number of bar exam passers. On average, successful applicants took the bar examination five times before passing.[12] Of note, neither legal studies nor a university degree were prerequisites for taking the bar examination.[13] However, most bar exam takers pursued and obtained a four-year law degree. In the three decades spanning 1960 and 1990, an average of only 500 applicants passed the bar exam each year.[14] In the decade from 1990 to 2000, the number of successful test-takers progressively increased until it hit 1,000 per year in 1999.[15] The low numbers resulted in severe shortages of licensed attorneys in rural areas and a lack of attorneys with specializations other than litigation. In fact, corporations engaged in transnational commerce had become increasingly frustrated with the poor quality and lack of training of Japanese lawyers, particularly with respect to nonlitigation services.[16]

Once a candidate passed the national bar examination in Japan, this individual would then enter the Legal Training and Research Institute ("LTRI," or *Shiho Kenshujo*), operated by the Supreme Court of Japan, for two years of additional study and practical attorney training. Trainees in the LTRI received a stipend paid by the government. Under the old system, the LTRI was really the only source of CLE as the curriculum and practical training of future lawyers rested exclusively with the Institute operating under the direction of the Supreme Court. The LTRI provided short-term, litigation-related training by present and retired judges, as well as temporarily assigned prosecutors and practitioners. This clinical-like training primarily focused on the drafting of pleadings, indictments, and judgments, as well as the application of facts to law.[17] After conducting internal training, the LTRI would then farm its trainees out to courts, prosecutor offices, law firms, and other entities to perform short-term apprenticeships.[18]

The LTRI-sponsored apprenticeships were unlike typical CLE or even professional legal education, however. Rather, they consisted mostly of passive observation of the practice of law. The LTRI felt that providing trainees with an opportunity to learn the practice of law through observation was sufficient for trainees to grasp and eventually follow legal practice.[19] Practical opportunities were not necessarily the focus. This is different from the typical legal clinical education model that encourages students to evaluate their own work in a hands-on, practical setting. At the end of the LTRI training, all attendees were required to take a practice-oriented examination.[20] Most students succeeded on the first attempt, and then became judges, prosecutors, or lawyers shortly thereafter.[21]

Legal Education Post-2004 reforms and CLE

Japan's establishment of new professional law schools in 2004 constitutes a monumental landmark in legal education. To effectuate its major legal reforms, Japan set out to increase the size and quality of its legal profession. Economic globalization combined with increasing societal disputes and the perceived need to reduce government fueled calls for strengthening the lawyer pool. To achieve this goal, the JSRC called for a legal training system that "organically connects legal education, the national bar examination, and apprenticeship training."[22] The Council recommended an interactive and broad curriculum that would enhance critical analytical ability, creativity, and skills in advocacy.[23] Ideally, the new law schools would raise accountability, include strict evaluation, and provide a bridge from theory to practice. They would also offer new training methods for aspiring lawyers that would enable students to learn to "think like a lawyer" and "practice like a lawyer" instead of simply focusing on memorization. This approach differed drastically from both the traditional legal education system and cram schools techniques that focused almost exclusively on memorization of the law and passing the national bar examination.[24] Remarkably, Japanese lawmakers quickly and uniformly adopted the JSRC's recommendations to revamp the legal education system without significant political infighting.

As a result, the country enacted a law facilitating the adoption of professional law schools (*houkadaigakuin*)[25] that led to the opening of 74 new law schools around the country between 2004 and 2005. Each school enrolled initial classes ranging from 30 to 300 students. As planned, the primary objective of these new law schools was to educate students aspiring to become attorneys. For the first time in the history of Japanese legal education, academics and legal practitioners were to collaborate in training future lawyers.[26] Students without a prior law degree could obtain a juris doctor degree from these law schools after a three-year course of study, while those with a law degree could obtain a juris doctor degree after two years. To infuse more diversity into the profession, the new law schools were encouraged to admit students from a variety of academic, professional, and socioeconomic backgrounds.

Many Japanese reformers believed that professional law schools based on the US model of legal education could produce a larger pool of high-quality lawyers that would help meet societal needs and embrace global challenges. In designing a new system, Japan looked at US law schools as a model. The system designers, including the Ministry of Education, noted many desirable characteristics in the US model that included varied curricula, rich pedagogy, diverse student bodies, small classes, strict student evaluation standards, and practical legal training opportunities including legal clinics. Accordingly, the new law schools looked to generally mirror the positive aspects of US legal education.

In accordance with the guidelines drawn up by the Ministry of Education, the new law schools set out to emulate the US legal education system in many respects. The schools sought to engage students through active in-class discussion, the case-method of study, and Socratic teaching methodologies. They also looked to integrate licensed practitioners into the faculty, offer practical skills courses, create legal clinics, provide externship opportunities, reduce class sizes, and utilize law school advisory committees.[27] From the time of inception, many of the new law schools also aspired to provide specialty courses and institute nontraditional methods of education in the form of skills courses, clinical programs, moot court programs, and law reviews.[28] In principle, the new institutions desired to bridge the divide between theoretical and practical education with an emphasis on comprehensiveness, diversity, and training.

Notwithstanding the similarities, though, the Japanese system deviated from the US model on several fronts. In an effort to appease the country's universities, the reformers allowed the continued existence of undergraduate law departments. Even more significantly, those individuals who pass the bar examination must still undergo training at the LTRI, albeit for a shorter duration. Although some insisted that Japan abolish the LTRI in light of the redefined role of the legal education system, it only condensed the LTRI training period to one year, with the expectation that it would split the training role with the new law schools.[29]

In correlation with the creation of new professional law schools, Japanese reformers believed that raising the national bar examination pass rate to around 70 percent would help ensure the success of the new law schools and facilitate skills training, including clinical education. If Japan could avoid an excessive emphasis on its bar exam, then students could ideally pursue knowledge beyond traditional bar subjects and devote time to acquiring skills directly transferable to the legal profession. Theoretically, law students could then develop an attitude and spirit of service toward clients and contribution to society that had been lacking in the past. By extension, this would lay the groundwork for successful CLE programs as well.

From an educational perspective, the expectations for the new law schools were not only facilitating the acquisition of legal knowledge but also outfitting law students with the ability to grasp cutting-edge legal issues, develop analytical abilities, think creatively, and acquire skills so that they could critically review and successfully resolve legal issues.[30] The reformers and many others understood that future members of Japan's legal community would be expected to have a heightened sense of humanity, greater sensitivity, broader expertise, flexible thinking, and abilities in persuasion.[31] Furthermore, there was a sense that to succeed, future lawyers would especially need "insight into society and human relationships, a sense of human rights, knowledge of up-to-date legal fields and foreign law, an international vision, and a firm grasp of language."[32]

As part of meeting these expectations, the new Japanese law schools have spent the last ten years experimenting with various measures, including CLE, with the aim of training law students and instilling a deeper sense of societal values. In contrast with undergraduate law programs, the curriculum has changed significantly in terms of expanded content, practice-oriented courses, simulation courses, externships, and even live-client clinics, which were introduced for the first time into Japanese legal education.[33]

Legal Clinics at Japan's New Law Schools: Success on the Horizon?

Although Japan's legal education reforms emphasized new learning techniques, professional values, and in-depth exposure to lawyering skills training, the JSRC recommendations did not specifically address CLE. Not only were the Council members largely unfamiliar with CLE, but also developments in CLE apparently were not on their radar screens.[34] Interactive learning and hands-on instruction designed to foster intellectual growth and practical skill development were strongly encouraged, however.

Tasked with a renewed mission, educators started honing in on legal clinics as a vehicle to help prepare students for the practice of law. Reformers, academics, and legal professionals came to view hands-on clinical education as a valuable tool within legal education. With the shortened apprenticeship period at the LTRI, however, law schools would need to step up efforts to provide additional skills training. Law clinics could help in this regard. Also, CLE could help bridge the divide between theory and practice that concerned the reformers. For example, hands-on law clinics generate interest in topics relevant to the legal profession that are less scholarly and more practical. If done properly, CLE can assist in promoting interactions between legal educators and practitioners as well.

Interestingly, the new professional law schools were not directly tasked with a social justice mission as part of the curriculum beyond improving the availability of quality lawyers particularly in underserved geographical regions.[35] As such, the initial interest in clinical programs did not necessarily arise from a concerted movement to provide more access to justice for marginalized people. The absence of an express social justice mission may have been due to the lack of educational tradition in this area. Alternatively, this could have arisen from Japan's historical inclination to sequester legal education from anything that might be perceived as a political movement or viewed as promoting a social justice agenda.[36] However, law schools operating clinics have been quick to emphasize the societal benefits arising from their efforts.

Opportunity to Offer CLE

Embraced by Many New Law Schools in Varied Forms

Because the JSRC's recommendations and resulting legislation did not require the inclusion of clinical education in the curriculum, each new Japanese law school was afforded the discretion of offering clinical courses or establishing a law clinic. The majority of the new law schools embraced the concept of clinical education, however, due to the vision for the revamped legal education system focused on practical legal education and skills training.

There is no fixed model of CLE in Japan. A survey taken in 2006 found that 56 law schools had implemented some type of clinical courses or programs.[37] The scope and subject matter of "clinic" courses or programs naturally varies among the law schools. Most law schools believe that CLE should take the form of providing students with a limited hands-on experience and more in-depth understanding about current legal practice, while others feel that students should be afforded the opportunity to more actively engage in a wider range of activities including client contact, interviewing, counseling, and drafting court documents.[38] In either event, many law schools feel that CLE should also benefit society and serve the surrounding communities.[39]

Despite the varied approaches, it is clear that the concept of practical education has taken root in some form at most law schools whether it involves real-client clinics, externship programs, or even simulation courses.[40] Most Japanese law schools will at least have students participate in providing some form of counseling exercises. This could simply take the form of shadowing an attorney and passively observing the legal counseling process, or it could involve active engagement under the supervision of a licensed attorney.[41] A good number of law schools provide a greater range of legal services, though.[42] A 2008 survey of all Japanese law schools focused on "real-client" clinical courses in which students have contact with real clients. Among the 74 law schools, a total of 38 schools reported that they offered real-client clinical courses, in which students have direct contact with clients.

CLE in Japan primarily focuses on civil, criminal, and family litigation matters. However, some law schools also offer specialized clinical courses that focus on a variety of subjects, including immigration law, asylum matters, women's legal issues, international human rights, disability law, and even labor law. In addition to touching various areas affected by the law, the critical benefit realized by integrating clinical education into the law school environment is being able to rely on instructors committed solely to the education of their students. Clinical instructors also can focus on bridging the gap between practice and lawyering theory.

In an effort to infuse expertise into the Japanese law school experience and provide students with an optimal education, many law schools decided to entrust their clinical programs to independent law offices outside of the university created specifically to facilitate legal clinical education. Essentially, a practicing attorney receives an appointment as an adjunct professor and oversees clinical courses and hands-on activities. Some law schools even jointly utilize law offices. For example, the Shibuya Law Office is a prime illustration as it offers a "legal clinic" staffed by approximately seven practicing attorneys and law students from four different Tokyo law schools.[43] This clinic handles a range of matters involving family law, finance, torts, real estate, corporate matters, employment, administrative issues, and crimes.[44] Additionally, over 15 Japanese law schools have established legal counseling offices for the purpose of conducting courses involving real clients.[45] In these specially created offices, clinical professors and students provide free counseling services for clients. In the case of both legal clinics and counseling offices, the underlying objective is providing legal representation to underserved clients.

To succeed in the long run, clinical faculty associated with Japanese law schools need to develop knowledge and expertise in CLE, including the relevant methodology and philosophy. This is difficult to achieve when relying on adjunct professors. To the extent possible, Japanese law schools need to turn to more training and stability with respect to clinical professors. Some law schools have directly hired clinical professors. However, many of these instructors have been appointed on a nontenure-track, part-time basis. Because these instructors have contracts of limited duration, the compensation is typically low, particularly in comparison with the time required to supervise students and operate a full clinic. Inadequate compensation may present as a disincentive for quality instruction simply because the instructor must find other work to provide a stable income. For CLE to take further hold in Japan, it is imperative that more law schools extend long-term contracts and compensation comparable to academic professors. This will enable a more concentrated focus on the clinics. It should be noted, however, that some law schools have attempted to involve traditional academic professors in the clinics. When the new Japanese law schools first opened their doors, most nonclinical faculty had little, if any, interest in clinic education. To generate additional interest and attempt to resolve the disconnect between theory and practice, about 20 of the law schools operating live-client clinics have made efforts to involve academic professors in the clinics. These efforts should continue.

Despite advances in clinical education in Japan within the university setting, the law schools and students are still wrestling with the role of clinics and clinical courses in several respects. In general, clinical courses are optional or only "mandatory optional," meaning that students must enroll in one course among a group of courses that include a clinic.[46] A legal clinic is not a prerequisite for graduation. Moreover, many students believe that clinics are not necessary due to the training provided in the LTRI after they have passed the bar examination. They perceive that the training offered through clinics does not significantly vary from the training offered through the LTRI. In addition, clinics participation typically counts only for two units of credit, or even no credits at all, making it difficult to quickly progress toward the 93 to 95 credits typically mandated for graduation.[47] Japan should explore offering clinics for more credits. In the United States, clinics are typically three-credit courses. Scheduling is also a significant issue at some schools. Unlike the US legal education system, in which upper-division students can typically schedule courses in a flexible manner due to block scheduling on alternate days, Japanese law school students typically attend classes from morning to evening five days a week. During their final two years of schooling, students generally only have one half-day to spend outside of class. Due to the full-time class schedule, students can be hindered from fully engaging in live clinics or other clinical activities. Absent making scheduling concessions, many students as well as the public may be shortchanged.

Notwithstanding, with the adoption of the new professional law schools, interest in clinical education has started expanding and taken root to a degree never experienced before. This is encouraging. Students are participating in clinics, and disadvantaged members of the population now have more opportunities to avail themselves of heavily discounted or free legal representation. There has also been an increased emphasis on communication and exchange. In addition to the university programs, the Japan Clinical Legal Education Association (JCLEA) was established in April 2008 with over 200 founding members. As the first Japanese academic society focused on legal education, the JCLEA was designed to facilitate a network of clinical law instructors that could share experiences, exchange pedagogical methods, and improve CLE. The JCLEA holds annual conferences and actively seeks to obtain information about clinical activities in different disciplines and legal clinical education overseas.

Model Clinics and Case Studies

To gain an even better understanding of the state of legal clinical education in Japan, it is useful to look at several clinics that operate in different contexts. The first illustration details two efforts by one of the largest law schools in Japan, and the other examines CLE at a smaller law school that has taken unique steps to meeting the needs of a local community.

Waseda University—Large Law School Clinic Experience

Waseda University Law School, one of the leading universities in Japan, is home to the largest clinical law program among Japanese law schools. From the start, Waseda has assumed a leading role in legal clinical education in Japan. In fact, two years before the new Japanese law schools opened, Waseda established the Institute of Clinical Legal Education with a special grant from the Ministry of Education, Culture, Sports, Science and Technology.[48] This enabled Waseda to start operating a clinical program starting in 2002.

In admitting 300 students per year to its law school and engaging 70 full-time faculty members, Waseda University anticipated that it could actively pursue CLE through both general and specialized legal clinics. It officially enrolled law students in its clinics beginning in the spring 2006 semester. Consistent with the objectives underlying the country's legal reforms, the legal clinics aimed to bridge theory and practice as well as offer students the opportunity "to learn by doing." Among other opportunities such as simulation courses and externships, Waseda Law School offers eight legal clinics, including a civil law clinic, family/gender clinic, criminal law clinic, labor clinic, administrative law clinic, clinic for foreigners, commercial clinic, and disability clinic.

The interest of Waseda law students in legal clinical education has been comparatively high, and their experience has generally been rich.[49] As of 2014, a total of 1,062 students have participated in clinics. Recent yearly enrollment totals around 130 students. Participants in Waseda University's clinics have commented that the opportunity to work with actual clients helped them gain a better understanding of the law, grasp legal theories, and think more like a lawyer. They also note that the clinics helped them to recognize professional goals and confirm career choices. However, Waseda's clinics have struggled to attract clients. For example, for 134 law students enrolled in Waseda's law clinics in 2013, there were only 42 clients accepted by the clinics from among 88 applicants. To attract clients, Waseda University advertised on buses in the surrounding community, placed information on the university website, extended services into the summer when law school clinics are typically closed, and even asked law professors to refer cases from their own law firms. However, these efforts have still fallen short. Recently, Waseda has turned to the Japan Legal Support Center, or *Hoterasu*, for client referrals.

To gain an even better understanding of the efforts of Japanese law schools to bridge the gap between theory and practical skills education, it is instructive to examine the civil law and criminal justice clinics operated by Waseda University.

Civil Law Clinic for Waseda Law Students

The Waseda Legal Clinic (WLC) is an actual law firm registered with the Daini Tokyo Bar Association with a mission focusing on education and community service. Although it handles civil matters, financial gain is not the objective. In 2004, Waseda founded this legal clinic on the principles of providing practical legal education and offering legal services to those individuals who are unable to afford legal fees.[50] The WLC is financially supported by Waseda University and other funding sources. From its clients, it only collects money for expenses (copies, phone, etc.) and a portion of any positive recovery.[51]

In essence, the WLC engages in three primary types of legal services, including clinical courses for educational purposes; free legal advice provided on certain weekdays by WLC attorneys for underprivileged clients regarding general civil matters, employment matters, family issues, and administrative issues; and traditional law firm services.[52] The WLC was also designated as a Japan Legal Support Center on June 13, 2013.[53]

In principle, all cases accepted by the WLC must have an academic purpose related to education and research. Otherwise, the WLC will not take the case.[54] For example, it does not make sense for the WLC to take simple cases of theft, fraud, or nonpayment as these cases have low educational value. Conversely, because the university setting is a source of expertise on a variety of matters, the

WLC can serve to handle more complex matters such as those involving intellectual property, issues faced by local organizations and public bodies, asylum and refugee matters, and even nuclear issues.

In principle, attorneys operate the clinic hand in hand with clinical students. As of 2014, nearly 15 licensed attorneys helped operate the WLC.[55] Student involvement in the WLC generally entailed teams of two to three students working on a single case together with one research attorney and one practicing attorney. In general, students in the WLC take the forefront in meeting with clients and conducting research. Naturally, the students working on a client problem will do so in consultation with the supervising attorneys. The students may be given the opportunity to lead client interviews, discuss legal issues with the supervising attorney, and then proceed to convey legal advice to the client. The supervising attorney will not only provide the students with feedback as they engage in a host of civil and litigation-related matters, but will also make sure that the clients receive high-quality legal services.[56] In turn, the students are able to develop and hone skills that will be useful in the practice of law.

Criminal Justice Clinic for Waseda Law Students

In addition, Waseda University Law School created its Criminal Justice Clinic during the summer of 2004, and first offered for-credit courses in the spring 2005 semester with a mind-set of educating through experience. At the time, two experienced criminal defense attorneys joined Waseda as faculty members to support the clinic. To date, the majority of the cases taken by the Criminal Justice Clinic have been acquired through the duty attorney system, which enables criminal suspects held at detention centers to obtain legal advice.[57] Through this clinic, students have the opportunity to negotiate with police and prosecutors, draft legal documents, and sometimes interact with judges. Although students are restricted from participating in confidential meetings or appearing in court, they can have the opportunity to meet with the accused, collect the facts and evidence, and strategize with attorneys.[58] These activities help shift students away from exclusive book learning, and prepare them for the practice of criminal law through hands-on activities.

University of the Ryukyus—Small Law School Clinic Experience

The University of the Ryukyus in Okinawa is one of the smallest professional law schools in Japan. It admits between 22 and 30 law students per year, who are taught by 16 full-time faculty members.[59] In 2008, the University of the Ryukyus commenced operation of a bilingual law clinic through its law professors and students.[60] The primary focus of this clinic was the community and providing foreign residents living in Okinawa with high-quality legal advice and assistance on matters typically challenging for foreigners, particularly cross-border family law issues. Due to a sizable US military presence, Okinawa is home to a heavy concentration of foreign residents, including citizens from the United States, the Philippines, Korea, and Thailand.[61] The interaction between local residents and transient foreign residents on a small island presents a wide range of complex legal and social issues that have historically not been adequately addressed by local legal professionals. These matters include international marriages and divorces; child custody and child support; adoptions; real estate purchases; negotiation and execution of contracts; immigration matters; and other family law matters.[62] With the foreign resident population and escalating number of mixed marriages in Okinawa, there has always been a sizable disconnect between society and the law.

Before the creation of a law clinic at the University of the Ryukyus that turned its attention to foreign-related matters, existing legal assistance providers were unable to meet the needs of the relatively large foreign community in Okinawa. The laws and procedures differ between Japan and other countries. There is also the language barrier for non-Japanese living within Japanese society. Local services were often inadequate. Although the city hall free lawyer consultation program, *Houterasu* (Japan Legal Support Center), and the Okinawa Bar Association have attempted to cover unmet legal needs, these groups largely could not assist potential clients who cannot speak Japanese or potential clients requiring assistance with a cross-border legal issue.[63] For US citizens, military legal offices could only provide advice on US law and could not assist foreign spouses due to language barriers, ineligibility for services, staffing constraints, or the inability to assist with long-term cases.[64] Some local attorneys have attempted to provide legal services to address cross-border issues, but their numbers have been insufficient. Additionally, other institutional barriers beyond legal representation have caused other frustrations. Vera Fry, international attorney and former professor at the University of Ryukyus Law school, noted that Japan is unlike the United States, where women can turn to state agencies and other organizations for assistance and child support.[65] As such, the law clinic at the University of Ryukyus was originally designed to provide assistance in these areas and fill the legal gap between US military lawyers specializing in US law and the community.[66]

Through the law clinic, underserved members of the community benefitted significantly. Ryukyus law students also had the invaluable opportunity of acquiring practical skills while learning about the intersection of Japanese and foreign laws (particularly US law). They were able to interview clients, conduct research, draft legal documents, and receive invaluable instructor feedback regarding their hands-on work. From a societal standpoint, the students could also positively impact children, mothers, and fathers who were at a disadvantage in terms of custody, financial support, and even citizenship issues.[67]

Like other Japanese universities, the efforts of the University of the Ryukyus to provide clinical opportunities have been hampered, however. Once Professor Fry departed and a replacement was not hired, it was very difficult to carry out an international and bilingual clinic. However, the university did continue with a general legal services clinic and has exerted efforts to branch out into the immediate and surrounding communities. The university continues to hold free legal advice sessions and look for ways to serve the underserved in the local community.

Challenges Facing CLE in Japan

Various challenges have negatively impacted legal education generally and clinical education specifically in Japan. In the decade since implementation, the new professional Japanese law schools have faced an increasingly rocky road, and their existence has even been called into question by the certain observations, bar associations, and bureaucrats. Since 2004, applicants to law schools have dropped significantly as a result of failed promises with respect to the national bar examination and other factors. This has directly affected the success and popularity of student clinics and practical skills training. It has also negatively impacted the future prospects of many institutions.

Low Bar Pass Rate Hampering Success of Clinics

The biggest obstacle facing CLE and many of the planned advantages of the new law school system is the national bar examination. In planning a new professional legal education system, the reformers realized that a low bar exam pass rate would detrimentally affect the proposed enhancements. Accordingly, the original blueprint for reform called for a bar exam pass rate around 70 percent to 80 percent.[68] Although the government moved forward with this recommendation, its own calculations were invariably flawed as it failed to correctly anticipate how many universities would meet the criteria to establish new professional law schools. Based on its original projections, the Ministry of Education, Culture, Sports, Science, and Technology estimated that enrollment in the new law schools would reach only 4,000 students per year. If the number of bar exam passers reached 3,000 by 2010, then the yearly passage rate would fall in line with its advertised goals.[69] With the approval of 74 new law schools, however, the initial enrollment swelled to about 5,800 students.[70] At this enrollment level, Japan would need to license 4,000 new attorneys each year to meet the 70 percent bar pass target. These numbers deviated substantially from the original plans.

Wary of entrusting market forces with more lawyers and believing it had committed a serious calculation error, Japan regulated and precipitously reduced the bar pass rate over the objections of students, professors, and universities that had substantially invested in the new professional law school system. For the first class of new law school graduates in 2006, Japan allowed a pass rate of only approximately 50 percent.[71] After this time, the government progressively reduced the bar pass rate until it leveled out in 2009 at around 25 percent.[72] In 2013, the bar pass rate was 26.8 percent as 2,049 individuals passed the national bar examination.[73] These results were significantly lower than the levels recommended for the law schools to succeed. However, the government felt compelled to limit the number of bar passers to around 2,000 individuals.[74] As demonstrated by the government's reaction, the national bar examination is not functioning as a qualifying exam for the practice of law. Rather, it provides a mechanism for law school graduates to simply compete for a limited number of seats in the LTRI.

Due to the lower than anticipated bar pass rate, Japanese law students immediately switched their primary focus to courses and other activities directly associated with passing the bar exam. Skills development and legal clinics took a back seat, particularly in light of the restriction that graduates of the new law schools have only three attempts to pass the bar examination within a five-year period.[75] In a very competitive environment in which only a quarter of bar exam takers pass the exam, law students naturally fear falling behind if they spend time on clinics, practical training, skills development, or specialty courses that only become relevant if they pass the bar exam. Also, the new Japanese law schools have overemphasized the bar examination despite the targeted changes in educational philosophy. In essence, their survival has directly depended on attracting and educating students who pass the national bar examination. If only a small number of students pass the bar exam at a certain university, then it is naturally assumed by the government and prospective students that the quality of education at such university is in adequate. In some respects, Japanese professional law schools have been relegated to the function of expensive cram schools. Interestingly, though, bar examination cram schools have still found their niche given that the new law schools focus on content and do not necessarily teach test-taking skills.

Another development that may hurt CLE has been the government's recent decision to offer a Law School Equivalency Exam (LSEE). The LSEE allows an individual the opportunity to possibly qualify as a lawyer without expending the time and money required to graduate from one of the professional law schools. Although the LSEE is difficult to pass (in 2012, only 116 of the 6,477 LSEE takers passed the exam, giving them the chance to compete with law school graduates on the final two portions of the national bar examination),[76] the existence of such an exam serves to undermine the legal education system and CLE. Allowing a select few individuals to test straight into the practice of law is counterintuitive in light of the legal reforms and Ministry of Education guidelines that focused on law schools teaching students how to think like lawyers while training them in the trade. In reality, it appears that little has changed from the prereform undergraduate law programs.

Another illustration of the fallout from a lower than promised bar examination pass rate is the rapid decrease in law school applications. Over the past decade, the number of law school applicants has dropped significantly, especially from nontraditional applicants or graduates from nonlaw disciplines. These are the potential students who reformers felt were key to expanding the reach and influence of the legal system. As of 2014, the Ministry of Education reported that Japanese law schools were only able to fill 59.6 percent of their available seats in their entering classes.[77] Additionally, the Ministry of Education had started decreasing subsidies to law schools with low bar pass rates, and plans only decreasing subsidies to those schools having difficulties filling their classes.[78] As such, the law schools face the decision of whether to lower admissions thresholds, educate a smaller number of students with less tuition income and smaller governmental subsidies, or close their doors despite their sizable investments of time, money, and other resources. As of May 2014, approximately 13 Japanese law schools whose graduates have not been consistently passing the bar examination and that had started losing financial support from the central government have started taking measures to close their doors.[79]Naturally, applicants and matriculants at these institutions have dropped significantly. For example, for the class entering in 2014, Toukai University was only able to matriculate one student, while Niigata University was only able to matriculate 5 percent of its enrollment quota and Kanagawa University only 8 percent of its quota.[80]

For years, observers have speculated that the Japanese government has secretly harbored a desire to see law schools merge or discontinue operations so that it can continue maintaining the number of bar exam passers at 2,000 per year or less, but also have the bar pass rate rise. If the bar examination pass rate increases due to the ongoing attrition of law schools, then it may be possible for Japan to more fully attain the goals underlying the recent legal reforms with respect to practical skills training. In turn, students may be more willing to take advantage of legal clinical education opportunities instead of focusing heavily on passing the bar examination. In any event, unless the passage rate on the new bar exam increases to the threshold originally envisioned by the reformers, Japan's legal education system will suffer pedagogically and clinical education will continue to face challenges.

To truly achieve the goals underlying the new law schools, the bar pass rate must increase significantly either by allowing the licensure of more junior attorneys or fewer law schools. If the bar pass rate exceeds the 70 percent threshold, law students should then feel more comfortable taking courses other than the standard "bar course" fare, particularly with institutional support.[81] Also, university administrators can then turn their focus to CLE with more confidence in student interest and more willingness to emphasize the benefits associated with legal education. Even if the bar pass rate does not rebound to the threshold originally promised, however, it is important that Japanese law school administrators and faculty advise students to take clinical courses for purposes of professional training and community service. This will help foster the development of a high-quality legal profession.

Other Challenges Hinder the Development of Clinics

Lacking a tradition in clinical education in a university setting, Japan continues to struggle with the distinction between law school clinics and the LTRI. Although some contend that the existence of the LTRI negates the need for clinical education at the university level, this contention ignores the hands-on nature of clinical work as opposed to the focus on observation in the LTRI.[82] It also unfairly dismisses the benefits that future lawyers can obtain by offering legal services to the community in a variety of contexts. Even more significantly, CLE in Japan is hampered by the lack of a student practice rule. The absence of attention to CLE in the JSRC recommendations combined with skepticism at the law school level about the appropriate involvement of students and the relative lack of tradition for apprenticeship trainees to actively participate in legal practice has led to uncertainties and practical problems.[83] For example, criminal justice clinics are quite rare given the position of the National Prosecutor's Office and National Police Agency that law students should not be able to participate in confidential interviews. Even in the case of civil litigation, clinic students cannot sit with their supervising attorneys in court, but rather must watch from the courtroom gallery. The inclination of the courts to treat law students as observers instead of participants inhibits the skills development of upper-division law students.

Conclusion

While CLE appears to be spreading in Japan, it still remains in its infancy. The reform of a legal education system does not take place overnight. The new pioneering law schools need patience, perseverance, and additional faculty training. The process of developing and refining new law schools will naturally take some time. At the same time, however, the law schools need to continue seeking ways to expand their CLE programs and encourage law students to avail themselves of this practical learning opportunity. Even more importantly, Japan needs to quickly address the obstacles and challenges inhibiting practical training and skills development at the university level. It should revisit the bar pass rate and explore additional avenues that will provide students the opportunity to learn by doing. Through hands-on learning in the context of a legal clinic, students can solidify their legal knowledge and develop foundational skills that will help them become quality lawyers. Legal clinic participation can also help ingrain a sense of societal service in future lawyers, while simultaneously benefitting the underserved in Japanese society.

Notes

1. Japan Federation of Bar Associations, "Justice System Reform," http://www.nichibenren.or.jp/en/about/ judicial_system/justice_system_reform.html,accessed May 27, 2014.
2. Justice System Reform Council, "Recommendations of the Justice System Reform Council: For a Justice System to Support Japan in the 21st Century" Ch I, Part 1 (2001)http://www.kantei.go.jp/foreign/ judiciary/2001/0612report.html, accessed May 27, 2014.
3. Ibid; Annelise Riles and Takashi Uchida, "Reforming Knowledge? A Socio-legal Critique of Legal Education Reforms in Japan" (2009) 1 *Drexel L. Rev.* 3, 4.
4. The *Shiho Seido Kaikaku Shingikai* (Justice System Reform Council or JSRC) was established by Prime Minister Keizo Obuchi to create official guidelines for Japan's judicial reforms. The JSRC consisted of 13 elite members from various political and economic sectors, including a former chief justice of the Hiroshima high court, a former chief prosecutor of the Nagoya Public Prosecutor's Office, two members from *Keidanren*

(Federation of Economic Organizations) and the *Keizai Doyukai*(Japanese Association of Corporative Executives), the former president of the Japan Federation of Bar Associations, the president of the Federation of Private Universities, a business professor from a private university, a popular writer, a vice president of the *Rengo* (Labor Union) organization, and the president of *Shufuren* (The Federation of Homemakers).

5. Setsuo Miyazawa, Kay-Wah Chan, and Ilhyung Lee, "The Reform of Legal Education" (2008) *Ann. Rev. L. & Soc. Sci.* 333, 341.
6. Masako Kamiya, "Structural and Institutional Arrangements of Legal Education: Japan" (2006) 24 *Wis. Int'l L. J.* 153; Mayumi Saegusa, "Why the Japanese Law School System Was Established: Co-optation as a Defensive Tactic in the Face of Global Pressures" (2009) 34 *Law & Soc. Inquiry* 365, 366.
7. Saegusa (n 6) 371; Kamiya (n 6) 154.
8. Kamiya (n 6) 153.
9. Ibid.
10. Riles and Uchida (n 3) 10.
11. Saegusa (n 6) 371.
12. James R. Maxeiner and Keiichi Yamanaka, "The New Japanese Law Schools: Putting the Professional into Legal Education" (2004) 13 *Pac. Rim L. & Policy* 303, 310.
13. Ibid.
14. Ibid.
15. Ibid.
16. Miyazawa et al. (n 5).
17. Ibid.; Supreme Court of Japan, "The Legal Training and Research Institute," http://www.courts.go.jp/ english/institute_01/institute/index.html, accessed May 27, 2014.
18. Ibid.
19. Takashi Takano, "Making a Criminal Justice Clinic in Japan" (2007) 25 *Waseda Bull. Comp. Law* 41.
20. Maxeiner and Yamanaka (n 12) 310.
21. Ibid.
22. Justice System Reform Council (n 2) Ch I, Part 3, 2(2).
23. Miyazawa et al. (n 5) 344.
24. Justice System Reform Council (n 2) Ch III, Part 2.
25. Ministry of Education, Culture, Sports, Science, and Technology, *Senmonshoku Daigakuin* (*Hokadaigakuin Kyoushoku Daigakuin*) [Professional Graduate Schools (Law and Teaching Graduate Schools)] http://www.mext.go.jp/a_menu/koutou/houka/houka.htm, accessed May 27, 2014.
26. Miyazawa et al. (n 5) 348.
27. Riles and Uchida (n 3) 12–13; Kamiya (n 6) 165. At least 30 percent of the faculty at the new Japanese law schools must be licensed practitioners. *Id.* at 169.Also, the target student to teacher ratio is 10:1. Miyazawa et al. (n 5) 170.
28. Setsuko Kamiya, "Law Schools Grope to Create Better Lawyers" *The Japan Times* (November 4, 2006) http://search.japantimes.co.jp/cgi-bin/nn20061104f1.html, accessed May 27, 2014.
29. Supreme Court of Japan (n 17).Previously, the time required at the Institute was two years. As the number of attorneys increased, the amount of practical training offered by the Institute decreased to 18 months. As of 2006, the required period was reduced to one year so that the Institute can accommodate more successful applicants.

30. Justice System Reform Council (n 2) Ch III, Part 2 (1)b.
31. Ibid.Ch III, Preamble.
32. Ibid.
33. Miyazawa et al. (n 5) 348.
34. Shigeo Miyagawa, Takao Suami, Peter A. Joy, and Charles D. Weisselberg, "Japan's New Clinical Programs: A Study of Light and Shadow," Ch 7, 108, in Frank S. Bloch (ed.) *The Global Clinical Movement: Educating Lawyers for Social Justice* (Oxford, 2010).
35. Ibid. 108–109.
36. Ibid.
37. Kamiya (n 28).
38. Ibid. 111.
39. *Ri-garu Kurinikku to ChiikitonoKyoudo* [Legal Clinics Cooperating with the Local Community], Ritsumekan University (March 30, 2009) http://www.ritsumei.ac.jp/acd/gr/hoka/special_program/houkoku_ 090421.pdf, accessed May 27, 2014.
40. Miyagawa et al. (n 34) 109.
41. Ibid. 110.
42. *Greeting from Director*, Waseda University Legal Clinic, http://legal-clinic.mylawyer .jp/ pc/free5.html, accessed May 27, 2014.
43. Shibuya Public Law Office, "Regaru Kurinikku Joukyu Saishu Houkokukai"[Legal Clinic Advanced – Report from Final Meeting](October, 2012) http://www.sbpb -law.jp/news/2012index.html, accessed May 27, 2014.
44. Ibid.
45. Miyagawa et al. (n 34) 112.
46. Ibid. 110.
47. Masanori Takeda and Vera Fry, "Legal Clinic Endeavour for International Family Law Clients in Okinawa"(2010) 82 *Ryudai L. Rev.* 1, 18.
48. Waseda University website, http://www.waseda.jp/eng/academics1/wasedalaw.html, accessed May 27, 2014.
49. Waseda University symposium, "Tenth Anniversary of the Establishment of Legal Clinics" (May 31, 2014), materials on file with author.
50. Koji Oumi, "Mission of Legal Clinics" Waseda Legal Clinic websitehttp://legal-clinic.mylawyer.jp/pc/, accessed May 27, 2014.
51. Ibid.
52. Ibid.
53. Ibid.
54. Ibid.
55. Ibid.
56. Ibid.
57. "Legal Clinics," Waseda University Law School websitehttp://www.waseda.jp/law-school/jp/about/ education/clinic02.html, accessed May 27, 2014.
58. Ibid.
59. University of the Ryukyus, http://www.law.u-ryukyu.ac.jp/information/information -outline/lawschool-outline/, accessed May 27, 2014.
60. David Allen and Chiyomi Sumida, *Free Law Clinics to Advise on Japanese Legal Issues* (Stars and Stripes, April 19, 2008).
61. Takeda and Fry (n 47) 14.
62. Ibid.3–14; Allen and Sumida (n 60).
63. Takeda and Fry (n 47) 15–16.

64. Ibid. 16.
65. Allen and Sumida (n 60).
66. Ibid.
67. Takeda and Fry (n 47) 17.
68. Justice System Reform Council (n 2) Ch II, Part 2, 2(2)(d); See also Katsumi Yoshida, "Legal Education Reforms in Japan: Background, Rationale, and Goals to be Achieved" (2006) 24 *Wis. Int'l L. J.* 209, 217–218.
69. Justice System Reform Council (n 2) Ch I, Part 3, 2(2).
70. Tomoya Ishikawa, Fumiaki Onishi, and Manabu Aoike, "Law School Quotas Set to be Slashed" *The Asahi Shimbun*(April 18, 2009) http://www.asahi.com/english/Herald-asahi/TKY200904180056.html,accessed May 27, 2014.
71. The Yomiuri Shimbun, "10 Law Schools Mulling Cutting Student Quotas"(May 22, 2008) http://www.yomiuri.co.jp/dy/national/20080522TDY02312.htm, accessed May 27, 2014; Dai Adachi, "Legal Sector Split on Raising Lawyer Numbers" *The Yomiuri Shimbun*(February 6, 2008) http://www.yomiuri.co.jp/dy/national/02/06/2008, accessed May 27, 2014.
72. "Bar Exam Pass Rate Hits Record Low" *The Mainichi Daily News* (September 11, 2009) http://mdn.mainichi.jp/mdnnews/national/news/20090911p2a00m0na013000c.html, accessed May 27, 2014.
73. Ministry of Justice of Japan, "Houkadaigakuinbetsugoukakushasutou" [2013 New National Bar Exam Passer Breakdown by Law School] http://www.moj.go.jp/content/000114386.pdf, accessed May 27, 2014.
74. "Law School and Bar Exam Reform" *The Japan Times* (October 3, 2013) http://www.japantimes.co.jp/opinion/2013/10/03/editorials/law-school-and-bar-exam-reform/, accessed May 27, 2014.
75. "Shihoshiken [5 nen 5 kai] nikanwa, 15 nenkaratekiyo he: Kaiseian Kakugi Kettei" [Relaxing the Bar Exam to Five Times Within Five Years from 2015: Reform Recommendation Cabinet Decision] *Nihon Keizai Shinbum* (March 3, 2014) http://www.nikkei.com/article/DGXNASDG0400U_U4A300C1CR0000/, accessed May 27, 2014.
76. Colin P.A. Jones, "Stop Thinking—The Test is About to Start: A Look at the Absurdities of Japan's Tests for Lawyers, Nurses and Caregivers" *The Japan Times* (December 18, 2012) http://www.japantimes.co.jp/community/2012/12/18/issues/stop-thinking-the-test-is-about-to-start/, accessed May 27, 2014.
77. "Houka Daigakuin no Teiin Shusokuritsu, Hajimete 6wari Shitamawaru" [Rate of Law School Entering Classes Falls Below 60 Percent for First Time Ever] *The Yomiuri Shimbun* (May 9, 2014) http://www.yomiuri.co.jp/ kyoiku/news/20140509-OYT8T50031.html, accessed May 27, 2014.
78. Law School and Bar Exam Reform (n 74).
79. "Niigata Daigaku, Houka Daigakuin no Boushu Chuushi" [Niigata University Stops Recruiting Students for Law School], *Nihon Keizai Shimbun* (March 17, 2014) http://www.nikkei.com/article/DGXNASDG1703F_ X10C14A3CR8000/, accessed May 27, 2014.
80. Houka Daigakuin (n 77).
81. Japan Federation of Bar Associations, "Recommendations to Improve the New Professional Legal Education and Training System" (January 16, 2009) http://www.nichibenren.or.jp/en/ activities/statements/ 090116.html, accessed May 27, 2014.
82. Miyagawa et al. (n 34) 113–114.
83. Ibid. 114.

CHAPTER 12

Legal Clinics in Turkey

Julian Lonbay and Musa Toprak

Introduction

Turkey has a classic two-stage legal education to prepare lawyers for practice as an *avukat*. The academic stage at the university was heavily influenced by the German legal tradition, and is reputed to be theory heavy, with little practical application of the law.[1] This climate of legal education is one reason why it is taking a while for the value of experiential learning, as reflected in the law clinic experience, to take hold in Turkish law faculties, which are not involved in the second stage of vocational training of lawyers. Another issue, discussed below, is that the bar associations are suspicious of the new legal clinics and consider that they breach the monopoly of the *avukat* in providing legal advice.[2] However, one can point to the 2007 Council of Bars and Law Societies of Europe (CCBE) Recommendation on Training Outcomes for European Lawyers,[3] which sets out the legal and practical skills that lawyers should have, without specifying at which stage of legal education they should be attained, as being supportive of legal clinics.[4]

Overall one cannot say "legal clinics" have yet found their proper place in the Turkish legal education system.[5] Until the last decade, the concept of legal clinics was practically nonexistent in Turkey, but as a result of the efforts of some law faculties over the last ten years, there have been important developments in this area. As Yasemin Işıktaç states, "Clinical legal education is not given a place in the standard curriculum. Some new private law schools give importance to this Anglo-American concept. However, even in these law schools there is no credit-course concerning clinical legal education."[6]

New law faculties are either starting legal clinics or announcing their desire to or interest in starting a legal clinic, and the number of legal clinics is increasing. Despite the improving awareness and visibility of legal clinics in Turkey, they are still in their infancy. This chapter aims to give an insight into the first examples of legal clinics in Turkey.

There is currently no legal definition of legal clinics in Turkish legislation, either in education law or in legal practice. We believe that examining the first examples of legal clinics in Turkey will create a floor that will enable discussion of potential developments and an airing the problems that legal clinics face, especially in their relations with lawyers and bar associations.

We will focus here on the legal clinics established in the law faculties of Bilgi University, Ankara University, and Anadolu University, because these were the first three clinics established in Turkey. Even though there were individual attempts, dating back to year 2000,[7] there were not any institutionalized legal clinics until the Bilgi and Ankara clinics were set up, as explained below.

Bilgi University Legal Clinic

The very first legal clinic in Turkey was started in 2003 at Bilgi University Faculty of Law in Istanbul.[8] The Bilgi University Legal Clinic declares that, while establishing its programs, it has taken the experience of other countries as a model for the Bilgi Legal Clinic. Bilgi started with two clinics: the Street Law Clinic and the Refugee and Private Law Clinic. The Open Society Institute assisted Bilgi in establishing these clinics, which were the first in Turkey. In that regard, *training-of-trainer courses* were offered for Bilgi staff in Krakow, Budapest, Prague, and in collaboration with American University[9] and Georgetown University in Washington, DC, and finally together with the University of Kwa Zulu, Natal, in South Africa.[10]

The Bilgi Legal Clinic is a two-semester elective course. The first-semester course is a non-credit-bearing one, but students can gain six European Credit Transfer System (ECTS) credits in the second semester.[11]

In the first semester, at the Bilgi legal clinics, the students are trained in the practical skills they will need for the second-semester sessions that will take place outside the classroom. During this semester, students learn to address subjects such as poverty, social exclusion, and empowerment through law, and they develop the skillsets that will enable them to interview and communicate with disadvantaged groups. In the second semester, these skills are deployed and practiced in the field. Typically, students have two options in joining a legal clinic. At the Private Law Clinic, they may choose to help those who cannot afford an attorney due to their socioeconomic situation by helping solve their legal problems. This involves interviewing them, researching the legal issue at hand, and writing legal memoranda. The students might also accompany these people on their visits to government offices and help them fill out application forms or write petitions. Alternatively, at the Street Law Clinic, with the approval of the Ministry of Justice, students may work on the prison seminars program, which involves visiting prisons in Istanbul to deliver seminars (lessons) to the convicts and detainees on legal issues they might need to know during and after their imprisonment. These seminars (lessons) last about nine weeks.[12]

Elveriş states[13] that the clinics are now accepting 12 to 14 students per year, although it was fewer initially—between four to six students in the first years of the legal clinic. They are admitting students only from the third or fourth year with a particular, high, GPA. Although it is an elective course, students do not have the option of choosing the course themselves. Instead, they are selected by interview. Elveriş states that everything has not worked out as the clinics had originally planned, but that they have developed their own paths. For example, the Private Law Clinic was originally envisioned as a Family Law Clinic, but because of the demand, it became instead a Private Law Clinic. Elveriş stresses that they are dealing with very few legal cases, and that "in the period of 2004–2013 the clinic [w]as involved with 123 cases, these are very humble numbers."[14]

Bilgi University states that

> in both legal clinics, students find the opportunity to practice theoretical knowledge that was obtained in other courses of the law faculty as well as to develop skills such as talking in a language that can be understood by disadvantaged people, speaking in public, interviewing, conducting legal research and writing—all of which will be beneficial to a great extent in their subsequent legal career. Moreover, the legal clinic experience also provides those students with further maturity by way of establishing links with people from different social circles.[15]

Bilgi University's efforts helped raise the awareness of legal clinics.[16] Although Bilgi Legal Clinic was the first in Turkey, legally speaking, it is nothing more than an elective course. Elveriş herself is a good example of the problems legal clinics are facing in Turkey. Elveriş was employed to run the legal clinics, but because the clinics have no legal status, she had to be hired as a member of the academic staff and has been officially assigned to the Philosophy and Sociology of Law department of the Bilgi Law Faculty. Moreover, she had to obtain a doctoral degree in order to remain at the university. Restrictive and inflexible employment rules for faculty members prevent legal clinics from having professionals who work only for the legal clinic.[17] This is likely to cause problems for the development of the legal clinics in the long term.

In 2005, the Street Law Clinic was selected as one of the "best practices in education" by the Sabancı University Education Reform Initiative.[18]

Ankara University Legal Clinic

The Ankara University Faculty of Law was the first law school established in Turkey in the Republican era.[19] Together with the Istanbul University Faculty of Law, this faculty plays, and has always played, a leading role in legal education in Turkey. For this reason, the legal clinic courses in the Ankara Law Faculty are very important for the visibility of legal clinics in Turkey. It will not be surprising if we see that the new legal clinics in Turkey follow the lead of Ankara University.

Legal clinics were started at Ankara University in 2005[20] through the initiative of Prof. Gülriz Uygur, chair of the Philosophy of Law and Sociology and Law Department. As we have seen, clinics have no legal definition in Turkey. Uygur states that they began in Ankara without the administration of the law faculty being notified. She states that, because the concept was unknown, she was afraid that their work might be stopped by the dean if they asked for approval, and thus they started to work *in a sort of secrecy* and *they awaited for good results to facilitate their acceptance.*[21]

Legal clinics at Ankara University follow a complicated system. Students take the courses called "legal clinics" in the fourth year, but they must take legal clinic courses as electives under different names in the second and third years in order to be able to attend the course in the fourth year. The courses are designed to follow each other. The first two years are aimed at preparing students for the practical course that is offered in the fourth year, which is the only one actually styled as a legal clinic course. The course in the third year is not a credit-bearing course, but rather a working group. Students may voluntarily join a working group if they are in the compulsory course, Philosophy of Law. Ankara Law Faculty staff would prefer to style these working groups as a course. But there was no room for a new course in the curriculum, and they therefore decided to call these courses working groups even though they consist of a ten-week program, which is almost completely separate from the compulsory Philosophy of Law course. The legal clinic courses in the third and fourth years are prerequisite courses, and students who did not successfully pass the prior courses are not allowed to take the courses that follow in the third and fourth years. For example, students who want to study gender must elect the course titled Law and Women in the third year. After that, they are allowed to join a so-called working group called Women's Rights, and finally they are permitted to work in the Domestic Violence Legal Clinic.

The legal clinic course in the fourth year is an elective, and students who choose this course are divided into many small groups. This is a strategy that was employed to avoid administrative conflicts. Instead of having eight to ten different elective courses, which would require an uncertain and difficult administrative path to be accepted into the curriculum, Uygur preferred to have one elective course consisting of several small groups. Legal clinic courses in the third and fourth year can be described as a *matrushka*. It seems as one course in the curriculum, but in fact there are eight more courses within it that are given by different people depending on the topics covered.[22] In this way, the legal clinic has the ability to be flexible. Instead of dealing with university bureaucracy to add a new course that is needed for a new legal clinic, they are free to start a new working area or to cancel or freeze an existing working area. For example, the working group on gender has decided to work on LGBT rights this year and described itself as an LGBT Clinic and prepared a ten-week working program in cooperation with NGOs working on the LGBT area.[23] Each group constitutes a different legal clinic under the supervision of a professor, with the help of research assistants. Students in all the groups of the legal clinic course are obliged to follow a common seminar.[24] The seminar aims at coordinating the work of all the groups and insuring that the educational aims of clinics are adhered to, something that otherwise might easily be overlooked due to a heavy workload.[25]

The legal clinics at Ankara University attempt to deal with some 800 students in total over three years. There are roughly 350 students in the second year, around 300 in the third year, and in the last year the numbers drop to around 150. This is a very large number of students for the Ankara staff to handle.

It must be stressed that the number of students at Ankara University is much higher than at Bilgi because Ankara is a state university.[26]

The clinics that were active in 2014, as part of the legal clinic course at Ankara University, are listed as follows:[27]

- Legal Clinic on Sexual Abuse
- Legal Clinic on Prisons
- Legal Clinic on Law and Art
- Legal Clinic on Refugees
- Legal Clinic on Patient Rights
- Legal Clinic on Gender-I
- Legal Clinic on Gender-II
- Legal Clinic on Being a Worker in Turkey

There are 135 students enrolled in these groups at the moment.[28] This number indicates that less than a third of the students who are interested in joining legal clinics remain in the legal clinics course for the entire three years.

Anadolu University Legal Clinic

The Anadolu University Faculty of Law is based in Eskişehir and is a state university. The Law Faculty was established in 1993, and it accepts around 400 students every year.[29] Anadolu University has a distance-learning faculty, with almost 1,500,000 students enrolled, which makes this university the biggest in Turkey in terms of the number of registered students.[30] In addition to Anadolu being one of the important law faculties in Turkey, its efforts to promote legal clinics gives this faculty a particular role in the field of legal clinics. The Anadolu University Law Faculty hosted two international events in Eskişehir in the last two years,[31] and is already planning another important international event for 2015.[32] The staff there also work closely with other law faculties and try to help to build new legal clinics in other law faculties.[33]

Anadolu legal clinic was founded in 2013 as a unit of the faculty.[34] "Units" are the smallest parts of the university's organizational scheme that can be set up according to academic or administrative needs. They are easy to start and can be defined depending on needs; thus, they differ from other institutional bodies of the university, which are defined by legislation. The Turkish higher education system has a hierarchical organization, and it is strictly bound by legislation, which leaves no room for the universities to build their own organizational structures, nor to define or to add different bodies depending on their institutional needs.[35] Units can be set up under faculties, and even though they have very limited scope, they still give some protection to the professors who are willing to work in their legal clinics if it is considered that, as explained above, there is no legislation on legal clinics. This is a creative solution.

Even though the Bilgi and Ankara clinics are about ten years older than the Anadolu University clinic, Anadolu is the first legal clinic that has officially called itself a "legal clinic." The Raoul Wallenberg Institute of Human Rights and Humanitarian Law (RWI) supported Anadolu in starting a legal clinic under the project entitled Strengthening Human Rights Capacity in Turkey (2011–2014). During the planning for this project, Anadolu and the RWI staff agreed to start a course prior to the founding of the clinic, and an elective course called Children's Rights in Practice, was offered in AY 2012–13 as a first step toward founding the clinic.[36] Children's Rights in Practice is a course that uses the techniques of Street Law. Nineteen students enrolled on this course, and they worked in high schools and delivered information to 69 high school students during the course. Ayşe Tülin Yürük conducted a survey to gather the results of this course for the students of the law faculty and the high school students. She also used the in-depth interview technique with stakeholders to understand their view on the legal clinics. She interviewed eight lawyers from Eskişehir Bar, five judges from Eskişehir Court, and two professors from the Anadolu University Education Faculty. Yürük states that the criticism of traditional educational methods that was made during the interviews was almost identical to the criticism indicated in legal doctrine.[37]

According to Yürük's study, both judges and lawyers criticize the "lack of practical information in the curriculum of law faculties" and the "lack of training in practical skills in trainings for trainee lawyers and trainee judges." Professors from the Education Faculty stated that "if the students have the possibility of practicing, they will not have fear during their traineeship, but if they do not have this possibility, their fear when practicing will stop them from starting a dialogue, which will cause them to act ineptly as a trainee, and which will in turn lead to their not being taken seriously, and in the end they will perform very badly as a trainee."[38]

Results of the Survey

Yürük conducted a survey of 69 high school students who attended the training delivered by the law students from the Anadolu legal clinic. The students were asked in the survey about the learning outcomes of the training that was received in the survey to see if they agreed. Here are the results.[39]

Table 12.1 Survey results from the Anadolu legal clinic

	Totally Agree + Agree
1. Informed me on human rights	91.58 %
2. Informed me in the methods to protect my rights	91.30%
3. Promoted me to approve legal authorities to protect my rights	89.85%
4. Informed me on the judicial system	88.40%
5. Made it easier for me to understand legal concepts	82.61%
6. Informed me on the concept of justice	81.15%

Yürük conducted another survey of 19 students who attended the Children's Rights in Practice street law course at the Anadolu legal clinic. The students were asked in the survey about the learning outcomes of the training that was received in the survey to see if they agreed. Here are the results.[40]

Table 12.2 Survey results from the Children's Rights in Practice street law course

	Midterm Exam *Totally Agree + Agree*	*Final Exam* *Totally Agree + Agree*
1. Helped me in my personal development	100%	100%
2. Improved my communication skills	100%	100%
3. Improved my research skills	94.74%	100%
4. Improved my self-confidence	94.74%	100%
5. Improved my process management abilities	94.74%	100%
6. Improved my abilities to deliver information	89.45%	100%
7. Created the feeling that I am working for justice	66.67%	85.71%
8. I cannot achieve in other courses the abilities that I achieve in this course	–	92.85%
9. I believe I have contributed to the community in this course	–	92.85%

The Anadolu legal clinic has been productive during its short existence. It has printed legal guides in several languages for Erasmus students; translated basic documents and handbooks on legal clinics; hosted an international symposium,[41] an international workshop,[42] and a national workshop;[43] and clinic members have attended several international meetings and study visits.[44]

Future of the Legal Clinics in Turkey

Legal clinics are expected to grow in Turkey over the next few years. At this time, there are almost fifty thousand law students studying at universities, of whom 42 percent are enrolled in so-called private universities. Law faculties can accept 15,500 new students per year.[45] Law faculties have no difficulty at the moment in finding students, but private faculties in particular are working hard to show that they can distinguish themselves from the other institutions and build up their reputations (brands) and so climb up the rankings. Promoting the social responsibility projects of students and adding practice skills training to the curriculum are good ways of doing that. Faculties are building courtrooms as part of their facilities for moot courts, and are asking lawyers, notaries, and retired judges to teach practical courses as *guest members* of the academic staff. The law faculties are also promoting students' affiliations to social projects. The emerging concept of legal clinics is being promoted more often day by day because it allows students to be in a social responsibility project and be trained in social and practical skills at the same time.

Currently, the law faculties of Istanbul University, Zirve University, Özyeğin University, Medipol University, and Yeditepe University also have legal clinic courses.

The Turkish Ministry of Justice has declared its willingness to promote legal clinics in the draft of the Justice Reform Strategy Document[46] as "Aim 9.1" of the Ministry of Justice under the heading "improve access to justice." The draft strategy document states that[47]

> The practices of legal clinics throughout the world support disadvantaged groups in solving their legal problems. Moreover, these practices also aim at realizing educational and social responsibility policies. Law students, who are pursuing their legal education in these faculties, may have the opportunity to help/support the legal consultation provided to disadvantaged groups under the supervision of their faculties. In this way, on the one hand, the needs of the neediest parts of the society will be addressed, while, on the other hand, the students will contribute to the society as a whole and, especially, law students will receive a sustainable and practicable legal education. There will be collaboration with universities to realize this goal.

The official naming of legal clinics in the draft strategy document has highlighted and drawn attention to legal clinics. The head of the Strategy Development Department of the Ministry of Justice states that he believes legal clinics may contribute a lot to both legal education and access to justice, which is why the department will be more supportive in this area in the near future.[48] The Ministry of Justice publicly announced its support for legal clinics and its willingness to amend legislation to provide space for legal clinics.[49]

An important lacuna is that the Ministry of Justice does not mention, in the draft strategy document, anything about cooperating with lawyers or bar associations.

In Turkey, *avukats* have a legal monopoly on representing people regarding legal issues and on giving legal advice.[50] These are protected rights for *avukats* and other professions are barred from these activities, so that only *avukats* registered with a bar association may perform these acts.[51] Lawyers are concerned about the legal clinics, and are feeling threatened because they believe clinics are a way of creating new rivals for lawyers' legal services.[52] Meral Öztoprak-Sağır conducted a study on "Legal Education in Turkey" in 2007 and 2008 with financial support from the Union of Turkish Bar Associations (UTBA), and published a study report by the UTBA.[53] Öztoprak-Sağır mentions the thirty-fifth article of the Code of *Avukats* and states that legal clinics cannot deliver consultancy even for free because of the clear and strict ban. According to the study, those who are against the legal clinics are employing the arguments outlined below:[54]

1. Law students have no liability nor insurance to cover their possible mistakes.
2. There is no code of conduct nor a disciplinary mechanism over the students such as the bars have over *avukats*.
3. Students have no privilege to protect the secrets of those who apply to legal clinics.
4. There is already a working legal aid system, which makes the clinics unnecessary.
5. In her report, Öztoprak-Sağır discusses the concept of legal clinics, the history of these clinics, and the US experience with clinics, relying on her research at Georgetown University in Washington, DC. Moreover, she points out that meetings have taken place in Alanya (Antalya) with the support of the Antalya Bar Association, among other supporters, on the subject of legal clinics.[55] This is important because it suggests that local bars and the UTBA (national bar) is trying to understand this concept and support academic work in this area.

Uygur states that she has been working together with the Ankara Bar since 2005 and that the bar has been more supportive of the Ankara Legal Clinic. She states that there is no tension between lawyers in their work, and if there is tension elsewhere, that means there is a problem of approach and a lack of dialogue.[56]

Avukat Rıza Öztekin, president of the Eskişehir Bar, states that the bar has no prejudice against legal clinics because, in addition to Article 35 of the Code of *Avukats*, there is also Article 76, which officially stipulates that bar associations have the duty *to protect the rule of law and human rights*. President Öztekin states that *avukats* are already doing pro bono work, especially on gender issues, and that they are in favor of legal clinics unless there is an infringement of lawyers' rights.[57]

Anadolu University is trying to build a platform to meet with other law faculties who wish to start law clinics and with bar associations. They express the fear that, if the status quo continues, different schools might use the concept very liberally and that this might lead to regular courses being defined as legal clinics because the concept is becoming popular, which will result in the concept of legal clinics being diminished in scope.[58] It is possible to find several law offices and consultancy firms that are claiming that they are offering "legal clinic" service, when in fact this is nothing more than a *free first consultancy* advertisement to attract new business.

Conclusion

As a civil law country, legal education in Turkey is, and has been, highly theoretical, and practical training has had little place in legal education. The practical training of new lawyers is considered more and more important for several reasons, including the increasing influence of Anglo-American common law (because of Turkey's improving economic relations), the changing legal market dynamics, the increasing number of law faculties in Turkey, the lack of sound initial training in the Turkish legal profession, and growing levels of unemployment in Turkey's legal profession. It is not wrong to say that, in the last ten years, legal clinics have had an incubation period and that they have started to attract more and more attention each year. Legal clinics are gaining momentum in Turkey, and they are growing evermore popular. Richard J. Wilson also points to this trend, stating that "the destabilization of the old guard in legal education, coupled with desire for European integration and donor focus on clinical legal education, led to rapid growth of clinical legal education offerings in such countries as Hungary, the Czech Republic and Turkey."[59] This development has pros and cons for legal clinics in Turkey. Traditionally, Turkish people are used to acting under specified and detailed legislation. Institutions, whether educational, professional, or administrative, tend to look for detailed rules that dictate how to act; however, even in the absence of such rules, legal clinics have flourished better than expected. This can be considered good in the sense that there is expanded awareness of their utility, but it has some negative aspects if one considers the traditional patterns of academic and commercial institutions in Turkey. The increasing number of legal clinics and the large and growing number of students involved in legal clinics show that this concept has been increasingly accepted by law faculties in Turkey. One can expect more legal clinics to be established in the coming years. The unregulated nature of legal clinics that have already started operations might cause some problems, because there is no legal authority to set their rules or to give them the name "legal clinic." Additionally, legal regulation would clarify their existence vis-à-vis the monopoly of the legal profession as regards the giving of legal advice.

Notes

1. For a short introduction to the legal education of lawyers in Turkey, see Julian Lonbay and Musa Toprak, *Legal Education in Turkey* (UTBA, 2014), 51.
2. Attorneyship Law numbered 1136 (dated March 19, 1969, published in Official Gazette issue no: 13168 on April 7, 1969).
   Work exclusive to attorneys.
   Article 35 – Amended as per Article 1238/1 dated February 26, 1970.
   Providing opinion in legal matters; litigating and defending the rights of real persons and legal entities before courts, arbitrators, and other bodies invested with jurisdictional powers; and managing all documentation associated therewith are the sole prerogative of attorneys enrolled with bar associations.
3. CCBE Recommendation on Training Outcomes for European Lawyers, which can be found on the CCBE website at http://www.ccbe.org/fileadmin/user_upload/NTC document/EN_Training_Outcomes1_1196675213.pdf, accessed October 20, 2014.
4. In this sense, see Richard Wilson, "Western Europe: Last Holdout in the Worldwide Acceptance of Clinical Legal Education– Part I/II" (2009) 10 *German L.J.* 823–846, http://www.germanlawjournal.com/index.php?pageID=11&artID=1123, accessed October 20, 2014.

5. For example, Seda K. Berk, *"Access to Justice" in Turkey: Indicators and Recommendations* (Türkiye Ekonomik ve Sosyal Etüdler Vakfı/Turkish Economic and Social Studies Foundation in 2011), 17 could write the following:

    The absence of initiatives such as pro bono services or legal clinics in Turkey is also another factor that impedes access to justice due to the limited availability of legal representation and advice.

    The Report goes on to recommend the establishment of legal clinics.
6. Turkish National Report for 18th International Congress on Comparative Law: The Role of Practice in Legal Education (Washington, 2010), written by Yasemin IŞIKTAÇ and Sercan GÜRLER based on the information that is collected from the Law Schools all around Turkey. This report was presented to the Congress but not published.
7. Dr. Carrie Louise Hempel of Irvine School of Law, University of California, organized and conducted, with Dr. Rod Uphoff (Oklahoma) and Dr. David Gottlieb (Kansas), a five-day conference on CLE for Turkish students, faculty, judges, and lawyers at Marmara University, Istanbul, Turkey, on December 2000. Clinical Legal Education Association Newsletter Vol. IX, No. 3 January, 2001, http://www.cleaweb.org/Resources/Documents/clea_newsltr_0101.pdf, accessed October 1, 2014.
8. See İdil Elveriş, IR 708, Social Policy Final Paper; Access to Justice for the Poor in Turkey: Can Legal Clinics Empower? (unpublished) 9ff.
9. http://insanhaklarimerkezi.bilgi.edu.tr/source/222.asp?lid=en&id=0, accessed October 9, 2014.
10. http://www.bilgi.edu.tr/en/programs-and-schools/undergraduate/faculty-law/law/page/bilgi-legal-clinic, accessed October 7, 2014.
11. International Symposium, "New Approaches to Legal Education: 'Legal Clinics'" Anadolu Üniversitesi Hukuk Fakültesi Yay, 2013, Eskişehir, 108.
12. http://www.bilgi.edu.tr/en/programs-and-schools/undergraduate/faculty-law/law/page/bilgi-legal-clinic, accessed October 7, 2014.
13. International Symposium, "New Approaches to Legal Education: 'Legal Clinics'" 111.
14. Ibid.
15. http://www.bilgi.edu.tr/en/programs-and-schools/undergraduate/faculty-law/law/page/bilgi-legal-clinic, accessed October 7, 2014.
16. http://www.hurriyet.com.tr/gundem/24955507.asp
17. International Symposium (n 13) 119.
18. http://www.bilgi.edu.tr/en/programs-and-schools/undergraduate/faculty-law/law/page/bilgi-legal-clinic, accessed October 7, 2014.
19. Ankara Law School was established in 1925, two years after the Republic was declared. Until 1978, there were only two law faculties in Turkey: Istanbul University Faculty of Law and Ankara University Faculty of Law.
20. An interview was conducted by the authors of this paper on May 2, 2014, at the Ankara University Faculty of Law with Olcay Karacan and Funda Kaya. Ms. Karacan and Ms. Kaya are both members of the academic staff of the Ankara Law Faculty, in the Philosophy of Law and Sociology of Law Department and both work for the Ankara University legal clinics.
21. International Symposium (n 13) 102.
22. Interview with Karacan and Kaya(n 20).

23. http://www.stgm.org.tr/tr/icerik/detay/ankara-universitesinde-toplumsal-cinsiyet-hukuk-klinigi, accessed October 10, 2014.
24. Common seminars are being announced as events in Facebook. https://www.facebook.com/events/1481289612158550/?fref=ts, accessed October 14, 2014.
25. Interview with Karacan and Kaya (n 20).
26. There are two types of universities in Turkey: universities owned by the state and universities owned by foundations, the so-called private universities. The number of students at state universities is much higher than at the private universities because it costs more than 20,000 TL (approximately 7,000 €) per year to attend a private university, while the public universities are generally tuition free. Accordingly, while the private Bilgi University accepts 200 students per year, the Ankara Law Faculty accepts 800 students per year.
27. http://ivr-turkey.org/content/section/6/73/lang,turkish, accessed October 3, 2014.
28. Collected by the authors from IVR Turkey's website; http://ivr-turkey.org, accessed October 5, 2014.
29. https://www.anadolu.edu.tr/tr/akademik/birim/genelBilgi/201/1/1, accessed October 10, 2014.
30. Anadolu University has 1,383,004 registered students in 2013. http://www.eskisehir2013.org.tr/index.php/tr/kent-rehberi/eskisehir/egitim, accessed October 10, 2014.
31. Anadolu University hosted an International Symposium titled "New Approaches to Legal Education: 'Legal Clinics'" on June 13–14, 2013, and an International Workshop titled "Law Clinics" on May 23, 2014.
32. Anadolu University will host the 8th Worldwide Conference of the Global Alliance for Justice Education (GAJE) on July 22–28, 2015, http://www.gaje.org/conferences/upcoming-conferences/, accessed October 11, 2014.
33. An interview was conducted by the authors of this paper, on May 3, 2014, at Anadolu University Faculty of Law (Eskisehir) with Dr. Ufuk Aydın, Dean of the Anadolu University Faculty of Law; Dr. Kıvılcım Turanlı, Head of the Anadolu University Faculty of Law Legal Clinics Unit; and Dr. Kasım Akbas and Dr. Duygu Özer-Sarıtaş, members of the academic staff of the Anadolu University Faculty of Law, who are also working in the legal clinics unit. After the long interview, the authors paid a visit to the rooms of the legal clinic unit to see their sample forms and file and archive system.
34. http://klinikhukuk.org/history, accessed October 10, 2014.
35. For further information on Turkish higher education system, please see Julian Lonbay and Musa Toprak, "From Ottoman to Bologna," in Shuvro P. Sarker (ed.) *Legal Education in Asia* (Eleven International Publishing, The Hague, 2014).
36. International Symposium (n 13) 164.
37. Ibid. 168.
38. Ibid. 171, 172.
39. Ibid. 173.
40. Ibid. 174.
41. International Symposium titled "New Approaches to Legal Education: 'Legal Clinics'" dated June 13–14, 2013; detailed information can be found at Symposium book, see (n 10).
42. International Legal Clinics Workshop dated May 23, 2014; detailed info can be found at http://e-gazete.anadolu.edu.tr/ayrinti.php?no=13979, accessed October 3, 2014.

43. National Legal Clinics Workshop dated September 26, 2014; detailed information can be found at http://e-gazete.anadolu.edu.tr/ayrinti.php?no=14163, accessed October 3, 2014.
44. Interview with Dr. Akbas and Dr. Saritas.
45. http://www.aksam.com.tr/yazarlar/hukuk-fakulteleri-her-daim-populer/haber-252574, accessed October 3, 2014.
46. Justice Reform Strategy Document Draft, September 2012, Ankara, Turkish Ministry of Justice.
47. Strategy Draft 28.
48. An interview was conducted by the authors of this paper, on May 3, 2014, at the Ministry of Justice building in Ankara with Alparslan Azapağası, head of the Strategy Department of the Ministry of Justice.
49. News about these announcements are also important to show the public opinion on legal clinics: "Free consultation to lawyers" http://www.haber365.com/Haber/Avukata_Danisma_Bedava/, http://www.tgrthaber.com.tr/video/1010.html, http://www.turkiyegazetesi.com.tr/gundem/104632.aspx, accessed October 3, 2014.
50. See generally Latham & Watkins LLP, *A Survey of Pro Bono Practices and Opportunities in Selected Jurisdictions*, 2010, http://www.probonoinst.org/wpps/wp-content/uploads/pro-bono-survey-sep2010.pdf, accessed October 20, 2014 at 220 ff and İdil Elveriş (n 8) at 8 ff.
51. (n 2).
52. Samil Demir, a lawyer from Ankara, writes on his law blog, "New Adversary to Lawyers Legal Clinics" http://www.samildemir.av.tr/2011/08/avukata-yeni-rakip-hukuk-klinikleri/, accessed October 7, 2014.
53. Güncel Gelişmeler Işığında Türkiye'de Hukuk Eğitimi Araştırma Raporu [Legal Education in Turkey under the Light of Current Developments, Study Report].
54. Ibid. 75.
55. Ibid.18.
56. International Symposium (n 13) 102, 123.
57. International Symposium 125.
58. Interview with Dr. Akbas (n 33).
59. Richard J. Wilson, "*Généraux du XVIIIème Congrès de l'Académie Internationale de Droit Comparé*" [General Reports of the XVIIIth Congress of the International Academy of Comparative Law/Rapports], in Karen B. Brown and David V. Snyder (eds.) *The Role of Practical Education* (Springer, 2012) 80.

CHAPTER 13

Pathways to Social Transformation through Clinic: Developing a "Social Justice" Culture in Hong Kong

*Luke Marsh and Michael Ramsden**

Introduction

Despite its outward appearance as a model of global economic success, Hong Kong is noted for its wide-ranging social problems.[1] Law schools inevitably play a critical role in producing socially responsible and public interest-oriented lawyers, who are essential to the delivery of justice and the protection of human rights. In Hong Kong there is a growing need to strengthen civil society and inspire student lawyers to advance the "public interest."[2] While clinical legal education (CLE) and student advocacy have become a core part of curricula around the globe,[3] there has been little exploration of how these two modes of experiential education can be combined convincingly to advance social justice. Our aim here, therefore, is to chart the pathways taken toward the goal of developing a "social justice" culture at university level and beyond through CLE.

This chapter will begin by tracing the development of CLE in Hong Kong by discussing the blue touch paper that led to its genesis: *The Redmond-Roper Report on Legal Education and Training in Hong Kong* (Redmond-Roper), published in 2001. In providing the context for understanding how CLE operates in Hong Kong, the authors will then briefly discuss the creation of the Refugee Rights Clinic, the first step in CLE at the Chinese University of Hong Kong (CUHK) and an initiative that has helped address the principal concerns raised by Redmond-Roper. Thereafter, this chapter will outline the authors' next steps in seeking to advance clinical teaching methods with an innovative clinic platform oriented along public interest legal issues. It will detail how the Clinic for Public

Interest Advocacy is able to fuse two areas of the law curriculum that often excite student interest and are distinct learning vehicles, in order to encourage students to contemplate public interest careers alongside legal skills development. In doing so our underlying teaching philosophy in developing these experiential learning initiatives will become apparent, in particular our commitment to course design that integrates theory with practice, promotes civic engagement while advancing social justice, and allows students to think critically beyond the letter of the law. Finally, this chapter will explore early insights drawn from these initial phases of the collective project to develop a sustainable culture of CLE within the faculty and map out directions for the future.

Building Foundations: Concerns with Legal Education in Hong Kong

This section is divided into two main parts. First, it will discuss the context within which CLE has surfaced in Hong Kong, largely triggered by a range of pedagogical concerns raised by Redmond-Roper. Second, it will demonstrate our efforts in addressing those pedagogical concerns through the development of a pilot clinic program—the Refugee Rights Clinic.

Following governmental awareness that there were growing concerns in Hong Kong that law school education was "not fit for purpose,"[4] a major inquiry conducted by Professors Paul Redmond and Chris Roper was held into the quality of legal education and training in Hong Kong.[5]Redmond and Roper spent nearly two years assessing Hong Kong's legal education system and the degree to which it met the needs of the legal profession before publishing their findings in August 2001. The consultant's report identified a number of pedagogical concerns with legal education, the most relevant of which we include here:

- It was found to be dominated by a "black-letter" approach to law. Rules were taught devoid of the social context in which they were formed and applied.
- It placed too much emphasis on traditional classroom teaching.
- It proved incapable of equipping graduates with the skills and values necessary to address the dynamic challenges of Hong Kong's legal market.
- Crucially, a dearth of experiential learning in the law curriculum was noted in the report, which advocated its uptake to provide the pedagogical change that was urgently needed.

Space precludes a full account of the various reforms recommended by the education consultants. Suffice to say, the importance of Redmond-Roper was that it sought to underscore the need for legal education to integrate theory with practice, contribute toward a broader liberal education, and promote professional and ethical responsibility in a particular societal context.[6] Redmond-Roper therefore provided the impetus for initiating substantial, concrete improvements to Hong Kong's legal education system. The most resounding of these improvements came in the form of a new law school.

A New Law School: A New Approach

A major governmental response to the Redmond-Roper reform proposals was the creation of a new law school at CUHK in 2005.[7] In its announcement, the university cited the importance of helping maintain Hong Kong's competitive advantage—the rule of law.[8] It sought to provide its law students with legal training that would help them adapt to evolving societal circumstances; work in a variety of legal and nonlegal contexts, including nonprofit sectors; and broaden their perspectives to incorporate a wider global awareness, with a particular focus on mainland China and greater Asia.[9]

The influence of Redmond-Roper on the establishment and development of Hong Kong's third law school appears significant. In describing the characteristics of its proposed School of Law, CUHK actively sought to address Redmond-Roper's most pressing concerns:

> CUHK aims to provide quality legal education that will *enhance the standards of legal practitioners*, by means of recruiting the best students to be interested in law, *making innovations in the teaching and learning of law*, and *leveraging on its strengths in the humanities and social sciences to enrich the study of law within the broad socio-cultural context*. The School of Law will establish its identity through its approach to the teaching and learning environment, its teaching [programs] and its emphasis upon and orientation towards research.[10]

Redmond-Roper thus provided a blueprint for change from which CUHK became a new provider of legal education in Hong Kong.[11] The School of Law's founding Vision Statement rooted itself in the learning of law in its social context. It placed emphasis on students being "encouraged to develop a deep and critical understanding of legal theory and practice" with a specific focus on the domestic context. Indeed the very raison d'être of the law school was to produce students who "possess the knowledge base, intellectual and lawyering skills and ethical values to become future leaders and serve the *needs of the community*."[12]

While the concept that one of the aims of legal education should be helping to create a "better society" is far from novel,[13] some innovation within the law curriculum was required if the perceived failings of its predecessors were to be overcome.[14] As a newly opened pathway to the legal profession, the way in which CUHK undertook its role in inculcating strong academic and legal skills in a community-driven context would be instrumental to its relevance in the modern marketplace of legal education.

Inclusion of Clinical Legal Education into the Curriculum

CLE is a method of experiential learning that places students in positions of responsibility to solve problems that are actually encountered in the practice of law.[15] Despite the multitude of benefits that can stem from this pedagogical construct, it is fair to say that until recent years, Hong Kong universities have had limited experience of CLE and their interest had been far from apparent.[16]

While the proliferation of CLE in other jurisdictions is in no way a guarantee of its suitability within the Hong Kong law school context, the scale of its successful implementation abroad meant the case for experimentation with experiential learning was a compelling one.

The reason for the slow growth of CLE in Hong Kong can be explained from different perspectives. First, the introduction of CLE is a symbol of the professional law school, and clearly indicates that law school aims at training lawyers. Even today, the idea of incorporating practical skills has not been fully accepted. But the gradual expansion of programs with a clinical element, such as mooting, is a positive sign that the value of experiential education is increasingly recognized, the fruits of which have led to invaluable exposure for a law faculty start-up like CUHK on the international stage.[17]

Second, in Hong Kong there is an inherent tension between producing internationally recognized scholarship and adopting a teaching pedagogy that satisfies the needs of the legal profession. CLE has the potential to have an impact on how legal scholarship is undertaken in Hong Kong. For the purpose of bridging the gap between legal theory and practice, CLE can play an effective role by reducing the distance between academics and practitioners. In order to facilitate CLE, the respective law schools in Hong Kong would benefit from including clinic-focused practitioners as well as academics.

This view is supported by Redmond-Roper, which emphasized the need for a bridge between legal theory and practice. The report recommended CLE, as it "may assist students to perceive more fully the value of various areas of the law" with the particular "benefit of exposing students to the legal problems of the poor."[18] Crucially, the consultants regarded CLE as an important way of giving students contact with, and commitment to, a "public interest subculture." This recommendation can be considered as the starting point for the development of CLE in Hong Kong.

The next major catalyst came in 2005 when Hong Kong University engaged Professor Stacy Caplow, the Director of Legal Education at Brooklyn Law School, as a consultant to report on the feasibility of introducing CLE in Hong Kong.[19] After extensive consultation with a variety of stakeholders in Hong Kong on the subject, Caplow submitted her report to the faculty in June 2006. While a full examination of her evaluation of clinical education prospects in Hong Kong is unnecessary here, some key strands of her research deserve mention.

First, although Caplow acknowledged that "constructing a live-client clinic is a major undertaking," her review led to the conclusion that "the ingredients for a successful program" were present in Hong Kong.[20] Despite this general endorsement, Caplow acknowledged "the US version of CLE cannot simply be superimposed on other countries."[21] Caplow felt the externship model was equally laudable in Hong Kong, preferably where students "would work on legal problems in the offices of government agencies, NGOs or law offices which perform *pro bono* work."[22] Indeed the reciprocal value of this type of clinic partnership was deemed plain, as students "quickly become indispensable resources for busy lawyers, particularly those in non-profit organisations with no budget to hire paralegal employees."[23] Whichever model Hong Kong would eventually adopt, Caplow stressed the importance of

> assuring that students interact with clients about legal matters and, whenever possible, give them tangible, useful assistance. The range and depth of this assistance is the key design question that must be addressed with educational and service goals in mind, and with an awareness of any professional structural limitations.[24]

Caplow mooted the possibility of "more advanced programmes" involving interdisciplinary skills on the basis that "many universities are recognizing the advantages of cross-fertilization of approaches to problem-solving, analysis, and holistic representation in the clinical context."[25] This could take the form of a clinic course that focused on the elderly, the disabled, or children. According to Caplow, in forming an intersection between law and social work, students can be placed in positions of responsibility in which they are able to collaborate on sociolegal issues to "provide non-fragmented services where the client's problems need multifaceted solutions."[26] This point is especially germane to the work of NGOs in Hong Kong, which can lack legal capacity to bring about desired reforms.

First Steps: The Pilot Clinic at CUHK

Although there was little development in the way of CLE immediately following Caplow's review, since 2009, CLE has been a strengthening feature of the undergraduate and postgraduate programs at CUHK. An important juncture in the trajectory was the growth of a clinical model that took the form of an "externship" in which students are placed in an organization that provides legal services.[27] To this end, CUHK forged a partnership with the Justice Centre Hong Kong,[28] a local NGO that provides support to asylum seekers and refugees against a backdrop of government hostility and stringent policies.[29] Our aim here is not to fully appraise the pilot program but to provide a brief overview of the clinic structure and how it developed.[30]

Through the Refugee Rights Clinic, CUHK law students are placed in positions of responsibility to address the unmet legal needs of refugees. This initiative provides a unique opportunity for law students to gain practical legal and advocacy skills in the context of asylum seekers and refugees seeking protection in Hong Kong and to experience the law and human rights advocacy in action outside the classroom through experiential learning opportunities. While supervised, students observe and conduct interviews with claimants and draft documents, including memoranda, testimonies, and legal briefs. Students are further able to learn how to critically analyze public policy and lobby the government, prepare submissions to domestic and international bodies such as Hong Kong's legislature or United Nations treaty monitoring bodies, and understand effective strategies to campaign for refugee rights and work with the media. In addition to performing these various tasks and services in aid of refugees, students are provided with seminar-based instruction led by the NGO. Combining clinical experience with academic courses assists students in perceiving the value of various areas of law so that their study does not become "book learning remote from daily work."[31]

A major success, therefore, of the Refugee Rights Clinic has been its ability to ensure that law students appreciate professional ethics and social responsibility. These attitudes have not only been inculcated in student behavior as a consequence of performing client-oriented tasks (such as those described above) but also through providing structured "theory" sessions, which, for example, take the form of simulated ethical problems and encourage students to self-reflect on their own professional responsibilities. As just one example, a student who had expressed their interest to continue working with this placement NGO after the clinic said, "The Programme was, at times, frustrating and challenging, especially with regards to my own values and principles, but ultimately this allowed me to develop a stronger sense of self."

While "social justice" externship-type programs in Hong Kong had been in existence before the Refugee Rights Clinic, none had taken the form of an academic course that integrated theory with practice and assessed the students by way of an end examination.[32] By using the seminar-based instruction and examination assessment method to bridge the gap between legal theory and practice, it was possible to persuade more traditionally minded faculty staff that the clinic program should bear course credits for those participating students.[33] This approach to securing academic credit for the pilot clinic has paid dividends in ensuring the quality of participants has remained high and ensuring the benefits derived from the relationship with our community partner remain reciprocal. Indeed, various stakeholders have praised CUHK students for their intrepid attitude toward learning and their ethical sensitivity and professional skills.[34] From the perspective of the law school, the pilot clinic has been instrumental in advancing its Vision Statement: to instill in its graduates the values of civil society and the responsibility to protect the most vulnerable members of the community.[35]

New Frontiers in Experiential Education: Clinic for Public Interest Advocacy

This section proceeds by discussing the next advance in CLE at CUHK with the creation of the Clinic for Public Interest Advocacy. This initiative presents universities with an unorthodox approach in using experiential education to advance social justice. It does so through its attempt to pioneer a teaching pedagogy that fuses clinical education geared toward public interest issues with student advocacy, two dimensions of the legal curriculum ordinarily distinct from one another.

Public interest law is in its infancy in Hong Kong. A distinction between "public interest law" and "class action" litigation must be made here, the latter being a term synonymous with American legal culture albeit with heavy associations to public interest lawyers. Existing law in Hong Kong does not allow any form of class actions per se. It does, however, provide individuals with the option to make a claim on the same issue as joint plaintiffs or lodge different claims if so desired.[36] The claimant brings the claim on behalf of the community at large or a sector of the community against the public authorities, on a matter that has wide impact on the society.[37] Thus, despite the disparity of avenues available to those seeking legal redress between the two jurisdictions, there is room for public interest lawyers in both.

When the term "public interest law" became popularized in the United States there was broad consensus in the mid-1970s about its general definition: "Activity that (1) is undertaken by an organization in the voluntary sector; (2) provides fuller representation of underrepresented interests (would produce external benefits if successful); and (3) involves the use of law instruments, primary litigation."[38] In fact, the term has since been subject to wide application, in part owing to the nebulous concept of "underrepresentation," leading, as some have argued, to a lack of agreement as to its perimeters.[39] The concept has therefore been "mobilized by different groups of social actors for different purposes."[40] For example, the "first wave" of public interest law in the United States focused on "civil liberties, civil rights, environmental and consumer protection, the expansion of welfare benefits and housing for the poor, media reform, and occupational health and safety."[41] Subsequently, alternative interests entered the public interest law arena, yet were in some opposition to groups belonging to the first wave.[42] At its root, public interest law represents the utilization of the legal system to resolve social problems that pose a threat to the stability of society. We therefore use the term "public interest law" here as an umbrella term: using rights-oriented solutions within the context of the legal system to help societies become more stable.[43]

Through this lens, the value of a public interest law clinic can immediately be understood as one capable of narrowing the distance between legal study and legal reality.[44] In this vein, Daniela Ikawa has persuasively argued that incorporating a public interest law perspective into the law curriculum serves as a "powerful teaching tool" that allows educators to bridge "law and reality" for their students, "as well as law and social change."[45] This is achieved by building upon the "problem-solving" approach to legal education "by encompassing complex issues that must be addressed not only from a legal perspective, but also from moral, social, and political perspectives."[46] In the Hong Kong context, this could involve students working alongside public interest lawyers who challenge government action, such as through the securement of State-funded schooling for the children of mandated refugees where none is guaranteed, or pursuing litigation as to whether abysmal housing conditions experienced by increasing numbers of residents of "cage housing" amounts to a justiciable human rights violation.[47]

The Need for Public Interest Lawyers

While the Refugee Rights Clinic model has proved successful in terms of steps made toward tackling a range of pedagogical deficiencies highlighted by Redmond-Roper, limitations do exist. In addition to low student capacity, its most apparent limitation has been its focus on a single marginalized group.[48] In light of these restrictions, any vision we might personally hold for our clinic initiative engendering what Redmond-Roper referred to as a "public interest sub-culture," remains optimistic.[49]

Here then, the difficulties of the nexus between universities and the legal profession are acutely felt: with no *top-down* solution in place in Hong Kong, law students seeking to engage with social justice work in a legal capacity face a quandary, cornered between uncompetitive salaries coupled with limited job placements, or working abroad, the latter route being of limited benefit to the territory itself. From our own experiences, a noticeable student perception found is the daunting level of risk associated with a career in this area, namely owing to financial burdens[50] and limited work opportunities. This barrier remains a key part of the problem.

Another major component to the general dilemma faced by students in Hong Kong has been a "public interest deficit," arising not just through a general neglect of the issues at university level but also within the legal profession itself.[51] Public interest lawyer Robert Precht has argued that, unlike North America and Australasia where this area of law has flourished, in Hong Kong "the pool of public interest lawyers is small and the city is depriving itself of a powerful resource for quelling social discontent."[52] However, signs of change are visible with the emergence of active public interest groups in Hong Kong who seek to place the topic firmly on the agenda.[53] A rise in the use of judicial review to combat social ills has also been an encouraging sign.[54] Indeed recent landmark decisions have sent tremors through Hong Kong society—both as a force for good and bad.[55] Of course, an increase in the supply of graduates remains a necessary component for this area to flourish.[56] While law can deliver justice and protect human rights, it does not happen automatically. Given the importance of judicial review as a mechanism to protect human rights and to advance the public interest in Hong Kong, it is essential that students be provided with training in how to effectively engage with the courts and administrative tribunals tasked with the supervision of government and legislative acts. Recent pronouncements from the Hong Kong courts have provided some measure of encouragement in this regard, suggesting that a key function of the courts is to protect minority rights.[57]

Our approach, therefore, in tackling this dilemma is to adopt a *bottom-up* approach, that is, utilizing effective pedagogies at university level to nurture public interest law-oriented graduates better able to tackle social problems. This approach is crucial as a catalyst to reverse the perception among law students of limited career pathways in Hong Kong in order to advance social justice. In confronting the "public interest deficit" that currently prevails, the authors have therefore sought to facilitate the growth of student interest in public interest work as well as augmenting student aptitudes when undertaking responsibilities in that career specialization. University-level endorsement provided through the running of such electives also assists in strengthening entry points to a career in this area by creating stronger networks between aspiring lawyers and NGOs. This endorsement is also a way of supporting the work of NGOs, which, in turn, can help them become more effective institutions through capacity building.

In taking our original clinic design implemented through the Refugee Rights Clinic back to the drawing board, we began wanting to fulfill five main objectives. First, we wished to instruct students in the theory and practice of public interest law in Hong Kong. Second, we aimed to give students an opportunity to develop their legal skills and ethical understanding. Third, we sought to encourage critical analysis of the law, the legal system, a client's place in the legal system, and the lawyer's role. Fourth, we aimed to provide service for unmet legal needs in the community. Fifth, we hoped to cultivate a pro bono ethic and long-term commitment to public service.

With these learning aims in mind, the innovative teaching pedagogy adopted for this clinic course is one that combines academic instruction with experiential education, not only in the form of "externship" responsibilities but also in a structured program of public interest-oriented advocacy exercises leading to a final advocacy-based assessment. Such assessment tests students' ability to pool their knowledge in one coherent and legally cogent oral argument. This fusion of "externship" responsibilities and student-centered assessment is in order to provide vital skills, knowledge, and experiences to help students develop as advocates better able to aid the vulnerable.

Forging Partnerships in the Community

In partnership with a selected number of community partners (legal agencies and NGOs), the Clinic for Public Interest Advocacy places up to 30 law students each term in organizations that focus on public interest work.[58] As discussed above, public interest organizations and law firms providing specialist pro bono services are an important tool for social transformation in Hong Kong. They serve to protect individual rights, advance social justice, and enhance interests common to the community. In this way, therefore, the CUHK Law Faculty is able to strengthen its founding commitment to "law in the community" by forging sustainable links with public interest organizations in a diverse array of areas.

Clinic partners are selected according to three criteria: (1) Does the organization have the capacity to provide an optimal learning environment for law students? (2) Does the work address an unmet legal need? (3) What opportunity for casework does the organization have to offer students? By adopting this broad threshold, students are able to undertake learning experiences in a variety of public interest organizations—extending beyond refugee protection work. The types of partnerships we have sought to forge encompass areas as diverse as immigration, housing, education, employment, and rights relating to those with disabilities.[59] Working in tandem with our community partners, students are placed in positions of responsibility to either (i) provide supervised assistance to disadvantaged and vulnerable members of the community or (ii) spearhead advocacy campaigns that are aimed at enhancing the legal interests of such individuals in Hong Kong.

Students are able to encounter a greatly increased range of possible clinic activities and engage with a diverse range of issues. For example, students may assist with the provision of legal advice, counseling and guidance to foreign domestic workers in Hong Kong to help them navigate the judicial process. They may become advocates for the fair treatment and protection of the rights of migrant mothers and their children, and assist with advice on legal and immigration matters. There may be issues of gender and sexual rights for them to tackle. There may be involvement with human rights education using social media to mobilize supporters. Their clinic experience may be dedicated to promoting civil and political rights among marginalized groups, or securing economic, social, and cultural rights.

In addition to the clinical placement, there is also a taught component thatis focused on developing knowledge and skills on *(i)* public interest law in Hong Kong, *(ii)* legal strategies to protect the rights of individuals, particularly via judicial review, and *(iii)* legal advocacy in a formal setting.

Modes of Learning

The Clinic for Public Interest Advocacy provides a unique three-component learning platform comprising theory, clinic, and advocacy. Students are required to participate in all three components of the clinic course in order to receive full academic credit.

The *theory* component involves students' learning the skills of advocacy, with emphasis on the particular demands of public interest law. All students are required to attend six seminars taught by faculty staff during the term. Seminars with advocacy exercises built in therefore assist students in understanding the role of judicial review in a changing society, while allowing them to explore the practicalities of such a supervisory mechanism as an engine for social change. To this end, we cover the following topics: (a) Introduction to Public Interest Issues in Hong Kong; (b) International Human Rights Systems and Mechanisms; (c) Domestic Human Rights Systems and Mechanisms; (d) Judicial Review Procedures; (e) Public Law Mechanisms: Administrative Review; and (f) Public Law Mechanisms: Judicial Review. As with the design aspects of the Refugee Rights Clinic, the theory component aims to counteract the dominance of a black-letter approach to law, in which graduates are perceived to lack an expanded view of the world.

The *clinic* component involves each student working under the supervision of a partner organization involved in public interest work. Students attend the office or center of the clinic partner on a weekly basis for one academic term. Clinic responsibilities may involve, but are not restricted to, casework, client interviews, team meetings, research assistance, and potentially a research or advocacy project related to a public interest cause. There will be involvement with real cases and contact with real people—be they from Kowloon or Kenya. Students gain unique experience of ethical issues, such as professional conduct, confidentiality, and conflicts of interest. Students are then able to apply knowledge gained through the clinic to practical situations. The clinic further enables the development of research and drafting skills. Building upon the benefits derived through access to real client problems in the Refugee Rights Clinic, this component ensures legal education is fully capable of adapting to the needs of Hong Kong society while promoting professional responsibility.

Finally, the *advocacy* component forms a fundamental part of the program, feeding in to both seminars and assessment. Advocacy plays an important role in exposing students to realistic exercises modeled on helping disadvantaged clients. Having been instructed in the skills of advocacy during the first half of the course, the second half is spent putting those skills into practice, culminating with a final advocacy assessment. Students participate in a number of simulated advocacy exercises during the seminars, leading to a final assessment pertaining to an application for administrative review. A particular focus is the preparation of a written "skeleton" argument for an oral application seeking leave for judicial review before the Hong Kong Court of First Instance. As was originally achieved under the Refugee Rights Clinic, this component continues to overhaul the traditional passive learning environment of the classroom, enabling student participation.

Assessment

Assessment is twofold. First, a reference from the Clinic Partner, confirming satisfactory completion of clinic duties, is required. An evaluation form is completed by all Clinic Partner Supervisors that incorporates unified criteria to ensure each student is assessed fairly and appropriate weight is given to his or her performance throughout the clinic work.[60]

Second, students are tasked with representing a (hypothetical) client in a simulated but integrated advocacy assessment that is based on their individual clinic placement experience. Students are examined on a legal issue in which a public law challenge is warranted in Hong Kong and then prepare an application for judicial review. The advocacy assessment will simulate the leave stage of judicial review proceedings, in which students will prepare written pleadings and make oral submissions to establish that their case has a realistic prospect of success if it advances to a full hearing.

Toward Lifelong Learning and Civic Engagement

In designing this new clinic model we have sought to provide students with an experience that trains them for future legal challenges in a way that previous cohorts have not been exposed to. Shifting what are traditionally viewed as practical skills into an academic setting carries the potential for transformation of the role lawyers play in society. We hope to bring about what Caplow describes as "cross-disciplinary conversations about professional responsibility, varying concepts of client relationships, and the connections between legal and non-legal problems and solutions."[61] To assist students in their useful engagement within this "conversation," we aim to equip them to be able to

1. explain to a client or prospective client the basic principles of administrative law/judicial review;
2. explain to a client or prospective client the remedies available to him or her for challenging government and legislative acts in Hong Kong;
3. identify, analyze, research, and gather support related to the legal and factual issues of a claim;
4. write a legal submission and/or legal brief;
5. advocate on behalf of a hypothetical client in regard to a public interest issue;
6. reflect critically on and take action to advance the theory and practice of a public interest law issue in Hong Kong, on the development of their professional skills and ethics, on the nature of the lawyer-client relationship, and on the value of pro bono service to unmet legal needs in the community.

Ultimately, our underlying aim in blending a clinical placement and a unifying taught component is to promote legal education that produces socially responsible lawyers. In enabling future students by providing them with a bespoke "toolkit" of skills as described here, it is the authors' aspiration that alumni from the program will become ambassadors for public interest advocacy in Hong Kong.

Conclusion

This chapter serves as testament to the crossroads at which CLE in Hong Kong currently finds itself. The direction in which legal education travels in Hong Kong is clearly of paramount importance to its success as an international hub in Asia. But often this guiding factor comes at the expense of more localized issues that impinge directly upon the lives of everyday citizens in Hong Kong. In giving this account of experiential education activities at CUHK, we have argued reducing that neglect is one function that CLE can usefully perform.

While not seeking to disregard the invaluable role the law of business and commerce plays in the elevation of the territory to an international player, this account of the authors' steps made in CLE serves as a timely reminder that "law schools [should] be centers of social justice, rather than merely vocational schools for lawyers who deploy professional skills to endow those with wealth and power with more of the same."[62] It also presents an opportunity to reflect upon the curious lineage within which this branch of legal education has developed. By chartings its origins from the catalytic findings of the Redmond-Report Report to its modern-day configuration, it is possible to take stock of developments and reflect upon the direction in which CLE is heading in this dynamic corner of the globe.

The collective CLE project in Hong Kong is less than a decade old. However, sufficient time has elapsed to make a number of observations. First, the concept of CLE s only starting to be an established one in Hong Kong. It remains the case that CLE is viewed, in some quarters, as anathema to the "drier" courses centered on legal theory. Reform or development of CLE in Hong Kong is therefore set against the need to strike a balance among interested parties. This balance has often resulted in contradictory elements (for example, the need at faculty level for "traditional" assessments for an essentially "clinical" course to ensure academic credit is granted). For the law faculty itself, perhaps the most fundamental issues concern integration of the clinical experience with the total education program. How will students reconcile the time commitment expected for clinical work with other onerous responsibilities? As the successful running of our pilot clinic has shown, these concerns have been rendered largely unimportant.

Second, while our faculty recognizes the challenge of training instructors in sound pedagogy, CLE is still viewed as a new discipline, despite its global proliferation in recent decades. Clinical initiatives, such as those described here, have surfaced owing to the motivations of a small group of proponents in the face of some ambivalence as to the goals of clinic programs. In response, we have been carefully studying foreign examples for clues on how to operate the new program to best achieve educational goals while pooling greater faculty support.[63] It does remain the case, however, that the clinic project at CUHK is largely contingent upon the motivations and efforts of faculty members with an interest in the field. Where this remains limited in number, there are obvious drawbacks to such dependence on a narrow pool of individuals for the delivery of such vital law school programs, not least the vulnerability posed to the sustainability of future cycles.

Third, although Hong Kong lags behind countries such as the United States and United Kingdom in terms of its CLE offerings, its unique context cannot be forgotten.Its visible position as "Asia's world city"[64] obscures from view the limitations both in terms of small geographical size and population[65]alongside which the three law schools in Hong Kong operate. While live-client clinics are now commonplace within law schools internationally, the challenges faced by those in Hong Kong arguably require a different approach. Space saves us from the task of a full discussion of the various merits and drawbacks of launching a live-client clinic at CUHK.[66] Nonetheless, there are some immediate problems that arise owing to the limitations outlined. Were the three law schools in Hong Kong to each run a live-client clinic, owing to their relative proximity to one another, an element of public confusion might arise as to the most appropriate venue for their specific problem. Capacity is another concern: if three in-house live-client clinics operated, there might be a shortfall of client footfall to warrant the expense that such an endeavor entails.

A bolder solution to meeting the prevailing unmet legal need in Hong Kong might be a unified clinic model involving collaboration between the three universities in order to most effectively utilize the various skillsets and specialisms on offer at the respective institutions. A unified approach might be able to better manage public awareness and expectations. As Caplow has argued, "[t]he legitimacy and acceptance of law clinics in Hong Kong legal education and by Hong Kong lawyers will be solidified if the two other law schools also offer them."[67] In this regard, we share Caplow's notion that the "concerted efforts of the three law schools will increase opportunities, perhaps even allowing students to practice in areas that today seem controversial or unthinkable."[68]

Despite being a proposal in the Redmond-Roper Report itself,[69] a unified clinic has not been explored as yet. To be sure, running a successful live-client clinic program is very resource intensive. Low student-to-faculty ratios make these programs expensive. One noticeable difference between the United States and Hong Kong in this regard is the paucity of significant private foundations and philanthropies with the mission of supporting this kind of activity in Hong Kong.[70] With a unified live-client clinic operating between the three major law schools in Hong Kong, sustainability would not be as dependent on the commitment of specific individuals in the same way that it currently is.

With full awareness that larger ambitions remain subject to smaller successes, the pathways on this journey shall be explored as the landscape in Hong Kong unfolds. Building upon our early efforts in delivering CLE through the Refugee Rights Clinic, the Clinic for Public Interest Advocacy was launched with a dual purpose in mind: to allow students to utilize the law for the benefit of marginalized communities but also think critically beyond the letter of the law. An intended corollary of the latest clinic is widening the talent pool of law graduates who currently face uncertain paths to a legal career advancing social justice. Our hope is that the creation of networks between aspiring lawyers and Hong Kong issue-focused NGOs will bolster the public interest subculture that has only recently emerged. We envisage that the support universities can lend NPO/NGOs by growing legal talent relevant to their goals, will make them more effective institutions for social transformation.

This initiative has been undertaken to further establish the presence of the somewhat undervalued pedagogical field of experiential education—a dimension of the law curriculum that can suffer from want of institutional support. By consciously addressing those more skeptical as to the role CLE can play in Hong Kong, this chapter has outlined the authors' efforts in seeking to advance innovative clinical teaching methods that encourage students to develop public interest careers and improve their lawyering skills, while ensuring civil society initiatives have a greater likelihood of success and impact in influencing law and policy. It has also provided insight into the early phases of the clinic's development and its plans for the future. We have demonstrated, where the legal landscape changes, CLE has the systemic capacity for self-renewal—a feature of Hong Kong's legal education that Redmond-Roper highlighted as previously lacking. Many obstacles lie ahead, not least the thorny question of whether a live-client clinic involving dedicated clinic faculty staff is viable, let alone desirable. Ultimately, though, the CUHK law faculty was established to help deliver on the *Redmond-Roper* package of reforms, to bring the law faculty into the community and the community into the law faculty. That compass in hand, we continue to navigate our educational goals further, confident that the direction in which we are heading is on course.

Notes

* We would like to express our continued appreciation to the many people who provided kind assistance to the development of the clinic programs discussed herein. Special thanks go to Professors Barbara Schatz, Stacy Caplow, Takao Suami, Shigeo Miyagawa, Satoru Shinomiya, and Edwin Rekosh

1. A survey of recent headlines from Hong Kong's leading newspaper—the *South China Morning Post*—demonstrate the extent of government failings: "Hong Kong 'a hot-bed for modern day slavery'"; "New town will leave 1,000 old people without homes"; "Ethnic minority pupils 'being set up to fail.'" See also Leo Goodstadt, *Poverty in the Midst of Affluence: How Hong Kong Mismanaged Its Prosperity*(Hong Kong University Press, 2013).
2. See *infra* n 39 and accompanying text.
3. This volume shows countries as widely spread as the Philippines, Maldives, Israel, Palestine, Japan, and Russia that have established clinical programs.
4. As was the view of a former Chief Justice in Hong Kong, prior to the publication of the Redmond-Roper Report. See Li Andrew, "Address at the Opening of the Legal Year" (January, 1999).
5. For a comprehensive study of the development of Hong Kong's legal education, see Luke Marsh, Michael Ramsden, and Christopher Young, "Legal Education in Hong Kong: A History of Reform," in S. P. Sarker (ed.) *Legal Education in Asia* (Eleven International Publishing, the Netherlands, 2013).
6. Ibid. 1.
7. The Chinese University of Hong Kong, "Announcement on the Establishment of New Law School" (2004) http://www.law.cuhk.edu.hk/news-and-events/news.php?events_id=1, accessed September 1, 2014.
8. Ibid.
9. The Chinese University of Hong Kong, "The School of Law of The Chinese University of Hong Kong" (2004) http://www.legco.gov.hk/yr04-05/english/panels/ajls/papers/aj0523cb2-1605-2e.pdf,accessed September 1, 2014.
10. Ibid. 2. Emphasis added.
11. Mike McConville, "What is the Role of the Dean Internally?" (2009)*Int'l Assn. of Law Schools*,http://www.ialsnet.org/meetings/role/papers/McConvilleMike%28HongKongChina%29.pdf, accessed September 1, 2014. Led by Founding Dean, Mike McConville, CUHK's School of Law started operations on schedule in 2006, admitting students to its inaugural LLB, Juris Doctor (JD), and Master of Laws (LLM) classes.
12. L C, Paper NoCB(2)1760/05-06(01) 1. Emphasis added.
13. G. Johnstone, "Liberal Ideals and Vocational Aims in University Legal Education" (1999) 3 *Web J. Current Legal Issues*.
14. They are, in order of establishment, the University of Hong Kong (HKU): law degree program first started in 1969; the City University of Hong Kong (CityU): law degree program first started in 1987.
15. See David R. Barnhizer, "The Clinical Method of Legal Instruction: Its Theory and Implementation" (1979) 30 *Legal Ed. J.* 67. For an introduction to the three classic

forms of clinical education, see Margaret Barry, Jon Dubin, and Peter Joy, "Clinical Education in this Millennium: The Third Wave" (2000) 7 *Clinical L. Rev.* 1.

16. Although note recent efforts to improve the prominence of this pedagogy at Hong Kong University (HKU) with the creation of the Gallant Ho Experiential Learning Centre (GHELC), http://ghelc.hku.hk/ http://ghelc.hku.hk/,accessed September 1, 2014.
17. For example, a team of law students from CUHK won the 2013 championship and the LAWASIA Trophy for Best Memorial at the 7th LAWASIA International Moot Competition.
18. Redmond-Roper (n 4) 166.
19. See Stacy Caplow, "Clinical Legal Education in Hong Kong: A Time to Move Forward" (2006) 36 *HK Law Journal* 229.
20. Ibid. 17.
21. Ibid. 6. For a brief but helpful summary of the "renaissance" of CLE in the United States as compared with other jurisdictions, see Kris Gledhill, "Establishing an International Human Rights Clinic in the New Zealand Context" (2013) 19 *Int'l J Clinical Legal Educ.* 295.
22. Caplow (n 19) 19.
23. Ibid.
24. Ibid. 17.
25. Ibid. 21. Seegenerally Symposium, "Promoting Justice Through Interdisciplinary Teaching Practice and Scholarship" (2003) 11*Wash. U. J.L. & Pol'y* 1.
26. Caplow (n 19) 21.
27. For a useful exposition of the merits (and limitations) of externships in a social justice context, see Liz Cole, "Externships: A Special Focus to Help Understand and Advance Social Justice," in Frank S. Bloch (ed.)*The Global Clinical Movement: Educating Lawyers for Social Justice* (OUP, 2011).
28. Formerly the Hong Kong Refugee Advice Centre.
29. For further discussion, see, for example, Michael Ramsden and Luke Marsh, "Hong Kong: Developing the Legal Framework for Socio-Economic Rights Protection" (2014) 14 *Hum. Rts. L. Rev.* 267; "The 'Right to Work' of Refugees in Hong Kong: MA v Director of Immigration" (2013) 25 *Int. J. Refugee Law* 574.
30. For more on this, see Michael Ramsden and Luke Marsh, "Using Clinical Education to Innovate the Law Curriculum and Address an Unmet Legal Need: A Hong Kong Perspective" (2014) 63 *J. Legal Educ.* 3.
31. Redmond-Roper (n 4) 166.
32. For example, HKU has operated a Social Justice Programme. When Caplow (n 19) conducted her survey of Hong Kong University law programs, her concern was that "it is a rather informal association with no sharing of perspectives."
33. Students' clinic work contributes to a maximum of 10% of their final grade.
34. Sonya Donnelly, "Clinical Legal Education: Maximising Student Learning and Social Justice Impact" (2014) Hong Kong Lawyer.Professor Carmel McNaught, former director of CUHK's Centre for Learning Enhancement and Research (CLEAR), described the clinic as "showing insight into a number of aspects of legal education, especially the need for authentic experience." Professor McNaught could "clearly see" that our program "looks for evidence of effectiveness based on reflections, and then seeks to adapt to students' learning needs in ways that will maximize their learning": The e-mail from Professor McNaught is with author (February 4, 2012).

35. For further discussion, see Luke Marsh and Michael Ramsden, "Fostering Civic Engagement through Legal Education: Observations from Hong Kong" (2014) 1 *Asian J. Legal Educ.* 57.
36. Under Order 15 Rules of the High Court. See generally Gary Meggitt, "Class Actions in Hong Kong—Yes, No, Maybe" (2013) 43 *HK Law Journal* 217; University of Hong Kong Faculty of Law, Research Paper No.2013/029, http://ssrn.com/abstract=2290116, accessed September 1, 2014.
37. Karen Kong, "Public Interest Litigation in Hong Kong: A New Hope for Social Transformation?"(2009) 28*Civil Just. Q*.327. See rules of *locus standi* in Hong Kong; see also Swati Jhaveri, Michael Ramsden, and Anne Scully-Hill, *Hong Kong Administrative Law* 2nd ed.(Hong Kong: Lexis Nexis, 2013) Ch 4.
38. Burton Weisbrod, *Conceptual Perspective on the Public Interest: An Economic and Institutional Analysis* (Berkeley, CA: University of California, 1978) 2.
39. Ibid. 29.
40. Amin Ghazani and Marc Ventresca, "Keywords and Cultural Change: Frame Analysis of Business Model Public Talk, 1975–2000" (2005) 20 *Sociological For.* 523.
41. Ann Southworth, "What is Public Interest Law? Empirical Perspectives on an Old Question" 62 *DePaul L. Rev.* 493.
42. Ann Southworth, "Conservative Lawyers and the Contest over the Meaning of 'Public Interest Law'" (2005) 52 *UCLA L. Rev.* 1223.
43. This broad definition is taken from http://www.justicelabs.org/. See *infra* n 55.
44. For an interesting perspective on two examples of community law clinics, see Anna Cody and Barbara Schatz, "Community Law Clinics: Teaching Students, Working with Disadvantaged Communities," in Frank S. Bloch (ed.) *The Global Clinical Movement: Educating Lawyers for Social Justice* (OUP, 2011) Ch 11.
45. D. Ikawa, "The Impact of Public Interest Law on Legal Education," in Frank S. Bloch (ed.) *The Global Clinical Movement: Educating Lawyers for Social Justice* (OUP, 2011) Ch 11.
46. Ibid.
47. See CESCR, Concluding observations regarding China (Hong Kong) under Articles 16 and 17 of the Covenant, May 11, 2001, E/C12/1/Add58 at 4.
48. Further examples of unmet legal needs include the following: Proceedings in which formal legal representation is not allowed; Proceedings outside the scope of Legal Aid, but in which the party cannot afford private lawyers (e.g., administrative appeals and refugee screening); Legal assistance beyond one-off preliminary legal advice but short of full legal representation by legal aid (or clients are not poor enough to obtain legal aid); Legal aid is unjustifiably refused on the "merits" ground: Presentation by Eric T.M. Cheung, "Setting Up a Legal Clinic in Hong Kong: Progress and Challenges," on May 9, 2014.
49. There are limited career opportunities in Hong Kong for those students who wish to exclusively practice law in this area, although notable exceptions exist. See, for example, Daly & Associates, a human rights law firm that has taken on a number of landmark refugee cases in Hong Kong.
50. Hong Kong rents are some of the highest in the world, comparable to major cities such as London and New York. See Hong Kong Government, "Hong Kong Property Review Monthly Supplement—Table 1.1" (Hong Kong Rating and Valuation Department, 2013)www.rvd.gov.hk/doc/en/statistics/full.pdf, accessed September 1, 2014.

51. Some leading academics go so far as to argue that "law schools breed a culture of . . . conformity, [which] exerts a constant pressure to make comparisons along a uniform axis . . . This culture is remarkably static, non-adaptive, and resistant to change, even in the face of strong pressure from significant constituents of legal education and evidence that law schools are not fulfilling core aspects of their mission.": Susan Sturm and LaniGuinier, "The Law School Matrix: Reforming Legal Education in a Culture of Competition and Conformity" (2007) 60 *Vand. L. Rev.* 519–520, 539–540.
52. Robert Precht, "More Public Interest Lawyers can Help Ease Hong Kong's Social Tensions"*SCMP*, September 17, 2013.
53. To give but two examples, the international organization Public Interest Lawyers Network (PILnet) recently established its first satellite office in Hong Kong. In addition, former China Director for PILnet Rob Precht recently founded Justice Labs, a start-up incubator for public interest innovators.
54. While recent government data shows application for leave to launch a judicial review reached a 1ten-year high in 2013 (182), the proportion granted leave (20%) plummeted to a record low. However, of those granted leave, the government lost its highest proportion of judicial reviews (32%) since 2001 (36%): Samuel Chan, "Record Few Given Their Day in Court" *SCMP*, April 10, 2014.
55. For example, the issue of welfare provision available to residents in Hong Kong recently arose in the Hong Kong courts: *Kong Yunming v. The Director of Social Welfare* [2013] HKEC 1995 (CFA). Although viewed by many as a "victory" for the underprivileged, the decision has arguably further highlighted the uncertain and hesitant relationship with mainland China and fueled underlying tensions that exist. See also sexual minority litigation discussed in Michael Ramsden and Luke Marsh, "Same-sex marriage in Hong Kong: the case for a constitutional right" (2015) 19(1) *The International Journal of Human Rights* 90.
56. One structural problem that also hinders a rise in the number of public interest lawyers is that, under Hong Kong rules, a lawyer can only represent a client directly when acting in the capacity of solicitor in a law firm. If a lawyer is employed by a corporation or the government, the client is the employer. If a lawyer were to be employed by a NPO, the NPO would be the client, meaning that the lawyer could not directly represent the people the NPO served, although he or she could give advice and assist in litigation.
57. *W v Registrar of Marriages* [2013] HKEC 716 (CFA) 220(Bokhary PJ).
58. This elective is offered to undergraduate and postgraduate students in the Faculty of Law at CUHK.
59. The clinic is run in partnership with a number of public interest organizations or legal agencies, including the Global Network for Public Interest Law (PILnet), Amnesty International, Asian Human Rights Commission, Daly & Associates, Helpers for Domestic Helpers (HDH), Path Finders, the Society of Community Organisation (SOCO), and Vidler & Co. More information about the work in which they are involved can be found on their respective websites.
60. The dual assessment method is weighted as follows: clinic component (30% of final grade); advocacy component (90% of final grade). Students who do not perform their duties competently and fail the clinic component are not eligible for the advocacy assessment.
61. Caplow (n 19) 21.
62. Sameer M. Ashar, "Law Clinics and Collective Mobilization" (2008) 14 *Clinical L. Rev.* 355, 357.

63. Since its establishment in 2009, the authors have been fortunate to visit and learn from other law schools and the way in which they operate CLE. In Tokyo, Japan, visits were made to the Waseda Institute of Clinical Legal Education and Kokugakuin University. Time was also spent at the law school at Columbia University, New York.
64. http://www.brandhk.gov.hk/en/#/, accessed September 1, 2014.
65. Hovering around the seven million mark, Hong Kong has approximately one million fewer inhabitants than London, England.
66. In 2010, a Clinical Education Course was introduced at HKU. One of the features of this course has been to operate a Free Legal Advice Scheme ("FLAS") on-campus and allow students to participate in supervised legal service delivery in real-life cases. In each FLAS case, a pair of students would take instructions from a client and then submit a case summary and legal research memo to the duty lawyer in charge, as well as attend any subsequent follow-up session: http://www.law.hku.hk/Files/Newsletter/A11.pdf,accessed September 1, 2014.
67. Caplow (n 19) 22.
68. Ibid.
69. Ibid. 166.
70. See Robert Precht, "US academic eyes fellowship for law graduates"*SCMP*, May 15, 2014.

Index

Anadolu (Faculty of Law) 219–21
Ankara (Faculty of Law) 217–19, 223

BABSEA CLE 163, 164, 167,168,169,171
Bar Council of India 180, 186, 189
Bar Ilan University 93, 96
Bilgi (Faculty of Law) 216–17

Carnegie Foundation 3, 55
CCBE 215
China, Center for Women's Law Studies and Legal Services 38, 43
China, Dalian University law school, law clinics 45
China, domestic violence law clinics 44–46
China, Harbin University School of Political Science, law clinic 44
China, Jiangsu Police Institute, law clinic 43–44
China, Northwest University of Politics and Law (Xibei), law clinics 39, 41, 43
China, Outstanding Legal Talent plan, 48
China, Peking University Law School, law clinics, 38, 42–43, 45
China, Peking University School of Transnational Law (STL), law clinics 41, 45–46
China, Renmin University, law clinics 38, 42–43, 46
China, Sichuan University, law clinics 39, 42
China, South Central University for Nationalities, law clinic 45
China, Southwest University of Political Science and Law, law clinics 45
China, Sun Yat-Sen University, law clinics 39, 42–43, 46
China, Wuhan Center for Protection of Rights of Disadvantaged Citizens 38, 41
China, Wuhan University, law clinics 38, 41, 44
China, Yangzhou University, law clinic 43
China University of Political Science and Law, law clinic 44
CMU Law Clinic 161–170
Committee for Implementing Legal Aid Schemes 179
Committee on Chinese Clinical Legal Education (CCCLE) 37, 39–41, 46–49

Expert Committee on Legal Aid 179

Ford Foundation 38–39, 48

Hebrew University 93, 99, 107

Japan, bar examination 196–97, 199, 207–209
Japan, clinical courses 202–203
Japan, legal clinic faculty 202
Japan, legal clinics 200–202
Japan, professional law schools 198–201, 207

Japan Clinical Legal Education Association 203
Japan Law School Equivalency Exam 208
Japan Legal Support Center (*Hoterasu*) 204, 206
Japan Ministry of Education 199, 203, 207–208
Japanese lawyers 196–97
Juridicare Committee on Legal Aid 179
Justice System Reform Council 195–96, 201

Law Commission Report of 2002 180
Legal aid 17, 21, 22, 23, 25, 26, 27, 33
Legal Aid and Advice Act 137, 138
Legal Aid Bureau 142
Legal Aid Initiatives 161
Legal Profession Act 141, 151
Legal skills 21, 25, 28
Legal Training and Research Institute 197–99, 207, 209
LGBT 218

Maldives 17, 18, 19, 20, 24, 25, 26, 27, 28, 29, 30, 31, 32

National Knowledge Commission 177
NUS Law Clinic 142–144

Öztekin 223
Öztoprak-Sağır 222

Phayao Law Clinic 171, 172
professional responsibility 3, 12, 22, 39, 46, 59, 82, 85, 94, 101, 139, 148, 239

Shari'ah law 18, 24, 29
SMU Legal Clinic 145, 148, 149, 150, 151, 152
SMU Pro Bono Centre 138, 144, 145, 146, 148
Social justice 3–9, 20, 23, 41, 94, 99, 124, 140, 177–190, 229
Street LAW 216–17, 220

Tel-Aviv University 93, 103, 105, 107, 110, 111
Turkish Bar 223,
Turkish legal education 215, 222–23
Turkish legislation 216, 222, 224
Turkish Ministry of Justice
Turkish Prisons 219
Turkish trainee lawyer 220

Underprivileged 2, 3, 4, 5, 101, 170, 177–190, 204,
United States India Education Foundation 188
University of the Ryukyus 205–206
UTBA 223,
Uygur 217–18, 223

Waseda Legal Clinic 204–205
Waseda University clinics 203–205

Yürük 219–20

CPSIA information can be obtained at www.ICGtesting.com
Printed in the USA
LVOW03*0826270915

455876LV00006B/23/P

9 781137 517524